Revolutionary Blacks

The SIEGE OF RHODE ISLAND, taken from Mr. Brindley's House.
on the 25th of August, 1778.

Revolutionary Blacks

Discovering
THE
Frank Brothers,
Freeborn
Men of Color,
Soldiers
of
Independence

Shirley L. Green

WESTHOLME
Yardley

Facing title page: "The Siege of Rhode Island," *Gentleman's Magazine*, London, February 1779. (*Library of Congress*)

Westholme Publishing, LLC
904 Edgewood Road
Yardley, Pennsylvania 19067
Visit our Web site at www.westholmepublishing.com

ISBN: 978-1-59416-406-4
Also available as an eBook.

Printed in the United States of America.

To my mother, Sarah Franklin Swan, who provided the story;

To my father, Marshall O. Swan, who gifted me the love of history;

To my son, Michael K. Green, Jr. and my grandchildren, who carry on the legacy.

Contents

ILLUSTRATIONS

Thomas Henry Franklin, Annapolis Royal, Nova Scotia. (*Gravestones of Acadie and other Essays on Local History, Genealogy and Parish Records of Annapolis County, Nova Scotia* [London: A. Smith & Co., 1929])

Introduction

The Mystery of the Landscaper

On a summer day in the late 1920s, Thomas Henry Franklin was interrupted in his familiar work of mowing, raking, and swatting mosquitoes in the peaceful and ancient cemetery at Annapolis Royal, Nova Scotia, Canada. William Inglis Morse, a local historian, interviewed Franklin about this small, tight-knit community. Franklin, a well-known and well-liked man, landscaped gardens throughout the community and operated the first transport service conveying passengers from the ferry station located across the river from Annapolis Royal. He knew everybody, and everybody knew him. He was the perfect person to question. Morse later reproduced part of their conversation in his book.[1]

> What is your name?
> My name is Henry Franklin—an uncommon name in these parts.
> My grandfather came from Africa.
> How old are you?
> I'm just turned seventy.
> What makes the mosquitoes bite so?
> I'll tell you. You smash one, and the others smell the blood and come
> and bite you worse.[2]

The huge, persistent mosquitoes did not seem to bother the landscaper who went about his work, paying little attention to the annoying creatures that were making Morse's life miserable as he studied the ancient gravestones scattered throughout the cemetery. Franklin's work attire illustrated his style and practicality. Wearing a three-piece suit with a buttoned-up vest, wrinkled from wear, to work as a groundskeeper demonstrated that

Thomas Henry took pride in his appearance, regardless of the task at hand. The ensemble also protected him against the attacks of the annoying mosquitoes. The bowler hat, worn at a stylishly cocked angle, also protected him from the sun. In the photo, he stands looking into the camera lens—relaxed but ready, rake in hand. In this pose, Thomas Henry comes across as a self-assured man who knows himself and his place in his community.[3]

Henry knew that he was a great landscaper. He was well known for his work in making the yards and landscape in the Annapolis Royal region beautiful and well maintained. But his life's work in the gardens and yards of his community was juxtaposed against the harsh reality of his personal life in which he had to deal with tragedy. He fathered six children; two died in childhood. He worked well into his old age as a landscaper and transport operator to make a living for his extended family. But these tribulations did not stop Thomas Henry Franklin from living a long and fruitful life and having a long marriage to Elizabeth Jane Ruggles. He passed away at the age of 76, married to Elizabeth for over fifty years. Until the end, Henry worked in landscaping (which he loved) and reveled in telling the tales of his own family's history (which he also loved) and expressed to William Morse on that day.[4]

Franklin—septuagenarian, family man, hard worker, and local historian's dream informant—knew his history. To many, like his attire, Franklin may seem out of place, standing in an ancient cemetery in Nova Scotia. But Franklin knew otherwise. He not only knew the connections among members of his local community, but he also knew where he and they came from. He could trace his roots to Africa. A century later, the words Morse recorded enabled one of Franklin's descendants to trace her lineage from Ohio through Nova Scotia to West Africa.

Thomas Henry Franklin of Annapolis Royal is my great-grandfather. He disclosed only a portion of the Franklin oral tradition to William Morse. The bigger story, passed down only through male members of the family, described how the first member of the Franklin family came to America from Africa by way of Haiti, an enslaved man who eventually gained his freedom. Two of his descendants—two freeborn brothers with the last name of Frank—fought together in the "Black Regiment" from Rhode Island of the Continental army during the American Revolution. It was a story about a manly struggle for liberty and acts of heroism. It was a wonderful story that pulsed with pride in the past.

I am part of the landscaper's story. In the early 1900s, Thomas Henry's son, John William Franklin Sr., left Nova Scotia looking for work and a better life in New York City. John served in World War I as part of an all-Black regiment from New York. He later married and settled in Massachusetts. His two sons, John William Franklin, Jr. and Benjamin Franklin, served in World War II and the Korean Conflict. John Sr.'s oldest daughter, Hattie Franklin Gilton, eventually settled in Rhode Island, and unbeknownst to her, lived thirty miles from the hometown of the Frank brothers. His youngest daughter, Sarah, attended college in Wilberforce, Ohio, met Marshall Swan, a native Toledoan, married, and settled in Toledo, Ohio. Sarah Franklin Swan is my mother.

My investigation of the Franklin family history began accidentally in a classroom at the University of Toledo in northwest Ohio. Taking copious notes during a lecture in an African American history class regarding the first great wave of emancipations after the American Revolution, I stopped short when Professor Nikki M. Taylor mentioned the migration of Black loyalists to Nova Scotia. During that lecture, I realized that I did not know a big piece of my family's history. Oral tradition did not explain how Thomas Henry Franklin got to Nova Scotia. I had always assumed that my grandfather's family had made their way to Canada by way of the Underground Railroad. But that was not true. The two Frank brothers who fought in the Revolutionary War were born free; they did not need the Underground Railroad. I had fallen victim to the trap (described by genealogist Barbara Thompson Howell) of thinking my family's story paralleled the well-known stories of African Americans.[5]

As it turned out, the real story was much more interesting than the assumed story. As soon as I left that classroom, I phoned my mother, who in turn phoned her older sister. Neither one had heard of the Black loyalists or our ancestor's connection to them. We then phoned the oldest surviving male member of their immediate family, my Uncle Ben Franklin. He recited the core element of the Franklin family's oral history—that two free-born brothers named William and Ben Frank fought for the "Black Regiment" of Rhode Island during the Revolutionary War. My aunt Hattie Gilton's proximity to and research in archives in Rhode Island helped begin an investigation into the Franklin oral tradition. However interesting and exciting, the story, as passed down through generations, did not explain why my grandfather was born and raised in Nova Scotia. I was left with two disconnected stories—the Frank brothers' service with the Continental army and its "Black Regiment" during the Revolutionary War and my grandfather's birth in Nova Scotia. It became my mission—a mission that started many years ago—to connect those two stories.

The answer to those disconnected stories came to light through the actions of the younger brother, Ben Frank. He and his older brother, William,
were unique in their status as one of the few identified pairs of African
American siblings to serve in the Revolutionary War. In terms of assignment and length of service, the brothers' experiences were like those of
other men of color who served with Rhode Island regiments. The brothers
were assigned as combat troops to the infantry corps. They were expected
to perform combat assignments and receive the benefits—pay, equipment,
and rations—that went along with that function, regardless of race. William
served for a total of six years, and there is no desertion or AWOL notation
on his record. Ben, however, is a different story. He served with the Continental army for a period of three years, a term of service shorter than the
average for the Black Rhode Island veterans but longer than most Continental regulars. He deserted and left during the war—never returning for
active service with the Continentals. Ben fled to British lines, became a
Black loyalist, and migrated to Nova Scotia as part of the loyalist migration
at war's end.[6]

Stories of freeborn Black soldiers are difficult to find and difficult to
verify due to limited primary sources, such as letters and/or diaries compiled
by these men.[7] However, some stories, like that of the Frank brothers, are
passed down by family members from generation to generation to memo-
rialize the actions of distinctive and/or esteemed ancestors. The Franklin
oral tradition omits the desertion of Ben Frank, the kind of "troubled si-
lence" described by Dee Parmer Woodtor as a method used by African
Americans to gain respectability by "casting off" negative aspects of their
past.[8] By omitting Ben's desertion, his descendants cast off the critical fact
that not only explains their presence in Nova Scotia but also explains how
their ancestor and other free Blacks made decisions about allegiance during
the American Revolution.

This book tells the story I uncovered—a rich and complex tale which
enhances the traditional narrative about African Americans in the revolutionary era—that enslaved Blacks received their freedom through military
service or by petitioning the courts. My ancestors, the Franks of Rhode Island, were already free before the American Revolution, which is part of a
lesser-known narrative. Only about 10 percent of African Americans can
trace their family's freedom to before the Civil War.[9] Historians have assigned free Blacks the role of bystanders—a small cluster waiting for their
ranks to be increased by manumitted slaves during the first great wave of
emancipation during and after the American Revolution. Studies rarely

show them as a dynamic group that shaped early American society. The Franks and other freeborn Blacks lived, worked, and prayed in cities, towns, and villages during the revolutionary era. Their "ordinary" stories and experiences are an important counterpoint to the lives of more famous persons like Crispus Attucks, Phillis Wheatley, Prince Hall, and Richard Allen, who have been the focus of narratives of African Americans in the revolutionary era.

In this book, I recount the lives of the Frank/Franklin families from the 1750s until the 1830s. I show how Frank men used their military service to assert their manhood, gain standing in their community, and help to create free African American and African Canadian communities. I show how their father, Rufus Frank, a veteran of the French and Indian War, established a free household in the colony of Rhode Island—a society with slaves. I show how his two sons, William and Ben, carried on a military tradition set by an older generation of Frank men and eventually served together in the First Rhode Island Regiment of the Continental army. I show how these young freeborn men of color came to the military from a different background and brought a different perspective than those who had been enslaved. Their service years included the segregation of the Rhode Island regiments and the marriage of the younger brother. I also show how William and Ben fared as Black veterans after the war and helped to build and stabilize free Black communities in New England and Nova Scotia.

Their descendant Thomas Henry Franklin knew and understood the importance of his family's history in North America. He understood how he came to live in Nova Scotia. He passed along a piece of his family's story to succeeding generations. The larger story provides an uncommon and lesser-told narrative about life for free people of color during the revolutionary era. If Thomas Henry Franklin knew the whole story about his ancestors, he did not tell it to historian Morse. This book tells that story.

What follows are the experiences of an extraordinary family which starts on the west coast of Africa, makes stops at Saint-Domingue (Haiti), Rhode Island, and Nova Scotia. At each of these points, their lives became intricately bound to the greater events and greater communities in which they lived. It is a story about the origins of America. It is a story about family, loyalty, and military service. It is a story about two young men who fought to free the American colonies from the tyranny of the British Empire. It is a story about my ancestors, the Frank family, and how they survived the American Revolution.

To RECONSTRUCT my family's history, I started with Frank/Franklin oral tradition, with all its challenges. For example, the story passed along in my family included the Frank brothers' service in the Continental army (the gratifying and heroic part) but omitted the "desertion" of Ben Frank (the uncomfortable part), even though the desertion explained the family's migration to Canada. Because my research expanded a treasured family story, my relatives did not take any of my discoveries for granted, no matter how rigorous my research. They scrutinized my findings, questioning me and providing guidance to make sure I was now getting the "real" story. I held myself accountable to them as well as to the historical profession; the resulting story neither exaggerates nor minimizes the accomplishments of my ancestors and adds a needed dimension to our understanding of the revolutionary era.

Often these oral family traditions are discounted or disregarded as gossip or judged as a way to perpetuate myths about family lore. But, if one views oral traditions as oral documents, as proposed by David Kyvig and Myron Marty, then one can extract and examine those traditions and memories as invaluable pieces of historical evidence which can open the door to stories about individuals and communities not generally captured in the more traditional narratives of early America.[10] These explorations of family histories provide what Francesca Mari calls "a unique angle overlooked by elite texts and master narratives."[11] The oral tradition of the Frank/Franklin family serves as the foundation of this story and is typical of family stories which focus on details important to the family but lack connection to a greater historical context. The details of the Frank/Franklin story—that two brothers with the last name of Frank fought together in the Rhode Island "Black Regiment," and their ancestor came to America from Africa by way of Haiti—have been supported by documentary evidence such as vital, census, and military records, along with genetic genealogy. When I encountered silences in the oral tradition and the archival sources, I turned to the community of people who lived alongside Ben and William Frank. Over fifty documented free men of color, Black and Native American, served in the "Black Regiment" with William and Ben. Together, these men left behind a satisfying amount of documentary evidence. As I built a picture of this community of people, I saw my ancestors' place in the whole. Frank/Franklin family members did not leave behind personal records such as letters, diaries, journals, or memoirs, but I found traces of them in public records. Village

and town records show how they were active members of their communities—turning in stray livestock and seeking financial assistance from town
fathers. Military records document the conditions of their service—brutal
battles, illness at camp, segregation, poor equipment, insufficient pay, and
desertion. Marriage records recognize that family-building continued during
extreme times of war. Census and other inventory records detail their freedom and sense of family. By piecing together various fragments of historical
documents and evidence, the story of my ancestors started to take shape.[12]

The first step in connecting the conflicting stories was a study of the
military records of William and Ben Frank. The compiled service records
housed at the National Archives and the military records at the Rhode Island State Archives and Rhode Island Historical Society provided the first
clues to solving the mystery of the Canadian Franklins' lineage. Learning
about the desertion of Ben Frank provided the potential bridge to Thomas
Henry Franklin and his ancestors and helped to explain how the Franklins
came to be in Nova Scotia.

The second and more challenging step was to connect Ben Frank to the
wave of Black loyalists who migrated to Nova Scotia at the end of the Revolutionary War. With the assistance of a local historian, an avenue of research was opened. The curator of the Shelburne County Museum in
Shelburne, Nova Scotia, indicated that a young man in loyalist records,
named Benjamin Frankum/Frankham, who was the same age as Ben Frank,
may be the missing link connecting Ben Frank of Rhode Island to Ben
Franklin of Nova Scotia. Using this information as a starting point, I began
to situate what happened to Ben Frank during this interim period by using
Franklin oral tradition, loyalist migration records, and general loyalists' histories. One of the pivotal resources when examining the migration of Black
loyalists to Nova Scotia is the *Book of Negroes,* also known as the *Inspection
Roll of Negroes.* This document was created by British officials as a means
to inventory Blacks behind British lines at the end of the war. I believe Ben
is listed as Ben Frankham in the *Book of Negroes.* In a subsequent document,
Ben is listed as Ben Frankum on the "1784 Muster Roll of Birchtown, Nova
Scotia." After 1785, in Nova Scotia land petitions and records, regarding
Black loyalists, Ben is listed as Ben Franklin. There are no further references
to Ben Frankham or Ben Frankum in the records. The discrepancies in
these records regarding his surname can be attributed to a number of factors
and could have been accidental or deliberate. The individuals responsible
for capturing the names and details may have misunderstood Ben's enun-
ciation of his surname—Frankham, Frankum, and Franklin are similar. Or

Ben may have deliberately changed his name to hide his desertion and/or service with the Continentals.[13]

The next step was to make the connection of Ben Franklin to my great-grandfather, the landscaper Thomas Henry Franklin. An investigation of the archival collections at the Annapolis Heritage Society in Annapolis Royal, Nova Scotia, provided another important piece of the puzzle. The Society's Genealogy Centre, housed in a former ship captain's home, is the repository of local histories and genealogical records. A binder containing the genealogies of local Black families held the genealogical key to connecting my great-grandfather to Ben Frank. There was only one Franklin family listed in the binder. I quickly located my great-grandfather's name in the listing: Thomas Henry Franklin, born March 3, 1853, Granville, Nova Scotia; died May 1929, Lequille, Nova Scotia. I then located my grandfather, John Franklin. Tracing back in time from John Franklin's name, I found the first name on the family lineage chart—Benjamin Franklin, born?; died after 1838, Granville, Nova Scotia; m. ca. 1788(?), Granville, Nova Scotia to Margaret Jackson, daughter of Edward Jackson, Black loyalist. This was the direct link to Ben Frank. The Franklin oral history originated in this part of the family tree. The story of two brothers who fought together in the Revolutionary War originated with the patriarch of the Canadian Franklins, Ben Franklin. But what were Ben Frank's origins?[14]

A combination of military, vital, and census records helped to answer this question. A Rhode Island military register of 1781 lists vital information about William Frank and placed his residence in Johnston, Rhode Island, before the war. John Bartlett's index of the 1774 Rhode Island colonial census provided another important step to piecing together Ben's family connection. The index lists one free family of color residing in Johnston with the surname of Frank. Rufus Frank headed this household composed of five free people of color. This index did not provide the composition of the Frank family members of 1774 in Johnston, Rhode Island. To solve that riddle, I visited the Rhode Island State Archives. A copy of the census taker's original record showed one adult male, one adult female, two males under the age of sixteen, and one female under the age of sixteen. Other vital records helped to assign names to the impersonal numbers listed in the columns of the 1774 census.[15]

I reconstructed the family of Rufus Frank of Johnston, Rhode Island, using a variety of records that enabled me to identify the three siblings in the household. William Frank's military records placed his residence in Johnston at the time of his enlistment and recorded his age as twenty-one.

At the time of the 1774 census, William would have been approximately eighteen years old. After his military service, William returned to his hometown of Johnston. This evidence supports that William Frank was one of the males living in the 1774 household of Rufus Frank. Marriage, vital, and settlement records helped me to locate Ben Frank/Franklin as the second male juvenile in the Frank household. Marriage records placed his hometown as Johnston. A 1784 settlement inventory of Birchtown, Nova Scotia, recorded his age at twenty-two, making Ben twelve years old in 1774. The young female in the household was almost certainly Hannah Frank, but the documentary evidence is not as rich. Marriage records listed her place of residence as Johnston; and Ben Franklin named his second daughter Hannah. In naming his daughters, Ben followed family tradition of naming offspring after family members: his first daughter was named after his mother-in-law; his second daughter was named for his sister.[16]

Regarding the early generation of Frank men in colonial Rhode Island there is an intriguing person who by 1694 had established himself in Providence, the hometown of Rufus Frank—father of William and Ben. This person was known as "Frank Nigro." He is mentioned in five documents which relate to his activities in Providence—a generation before Rufus Frank. Rufus and other Frank men of his generation more than likely followed an African custom of adopting a revered ancestor's first name as their last. There is no documentary evidence that Frank Nigro bears a direct link of consanguinity to Rufus Frank, the Frank brothers, or their family in Johnston, Rhode Island. However, Rufus Frank resided in Providence before the French and Indian War. And given the small population of Providence in the years before the French and Indian War, Frank Nigro is most likely the ancestor of Rufus Frank.

Most of the evidence I used to reconstruct the Franklin family narrative came from archival documents. But I also turned to more unconventional and new methods. Locating records that documented the link to Ben Franklin and an ancestor from Africa by way of the Caribbean was next to impossible. Instead, I used DNA genealogical testing to trace the Franklins' transatlantic origins. Genealogists and family historians have used genetic genealogy as a method to connect African Americans to their distant African roots. For many African Americans, the search for their past ends at the western edge of the Atlantic Ocean. This was not the case for my family.[17]

Genetic genealogy helped to build a bridge to my ancestral roots. Most African Americans do not have written documentation and records to link us to our ancestral past. Some like my family have oral histories that have been passed down from generation to generation, which help to link the present to the past. The Y-chromosome DNA pattern, passed from father to son, moves along generational lines like surnames.[18] The path back from my Uncle Ben to family patriarch Ben Franklin is a direct male ancestral line—tracking the Franklin/Frank surname. The results of Uncle Ben's test corroborated Franklin oral tradition. His sample matched an individual residing in the Dominican Republic. This match puts the Frank/Franklin ancestral line remarkably close to its Haitian origins as related in my family's oral tradition. Another result showed an ancestral link to the Ewe Peoples of West Africa with a match to an individual residing in Togo.[19] This supported what Thomas Henry Franklin told local historian William Inglis Morse—that "my grandfather came from Africa."

The process of determining the appropriate racial or ethnic identity of members of the Rhode Island Continental army regiments has been challenging. The racial identifiers attached to minority members of the Rhode Island Continental line during the revolutionary period are not exact. For the most part, military records did not denote or identify the race or ethnicity of individual soldiers. Muster rolls and other returns do not offer this information. However, a Rhode Island regimental listing of 1781 does offer a descriptive listing of its soldiers, including racial labels assigned by the recording officer. To identify these men, I used other records to determine, verify, and crosscheck military returns and lists. Pension applications, completed with the assistance of veterans and their families, detailed the race or ethnicity of the applicant. I also used colonial and federal census records as well as church, court, and other local and vital records.

When noted in the records, a variety of terms have been used to racially mark the men of color who served as Rhode Island regulars. Some of the terms used to describe profiled soldiers are easily interpreted and recognized—"Negro," "colored," "black," or "Indian." Other terms are more physically descriptive, but less racially identifying, like the term "yellow," which could indicate a Native American or person of a mixed race background. Some are confusing and indicate the confused nature of racial labeling in the revolutionary period. "Mustee," "mulatto," or "man of color" could indicate any combination of nonwhite individuals. By the 1770s, adding to this confusion was the use of the terms "black" or "colored" by whites to refer to all people of color. Throughout this book, I use the phrase "men of color" to include Black, Native American, or mixed race individuals. When appropriate, I also use racial and ethnic identities as documented by terms used in official records.[20]

CHAPTER ONE

The Possible Ancestor:
Frank Nigro in
Colonial Rhode Island

THE ANCESTOR OF William and Ben Frank, who would serve together in the First Rhode Island Regiment in the Revolutionary War, was the first free member of this family line in America. This possible ancestor was known as Frank Nigro and, by 1694, he had established himself in Providence, the hometown of Rufus Frank—father of William and Ben. Frank Nigro's story illustrates the possible deep roots of this family in America. Frank gained his freedom at the turn of the eighteenth century and lived in a place central to the slave trade in North America. The surname of "Nigro" served as a racial identifier and an indication of his legal status—enslaved or previously enslaved. A surname rooted in his ancestral and familial origins was not a luxury afforded to Frank and other Blacks in colonial Rhode Island. So, Frank lived in a social system where the presence of slavery with all its restrictions and economic concerns dictated the lives of free Blacks as well as the enslaved.[1]

Five official records capture and document the status of Frank Nigro in colonial Providence and his attempts to survive his condition as an enslaved man, referred to as a "servant," before slavery became deeply entrenched in colonial Rhode Island and throughout the American colonies. These documents provide a glimpse into the life of this industrious man and show him as an engaged participant in a system designed to actively control his life and how he navigated that system. The documents confirm that he was a purchaser of land; was a landowner who leveraged his property for money; was the finder of a lost colt; and finally, was a victim of an assault. Frank's actions as detailed in the documents illustrate his attempts to gain economic competence but also to acquire status in his community. Respectability could be gained by a Black man in colonial America through his ability to take care of his family, own land, and foster relationships with "well-meaning" white men. The five documents provide a roadmap as to how Frank Nigro became "respectable" in the Providence community and set an example for succeeding generations of Frank men—which was foundational to their understanding of manhood.[2]

In 1694, Frank, as an indentured servant or enslaved by Silas Carpenter, purchased land in the township of Providence from Ephraim Carpenter (Document 1). The land sat near what would become the border between Providence and Johnston, Rhode Island. Frank acquired the £7 sterling necessary for the purchase by persistent, hard labor. His purchase of land from his master's nephew indicated Frank's connection to the larger Carpenter clan. Even though his enslavement did not prevent his purchase and ownership of land, the institution of slavery in colonial Providence permeated every aspect of his life—starting with the arrival of Frank or his ancestor to New England.[3]

Frank Nigro or his predecessor was a survivor of the transatlantic slave trade. Massachusetts and Rhode Island were the slave trafficking leaders in New England. Major ports of departure for slave ships were Boston, Salem, and Newburyport in Massachusetts and Newport, Providence, and Bristol in Rhode Island. The results of the slave trade can be seen in the Black population of New England. By 1680, there were an estimated 470 enslaved persons in New England. The growth continued with 1,680 enslaved in 1700 and 10,982 by the 1750s in the years before the French and Indian War.[4]

At the time of the Franks' arrival, in the second half of the seventeenth century, white New Englanders satisfied their need for unpaid labor with both Native Americans and Africans. Early on, as the English colonies grew and expanded commercial enterprises in the Caribbean, colonists initially turned to Native American captives as a source of labor on farms, in their shops, and in their households. After a crushing defeat in the Pequot War (1636–1638), Native American survivors were dispatched to

[**432**] Memorandum That I Ephraim Carpenter now Resident into Pautuxett in the Towneship of Providence in ye Colloney of Rhode Jsland have & doe Sell make & pass over from me, my heirs Exsecutors Administrators & Assignes unto ffrank Nigro Servant of Silas Carpenter of the Towneshipp & Collony aforesaid his heirs Exsecutors, Administrators & Assignes all that Right of land wch is mine or that doth any wayes belong unto me without the line by the Towne of Providence Called ye Seven mile line. (videlicet) a Right or shier of land which was Given to me by my Honored Grandfather William Carpenter deceased, as it appeares in his last will & Testament All which said Right or shier of land aforsaid for & in Consideration of Seven pounds Sterling in hand already well & truely payd unto me by the sd ffrank Nigro I doe sell & pass over from me my heirs Exsecutors Administrators & Assignes unto the aforesaid ffrank Nigro his heirs Exsecutors Administrators & Assignes To have & to hold the said Right or shier of land & to be for the only proper vse & behoofe of the said ffrank Nigro his heirs Exsecutors, Administrators & Assignes for Ever Clearely & freely Exonerated Aquitted & discharged, or otherwise by me the said Ephraim Carpenter Sufficiently Saved & kept harmeless from any Challing clayme or demand whatsoever which I or any from, by, or under me shall Challinge Clayme or demand in or to the·land above bargained, And [**433**] in wittnes hereof I have hereunto sett my hand & seale this Thirtieth day of June Anno Domini Nostri one thousand Six hundred & Ninty foure.

Signed Sealed   Ephraim Carpenter jun^r.
& delivered in
the presence of us
James Dexter
            his
Richard X Marshall
           mark
Stephen Arnold Junr:

Document 1. Land purchase of Frank Nigro from Ephraim Carpenter. (*Horatio Rogers, George Moulton Carpenter, and Edward Field, editors. The Early Records of the Town of Providence, Volume V. Providence: Snow & Farnham City Printers, 1894*)

the Caribbean and exchanged for enslaved Africans to take their place in the fields, industries, and households of white New Englanders. In this manner, Native American slavery foreshadowed the nature of slavery for Africans in New England.[5]

In seventeenth-century New England, enslaved Blacks comprised a small fraction of the population and its overall growth in New England was slow-moving. Most worked in the households of their owners. Some men were trained in the trades and became skilled laborers. Others worked on the land and farmed alongside their enslavers. They existed in a position between indentured servitude and chattel slavery where the enslaved were seen as pieces of property. They were often referred to as "servants" instead of "slaves." But for taxation purposes, they were regarded, in Massachusetts, as both persons and property. In Rhode Island and New Hampshire, laws treated them similar to livestock. And even when recognized as persons before the law, they only had rights as given by their enslavers or granted by specific laws—unlike indentured servants, who were regulated primarily by their contracts.[6]

By the early 1700s, Rhode Island merchants had become leaders in the slave-trading business. Newport was the second largest slave-trading port in New England. Rhode Island enslavers sold enslaved Africans primarily in the West Indies, with two-thirds of their African cargo sold in the Caribbean and one-third sold in mainland North America. The slave merchants rarely reserved whole shipments of enslaved Africans for the New England market. They sold most of their shipments in the plantation colonies; however, merchants did carry a few enslaved persons back to Rhode Island for sale. In May 1696 fourteen enslaved Africans became the first documented group of Blacks purchased directly from Africa. These unfortunate souls arrived in Newport aboard the Boston-owned ship *Seaflower* as part of a cargo of forty-seven enslaved Africans and were sold for £30 to £35 each. Four years later, in 1700, Rhode Island's first documented slaving voyage embarked to the west coast of Africa, eventually bringing a shipment of enslaved Africans to Barbados.

The first Blacks brought to Rhode Island were not legally enslaved in perpetuity. Rhode Island's 1652 statute prohibited lifelong servitude and was followed for a time. But that time was brief. Within a decade of the enactment of the 1652 statute, Rhode Island officials passed a series of laws which legalized a system of race-based slavery. Starting in 1703, the Rhode Island Assembly passed laws controlling the movement and activities of Black and Native American servants, i.e., prohibiting householders from entertaining these servants without their owner's permission. In totality, the statutes legally recognized the enslavement of Native Americans and Blacks. However, in 1715, the Assembly prohibited the importation of enslaved Native Americans to the colony, as did other northern colonies during this time period. As a result of this and other factors, such as war, disease, and banishment, Native American slavery in Rhode Island had lessened by the turn of the eighteenth century. Wendy Warren argues that "the work of colonization had proceeded thus: Indians and Africans had replaced each other in ways orchestrated by settler colonists, for the purposes of profit and expansion."[7] By 1750 Rhode Island had the highest percentage of slave ownership in New England. Frank Nigro lived in the slave capital of New England, where the institution of slavery stood at the center of its commercial interests.[8]

Since the Frank forefather arrived during the period of recognized but not legalized slavery, there was a pathway in place for him to gain his freedom. Blacks at this time were often treated like indentured servants and released after ten years. Even in a society with slaves, there were opportunities for the enslaved to gain their freedom. Some enslaved persons purchased their own liberty. Some were freed by grateful enslavers after many years of service. Some were freed upon their enslaver's death. Others earned their freedom through military service.[9]

If enslaved, the Frank ancestor was forced into a system of enslaved labor that had developed in the colony over years. There were three types of slave-holding in colonial Rhode Island. In the wealthy slave-trading seaport of Newport, most enslaved Blacks were house servants or worked on ships, on the wharves, or in the shops of merchants. In the southern part of the state, in regions like Narragansett Country, the enslaved worked on the large farms in the area, producing wool, agricultural products, and livestock on the hoof for sale to Caribbean plantations to feed their enslaved workforce. In urban areas, like Providence, the enslaved worked at a variety of trades, which included distillery work, blacksmithing, carpentry, fishing, shoemaking, and domestic service. Enslaved Blacks worked and lived closely around whites. They also lived an isolated life—separate from other Blacks, enslaved or free. They lived in attic spaces, cellars, kitchens, and small garrets. They survived off the food scraps of their enslavers and, like other members of the bound labor class and the poor, they suffered from malnutrition.[10]

Frank Nigro's status in the community was tied to his relationship with the Carpenter family of Pawtuxet, Rhode Island, and by 1694 he was enslaved or bound to Silas Carpenter, the youngest son to the Carpenter patriarch, William. For the Carpenters and others, the use of bound labor enhanced their circumstances to shape and control their communities. Carpenter family lore asserts that William Carpenter was the first person with the surname of Carpenter to permanently settle in North America. William arrived at Roger Williams's dissident colony from the parish of Amesbury, England, in April 1636. And whether he holds the distinction of being the first, William was the patriarch of the Providence line of the Carpenters in the American colonies—heading a family that acquired important positions and land holdings in early Rhode Island. He married

Elizabeth Arnold about 1637 at Providence. They had a total of eight children.[11]

For the Carpenters, the early accumulation of land in Providence, then Pawtuxet, led to their status as leading figures in colonial Rhode Island. Founded in 1638 by William Arnold, William Harris, Zachariah Rhodes, and William Carpenter, Pawtuxet is one of Rhode Island's oldest communities. It gained its name from the Sononoce, a clan of the Narragansett Native American Nation. The village sits at the mouth of the Pawtuxet River in the present cities of Cranston and Warwick. However, the original settlement was part of Providence—where William Carpenter was listed on the initial deed, dated August 8, 1638, drafted by Roger Williams at the time of its settlement. Carpenter, along with his father-in-law William Arnold, William Harris, and Zachariah Rhodes exchanged their initial holdings at Providence for a large tract of land at Pawtuxet in the "Towneshipp of Providence." It was described as a "beautiful meadow-land, about four miles southerly from Providence, bounded on the east by Narragansett Bay and on the south by the Pawtuxet River."[12]

William Carpenter built a homestead, raised his large family, and spent the remainder of his life, fifty years, in Pawtuxet. His life there is well chronicled due to his friendship with the colony's founder, Roger Williams, and his status in the community. He served for over a decade on the General Court of Trials. As elected members of the court, he and his son, Ephraim, and grandson, Silas, Jr., were tasked with administering justice in cases of serious criminal offenses and important civil disputes as dictated by Rhode Island's code of laws. He was appointed as Deputy of the General Assembly in 1679 and performed the role of the magistrate at judicial tribunals. As a community leader, he served on various commissions charged with infrastructure building, like laying out roads and determining locations of bridges.[13]

William was not content with his initial landholdings, and he continued to expand his Pawtuxet empire. Twenty years after the founding of Pawtuxet, he purchased additional land. He acquired the "Land laying below Pawtuxet Falls . . . of that place commonly called the Vinyard" from John Greene, Jr., including the land and water rights near the Pocasset River. The acquisition of this land and other holdings allowed William to increase his commercial enterprises.[14]

William Carpenter supplemented his holdings by running a sawmill. William operated the mills with his youngest sons, Silas and Benjamin. The Carpenters operated at least two sawmills in the region—one at

Pawtuxet and the second in the meadowlands near the gristmill operated by miller John Smith. The mills were an integral part of a flourishing trade system between the colony and the West Indies, providing products and timber used to build ships and barrels to carry foodstuffs to Caribbean plantations from Pardon Tillinghast's warehouse and wharf—the first built in Providence in 1679. The Pawtuxet trade included tobacco cultivated by Warwick farmers and beef packed in barrels from the Pawtuxet region. These products and others were transported by traders to the Caribbean. The Brown family of Providence engaged in this type of intercolonial trade by supplying the slave societies of the West Indies with necessities like cheese, horses, and tobacco.[15]

Upon his death, William bequeathed substantial landholdings to his children. His bequest to his two youngest sons, Silas and Benjamin, focused on their joint ownership of the sawmills. The land in Pawtuxet Neck and the Vinyard was left to the brothers—possibly the site of the two mills. Additionally, the brothers were taxed jointly in 1688 for the land owned in Pawtuxet. A portion of middle meadowlands was left to William's fourth child, Timothy. However, William made sure to set aside the rights of passage through that land for Silas and Benjamin—making sure that there was a "suficient high way at all times" to traverse that section of the meadow. This was possibly done to allow for the movement of product from the mills to town. He left the tools of the trade and carpentry for his sons, "Carts, Ploughs, & all tacklin." The term "tacklin" described a variety of mill equipment such as axes, saws, augers, irons, and chisels. The inventory of William Carpenter's estate does not list any holdings of enslaved persons. However, the operation of his sawmills more than likely benefitted from the bound labor of Frank Nigro.[16]

By 1690, Frank Nigro was the documented "servant" of William's son Silas. His documented status as a servant or as an enslaved man was unclear in seventeenth-century Rhode Island. Many enslaved persons were referred to as servants in official records and treated more like indentured servants. As stated earlier, Rhode Island had passed a statute in 1652 prohibiting lifelong servitude and limiting involuntary servitude to ten years—however, this statute was not followed. Therefore, Frank Nigro served Silas Carpenter in a loosely defined state of enslavement. Silas was born at Pawtuxet around 1650–1651. He died a decade after his father at the age of 45–46 years in 1695. Following in the footsteps of his father, Silas also married into the Arnold clan. He married Sarah Arnold in 1680. Four children were born of this union.[17]

As co-owner of the Carpenter milling enterprise, Silas would have used Frank's labor in the operation of the sawmills. Working alongside his owner, Frank gained firsthand knowledge of milling and the skills needed to get a product to market and interact with customers, which was typical of the lives of skilled enslaved men in New England. These skilled enslaved laborers were afforded more opportunity and autonomy than enslaved women and unskilled laborers. And Frank was learning a valuable skill. Sawyers (men who processed timber by sawing or who owned a sawmill) were important members of the community. They were multitalented men who owned the land as well as the mills that sat on the land. They had to have a knowledge of the trade, understand the marketplace, and be able to maintain mill equipment. That was the case for the Carpenters. Sawyer's fees were not cheap—expected costs were generally one-quarter of the lumber processed. An additional skilled hand, like Frank, enabled the Carpenters to mill more wood, thus making more money. For instance, a skilled sawyer with the help of an assistant could make over 1,000 feet of pine boards in a day. Frank working in proximity at the sawmill with the Carpenters gained the skills and social connections that could advance his standing in the community even though still held in bondage. If allowed to market and sell his acquired skills to others then Frank could acquire the funds necessary to purchase property.[18]

Many enslaved Blacks were used as skilled laborers throughout New England, including Rhode Island. Free sawyers, carpenters, and coopers could operate under a piece-wage system which allowed skilled laborers to be paid by the piece. They performed an important part of an economic system developed in Rhode Island whose chief commodities included "lumber of all sorts" for shipment to the West Indies. Bound laborers, like Frank, also played a role in this work. If not used in their enslavers' enterprises, enslaved artisans were sometimes rented or hired out by their owners. When an enslaved person was hired out, the enslaver and the employer completed a contract that stipulated the length of service, the type of work performed, and the compensation paid to the owner. Conversely, the enslaved could self-hire, procuring short-term and long-term employment on their own. Enslaved men had greater opportunities in urban areas like Providence, to sell their labor to individuals who were not their enslavers. Their owners, of course, would share in the earnings of the enslaved laborers, but sometimes the enslaved were able to keep portions of their earnings. If Frank could hire out his services and keep his wages, then he would be able to purchase land from his owner's nephew with his own money.[19]

Frank Nigro was in servitude to Silas Carpenter when he purchased land from Ephraim Carpenter, his owner's nephew in 1694. The enslaved in New England could legally possess and transfer landholdings. And for Frank Nigro, land ownership afforded a level of status in his community. Historians Elizabeth Pleck and Catherine Adams argue that respectable Black men displayed courage, took advantage of good land deals, and made "alliances with well-meaning whites." Frank Nigro fits this profile. He took advantage of his relationship with the Carpenter family and purchased land. The land in question was bequeathed to Ephraim by his grandfather upon his death in 1685.[20]

The ownership of land placed Frank into a very small community of landowning blacks. And in the minds of free and enslaved Blacks, land ownership was tied integrally to their definition of freedom. They understood that economic independence relied on owning one's own land or business. The land purchased, while not granting Frank the privilege of the vote, did allow him to leverage his land and acquire funds to support a family—eventually as a free man.[21]

The second document details the mortgaging of Frank Nigro's property—possibly an indication that the servant needed seed money to start a farming enterprise or had immediate needs to provide for himself or his family (Document 2). A few days after the initial purchase, Frank used the land as collateral on a loan of £5 sterling from Stephen Arnold, the father-in-law of Frank's owner, Silas Carpenter. This loan called for the repayment of the original loan of £5 and an annual interest rate of 6 percent. During the period of the mortgage bond, Stephen Arnold held the rights and share of the mortgaged land for his (Arnold's) own benefit.[22]

In the aftermath of mortgaging his land to Stephen Arnold, a major change took place in the life of Frank Nigro. In a close review of the five documents, between the time he purchased and mortgaged his property and repaid the loan, Frank gained his freedom from Silas Carpenter. Sometime between the date of the mortgage bond, July 2, 1694, where he is still listed as a "servant" of Silas Carpenter, and the death of said Carpenter in December of 1695, Frank became a free man. He did not appear in the will or inventory of the movable estate of Silas Carpenter. The will was composed two days before Silas' death, and he was aware of his imminent demise when acknowledging such in his last will and testament. Could Silas have freed Frank in the days before his death as a reward for years of dedicated service? It was not unusual for owners to manumit enslaved persons for long service or for performing

[**47**] Be it knowne unto all PerSons That I ffrank Nigroe Servant to Silas Carpenter of Pautuxet, in Providence, in the Collony of Rhode Island & Providence Plantations in New England, have Granted Bargained & Sold & paSt over from Me my heirs Executors AdminiStrators & ASsignes unto Stephen Arnold of Pautuxet in the Towne & Collony aforeSd, his heirs Executors AdMiniStrators & ASsignes, all that SSs land or lands, devided or Undevided Which is mine or doe anywayes belong unto Me, Which Right I bought of Epharaim Carpenter junior, on the WeSt Side of the line Called the Seven Mile line Which is in the TowneShipp & PreSinckes of Providence Towne, as in & by a deed beareing date yᵉ thirtyeth day of June 1694 doth therein plainely appeare; All Which Share & Right, of land aforeSd, for & CoNSideratioN of the Sum of five Pounds in Sterling Money in hand already Received by Me the aforeSd ffrank Nigro I doe Grant, Alien, Enfeoff, Bargaine, Sell & Confirme unto the aforeSd Stephen Arnold, his heirs Executors, AdminiStrators & ASsignes forEver To have & to hold all the foreSd Right *[of land] or Share of land, and to be for the Only Proper USe & benefit of the aforeSd Stephen Arnold, his Heir Executors, AdminiStrators & ASsignes foreVer, Clearely Aquitted and diScharged from all troubles, MoleStations, & from all juSt & lawfull Claimes I Will Warrant & forEver defend by theSe preSents; AlWayes Provided & it is NevertheleSs agreed; That if I the foreSd ffrank Nigroe, My heirs, Executors, AdminiStrators or ASsignes doe betweene the day of the date hereof & the Second day of July, Which Will be in the yeare one ThouSand Six hundred Ninty Eight, doe pay or CauSe to be payed unto the foreSd Stephen Arnold his heirs Executors AdminiStrators or ASsignes, or by either of their Order the full & juSt Sum of five Pound in Current Silver Money in NeW England, and alSo to pay the yearely IntreSt of the foreSd five Pound after yᵉ Rate of Six Pound in the hundred, & to pay it ANNually in yᵉ like Silver Money at yᵉ houSe of yᵉ foreSd Stephen Arnold at Pautuxet; And if it be all paid according to yᵉ Contents of theSe preSents; Then this bargaine of Sale Shall be Voyd & Null & of None Effect, anything herein Contained NotWithStanding; But if it be Not performed according to the Contents hereof, then this deede of bargaine & Sale Shall Stand firme in full force Power & Vertue in the laW to all intents according to yᵉ Meaneing & true intent of theSe preSents: In WitneSs of this My Reall act act & deede, I doe hereunto Set My hand & Seale, this Second day of July one ThouSand Six hundred ninty foure; Memorandun that the Word; of: in yᵉ ninth line; & the Word: Pound: in yᵉ twentieth line, Were interlined before Signeing & Sealeing.

Signed Sealed & delivered	his
in yᵉ preSence of, Viz	ffrank F Nigroe L. S.
Ephraim Carpenter junʳ:	mark
his	
Richard R MarShall	Recorded September yᵉ
mark	17ᵗʰ 1706 ꝑ Me
James dexter. /	Tho: Olney Towne Clerk. /

Document 2. Land mortgage of Frank Nigro to Stephen Arnold. (*William E. Clarke, The Early Records of the Town of Providence, Volume XX Providence: Snow & Farnham Co., City Printers, 1909*)

"extraordinary" acts. For example, the manumission record for "Peter Palmer (negro man) late servant to William Randall" in 1702 contained language such as this. The document stated that "the good faithfull service done by the said negro . . . give him said Peter Palmer his freedom for ever." Many manumissions were generally carried out in the wills of grateful owners. But Silas' will did not contain such a manumission. Frank was freed from his servitude before Silas died on Christmas Day 1695.[23]

[**65**] Whereas ffrank Negro of Providence in the Collony of Rhode Island & Providence Plantations in the NarraganSet Bay in New England did for the ConSideration of five Pounds in Silver Money Which he received of Stephen Arnold of Pautuxett in the TowneShipp of Providence aforeSaid (now deceaSed,) by a mortgage bond beareing date the Second day of July one ThouSand Six hundred Ninty foure, PaSs, Make Over & lay to Pawne all his Right of laNds devided & undevided lieing & being on the WeSt Side of the line Called the Seven Mile line in the TowneShipp of Providence aforeSd unto the aforeSaid Stephen ArNOld his heirs, Executors, AdminiStrators & ASsignes, forever, for Securitye of the paying back of the Said five Pounds in Money & the USe according as the CoNditions of Said bond doth ExpreSs; The which Sd bond is Recorded in Said Providence Records in the booke for Entry of deeds or land Evidences NuMber two, & in Page forty & Seven: and in CaSe Said Money were all Paid according to the Contents of the Said InStrument Then that the Said inStrument Should be Voyd & Null, & of NONe Effect. Bee it therefore knowne unto all People by theSe PreSents, That wee Stephen ArNold & EliSha Arnold both of Pautuxett in Providence aforeSaid, Sons unto the aforeSaid deceaSed Stephen Arnold, & Executors of his laSt Will & TeStament doe oWne & ackNOWledge that We have of the Said ffrank Negro Received all & whole the Said Moneys in the Said bond or inStrument ExpreSt & injoyned to be Paid, & that the Sd ffrank Negro hath fully performed all the Conditions in the Sd InStruMent Contained, whereby the Said inStrument is Wholy & fully Evaqueated, made Null & Voyd & become as if it Never had been Made, & the aforeSd Record thereof to be of NO fOrce NOr Value: And Wee doe hereby aquit & fully diScharge the Said ffrank Negro of all Moneys & PayMents in Sd inStruMent Engaged unto; In WittneSs of the PremiSes Wee the Sd Stephen Arnold & EliSha ArNold have hereunto Set our hands & Seales the TWentyeth day of ffebruarey ANNo: one thouSand |Seven| *[Six] hundred & Six or Seven.

Stephen Arnold L. S.
EliSha Arnold L. S.

Signed, Sealed, & delivered
in the preSence of us
JoSeph Williams ASsiStant
The Mark of **A** Abell Potter

Recorded ffebruarey yᵉ 25ᵗʰ
170⁶/₇ ℔ me Tho: Olney
Towne Clerk. /

October yᵉ 16ᵗʰ: 1707 ffranke Negro: of Providence gave notice that he hath taken up a horse Coult, a stray, of Colour black, no white, neither Eare marked nor branded; about two yeares old & vantage, proclaimed, & Enteed October 16ᵗʰ 1707: ℔ Tho: Olney Towne Clerk. /

Document 3, top. Mortgage repayment of Frank Nigro to the heirs of Stephen Arnold. (*William E. Clarke, The Early Records of the Town of Providence, Volume XX Providence: Snow & Farnham Co., City Printers, 1909*) Document 4, bottom. Notice that Franke Negro found a lost colt. (*Horatio Rogers, George Moulton Carpenter, and Edward Field, editors. The Early Records of the Town of Providence, Volume IX. Providence: Snow & Farnham City Printers, 1895*)

Frank Nigro repaid the loan to the heirs of Stephen Arnold in February 1706—meeting all conditions of the original mortgage bond (Document 3). He paid "all and whole" of the money imposed by the original agreement to Stephen and Elisha Arnold, which amounted to £5 sterling. Frank had also been required to make yearly interest payments to Stephen Arnold and his heirs, to be delivered annually to their home in Pawtuxet, in the amount of 6 percent of the original loan. The repayment of the loan solidified

Frank's position as a hard-working and reliable member of the Providence community.[24]

Eight months after paying off the mortgage bond, Frank turned in a lost colt to the local constable—hoping that the colt would eventually become his property if no rightful owner was found (Document 4). By the early 1700s, horses proliferated in the Rhode Island landscape. William Harris, one of the original proprietors of the colony, lamented that the colony was overrun by horses. So finding a lost colt was not an unusual occurrence. And Frank's delivery of the colt to the town constable was decreed by a local statute, since most New England towns required townspeople to bring lost and stray livestock to the constable or designated pound. Along with land, ownership of livestock was another method of gaining economic competence and stability. Most New England colonists used their farm lots to produce enough to sustain their own families, and the achievement of that goal was aided by the ownership and use of livestock. The addition of a colt may not have been as beneficial as acquiring other livestock, like oxen (used for plowing and hauling) or hogs (used for eating), as horses were used in a limited fashion for carting items and riding. And if not used on the farm, Frank could have sold the colt to an interested neighbor. Overall, the acquisition of land coupled with livestock ownership provided Frank the tools to achieve financial stability.[25]

The fifth document provides an example of Frank Nigro's knowledge and understanding of his place in the Providence community (Document 5). As a testament to his status in his hometown, Frank sought and received justice for an assault committed against him. Frank obviously understood the workings of the legal system and how to make it work for him. Even though Blacks could not serve on juries in the New England colonies, they did hold some rights in the courts. The initial judicial system established in Providence used arbitration as the means to settle disputes in the colony. If an arbitration did not meet the needs of the petitioners, then they could appeal the decision at general town meetings. The union and charter of the four original towns of Rhode Island in 1644 led to the establishment of a General Court of Trials to adjudicate crimes and civil cases. Under the Royal Charter of 1663, the Royal Governor, Deputy Governor, and Assistants were designated to serve not only in an executive function but in a judicial capacity as well—holding the General Court of Trials twice a year at Newport to handle civil cases and serious criminal offenses. Additional courts were also established at Warwick and Providence to handle lesser offenses. Frank Nigro may have obtained knowledge about

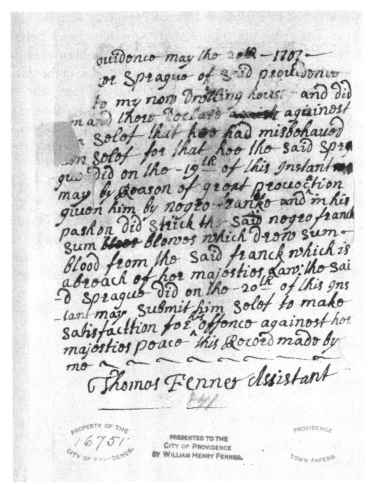

Document 5. Legal record of "Negro Franck" as a victim of assault. (*Rhode Island Historical Society. Providence Town Papers. MSS 214, Series 1, Volume 39A, No. 16751*)

the court system from his relationship with the Carpenter family. William Carpenter served for over a decade on the General Court of Trials. His son Ephraim, from whom Frank purchased land, also served as an elected member of the court, tasked with administering justice in cases of serious criminal offenses and other disputes.[26]

The assault occurred in May 1707, after Frank had paid off his debt to the Arnold family. The criminal complaint named "negro franck" as the victim. It is important to note that in general, Blacks in colonial New England were forbidden to strike or defame white persons. In this case,

Frank was attacked by a fellow resident of Providence with the last name of Sprague. The complaint summarized the vicious attack perpetrated against Frank by Sprague, which appeared to have been prompted by actions taken by Frank. Sprague was not only charged with the assault but convicted and fined an amount of two shillings and four pence for his "misbehavior" against a Black man—possibly a Black man who had earned his freedom, owned land, and had ties to prominent members of the Providence community. Frank Nigro was a Black man who understood his status in his community.[27]

The life and experiences of Frank Nigro provide a glimpse into a bound man who survived his condition as a "servant" by skillfully navigating a system created to control his life and impede his survival. He obtained the attributes of respectability—skilled trade and land—by using his learned skills and relationships with prominent citizens. His work and tenacity are characteristics that would be illustrated in the lives of those succeeding generations of men carrying the Frank name.

CHAPTER TWO

The Frank Family
Before the
Revolutionary War

FRANK NIGRO LIVED in Providence at least one generation before one young freeman who held the surname of Frank—following the West African custom of adopting a revered ancestor's first name as a surname. If this young man was indeed the descendant of Frank Nigro, then as a freeman, Rufus Frank continued a tradition of family-building and began a family tradition of community involvement which included military service. Rufus served in the Providence militia during the French and Indian War. He was at least sixteen years of age, at the time of his service, since the required age of militia service was sixteen to sixty years of age. After the war, Rufus and his young family established a household in Johnston—a satellite community of Providence.[1]

Even without a documented connection between Frank Nigro and Rufus Frank, he (Frank Nigro) appears to be the first one of a growing population of Black individuals with the name of Frank in Providence and Rhode Island during the colonial period. So, Rufus Frank was not alone. He resided near other Black Franks, enslaved and free, who participated in the daily rhythms of life known to African Americans in that New England colony. For example, Job and Mary Frank, both of Barrington, Rhode Island, made intentions to be married at the Congregational Church of that town on December 18, 1738.[2]

Of particular interest to this study is a collection of Franks who resided in the Providence community before the French and Indian War. Of those individuals, Phillip Frank had a direct connection to Rufus because he (Rufus) was named the administrator of Phillip's estate in 1758. The probate records do not provide the exact relationship between Phillip and Rufus, but Rhode Island statute required that the administration of the estate of any person who died intestate be granted to the next of kin. It was the duty of the next of kin to provide notice of the deceased to the county court in order to be named administrator of the estate. Phillip Frank was also a resident of Providence. He served in the militia, in Lt. Colonel Angell's Company, for one campaign during the French and Indian War, a year before Rufus started his service in 1757. Given the date of his death, Phillip was possibly a generation older than Rufus. Was Phillip actually Frank Nigro? He did own some sort of property which precipitated an administration bond for his estate. However, Phillip served in the Rhode Island militia during the French and Indian War, almost fifty years after Frank Nigro's assault case in 1707 and sixty-two years after Frank Nigro's purchase of a parcel of land from Ephraim Carpenter. In general, militia service required able-bodied men between the age of sixteen years and sixty years to serve. During times of alarm, all men were required to turn out. If still living, Frank Nigro would be well past the age of required service or able-bodied during the French and Indian War. If there was a familial connection between Frank Nigro and Phillip, it could be as siblings or more likely as father-son or uncle-nephew.[3]

There is another Frank who passed away three years before Phillip's death—probably making him a member of the same generation as Phillip, possibly a brother. Like Phillip, Andrew Frank grew to manhood in the generation before Rufus Frank. Andrew married in 1742. "Josiah Cotton minister gave notis that he had Joyned together in marriage Andrew Frank and Sarah a negro on 25 of April 1742."[4] There is indication that Andrew Frank served in the militia. There is also an indication that Andrew and Sarah had a child named after his father. Seven years after his marriage, on October 15, 1755, Andrew died and was recognized as a veteran of colonial wars. He left personal property worth more than £22. He owned a note of hand, an IOU of possibly money owned to him, worth £60, clothing, an old Bible, 2,400 pounds of hay, a cow, two calves, and a gun. He also left

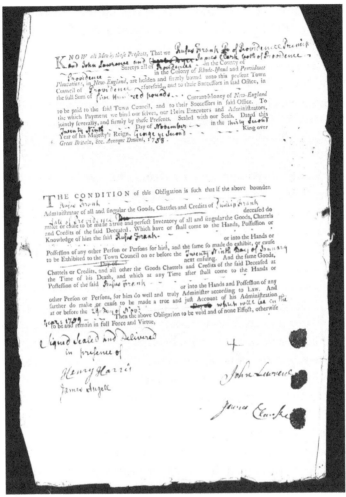

Administration Bond of the estate of Phillip Frank, 1758, naming Rufus Frank as administrator. (*Providence Old City Hall Archives. Wills and Probate Records, 1582-1932*)

behind a son, Andrew Frank, who would later serve with the Rhode Island militia during the Revolutionary War.[5]

Another Frank, Samuel, also served as a member of the Providence militia during the French and Indian War. He served in the 1756 and 1760 campaigns, as a member of Captain Christopher Harris' company. Samuel Frank is enumerated as Black or Native American in the 1800 and 1810 Federal Censuses, living in Johnston, Rhode Island. Since Samuel survived until the early nineteenth century, he was likely a member of the same generation as Rufus Frank. And since he was not named as administrator of the estate of Phillip Frank, it does not appear that Samuel was a son or could usurp Rufus' connection to Phillip.[6]

The elder Andrew's death in 1755 prevented him from serving in the French and Indian War. Rufus, as a freeman, served and received payment for his service which spanned from 1757 to 1762, ending with the Siege of Havana in 1762. His service carried on a pattern of military service set by Andrew and Phillip Frank and continued by the next generation of Frank men.

Rufus Frank served at a time of change for the British military. The crisis of the French and Indian War pushed the British enlistment system to the breaking point. Many New England towns were unable to supply their quota of soldiers for the colonial forces from the white population. Because of these shortages, recruiting officers gladly accepted free and enslaved Blacks and Native Americans into military service. At the time, the general policy in colonial America excluded Blacks from military service and from bearing arms. Most state laws precluded Blacks from militia responsibility or service. Massachusetts was the first colony to institute the practice of labor service over service in arms. A 1707 statute stipulated that Blacks shared the benefits of military protection and should earn that protection by performing "service equivalent to trainings." This translated into street cleaning, highway maintenance, and other public service details.[7]

Rhode Island preferred real military service over labor service. In 1667, the Rhode Island legislature required that all men between the ages of sixteen and sixty serve in the militia, except for civil servants. In 1676, the state legislature proclaimed that "a man capable of watch . . . shall be liable to that service." Watch service, however, did not require arms-bearing. The 1676 act also voided a clause exempting conscientious objectors from militia service. There were no other exemptions listed in the act. A 1718 act required all men to serve in times of alarm, even if they did not train with the militia. After 1700 the militia included free Blacks, Native Americans, and transient white males—people who had previously been excluded from militia service.[8]

As indicated by the militia service of Andrew Frank, this legislation did not prevent Black service. Rhode Island's militia acts did require men of color—Blacks and Native Americans—to perform community service. But the service for men of color was limited to watch service and not bearing arms. For the most part, Blacks in the militia served in noncombatant roles performing construction and repair work or serving as drummers and fifers.

Blacks—free or enslaved—were excluded from bearing arms, unless in exigent circumstances. However, if the need was great enough, officials turned a blind eye to their exclusionary statutes. Rhode Island acts regarding Black participation in the militia fall within the "did not exclude" category since most of these acts did not exclude Blacks from service. This atmosphere may have provided the best opportunity for Black soldiers to serve equally with whites, since they made no stipulations about Black service. Blacks served in the colonial defense as members of integrated fighting units. The records do not indicate any difference in treatment due to their race. Black soldiers received the same pay, but enslaved soldiers had to give all or half of their wages to their owners. Additionally, free and enslaved Blacks were still bound by Black Codes that regulated their behavior throughout the colony. Statutes of exclusion enacted by other colonies broke down during times of war, when limited manpower led to the acceptance of Black recruits, both slave and free. This policy of semi-exclusion was so prevalent it became a basic feature of American military history.[9]

The first documented incident of Black military service in New England occurred in 1690. In that year, an enslaved man was killed by enemy forces while in service aboard a British ship. British officials reimbursed his master for his loss at £20. In 1713 a New Hampshire enslaved male fought at Fort William Henry and his master was compensated for that service. Blacks fought in King William's War (1690–1697), Queen Anne's War (1702–1713), King George's War (1744–1748), and in the French and Indian War (1755–1763). In the French and Indian War, Black soldiers served in a greater military capacity as soldiers, scouts, and waggoners. Connecticut saw Black soldiers serve in twenty-five different companies. Blacks saw service in Massachusetts, as well. The town of Hingham recruited Primus Cobb and Flanders for Captain Edward Ward's company. The servant of James Richardson of Stonington, Connecticut, served in the Rhode Island militia. Rhode Island Blacks bearing names of James, Caesar, and Benjamin Negro also served in the Providence militia.[10]

Rufus Frank joined this group of Black soldiers in service and mustered out of Providence during the war. Rufus's service included the campaigns of 1759 and 1762 and posting at Fort Stanwix in 1761 with service in the companies of Captains John Whiting, Daniel Wall, Christopher Harris, Burkitt, and Eddy. Rufus and other free Black soldiers received pay like their white counterparts, but owners received the salaries earned by enslaved soldiers. Rufus received payment on January 23, 1758, in the amount of over £43 for his service in Captain Whiting's Company and received an additional £12 in the following year.[11]

Rufus Frank may have served in a support capacity with occasional combat experience, possibly experiencing fierce conflict.[12] The actions of William Smith, another member of Captain Whiting's Company, illustrated the tough fighting that occurred at the Battle of Ticonderoga. In a letter written at Lake George on July 26, 1758, Smith's commanding officer wrote about his skill at fighting:

> William Smith a Private of Capt. Whiting's Company, in the Rhode Island Regiment, when the Attack was made at Ticonderoga, conceal'd himself under the Enemy's Breast Work, and when any Opportunity, offer'd, he improv'd it, by discharging his Piece, with which he killed and wounded, many . . . a Frenchman stept upon the Parapet, and turned the Muzzel of his Gun, mow'ed a brace of Balls, which penetrated his Shoulder, and enter'd his Body. This Treatment greatly exasperated him; but when he had recover'd from the shock which it gave, he was determin'd to destroy as many more of his Enemies as possible; loaded, and with great difficulty rais'd himself upon the Lines, and kill'd one; upon which another endeavour'd to get rid of him, by aiming a Blow at his Head with a Tomahawk, which with more Fortitude and Dexterity, than Strength, he avoided, by opposing his Hatchet to prevent it, and immediately disparch'd him also, the Hatchet entering his Skull, wich requir'd some Time to force it out, for further execution.[13]

Rufus continued his service into 1759 along with other Rhode Island soldiers who participated in the campaign of that year. The Rhode Island General Assembly ordered their retention and ordered new enlistments to fulfill their pledge of 1,000 men for the campaign. The Assembly offered a bonus of two months' pay to encourage enlistments. Rhode Island involvement in that campaign dissolved when General Amherst delayed preparations and the weather became too cold to march northward to Canada. In 1760, Rufus marched with Colonel Christopher Harris' regiment to Albany to join the larger forces of Lord Amherst. This main force under the direction of Amherst advanced to Montreal, where on September 8, 1760, Montreal surrendered to the British forces. Weary and tired of war, the Rhode Island militia "demobilized themselves" and went home. This did not end Rufus' service during the war. In March 1761, the

General Assembly voted to raise a force of over 600 soldiers for the next campaign. Rufus' former commander, Captain John Whiting, was promoted to colonel. Custom dictated that commissioned officers enlist a certain number of men to earn their commission. Captain Whiting likely sought out former subordinates, including Rufus, to fill his quota. Rufus marched with sixty-five other men to Fort Stanwix in upstate New York, where they were detailed to serve until November.[14]

Rufus' final service during the war involved a siege at Havana, Cuba, during the campaign of 1762. In February of that year, Rhode Island voted again to raise 666 men for that year's campaign. However, instead of fighting the French or Native Americans, the British turned their attention to the Spanish. With the surrender of French Canada in 1760, British forces concentrated on Spain. In the summer of 1761, Spain jumped into the conflict on the side of the French. The British military strategy involved the capture of Cuba. With Cuba under British control, the conquest of Florida and Louisiana would be simpler. An expedition under the overall command of Lord Albemarle consisted of soldiers from England and the Caribbean, and over 2,300 troops from Rhode Island, Connecticut, New York, New Jersey, and South Carolina. Rhode Island supplied 212 troops. Colonel Samuel Rose and Lieutenant Colonel Hargill commanded the Rhode Island detachment. The detachments made their way to New York and sailed to Havana. British naval forces closed the harbor at Havana and laid siege at Castle Moro at the harbor's entrance. American forces arrived in the summer of 1762. On July 29, 1762, three explosive mines were detonated, allowing British forces to successfully take the castle, and end the siege.[15] Former slave and soldier Jeffrey Brace remembered the battle at Havana: "The Spanish made a sally from the fort, placed their cavalry in front, who commenced the attack on their part. They were met by a regiment of Scotch Highlanders, who fought with broad swords, and with great dexterity cut one rein of their horseman's bridles, which turned them round upon their foot and created great confusion and prodigious slaughter, which decided the battle."[16]

Of the combined British forces over 4,700 died of yellow fever during the siege. A total of 560 lost their lives in combat. Of the Rhode Island contingent, 110 died of the fever, two died from combat wounds, three were wounded, and ninety-seven returned home unscathed. Rufus Frank served eleven weeks and one day during this campaign and was a fortunate survivor of the siege. He received payment for his service and returned home to his family.[17]

Not only Rufus Frank benefited from his military service in the campaigns of the French and Indian War. His entire family benefited from Rufus' new standing. His sons, William, and Ben, both more than likely born during the war, were evidence of Rufus' commitment to family life. With his wages from the military, Rufus was able to sustain a household in Johnston, Rhode Island, a smaller village northwest of Providence where he might be able to purchase land more cheaply and create a homestead. Or is it possible that Rufus created a household on land bequeathed to him by Phillip Frank or passed down by his possible ancestor, Frank Nigro? The Seven Mile Line mentioned in Frank Nigro's property is the west boundary line of Johnston.[18]

The combination of military service, building a family, and moving to a new town illustrated Rufus' status as a manly member of his community. In the period before the American Revolution, "real men" were required to first find work and then a wife. African Americans in New England in the eighteenth century created their own formula for ideal manhood, drawing on West African and Anglo-American traditions. For example, in his autobiography, Venture Smith offered his ideas of manhood heavily influenced by his father and other males in his culture. Smith, a survivor of the transatlantic slave trade, grew up in West Africa. In his eyes, his father was the ideal man who died protecting his people. Smith came from a patriarchal culture that informed his sense of manhood and centered on the father figure as the location of male identity and manhood.[19] In his memoirs, Jeffrey Brace, another victim of the transatlantic slave trade, tied manhood and status in the community to fighting prowess: "But for those who have signalized themselves in battle or by extraordinary feats of military skill and bravery or wisdom in the war council are invited to partake of the feast with the King himself."[20] Rufus Frank maintained this sense of African manhood as described by Jack Cardoso: "the essence of African manhood was preparation for the life of the warrior, who was, as in all military units, the basic fighting factor."[21] Rufus Frank fulfilled two roles that defined manhood in West African society—soldier and father. But for his sons to gain that status, they would have to learn how to navigate the difficult environment for free men of color in revolutionary era Rhode Island.

By 1774, Rufus Frank led his own household in Johnston, Rhode Island—a town that did not exist until 1759. Disgruntled residents of West Providence had petitioned the General Assembly to create their own town. In the petition, over 400 freemen argued that the ten-mile distance to Providence to attend town meetings presented a burden for them. Their

Listing of the Rufus Frank family in the 1774 Rhode Island Census for Johnston. (*Rhode Island State Archives*)

request was granted, and Johnston partitioned from the western part of Providence in 1759. It is unknown if the Franks already resided in the area of Providence that hived off to form its own locality. If Rufus and his family lived in the fledgling communities created by free Blacks in Providence, then he and his family physically relocated since those small communities were not in the section of Providence that became Johnston. By the mid-1700s and early 1800s, free African Americans of Providence created their own communities in the Smith Hill (also known as Camp Hill) region in present-day downtown Providence near the state capitol. These communities became known as Hard Scrabble and Addison's Hollow in the 1800s.[22]

Whether a physical or jurisdictional move, residence in the "new" town of Johnston did not ease the burden of their status as free Blacks. The community that Rufus and his family lived in was a rarity in pre-revolutionary America. There were few free Black households in Rhode Island. Most free Blacks lived in large urban areas where they found safety and support in larger numbers. Overall, the 1774 Rhode Island colonial census reported 3,761 Blacks residing in Rhode Island. Providence boasted more free Black families than Johnston—forty-six in Providence, seven in Johnston—and Johnston's proximity to Providence suggests that these seven families were "hived off" from Providence: connected to the Providence free Black community, but building their own community nearby, so that people, goods, and information could move back and forth.

The demographics of Providence and Johnston were similar since most households were headed by men. Those households in Providence had an average size of four. The average size of the free households in Johnston totaled 5.5 persons per household. Even though the size of their households were larger than their Providence counterparts, the scarcity of their numbers allowed for little institution-building other than their own families. But Black communities did take hold if Blacks met and interacted on a regular basis, and other Black patriarchs in Johnston like Prince Angell, a former member of the Providence militia, were also in the process of family and community building. Angell married Mercy Baker in January 1770 and like Rufus, moved his small family from Providence to Johnston. Prince was more than likely "Negro Angell" who served in the Providence militia and marched out of Providence on the alarm of August 1757. It is difficult to determine the origins of the free Johnston households headed by Bristor, Caesar, Prince Lewis, and Jack Sweet. Rufus Frank's household was the only Frank household in Johnston in 1774, indicating his independence and courage moving from a known environment to a racial frontier. There he raised his three children, William, Ben, and Hannah.[23]

Johnston, a much smaller version of Providence, was a quiet farming village and populated with small enterprises—a sawmill, blacksmith shop, and gristmill—and it reflected the society of early New England. The opportunities available to free peoples of African descent were limited by pervasive social prejudices and legal prohibitions including Black Codes designed to govern activities of free Blacks. The Franks of Johnston were in fact second-class citizens. Legally, they were constrained by the laws and regulations enacted to control the lives of enslaved Blacks but that also regulated the activities of free Blacks. Economically, they were relegated to menial, lower-paying jobs. And socially, they faced discrimination in terms of housing, schooling, and religious practice. But despite these difficulties, many free blacks were able to build homes and communities. By building a free black household in a difficult social and economic environment and forging an identity for himself in the community because of his military service, Rufus set an example of how to achieve manhood for his sons.[24]

The legal status of the Franks and other free Blacks was not much better than elsewhere in colonial America. Legally, free Blacks held an intermediate status somewhat higher than the slaves, but lower than free white persons. Legal punishment for free African Americans was the same as for whites. However, nowhere in New England could free Blacks vote. And they could not serve on juries. A free Black's elevated material or community status did not change his rights. Anthony Kinnicutt, a property and business owner, could not vote in his hometown of Providence. In 1778, Kinnicutt petitioned the town council for the right to vote since he was a tax-paying citizen of the town. The Providence town council declined to hear his petition. It became obvious that a free African American, no matter how substantial his wealth or community standing, would not be the civic equal of a white voter. The Franks, of far less social and economic status than Kinnicutt, struggled against the injustices of second-class citizenship that, among other things, equated them with enslaved people and dispossessed Native Americans in the application of Black Codes.[25]

Black Codes, promulgated against free Blacks, were designed to govern their activities and assign punishment for alleged violations. The Black Codes enacted in colonial Rhode Island were more prohibitive than elsewhere in New England, due to white magistrates' concern over the larger concentration of slaves and free Blacks. A 1703 colonial statute stipulated that disorderly free and enslaved Blacks and Native Americans should be punished with at least fifteen lashes. Free African Americans could not legally walk on the streets after 9:00 p.m. without a pass. They could not legally use ferries without a pass. These codes were intended to prevent free Blacks from going beyond their town limits. By these laws, free Blacks could not legally entertain Native Americans or Black or mulatto slaves. A 1718 Kingstown, Rhode Island, law barred the enslaved from visiting the homes of free Blacks. If caught, violators were whipped. These codes also inhibited the ability of free Blacks to make a living. The law prohibited the enslaved from commercial transactions with any free person. Free Blacks also could not own certain types of property. In South Kingstown, Rhode Island, free African Americans could not keep horses, sheep, or any other domestic animals. These types of prohibitions limited how free African Americans could earn a livelihood for themselves since ownership of livestock provided some economic stability. A harsh punishment was meted out to free African Americans if they were convicted of keeping a disorderly house. The punishment for a freedman was possible reenslavement. The town council records reveal that many people ignored these various laws, and local officials enforced them inconsistently, but free Blacks like the Franks would remain constantly informed and aware of the rules that were designed to keep people of color at the bottom of the social hierarchy. Finding ways to live with and work around these codes would have become part of daily life for the Frank family.[26]

People of color inhabited other localities in Rhode Island before the Revolutionary War. Tiverton was home to ten households of color, composed of African and Native Americans. Four of those households included Blacks. William and Solomon Wanton headed households of seven and five, respectively, both including one Black each. Blacks also lived in the households of Joseph Gray and Deborah David. These households illustrated the interaction between Blacks and Native Americans. Marriage between Native Americans and Blacks was not unique. Social interaction occurred more between Black males and Native American women. And marriage between the two groups was not uncommon. The couples met at taverns in town or as servants working for the same employer. The Black husband in these alliances gained tacit control of his wife's land but could not gain title to it.[27] In 1764, Reverend Ezra Stiles wrote about the lack of Native American males in the town of Grafton, Connecticut, prompting the marriage of Native American women and Black men: "At Grafton, saw the Burying place and Graves of 60 or more Indians. Now not a Male Indian in the Town and five Squaws who marry Negroes."[28] Native American men also interacted with Black women through marriage and parenthood. Generally, these couples lived in English towns, not in Native American communities. These unions led to a multicultural nature of New England before the war.

A larger community of free Blacks resided in Newport. In seaport towns like Newport, Blacks mingled with other members of the lower sort to establish an interracial community of poor peoples. Free Blacks, Native Americans, enslaved persons, and poor whites interacted at work and play. Forty-one Blacks headed households in Newport prior to the war. Most were sailors who left behind their families while at sea. The larger numbers of Blacks in Newport allowed them to gather and plant the seeds of formal institution building. The Great Awakening, a religious revivalist movement of the 1740s, brought free and enslaved Blacks into evangelical churches. Leading ministers of the movement, like George Whitefield and Gilbert Tennent, preached that all could experience God's grace, regardless of race. Starting in 1765, Sarah Osborn held religious meetings for Blacks in her Newport household as a result of the teachings of the Great Awakening. Blacks also received instruction in reading and writing at these gatherings. The Blacks that attended these meetings formed their own group, an Ethiopian society, which consisted of over eighty men and women. The seeds planted by these individuals would expand after the war to produce the first Black social institutions in Rhode Island.[29]

Rufus Frank and his family lived at a distance from the activity of free Black people in the seaport of Newport. Rufus' move to Johnston after the French and Indian War brought his family into a smaller Black community. Out of this household and community came two sons who continued the Franks' journey in North America. Their lives would move in different directions than their father's, even though they chose the military as their means to advance. Their choices took the family's story into the heart of the American Revolution.

CHAPTER THREE

Brothers to War:
Race, Masculinity, and
Frank Family Tradition

THE REVOLUTIONARY WAR PROVIDED an avenue for William and Ben Frank to obtain the accoutrements of adulthood—their own identities, families, and economic competence. They could also continue the Frank family tradition of military service. They enlisted for military service with Rhode Island regiments in the spring of 1777, two years after the initial battles at Lexington and Concord. Both were young men in their teens. In April 1777 William Frank enlisted for military service with one of the Rhode Island state regiments which were created in response to the British occupation of Newport and the entirety of Aquidneck Island. Recruited and enlisted by Ensign Nathan Westcott, William joined Colonel Joseph Stanton's regiment with Captain Peleg Slocum's company on April 20, 1777. Stanton's regiment was created in December 1776 for a duration of fifteen months. However, William's service with the state forces did not last long. A month later, Ben enlisted on May 12, 1777, at Providence as part of the Rhode Island's General Assembly push to recruit and enlist five hundred men by May 1777 for service in Rhode Island's Continental regiments. Both brothers were members of the Second Rhode Island Regiment by late spring. Their willingness to serve was a viable option for

William and Ben as an important step to gain manhood and competency in a family and a society that valued military service.[1]

At the time of enlistment, they were among the large group of common laborers attempting to eke out a living in revolutionary Rhode Island. As opportunistic young men, they were joining the growing ranks of Rhode Islanders who were fighting for ideological and/or economic reasons—seeing the war as a means to advance their vision of an America free from British rule or as a means to improve their economic standing from the rewards of military service. As young men of color, they were joining a group of free men of color fighting to gain equal footing and opportunity in a country where both were often denied to them. And as young men of the Frank family they sought to replicate the example set by their father—to create and support their own families. But was the new government ready to accept their service?

George Washington took command of the militia-based army laying siege at Boston, under the auspices of a Continental Congress order dated July 4, 1775. He was charged with creating and maintaining a Continental army with a centralized chain of command and cadre of professional soldiers from a militia force of approximately 17,000 soldiers. With the adoption of these troops, Washington and Congress also acquired their terms of service. As militiamen, they were accustomed to short-term enlistments to fight in wars against Native Americans, and they lacked the motivation for long-term service. Others had signed on for service with state troops that required a longer commitment of service. Overall, most terms of service for the initial troops serving in the Army of Cambridge expired at the end of 1775, causing immediate problems for Washington and Congress.[2]

The issue of manpower and the lack thereof plagued Washington for the duration of the war. Shortly after Washington's arrival in Boston, the Congress agreed that each colony would continue to field its own militia for local defense, but Washington could also use these troops for occasional operations. Additionally, Congress mandated each colony to provide men for the Continental army. Originally, Congress called for a Continental army of approximately 20,000 men, organized into twenty-six battalions or regiments of infantry composed of 728 men each. Congress also authorized two regiments of riflemen and artillery. By the end of December 1775, the army had shrunk from a high of approximately 18,500 in August 1775 to approximately 15,000 soldiers present and fit for duty. The decrease was a result of desertions and expiration of enlistments, which forced Washington to request an extension of then current militia enlistments.[3]

Rhode Island supplied three battalions during the early months of the war. In the spring of 1775, incited by British officials' control of Narragansett Bay and Newport, the state assembly passed a resolution "that a number of men be raised, properly armed and disciplined to repel any insult or violence and to march out of this colony and join with the forces of the neighboring colonies."[4] This resolution resulted in the creation of three battalions, the First, Second, and Third Rhode Island regiments, organized in May 1775. Colonel James M. Varnum led the First Rhode Island Regiment with volunteer troops from Kings and Kent Counties. Colonel Daniel Hitchcock commanded the Second Rhode Island Regiment with troops raised in Providence County. The manpower allocation for each of these regiments was set at 610. Each regiment was divided into ten musket companies, commanded by captains, and composed of sixty troops. The Third Rhode Island, commanded by Colonel Thomas Church, was raised in Newport and Bristol counties with an authorized strength of 550 men, distributed throughout nine musket companies. In June 1775, all three regiments marched to Boston and were taken into Congressional service and pay.[5]

In September 1776, when it became obvious that the war would not be of short duration, Congress increased the allocations for Continental soldiers and required all states to provide several battalions according to their population. This revision raised the number of battalions to eighty-eight with each state's apportionment based upon their population. This reorganization of the federal army increased the number of soldiers present and fit for duty to approximately 27,000 in September 1776. The highest number would reach over 28,000 in October of the same year. A low point would occur in December 1776 when the total of officers and rank and file available for assignment totaled approximately 6,000 men. Under the new configuration, Rhode Island was tasked with providing two battalions—the 9th and 11th Continentals, under the command of Varnum and Hitchcock, respectively. Many officers and men from the disbanded 1775 regiments of Varnum, Hitchcock, and Church volunteered to serve in the new regiments. The authorized strength for each regiment was 600—with eighty-eight officers and men assigned to each of the eight musket companies. The actual totals—troops present and fit for duty—would never reach or exceed those totals.[6]

Men of color participated from the outset of the war as active members of the militia companies that served in the Army of Cambridge. William and Ben, as sons of a Black military veteran, were probably aware of the exploits of Black soldiers who had defended American soil early in the war. As opposition to British rule grew, especially after the Boston Massacre in the fall of 1770, the Continental Congress recommended that all able-bodied men in each colony form militia companies, including the most reliable, enthusiastic, and physically abled—the origins of the celebrated minutemen of Lexington and Concord. Initially, nonwhites were admitted to these militia companies, notwithstanding policies enacted against their service. When the actual fighting broke out, men of color fought alongside white minutemen at Lexington, Concord, Lincoln, and Bunker Hill. At Lexington, Prince Easterbrooks, a Black man, was carried on the list of the wounded. Other Blacks who participated in the short initial battles at Lexington, Concord, and Lincoln include Peter Salem, Pompey, Prince, Cato Stedman, Cato Bordman, Cuff Whittemore, and Cato Wood.[7] His fellow soldiers recognized freedman Salem Poor for bravery and valor at the Battle of Bunker Hill. In a petition to the General Court of Massachusetts, a request was made that the Congress bestow upon Salem Poor a "reward due to so great and Distinguisht a Caracter."[8]

In 1850, Benjamin Cowell attributed early participation on the part of Rhode Islanders to *rage militaire*. He described the Rhode Islanders' early participation in the war as "a fire . . . kindled in the hearts of men which burnt up the tory stubble in every colony and was not extinguished until Great Britain herself acknowledged our Independence."[9] Cowell's patriotic hyperbole in describing the motivation of Rhode Island soldiers is understandable given his relationship with veterans of that war. As a state's attorney, he spoke personally with surviving veterans and served as their advocate in their crusade to obtain promised benefits. Whether the Frank brothers understood or felt this impassioned fire, as adolescents they must have witnessed the departure of Rhode Island militiamen as they marched to Boston and joined other militia troops from throughout the colonies to lay siege to Boston.

Among those who marched to Boston were Black soldiers, including probable Frank family members. Andrew Frank lived in the small village of Troy, Massachusetts, at the border of Rhode Island near Tiverton at the beginning of the war. At one point, he also held residence in Johnston, Rhode Island, the hometown of the Frank brothers, and was a member of the very small free Black community of that village for a period. Andrew was one of the militiamen who "turned out in the alarm in said Captain Slocum's Company and marched to Boston."[10] Andrew's service at Boston lasted only two days but he pointed to his participation at the Battle of

Bunker Hill as a highlight of his activity during the siege of Boston. Another Rhode Island native, Winsor Fry of East Greenwich, signed up for duty in early 1775 as a member of Captain Thomas Holden's Company in the regiment of Colonel James M. Varnum. He served at the siege of Boston from July to December 1775.

So as William and Ben Frank stepped forward to serve their country, they were following in the footsteps of others, Black and white Rhode Islanders, who decided to take up arms against their mother country. However, the road to their enlistment and service was deeply affected by the political and social customs of the time.[11]

Washington's vision of a professional Continental army at first did not include Blacks. He may have been surprised to see the numbers of Blacks bearing arms upon his arrival at Boston. Black soldiers of New England regiments were accepted members of the various militia groups now under Washington's command. The spontaneous integration of these militia units proved problematic for Washington and Congress. Washington would temper his recruitment policies to reflect the general prejudice of whites against Blacks during that time. He was especially sensitive to the fears of southern whites concerning the arming of Black soldiers.[12]

Discrimination and fear, particularly by southern slaveholders, played a large role in the lack of recruitment and enlistment of Black soldiers. Upon assuming command of the Continental army, Washington instructed his recruiters to secure replacements and additional troops. On July 10, 1775, he instructed his recruiters to "engage men of courage and principle to take up arms. You are not to enlist any deserter from the Ministerial army, nor any stroller, negro, or vagabond, or person suspected of being an enemy to the liberty of America."[13] Thus Washington equated Negroes with enemies of the state, a state allegedly built upon the equality of all men. While this order fell short of dismissing Black soldiers in active service, it did forestall the recruitment of new Black soldiers and the reenlistment of Black veterans.

In the latter half of 1775, Washington and the Congress strengthened their policy against the service of Blacks in the Continental army. In a document to his War Council dated October 1775, detailing the decisions to be made during the next meeting of the council, the general asked "Whether it will be advisable to enlist any negroes in the new army? Or whether there be a distinction between such as are slaves and those that are free?"[14] On October 23, 1775, the council recommended to Congress that all Blacks were deemed improper by the Council of Officers. And they "Agreed, that they be rejected altogether."[15] On October 31, 1775, Washington directed the supply master to provide clothing to all who reenlisted except African American soldiers, who were prohibited from reenlistment by Congressional policy. In General Orders dated November 12, 1775, Washington reiterated that "Neither negroes, boys unable to bear arms, nor old men unfit to endure the fatigues of the campaign are to be enlisted."[16] By December 1, 1775, the Continental army, raised to protect liberty and defeat tyranny, was an army fueled by strict regulation and individual prejudice and officially represented only by white soldiers.[17]

As a result of this racist policy, the Frank brothers were unable to offer their services to the American cause in the early months of the war. Nonetheless, between 1775 and 1777, military policy regarding the enlistment of free Blacks evolved through three distinct stages: purging and rejection of Black troops; enlistment of free Black veterans; and the enlistment of all free Blacks, which allowed for the recruitment, enlistment, and service of William and Ben Frank. The change of policy was also influenced by New England, particularly Rhode Island and Connecticut. This was due in part to the larger number of Black soldiers furnished by the New England states. These influences and the reality of war forced Washington to change his policy of racial exclusivity.[18]

A major blow against racist military policy came in the form of an act promulgated by the royal governor of Virginia. John Murray, Earl of Dunmore and royally appointed governor of Virginia, issued a proclamation on November 7, 1775, that invited the enslaved to leave their masters and join the British forces. He promised that "all indented Servants, Negroes, or others, (appertaining to Rebels,) free that are able and willing to bear Arms, they joining His MAJESTY'S Troops as soon as may be, for the more speedily reducing this Colony to a proper Sense of their Duty, to His MAJESTY'S Crown and Dignity."[19] As a result of their service, the enslaved could earn their freedom. This proclamation was not directed at the enslaved of loyalists, only at those enslaved at the hands of the rebels and who were willing and able to bear arms against their former owners.[20]

Dunmore's proclamation was not an isolated act. It was part of a grander scheme by British officials to aid their war effort. Earlier in the year, the British command had outlined a plan to reinforce British forces in the south. The plan had three elements: enlisting enslaved men, raising a corps of Irish troops under the command of Protestant commanders to assist Dunmore in Virginia, and recruiting a large army of indentured servants and convicts from the Chesapeake region. So, Dunmore's proclamation was not meant to be radical in nature but part of a more elaborate scheme to ensure British success and to limit American resources. His ploy resulted in the enrollment of 300 formerly enslaved men, officially designated as Lord Dunmore's Ethiopian Regiment. Dunmore's promises were ill-fated. At the Battle of Great Bridge in December 1775, loyalist troops, including the Ethiopian Regiment, were routed. The regiment did suffer some losses; however, many of the remaining troops died due to an epidemic of smallpox in the spring of the following year.[21]

General Washington's response to Dunmore's initiative was immediate. He termed Dunmore's plan diabolical. He gave credit to Dunmore's tactic, believing that success lay with the side that armed Blacks the fastest.[22] In General Orders dated December 30, 1775, Washington allowed recruiting officers to enlist free Blacks to prevent them from flocking to British armies. The order stated: "As the General is informed, that Numbers of Free Negroes are desirous of inlisting, he gives leave to the recruiting Officers to entertain them, and promises to lay the matter before the Congress, who he doubts not will approve of it."[23] He wrote to John Hancock requesting that free Blacks be allowed to enlist for service because "they (free blacks) were very much dissatisfied at being discarded and may seek employ in the Ministerial Army."[24]

The dissatisfaction that Washington referred to in his request to Congress came from two groups. Many commanders and other fellow officers of Black soldiers defended their service and championed their right to fight in the new Continental army. They lodged their collective protests against the barring of their former comrades and subordinates to General Washington and his staff. The second group was free Blacks themselves. Prince Hall, as the leader of the Black Freemason movement, had petitioned Washington, as early as the summer of 1775, against the "racial exclusivity" of the American regular army. His first appeal was made to fellow Masons Joseph Warren and John Hancock, leading members of the Safety Committee of the Continental Congress—the group that oversaw the actions of the commander-in-chief. Hall pled for the right of Black men, free and enslaved, to enlist and serve. The Committee of Safety initially rejected his plea for Black inclusion, concerned that it would prompt Black insurrectionary ideas. However, they would reverse their decision at the prompting of General Washington.[25]

The commander-in-chief's attitude regarding the use of Black troops was conflicted and reflected his upbringing as a southern gentleman and slaveholder. He was torn between the need for the manpower that Black troops provided and the perceived danger of arming Blacks. Washington's exclusionary policy regarding Black troops can be linked to the disdain southern gentry held for the enslaved and his own discomfort regarding the presence of Black soldiers in a "strong and respectable army."[26] The idea of arming slaves was anathema to most slaveholders—the use of free Black troops ran a close second. Additionally, white soldiers were put off by the taunts of British regulars that made disparaging comments about the composition of the American forces.[27]

Washington and his commanders also had to deal with a grassroots move toward integration.[28] There were those who felt that the principles elucidated in the Declaration of Independence called for a change in thinking. James Madison, when referring to the "negro bounty" of his state of Virginia, argued: "without deciding on the expediency of the mode under their consideration, would it not be as well to liberate and make soldiers at once of the blacks themselves, as to make them instruments for enlisting white soldiers? It would certainly be more consonant to the principles of liberty, which ought never to be lost sight of in a contest for liberty."[29]

Washington may not have shared Madison's idea about arming slaves, but he was sympathetic toward the complaints of free Black veterans and did petition Congress for their acceptance in December 1775. Additionally, as stated earlier, Washington worried that these experienced soldiers would migrate to the British cause. Also, the general could not ignore the integrated nature of the troops under his command. His actions were an attempt to manage in-service troops and appease the concerns of southerners and others against the use of Black troops. But, regardless of his status as a slaveholder and upbringing as a member of the gentry class, Washington was at the very least a practical man who tied an American victory to a protracted war that would eventually wear the enemy down. This protracted war depended on the availability of troops.[30]

In the end, the American policy was revised to recruit and enlist free Black veterans. In January 1776, Congress approved Washington's request for the enlistment of free Blacks "who have served faithfully in the army at Cambridge may be re-enlisted therein but no others."[31] No others needed to apply. This new policy did prevent the loss of experienced Black soldiers to the British cause. However, it did not make use of the available and willing manpower resources to be found among the population of the enslaved and free Blacks, like William and Ben Frank, who did not have prior military experience.

In January 1777, Washington again revised his stance toward the enlistment of free Blacks—free African American males were approved for enlistment with the Continental army, most coming from New England. In a memo to recruiting officers dated January 12, 1777, Washington charged them to "inlist none but Freemen, above the Age of seventeen, and under that of fifty, of sufficient Stature and Ability of body."[32] However, service and pension records of Black soldiers indicate that revisions in policy had already taken place at the grassroots level. As Washington and the Congress reconsidered their original recruitment policies and reversed themselves on the use of Black soldiers, reality, in the form of manpower shortages, convinced recruiting officers, state officials, and census takers to expand their way of thinking. Despite the clear policies enacted by Washington, Congress, and state governments that no Blacks and then only free veteran Black soldiers could enlist, many commanders and recruiting officers interpreted the policy as *carte blanche* to recruit and enlist all free Black men.

To deal with this tough recruitment environment, command officers for Continental forces paid little heed to the racial identity of a recruit; they sought only to fill their ranks with able-bodied soldiers. The Congressional quotas of 1777 drove recruiting officers to send Blacks whenever available to fill the number of soldiers called upon by Congress. Muster officers often ignored the restrictions regarding the recruitment of Black soldiers and enlisted the enslaved and free Blacks at will. James Murphey may have been one of those beleaguered recruiting officers. In 1777, he received punishment for his involvement in the recruitment of Black soldiers. Charged and convicted with "endeavoring to persuade Negroes to enlist" and intoxication, Murphey received fifty lashes for his infractions. But the potential for harsh punishment did not dissuade recruiting officers. Often paid by the head, they were not very diligent in their refusal of African American recruits. Recruiting officers, sometimes assigned to specific districts, were dispatched to drum up recruits and paid up to eight dollars a head. Adding to the tough environment for recruiting officers were the attempts by states and local jurisdictions to fill their own state and local militia. The competition for available manpower between the Continental army and individual colonies was ongoing throughout the war, with the advantage going to state regiments since enlistees preferred to serve closer to home.[33]

The institution of the draft only increased the enlistment and use of Black soldiers. Massachusetts and New Hampshire initiated the draft of militiamen into the Continental army in 1777. The remaining colonies followed suit in 1778. Most states allowed draftees to engage viable substitutes to serve in their place. For instance, Connecticut exempted men from actual service if they procured an able-bodied substitute for a period of three years. Free and enslaved Blacks often filled in for whites when states drafted soldiers. New York allowed the enslaved to serve in the place of their owners. Rhode Island also allowed substitutes to serve, regardless of their race or ethnicity. Additionally, some slaveholders used enslaved men at the state level as substitutes for their own service. William Wanton of Tiverton provided his services as a substitute on numerous occasions. Wanton's service at the state level illustrates how state and local officials were also willing to overlook policies promulgated at the local and state level:[34]

> As he is a colored man he was not able to be enrolled and ordered into the public service as one of the militia but that he served in the militia as a substitute for the following named person, being hired by them to take their place for one month each. That is to say he took the place of Judge Will Anthony as a substitute in the militia company commanded by Capt Alexander Thomas . . . guarding the shore of Narragansett Bay in Tiverton . . . he thinks was in the early part of the year 1777 as the British troops had had [possession] of Rhode Island at that time only for a short period of time.[35]

Census takers did not alleviate the confusion regarding the recruitment and enlistment of soldiers. There were inconsistencies among Rhode Island military census takers, who were charged by town officials to enumerate white males eligible for military service. Blacks and Native Americans were also to be counted and noted. However, census takers interpreted their responsibilities in different ways. Some refused to distinguish men of color in their listings. Some did not record complete information for Blacks and Native Americans. And others were named but not designated by age or ability. This confusion on whether to enumerate Native Americans and Blacks as possible soldiers did not deter the actions of recruiters who targeted men with the least to lose—unpropertied, transients, indentured servants, Blacks, and Native Americans—for long-term service with the federal army.[36]

One example of this confusion is the documented military service of Winsor Fry with the Rhode Island Continental line. It is difficult to determine the racial identity of Fry. In vital and military records, he is listed alternately as a "man of color," "mustee," "Indian," or "Negro."[37] His designation, as a man of color, Black, or Native American, would have prevented his service during the early years of the Revolutionary War. State and local authorities had enacted laws prohibiting the enlistment of Blacks, both free and enslaved, as well as Native Americans.[38] In a sworn pension affidavit, Winsor Fry stated he enlisted in the month of March 1775 as a private in Varnum's Rhode Island Continental regiment. He attested: "I may say . . . during all that time having been absent but once."[39] Fry's testimony matches the configuration of Varnum's regiment, organized in May 1775 and disbanded in December 1775. His recollection of his enlistment month may be in error, but Fry's memory of the command structure is accurate. His sworn testimony of service contradicts the official policy promulgated by Washington and the Continental Congress that no Blacks need apply or serve. He continued to serve during and after the purge of 1775 as a member of the Rhode Island Continental line.[40]

William and Ben Frank joined fifty-two other documented Black and Native American soldiers who had been free for varying lengths of time before their enlistment—thirty-five are listed on a document titled, "Return of Freemen inlisted during the war."[41] The return appears to have been initiated to identify and enumerate the members of the regiment who were not freed because of the Slave Enlistment Act of 1778 (addressed in Chapter 5). The undated document lists thirty-five privates distributed throughout five companies. Nineteen have been identified as "black," six as Native Americans, and three as "mustee." The racial identity of the remaining seven has not been determined.

Of the men enumerated on the "Return of Freemen," twenty-five enlisted prior to the Slave Enlistment Act. Seven of the freemen did not enlist until after the passage of the act—in the spring of 1778—the latest enlistment date being in March 1779. So, the list could not have been formulated before that date. A review of pension applications for eight members on the list shows no indication of enslaved status before or during the war. The pension records of the formerly enslaved refer to their enslavement. Additionally, the soldiers of the return are not named on various documents listing slaves emancipated for their service. It appears that the return lists men of color who were free before their service. So, for the purpose of this analysis, the return was used as a basis to determine the validity of official policy regarding the recruitment and enlistment of men of color, particularly Blacks. As part of this analysis, records indicating enlistment and muster dates were examined for those soldiers.[42]

Of the thirty-five included in this data set, seven freemen enlisted after February 1778, when the Rhode Island State Assembly allowed the enlistment and service of former slaves in exchange for their freedom. Twenty-one free men of color enlisted prior to that date. Seventeen of these soldiers

Return of Freemen in the papers of Colonel Christopher Greene. (*Rhode Island Historical Society. Revolutionary War Military Records. MSS 673*)

enlisted during the period of open recruitment and enlistment of all free Blacks, including the Frank brothers. Of the remaining numbers, one enlisted in 1775 (Winsor Fry); six in 1776 (Thomas Amos, William Coopin, Asa Gardner, Pharoah Hazzard, Richard Potter, and Thomas Smith); and three in early January 1777 (James Daley, Francis Gould, and James Greene).[43]

An analysis of the six enlistees of 1776 (Amos, Coopin, Gardner, Hazzard, Potter, and Smith) illustrates how recruiters ignored both federal and state policies. Apart from William Coopin, all were identified in census and military records as Black. Coopin, a resident of Charlestown, Rhode Island, was the sole Native American in the group. The official federal requirement for Black enlistment at the time was prior service. The official policy for service with Rhode Island state troops called for Blacks to participate as members of the watch but prevented the bearing of arms. By 1776, Rhode Island fielded five regiments in the war for independence—

three in the Continental army and three state regiments. However, in May of that year, the two state units came under the control and supervision of the federal army and as such were bound to follow its policies. The two provincial regiments fell under the command of Colonels William Richmond and Christopher Lippett. Richmond's regiment was organized in November 1775, while Lippett's battalion was organized in January 1776. Both were pressed into Continental service in May 1776. As members of Lippett's regiment, William Coopin and Pharoah Hazzard served under the command of Captain Christopher Dyer and both are listed on the regimental payroll in September 1776. Private Asa Gardner served under the immediate command of Captain John Topham, a farmer from Newport County, and was carried on his payroll for 1776. During the spring and summer of 1775, Topham led a musket company under the direction of General Thomas Church. However, in September 1775, Topham was reassigned to a force of 1,100 troops led by General Benedict Arnold given the task of capturing Quebec City from the British. Over 100 Rhode Island troops volunteered for the mission. If Gardner became a member of the Arnold expedition, his lot was not a happy one. The capture of Quebec City failed spectacularly. Four hundred were either killed or captured. The remaining 700 became sick or turned back sometime during the march to Canada.[44]

The initial service of Thomas Amos and Richard Potter was in blatant defiance of military policy. Potter enlisted in May 1776 and served as a private in Captain Ebenezer Flagg's company of Varnum's regiment. The 9th Continentals under Varnum's command were part of the initial force of Continentals and as such bound by Washington's exclusionary rule. Thomas Amos and Thomas Smith became members of the same regiment later in the year, after command was given to Colonel Archibald Crary in October 1776. However, there is no indication of prior service on the part of these men—the prerequisite for the enlistment of free Black men during this period.[45]

The three soldiers who enlisted in early January 1777 were already serving by the date of Washington's directive allowing the admission of all free Blacks. The records of James Daley and Frances Gould also do not indicate any prior service. However, this does not mean that they did not serve with local militia companies prior to their Continental service. But Washington's directive regarding the status and service of free veterans required previous service as members of the Army of Cambridge—the ragtag group of militias that laid siege at Boston during the summer of 1775. If Daley and

Gould were not veterans of that engagement, then their enlistments conflicted with the policy that dictated prior service.[46]

It was this third revision of the recruitment policy that allowed the enlistment of William and Ben Frank as freemen in the spring of 1777. Records indicate that William enlisted on April 20, 1777, with the state regiments and eventually joined with Continental forces at Tiverton, Rhode Island later that spring.[47]

At the time of his initial enlistment with Rhode Island forces, William was residing in the village of Tiverton across the state from his hometown of Johnston, Rhode Island. There is little evidence to indicate his purpose for staying in Tiverton. He was no longer under the care of his parents since Tiverton was too far for him to return to Johnston daily. He may have been residing with a relative named Andrew Frank who lived in nearby Troy, Massachusetts. By 1777, a young man, like William, had the possibility of finding work there on a whaler, as a ferryman, or alongside a blacksmith or farmer. Small sawmills and gristmills also populated Tiverton—a throwback to the work performed by William's possible ancestor, Frank Nigro in Providence. If William found steady work at any of these occupations, it was short-lived. The American war effort was very active in the Tiverton area. In 1776 and 1777, Forts Durfee and Barton were constructed as protection against British vessels in the passage between Tiverton and Portsmouth.[48]

William initially enlisted with Colonel Joseph Stanton's Rhode Island state regiment. He may have enlisted with a number of other Blacks and Native Americans in early 1777. By late spring, he was a member of Captain Potter's Company of the Second Rhode Island Regiment. William, as the older son, may have been motivated to strike out on his own to seek out a worthwhile occupation or livable wages. The economic climate of New England was devastated by the war. Fishing and agricultural enterprises collapsed due to the loss of their major trading partner, Great Britain. The British occupation of major seaports added to the loss of commerce, which translated to the loss of jobs for general laborers like William and Ben Frank. The poor prospects of obtaining a trade or making a suitable wage may have convinced William to accept service with the military. Or the change in recruitment policy may have offered William the chance to follow in his father's footsteps, a chance to prove his manhood and worth in the community.[49]

Benjamin Frank enlisted a month after his brother, in the town of Providence, near his hometown of Johnston. As a teenager, Ben was still living at home. His occupation was not listed at the time of his recruitment; no special skill or trade was noted on his enlistment record. Ben, like his brother, was a common laborer, but still living at home with his parents and his younger sister, Hannah. After William enlisted, family members may have pressed Ben to enlist as well. Or Ben, attempting to establish himself as an adult, could have chosen the military service to accomplish that goal.[50]

Both brothers were drawn to the recruitment system established to ensure that Washington's army had enough soldiers to defeat the British. Continental army recruiters in Rhode Island were hard-pressed to raise troops for the Continental battalions. Overall, the thirteen colonies were unable to fill the authorized strength for the new battalions. Men refused to enlist, and early in the war effort, legislators refused to initiate a draft. Difficulties recruiting soldiers for the Rhode Island battalions were typical. Rhode Island men had special reasons to stay at home and refuse service in a regular army. The small colony had over 400 miles of coastline to defend. The occupation of Newport and Aquidneck Island by British troops, along with the fact that British ships controlled Narragansett Bay, prompted many Rhode Island men to stay at home to protect their homesteads and families. Rhode Islanders also had options for military service other than the Continental army. Many chose to serve in state or local militia units. Another drain to the recruitment of Continental soldiers was the State Assembly's actions to protect the state by raising state troops, totaling 1,800 men to serve for eighteen months.[51]

William Frank's recruiter was Ensign Nathan Westcott, assigned to Captain Peleg Slocum's Company of Colonel Joseph Stanton's state militia. William was later recruited into the Continental army. Recruiters used a variety of inducements to lure William Frank into military service. They attempted to attract potential enlistees with a message of personal upward mobility through service. In exchange for personal sacrifice in the short run, there was the opportunity of something greater in the long run. Typical recruitment ploys at the time included cash and land bounties. The initial Congressional bounties established at the start of the war included a ten-dollar bounty, along with monthly pay of forty shillings for three years of service or the duration of the war. By the time of the Franks' enlistments, Congress had doubled the bounty and added the bonus of 100 acres of land per man at war's end. Congressional bounties and rewards were supplemented by state and local bounties. Black enlistees in New Hampshire received the same bounties and rewards that whites did. The average bounty awarded by New Hampshire towns was £10, augmented by the state enlistment bounty of £10 and pay of eighteen shillings per year. For free Blacks, hard-pressed to earn subsistence wages, the bounties offered, and the promise of food, clothing, and shelter, were quite compelling.[52]

The many soldiers who were recruited to fight with Washington's army after 1776 were not from the ranks of the "yeoman farmer," nor were they the "rabble" or "sweepings" of the street. But they were among the poorest, most oppressed, and most repressed segments of colonial society. Many of them included drifters, unemployed laborers, and indentured servants. Very few of these "regulars" had experienced economic prosperity or full political liberty before the war. As a group, they had much to gain from military service. Most Black enlistees were on the lower rungs of the socioeconomic ladder of colonial society. Charles Patrick Neimeyer's survey of fifty African American soldiers' pension records showed that one-fifth listed laborer or servant as an occupation. Other occupations listed were semi-skilled laborers, such as weavers or waggoners. William and Ben Frank were among this mass of struggling laborers. The cash bonuses and bounties offered by recruiting officers would have been particularly appealing to them. By 1777, the time of the Franks' enlistments, Congress had authorized a minimum cash bounty of twenty dollars. Free Blacks like the Franks received bounties equal to those of whites for their enlistment. William's motivation for enlisting at Tiverton may have been prompted by an even higher bounty offered by the town council there.[53]

Along with cash bounties, the appeal of steady pay for steady work was very strong for common laborers like William Frank. It was hard for free Blacks to find work that would provide an economic competency for themselves and their families. The ability to earn an independent living was frequently denied them due to their race. As free people, they were dependent upon themselves for the sale of their labor, but they also had to face the competition of white working men. Whites not only resented the appropriation of available jobs by free Blacks but sometimes showed their resentment by violence. During the hard times prior to the Revolutionary War, free Blacks in Boston were often verbally and physically assaulted by mobs of poor whites in the streets. The type of work performed by free Blacks was usually like that performed by the enslaved. Freedmen were taught a variety of skills and trades while in servitude to their masters. They learned trades ranging from blacksmithing and carpentry to shoemaking and tanning. However, the ability to ply their trade, once free, was limited by white resentment and harsh economic reality. Some free Blacks found work on farms, but most worked in towns where employment opportunities were more varied. However, in towns and villages, most free Blacks worked as domestics or common laborers. Some did work at the trades or located work on whaling or coastal vessels, but most free Blacks were common laborers like William Frank. If William was living in Tiverton and trying hard to exist on a common laborer's wages, the offer of steady pay, food, and living quarters had its appeal. Ben, on the other hand, may have been impressed with the opportunity to make his own wages; he would find the harsh living conditions of a soldier's life to be a striking contrast to living at home, however.[54]

A greater economic incentive for the brothers to enlist was the opportunity to own land. There is no documentary evidence that Rufus Frank owned farmland at the time of their enlistment. The enlistment of both sons to serve with the Continental army, leaving only an adult female and a young girl to assist with the tasks of keeping up a farm, suggests that Rufus Frank had little land or other property to bequeath his sons. There were a few examples of land ownership among the free Black community of Rhode Island. Anthony Kinnicutt not only owned a house and lot, but also operated a successful victualling business on the docks of Providence. His successful business enterprises gave him the opportunity to purchase a share of a privateering vessel during the war. But Kinnicutt's successes were unusual and were not indicative of the conditions for free Blacks in Rhode Island. Service with the "regulars" may have been the only avenue open to the Frank brothers in a quest to obtain their own land. To encourage enlistments, Congress also authorized the promise of land allotments of 100–500 acres, depending on the state and the rank of the soldier. The Franks, as members of a colonial society, were aware of the importance of land ownership in determining one's social and economic status. The promise of land ownership doubtless appealed to William, who signed on to receive a land bounty upon war's end.[55]

As members of the small population of free Blacks living in Rhode Island, the Franks' opportunity for gaining economic competence and community status were severely limited. By 1774, free Blacks living in their own households comprised less than 10 percent of the Black population. Free Blacks lived in a society that had thrived on the system of slavery. Rhode Island served as one of the focal points of the slave trade in America. The colony still had the greatest percentage of enslaved persons in New England. Rhode Island's free Blacks lived under many of the same sanctions and laws used to control their enslaved brethren. Free Blacks could not vote. Very few of their children attended the public school systems provided for white children. Due to low incomes and white prejudice, free Blacks were more than likely restricted to less than desirable living quarters in towns and villages. In colonial New England, most free Blacks lived near the docks or riverfronts or in alleys. However, there are records that indicate some racial integration between whites and Blacks of the period. Boston town council records indicate white neighbors suing Black neighbors. The Rhode Island census of 1774 shows free Blacks living near whites. And if provided with capital, free Blacks operated their own businesses, like Anthony Kinnicutt of Providence. However, free Blacks struggled to survive and thrive in revolutionary era Rhode Island.[56]

Even those recently freed were forced to understand the tenuous nature of their freedom in terms of survival and establishing economic competence. And freeborn men like the Frank brothers looked to military service to do so.

Francis Tifft enlisted on the day after his manumission on May 29, 1777. Francis was enslaved to Daniel Tifft, a blacksmith of Providence. The manumission of an enslaved person was not a casual act. Local statutes require certain stipulations. Daniel had to provide a security bond to the town to cover any expenses incurred by the freed Francis in case he was unable to support himself. It was important for Francis and his former owner that he find viable employment—and military service fit that need.[57]

Many Blacks who decided to bear arms against the mother country hoped that the Revolution would be a true fight for independence that incorporated a change in the status quo—an opportunity for a better life for those on the fringes of society, the poorer sort, and racial minorities. Their motivation and desire to serve should be considered from the perspective of the larger community of free Blacks—some of whom welcomed the advent of a war for freedom and equality.[58] Historian Benjamin Quarles assessed the loyalty and motivation of free Blacks during the revolutionary era in the following manner: "Their loyalty was not to a locality in which they were propertyless, not to an assembly in which they could not sit and not to a social order that denied their worth. They reserved allegiance for whoever made them the best and most concrete offer in terms of man's unalienable rights."[59]

Free Blacks did, however, feel a strong affinity to their homes, families, and communities and these were the driving factors behind their actions during the war. This was the mental and emotional state of some free Blacks at the advent of the Revolutionary War, this was their *rage militaire*—a fierce urgency to protect their homes and families and a fierce need to obtain their fair share of America's promise to make better lives for themselves and their families. So, young men, like William and Ben Frank and other young men of color, may have seen the war as offering hope for a better life and standing in their communities; opportunity for economic competency; and excitement for young men whose experiences were stunted by stifling Black Codes which regulated their behavior.[60]

If the reasons for service among free Blacks do closely resemble those of poor whites, even though their social circumstances were much more pressing, then maybe some insight can be gained by looking at the memoirs and narratives of white soldiers during the war. Like many young men, Revolutionary War soldier Joseph Plumb Martin was seeking adventure and freedom from his tedious life on the family farm. Martin was also seeking economic opportunities as well. In his memoirs, he wrote that "My spirits began to revive at the sight of the money offered . . . O, thought I, if I were but old enough to put myself forward, I would be the possessor of one dollar."[61] Martin was also concerned about proving his worth on the battlefield: "I was now what I had wished to be a soldier. I had obtained my heart's desire; it was now my business to prove myself equal to my profession."[62] Issues of patriotism and masculinity prompted Jeremiah Greenman's service with the Rhode Island Continental line. He went to war "to make a man of himself and help in the birth of a nation."[63] In his pension application, Greenman offered a more practical side to his enlistment: "And where it not for the leisure hours I spen while in the army in the Study of Navigation under the pupilage of Maj. Genl. Schuyler at the close of the War I should been plunged on the world destitute of employment."[64]

Motivation and desire are elusive things to analyze, especially given that neither of the Franks left personal accounts detailing their reasons for service. But if military service is a loyalty-defining experience, then perhaps the actual service of free Blacks indicates a sense of personal and professional commitment to the patriotic cause. Also, the memories of these soldiers, captured in their pension records, provide insight into their reasons to serve.[65] Veteran Winsor Fry asserted his commitment to the patriotic cause by pointing to his length of service. Fry declared: "in the month of March 1775 I enlisted as a private soldier in Thomas Holden's Company and Col. Varnum's regiment afterwards Col. Greenes, in the continental army of the United States on . . . the Rhode Island line, in which . . . I continued during the whole war between this Country and Great Britain and think I may say without, during all that time having been absent but once at the close of the war."[66]

William Wanton declared his commitment to service as a member of the state militia by swearing "that he faithfully and truly served out the terms aforesaid in the defense of his country in the war of the Revolution."[67] These statements and declarations may indicate a personal commitment to the patriotic cause—or a very real need to present a compelling story to the pension board. However, if taken at face value, these assertions indicate a sense of personal and professional commitment and responsibility on the part of the veterans. It is safe to assume that like other free Blacks of the era, William and Ben Frank had to grapple with these feelings of responsibility and patriotism, as well as inequality, as they made their decisions to serve.

William and Ben also had to deal with their youth and eventual passage into the adult world. As teenagers embarking on military careers, both were part of what historian Caroline Cox described as a "shifting and variegated landscape" that saw the age that adults believed children could rightfully and legally participate as adults shift from fourteen to twenty-one years during the revolutionary era. John Resch's study of veterans of the war indicates that from a selection of 877 Continental army enlistees, a majority were above the age of eighteen at 78.5 percent. However, the need for able-bodied soldiers allowed for the use of "boy" soldiers throughout the war. Both Frank brothers must have been deemed physically suitable to fill the role of a Continental regular since soldiering was physically demanding. And both were looking for ways to gain economic independence, like other young men of the laboring class. Military service provided an avenue for steady income lacking for poor or unskilled youth. The enlistment of Ben Frank at the age of fifteen more than likely was an indication of the family's financial status. The ability to earn his own way may have been motivation for him to seek enlistment with the Continentals with his father's approval. To protect his younger son, Rufus, like other fathers of the era, may have accompanied Ben to the enlistment site at Providence to assure that he was assigned to the same regiment as his older brother.[68]

As members of a minority group and living on the margins of society, the Frank brothers were susceptible to offers of cash or land. Their motivation and desire to serve should also be considered in more practical and personal terms—their social and economic status at the time of their enlistments. Did they believe that military service would open the doors for better economic and occupational opportunities? Additionally, aside from material gain, more personal reasons may have also affected the Frank brothers' decisions to enlist. There may have been other familial and social conditions that affected their decision to enlist. Documents indicate that other Frank males, including their father, had served in the colonial wars. Did military service lead to greater status/standing within the colonial community, especially for Black males? Or were the brothers simply following a family tradition of military service?[69]

Another important factor for the brothers may have been their perceptions about what constituted manhood. Their primary role model for Black masculinity was their father. He set an example of manhood that included building a free Black household in a difficult social and economic environment and forging an identity for himself in the community by enlisting for military service. Quite possibly, for the Frank brothers, a very active component of their desire to serve reflected their need to incorporate those aspects of masculinity into their own adult lives.

In revolutionary America, masculine ideals were in flux, changing to deal with rhetorical language of freedom, independence, and liberty. The pre-revolutionary man of the middling sort or gentry elite was the head of a household that respected his authority. He was responsible for the lives and conditions of everyone who lived in his household, including servants and the enslaved. Members of the elite came to be associated with masculine ideals defined as the genteel patriarch. These propertied members of the gentry elite were dispassionate and concerned foremost with political stability, civic duty, and family responsibility. Their greatest concern was to control competing masculine ideals that they believed usurped civil authority and their place in society. The genteel patriarchs were threatened by the actions and voices of those whom they viewed to be unstable—itinerants, criminals, slave owners, slaves, and the poor.[70]

The revolutionary-era rhetoric of freedom and equality spawned a sense of righteous masculinity—where Locke's natural rights of man met the Christian ideal of correct moral action. Fighting for the twinned causes of liberty and property drew men of all sorts, occupations, and persuasions to a common purpose. However, members of the dependent class—wives, servants, the enslaved, and by extension free Blacks—did not have the power to protect their natural rights and could only claim the lofty title of "American" if willing to support the "rebellion of free men."[71]

These shifting ideals of American masculinity found a home in the persona of the heroic artisan. These heroes thought little of wealth, advantages, and prerogatives that had been fostered at the highest levels of American society. Personified by the craftsman Paul Revere, heroic artisans were members of the middling sort who were deemed hardworking, independent, and civic-minded. They were seen as the stalwarts of republican man-hood, protecting "liberty against the corrupting force of power."[72] These uplifting ideals of masculinity were expected to translate to members of the poor and working classes—the lower sort. However, for those men living on the margins of American society, unpropertied and poor, manhood was still defined in terms of physical strength and bravery. Men were expected to react strongly to any assault on their body or their honor. These reactions oftentimes took the form of physical retaliation. The Revolutionary War became an outlet for many men to prove or disprove their manliness.[73]

There was also a racial motive for fighting well that was common among the poor, immigrants, or other marginalized groups—a chance to increase respect for their race or group.[74] "Are you men?" This was the call to Black men during the revolutionary era.[75] For free Black men, the ability to assert their own manhood was taken away by the rules and norms of American society. Any attempts on their part to assert their masculinity were coun-tered by a series of societal restrictions in the form of codes which restricted their activities and opportunities. In Revolutionary era Rhode Island, William and Ben Frank and other free Black males were constrained by legal and political limitations and other unwritten social norms. These lim-itations have their origins in earlier codes enacted to regulate enslaved and free Blacks in the years prior to the Revolution. However, the stigma and restrictions attached to those codes would affect free Blacks living through-out the state during and after the Revolution. Of great importance to slave-holders was the power of these codes to control the activities of free Blacks and regulate the interactions between free and enslaved. The codes were a vivid reminder of the limited opportunities afforded free Black males in Rhode Island society.[76]

The weight of these codes and other limitations affected gender rela-tionships in the Black community, as well. In a justification of slavery, slaves were reduced to a submissive and dependent state. Enslaved males, made powerless by their servitude, were deemed unable to protect and provide for their families. Some free African American males were dismayed and embarrassed by the lack of manliness displayed by their enslaved brethren. They attempted to counteract this association with enslaved men by em-phasizing their physical and mental toughness. Subordination, timidity, or weakness did not have a place in their ideal vision of Black manhood.[77] Freedman G. W. Offley, a boxing instructor, tied slavery to cowardice: "no one is so contemptible as a coward. With us a coward is looked upon as the most degraded Wretch on earth and is only worthy to be a slave."[78] Offley did not acknowledge that the system of slavery was devised to rob enslaved men of their manhood. Similarly, former slave William Grimes believed that cowardice was unmanly and real men physically retaliated against anyone who assaulted them.[79] He related his physical altercation with a white butcher: "The trouble I got into was, that a large butcher one day insulted me and I knocked him down. I was then younger than I am now, and if anybody meddled with Grimes, he was sure to be punished, if he wasn't stronger and a better man than I was."[80]

But enslaved men also had their own ideals of manhood, centered on physical prowess, as revealed in many slave narratives. For example, William Davis warned his overseers who were threatening to whip him: "Boys, I am only a poor boy and you are grown men, but if either of you touch me, I'll kill one of you that I'm bound to."[81]

Any Black masculine ideal fostered and sought after had to compete with the image perpetuated by runaway advertisements in newspapers and advertisements throughout the colonial and Revolutionary periods. These advertisements offered the most typical depictions of Black men and misrepresented Black masculinity by generalizing and degrading their physical and emotional attributes. The generalities of "very thick lips" and "curled head of hair" illustrated the vagueness of Black male visualization in early America.[82] Very general physical descriptions were used to represent an assortment of fugitive slaves, such as "A handsome well made Fellow," "a tall Fellow," or "a fellow of middling stature."[83] However, sometimes scars and other facial markings were listed in an attempt to assist with the quick identification and return of runaways—"has got a Guinea Mark on each Cheek," "has a Scar near his left Eye about an inch long," [84] "has a remarkable scar on one side of his neck."[85] Occasionally, skills and talents were listed to distinguish a missing enslaved person—"plays well on a violin," "understands all Sorts of farming Work," "speaks tolerable good English, and some French."[86]

In most advertisements, the names of fugitives were listed along with their physical descriptors. However, there are instances in which no name is listed—an indication that the fugitive was considered less than human—a piece of property with no name. For example:

> Run away from the Subscriber, on the eighth of June, at Night, a
> Negro Boy, about 17 years of Age: Had on, when he went off, a dark
> coloured Cloth Jacket, and Trowsers and is branded on the Breast De-
> lamote.[87]

Ran away from the subscriber, of Tiverton, on the 2d instant, a NEGRO MAN, about 26 years old, 5 feet 5 or 6 inches high . . . and carried with him, a blue outside sailor's jacket, bound with white, a green jacket tied with strings at the button-holes, a white tow shirt, a small brimm'd hat, bound with red, ear-rings in his ears, a pair of pumps, which had been new-toed, a moss coloured sailor's great-coat, and striped blue and with tow-trowsers.[88]

Most advertisements included description of the clothing worn by the fugitive. These descriptions were precise, detailed, and individualized, different from the general and sometimes detached summaries provided regarding the personalities and physical composition of fugitive slaves. The imagining of Black men by ubiquitous fugitive advertisements bound their image to a certain space in society—a space inhabited by livestock, home furnishings, and farm tools. The ability of Black men to chart out their own masculinity was in direct conflict with pervasive and prevalent fugitive slave advertisements describing Black males as pieces of property as opposed to human beings. As free Black men tried to define their own masculinity and carve out a niche in American society, they had to deal with these often negative and persistent images of the Black male.

Black Freemasonry was one of the first opportunities for African American men to define their manhood. Black Freemasonry attempted to transform all Black men into "symbolic artisans" and members of a larger Black masculine body. The origins of the movement go back to the beginnings of the Revolutionary War. Six weeks before the battles at Lexington and Concord, Prince Hall of Boston, a free Black artisan, and fourteen other free Black men of Boston entered a British encampment at Massachusetts' Bunker Hill to gain entry into the Masonic order. Hall and his group were initiated into Masonic Army Lodge No. 441 by an outfit of Irish Freemasons. At the cost of twenty-five guineas each, Hall and his companions became members of the Ancient and Accepted Order of Freemasons. They immediately formed a lodge of their own, Provisional African Lodge No. 1, naming Prince Hall as its first Grand Master.[89] Maurice O. Wallace describes the appeal of Hall's Black Freemasonry deriving from its "gendered identity of the artisan but equally on the historical relevance and respectability of the artisan as a racialized identity."[90] This ideal incorporated the history and tradition of Black tradesmen in America to the emerging symbolism of the heroic artisan.

Prince Hall, as the founding leader of the Black Freemasonry movement, served as an example of the heroic artisan. To provide the opportunity for all Black men to claim and assert their masculinity, Hall advocated for their involvement in the two institutions that provided "masculine authentication" in the Revolutionary era—Freemasonry and the military. As shown earlier, Prince Hall was the vocal leader of the free Black community in Boston that petitioned General Washington to allow the enlistment of African American men as soldiers in the Continental army. He also pushed for the recruitment and indoctrination of Black males as Freemasons. Individuals like Prince Hall illustrated how Blacks formed their own version of the heroic artisan—seeking to "link their manliness to the building of nationhood."[91] In the spirit of the heroic artisan, free Blacks welcomed the beginning of the war. They joined the army, but also drafted petitions lodging their protests against unequal and unfair treatment—particularly the denial of the right to vote even though they paid taxes—offering up their own protest concerning taxation without representation.[92] Entrepreneur Anthony Kinnicutt of Providence used Revolutionary rhetoric to push his case for the right to vote. If not given the franchise, then Kinnicutt reasoned that he should not be made to pay taxes. As a taxpaying citizen, Kinnicutt petitioned town officials to "make an explicit and clear Declaration whether they will wholly forbear to tax him, or grant him the Privilege of being a Freeman of the Town like another Man if his real Estate should be of sufficient Value. He thinks his Request reasonable and thinks that if he cannot be admitted free of the Town if his Estate be enough, he ougt to [be] exonerated from the Payment of any Rates and Taxes."[93]

It is also likely that free Black men tied their masculinity to the notion of freedom and the ability to freely express their own ideas, make their own decisions, and to earn a living, raise and support a family, and live in their own homes. These ideals of Black masculinity can be seen in the life of Venture Smith, who lived in Connecticut throughout the colonial and revolutionary eras. Through hard work and perseverance, he not only gained his own freedom but also purchased the freedom of his wife and children. His narrative, created at the end of his life, is filled with his prideful recollections of becoming self-sufficient in terms of land ownership, home ownership, and steady employment as a general laborer and entrepreneur.[94] He rejoiced in his ability to purchase family members and provide for them as the head of the household: "Being about forty-six years old . . . I had already redeemed from slavery, myself, my wife and three children."[95] His recollections bespeak his commitment to hard work and frugality. "In the space of six month I cut and corded upwards of four hundred cords of wood. Many other singular and wonderful labors I performed in cutting wood there, which would not be inferior to those just recited, but for brevity sake I must omit them." He went on to add: "this money I laid up carefully by me . . . as for superfluous finery I never thought it to be compared with a decent homespun dress, a good supply of money and prudence."[96] Above all, Venture valued his freedom, and he attributed his liberty to his successes in life: "My freedom is a privilege which nothing else can equal . . . I am now possessed of more than one hundred acres of land, and three habitable dwelling houses. It gives me joy to think that I have and that I deserve so good a character, especially for truth and integrity."[97] But the greater rhetoric of freedom and liberty recited during the revolutionary era did not seem to mean much to him. His son's service with the Continental army goes unmentioned in his narrative—a nod to Venture's belief in hard work and action to ensure liberty and equality for Blacks in the new nation.[98]

Where did other freemen of color, who enlisted along with the Franks, stand in this conflict of warring ideals? A variety of diverse and varied motivating factors and beliefs can be attributed to the freemen—based on their backgrounds and experiences. Twenty-nine identified African Americans enlisted in 1777—the same year as the Frank brothers. These men came from a variety of backgrounds and experiences. All came from the working class and were susceptible to the opportunity of earning steady wages and promises of land. Their father figures were more than likely enslaved or formerly enslaved and had to fight against the negative perceptions. These father figures more than likely did not have the resources to assure that their sons embarked on adulthood with necessary resources—land and money. The opportunities promised by the military would provide those resources. Most, like Winsor Fry, Cesar Sabins, and others, were listed as common laborers on the rolls. As such, their ability to become men—by providing for themselves and a family—was limited. Even those with a skilled trade were not immune to the benefits provided by military service. Cobbler Prince Babcock and tailor Plato Vandorum sought out military service to improve their situations. Even with those skills, Babcock and Vandorum were subject to the whims of the marketplace and had to deal with competition from white workers.[99]

Mariner Francis Gould came from an environment much different than his fellow comrades. First, he was older than the Frank brothers upon enlistment. As a twenty-three-year-old, he was an adult. And where most of his fellow enlistees stood under six feet tall, Gould measured six feet one inch in height. He was one of the few who was born and raised outside of New England. Gould's home was New York City and as a sailor, he traveled throughout the western boundary of the Atlantic world. Gould's work led him to the busy seaport at Newport, Rhode Island—his listed place of residence at the time of his enlistment. By 1777, however, Newport was under the control of British forces, who began their occupation of the seaport early during the war. That occupation drove many sailors and others to seek a livelihood elsewhere. Francis Gould saw an opportunity in military service.[100]

Where did the young Frank men stand in their understanding of why to serve? They were most likely inspired and driven by their father's example. But which of these ideals was the closest to the reality set by Rufus Frank? The Frank family was part of a history of Black Americans who already had a tradition of military service. Historian William Cooper Nell wrote about the exploits of Charles Black, a victim of race riots in Philadelphia in August 1842. Black was impressed as a sailor on a British ship during the War of 1812, but he refused to fight against Americans and was jailed aboard a prison ship for a period during the war. Upon his release, he fought with American sailors on Lake Champlain. Black's father served in the Revolutionary War and fought at Breed's Hill. Black's grandfather fought during the French and Indian War. This tradition of military service is quite like the Frank family's involvement with wars that were pivotal to the creation of the American nation.[101]

But was there another aspect of this military tradition fostered by members of the Frank family? Did the Frank forefather instill a sense of Africanness into his heirs? Were William and Ben recipients of this heritage? A sense of pride in their homeland was passed down through each generation of Frank men. Did part of that heritage include a sense of the African warrior spirit? If so, then they were the recipients of a valuable commodity. Many enslaved African men brought to the Americas had been warriors in their native land and brought that military experience with them to their new place of residence. Large numbers of enslaved males were captured in African wars and as such had some experience with military systems and if from a more traditional martial culture saw military service as a way to retain their warrior tradition—a chance to illustrate their manhood through physical prowess, strength, skill, and character. If the Frank forefather had experience as a warrior in his homeland, he could have passed down to his male descendants a sense of this warrior tradition.[102]

There was a tradition of military service among Frank men in the colonial era. As stated earlier, Rufus Frank served in various campaigns during the French and Indian War. Rufus' probable father, Phillip Frank, also served in that conflict. Another possible ancestor, Andrew Frank (I), is listed as serving in colonial conflicts before his death in 1756. And Andrew Frank (II), a probable relative from Providence County, served as a member of the Rhode Island militia during the Revolutionary War. He settled in William and Ben's hometown of Johnston, Rhode Island, after the war and received a pension for his service, starting in 1831 at the age of eighty. These examples may have motivated the young brothers to serve.[103]

In 1777, conditions were in flux for two young Black men embarking upon adulthood. Their father, Rufus Frank, was one of the few Black heads of households in Johnston. If his status in the community was the result of his service during the French and Indian War, he was likely an advocate for his sons to enlist. His sons' decisions to enlist in the service may have been prompted by their attempt to rise above the other Black males in their community and eventually gain status and public gratitude as veterans of the war that liberated America. Additionally, Rufus set an example of manhood that included forging a free Black household in a difficult social and economic environment and forging an identity for himself in the community by enlisting for military service.

The brothers were joining a group of Blacks and other men of color who served long-term enlistments with the regular army, as opposed to short-term stints with the militia or state regiments. As Continental soldiers, Blacks usually enlisted for a longer term, sometimes three years or the duration of the war. As enlistment restrictions against Blacks subsided, the number of Black soldiers increased. Over 5,000 African American soldiers would eventually serve during the Revolutionary War, mostly distributed in battalions raised in New England. The Franks were two of these soldiers and the First and Second Rhode Island regiments were two of those battalions.

CHAPTER FOUR

Brothers at War:
The First Year

THEIR CAMP WAS A HOT, humid, sickly mess during the day and often
cold and dreary at night. Amid breaking winter encampment, William
and Ben Frank and other members of the Second Rhode Island Regiment
were stationed in and around Morristown, New Jersey, in the late spring of
1777. William may have arrived at winter camp as part of the Continental
troops arriving daily at Morristown. Benjamin may have arrived with other
new troops and the recently promoted Major Samuel Ward during the first
weeks in May. The brothers' first year of service started with a series of
marches and maneuvers designed to sometimes engage and oftentimes
avoid British regulars stationed in the New Jersey countryside.[1] Their commander, Colonel Israel Angell, lamented their tough situation. In a letter
to the governor of Rhode Island dated August 1777, Angell described the
state of his regiment as "scandalous in its appearance in ye view of every
one—and has because of this incurred from surrounding regiments from
ye inhabitants of Towns thro which they have lately passed, ye disagreeable
and provoking Epithets of the Ragged, Lousy, Naked regiment—Such
treatment, gentlemen, is discouraging dispiriting in its tendency."[2] From

Angell's description, it appears that the Frank brothers enlisted into a hell-hole of an experience and they were not even appreciated by their fellow countrymen and women.

As they endured their first year as members of the Rhode Island regiments, the Franks and other free Black men of the Rhode Island Continental Line became part of the population of "hardcore" soldiers who were long-serving and long-suffering in their length and breadth of service. These soldiers served for long periods of time, often without pay and proper equipment, lived in wretched camp conditions, and formed tight bonds with fellow soldiers. The post–1776 Continental regulars mostly came from the working and poorer classes in revolutionary America. They were young men from meager circumstances who had little property or economic ties. They were dependent upon others for their livelihood and looked at military service to gain "personal socioeconomic mobility."[3] For the Rhode Islanders among them, they served as members of integrated regiments composed of former common laborers who had been attempting to eke out a living in revolutionary Rhode Island.

William and Benjamin enlisted at a time when the recruiting of men into service away from their home state was tough. British occupation of Newport and Aquidneck Island led many Rhode Island men to want to stay home and protect their home turf. Throughout the spring of 1777, there was a competition between state needs, led by Governor Cooke, and the requirements mandated by the Continental Congress for able-bodied men to fill the ranks of the state regiment and/or the Continental forces. The post–1776 configuration of the Continental army changed from its original alignment. In 1776, Rhode Island's contribution to the Continental forces was reduced by Congress from three regiments to two—the 9th and 11th Continentals, under the command of Generals James Varnum and Daniel Hitchcock. At the end of 1776, the Rhode Island General Assembly voted to raise two regiments, the First and Second Rhode Island regiments, with an authorized strength of 1,424 men. The recruiting did not go well. By February 1777, only fifty men had enlisted. By March, the two regiments had a total of about 400 men. Additionally, a change was made to the command structures of the reorganized regiments. Colonel Israel Angell was appointed commander of the Second Rhode Island. Angell was a veteran of the campaigns of 1776 who saw action as a major with the 11th Continentals at Trenton and Princeton. Angell also saw military command prior to the war. He commanded a militia company in his hometown of Johnston, Rhode Island. In that position, Angell was more than likely aware of the Franks and the two young men who were part of that family. Angell's compatriot in the command of the Rhode Island regiments was Christopher Greene, who was appointed commander of the First Rhode Island. Both were promoted to their positions at the recommendation of General Washington. Because Greene was still a prisoner at this time (he was captured during the Arnold expedition to Quebec), Lt. Colonel Comstock was put in command until Greene could join his unit. Colonel Greene returned to his unit after his parole from British captivity in July 1777. Upon arrival at the American encampment in Morristown, New Jersey, the Rhode Island regiments were brigaded with the Fourth and Eighth Connecticut regiments. All four units were placed under the command of General Varnum, now a brigadier general in the Continental Line. After the enlistments of William and Benjamin Frank, the two Rhode Island regiments peaked in strength at 600.[4]

The men who filled the ranks of the Rhode Island regiments came from locations throughout the small state. At the beginning of the war, Rhode Island's population was approximately 60,000, with 54,000 whites and over 6,000 Blacks and Native Americans. The diversity of its population was reflected in the multiethnic composition of both regiments. Most of the soldiers were of European American descent, as evidenced in their English, Scotch, Irish, and French names. Men of color sometimes came from biracial backgrounds—the children of European fathers and Native or African American mothers—sometimes sharing the European names of their fathers. The formerly enslaved may have also taken on the names of their former owners. Members of the Rhode Island regulars were primarily from farming communities but also participated in commercial and noncommercial activities connected to the Atlantic Ocean and Narragansett Bay. Many among them came from large towns like Providence and Newport and others came from small towns like East Greenwich, Warwick, Bristol, and Coventry. They were coopers, rope makers, mariners, fishermen, and general laborers. An integral part of these regiments was a coterie of Black soldiers who were freeborn or free at the start of the war. These men, like the Franks, committed to service for a variety of reasons, as discussed in the previous chapter.[5]

As members of the Second Rhode Island, William and Ben served under the overall command of Colonel Israel Angell. Black, Native American, and white soldiers of the Second Rhode Island suffered together. The regiment included many free men of color—a mixture of Native Americans, mulattos, and Blacks who served as foot soldiers. Ben served in Captain

Thomas Hughes' company of forty-six regulars. The muster roll for December 1777 shows at least eleven soldiers of color serving alongside more than thirty white soldiers. Edward Anthony, Jonathan Charles, William Coopin, Toby Coys, Gideon Harry, Simeon Niles, Joseph Nocake, Cuff Peckham, Richard Pomp, and Fortune Sailes all became members of the battalion during the early months of 1777. All were free men before their enlistments. In January 1778, William served in the company led by Captain William Potter which included at least five other men of color (John Daniels, Francis Tifft, Henry Hazzard, Noah Sisco, and Ceasar Cook) who served alongside white privates.[6]

Captain Thomas Hughes was born in Newport, Rhode Island, in 1752 and lived there before the war. Newport was an especially important seaport, as the town's leading citizens and merchants were involved in the transatlantic trade centered on molasses, rum, and enslaved Africans. By 1750, Newport was the leading slave market on the Atlantic Coast and its population reflected that involvement. Newport had the largest enslaved population in New England at 1,084. The 1774 Colonial Census of Rhode Island shows 7,917 whites, fifty-two free Black households, and 162 free Blacks in Newport—1.7 percent of the Rhode Island population and 13 percent of the Black population. Hughes was not a slaveholder but he lived in a town that tolerated slave trading. Newport was also home to an active abolition movement. Where Hughes stood on this spectrum is unknown. Of the free soldiers of color that eventually came under his command, none came from Newport. At the beginning of the war, Hughes served as an ensign in Colonel Thomas Church's regiment which was raised in his hometown and Bristol County. Hughes saw service at the siege of Boston from June 1775 until March 1776. By the time of his promotion to the command of his own company, Hughes had already fought in important battles at Long Island, White Plains, and Princeton, sustaining a wound on Long Island. A "small wirey man" with reddish-colored hair and blue eyes, he was a capable command officer. Hughes' personal experiences from his upbringing in Newport, surrounded by a collection of free and enslaved Blacks, and his wartime experiences from early in the war may have prepared him for the command of a diverse collection of foot soldiers whose origins ranged from Native communities in Charlestown and free Black communities throughout Rhode Island.[7]

John Charles, William Coopin, Gideon Harry, Simeon Niles, and Joseph Nocake became members of this diverse group when they enlisted in March 1777. Nocake joined after serving with the Rhode Island Brigade and after a stint on board the sloop of war *Providence* during the early months of the war. Toby Coys joined them at the age of seventeen when he enlisted in May. All signed up for the duration of the war and all have been identified as being of Native American descent. It is unknown where John Charles resided before the war. Coopin, Harry, Coys, Niles, and No-cake resided at Charlestown, Rhode Island, prior to their enlistment—an indication that they may have been members of the Narragansett Native American community that was concentrated in that area. For example, Coys hailed from a household of four individuals who resided in Charlestown. All these men were assigned as foot soldiers and served for an average of four years.[8]

Five other men of color also served alongside Ben in Captain Hughes' company. Edward Anthony, also known as Ned, signed up in April 1777, at the same time that William Frank began his service with Colonel Stanton's state militia. Like William, Anthony also served time with the state militia before his enlistment with the Continentals. Anthony, of mixed race descent, resided in South Kingstown before the war. Cuff Peckham signed up for the duration of the war in March 1777. He also resided in South Kingstown before the war. Richard Pomp also enlisted in March 1777 for the duration of the war. Fortune Sailes enlisted in May 1777.[9]

Captain William Potter, William Frank's initial company commander, began his Continental service early. He served as ensign in Hitchcock's regiment (14th Continentals) from June to December 1775. The regiment was originally raised in Providence County in May 1775. He was promoted to the rank of lieutenant in January 1776, as a member of the 11th Continentals where he served from January 1776 to January 1777. He became a member of Second Rhode Island Continentals starting in January 1777 as captain and eventually retired in April 1779.[10]

At least five men of color served alongside William in Potter's company. Native American John Daniels enlisted in April 1777 for the duration of the war. He resided in Charlestown before the war. The remaining soldiers have been described as Black. Ceasar Cook enlisted in May 1777 for the duration of the war. Henry Hazzard also enlisted in April 1777 for a term of three years. Noah Sisco enlisted in April 1777 for the duration of the war. Sisco possibly resided in Providence prior to the start of the war. As stated in the previous chapter, Francis Tifft enlisted at the end of May for the duration of the war. He resided in Providence in the household of his owner Daniel Tefft before the war and gained his freedom before signing up to serve.[11]

A close inspection of the Franks' first year of service shows their introduction into the ranks of the hardcore Continental regulars was based on class, as opposed to race—an important distinction for the Franks seeking to gain economic and community standing. Like most of the working-class poor that composed the Rhode Island regulars, Black soldiers were motivated to follow American leaders, as opposed to the British. The first-year experiences of William and Ben paralleled the service of white soldiers like Joseph Plumb Martin and illustrated the common experience shared by Continental regulars.

New recruits like William and Ben were subject to rudimentary training and constant drilling in camp in preparation for long marches and violent battles. The most important aspect of their training was instruction on the loading and firing of the musket. Black soldiers assigned to infantry units were issued muskets and bayonets as their primary weapons. The main infantry weapon of the period was the muzzle-loading, smoothbore, flintlock musket. The military tactics of the era called for opposing troops to line up shoulder to shoulder, two ranks deep. From this position, the troops either fired their volleys or charged their opponents. The idea was to lay down a field of fire as quickly as possible. To accomplish this task, the Continental soldier had to complete twelve orders: 1. Poise firelock; 2. Cock firelock; 3. Present; 4. Fire; 5. Half cock firelock; 6. Handle cartridge; 7. Prime; 8. Shut pans; 9. Load cartridges; 10. Draw ramrod; 11. Ram down cartridge; 12. Return ramrod. This training would serve them well as they embarked upon the first major campaigns of their military careers.[12]

As incoming soldiers, William and Ben received the typical uniforms and equipment given to the common troops. Many soldiers favored hunting shirts, loose garments like smocks worn by farmers and workmen. The shirts were durable, practical, and large enough to wear over other clothing and gear. They were fastened with straps or buttons embossed with "USA" for Continental troops. Oftentimes the only clothing/uniform available to a soldier was a blanket draped around the body and tied with a sash at the waist. Shoes were always in short supply. Wealthy officers could afford boots; most common soldiers were equipped with simple shoes, when possible. Shoes were of the buckle variety. Soldiers used leather, canvas, and other coverings to wrap their calves to protect them from muddy, rough terrain. It was not uncommon, however, for the soldier to walk barefoot in the summer and endure the winter with nothing but cloth to wrap the feet. Soldiers usually wore headgear made of leather or knitted wool. A unifying symbol of the American troops was a single sprig of evergreen or other greenery worn in the cap.[13]

Among other supplies issued to the common soldier were blankets and cooking gear. Wool blankets were prized possessions and were usually carried by the soldiers so that they would be available even if supply wagons could not get to their location. Blankets were the first thing discarded in a fight and the first thing recovered from the battlefield once the fighting stopped. The quartermaster also supplied firewood and cooking utensils when possible. Usually, soldiers gathered firewood from forests near their camps for cooking and warmth. Iron kettles were issued based on one per every six or eight men to provide soldiers with a utensil to combine rations into a "squad mess" while in camp.[14]

Privates like William and Ben Frank received one ration of food which translated into three meals per day. A normal daily ration consisted of:

1 lb. beef, or ¾ lb. or pork or 1 lb. salt fish
1 lb. bread of flour
3 pints of peas or beans per week
1 pint of milk
1 half pint of rice
1 pint of Indian meal (corn) per week
1 quart of spruce beer or cider.[15]

Additionally, companies were allotted supplies of molasses, candles for guard duty, and soap. Vinegar was also commonly issued to flavor food, make water drinkable, and serve as an antiseptic. In camp, soldiers usually pooled their rations and took turns as cooks. In the field, soldiers would broil meat over an open fire, coupling that with hastily made bread for a meal.[16]

Food provisions were usually in short supply, which forced the common soldier to forage or acquire his own daily rations. The average soldier spent much of his day searching for food or performing guard duty. Items such as fresh milk, rum, or whiskey and sometimes pork and salt fish often did not make their way into the daily rations provided to the line soldier. Beef and flour of questionable freshness were often the only food issued. Soldiers hunted, gathered, and otherwise appropriated foodstuff on their own. The farms, orchards, and gardens of civilians, especially loyalists, were the targets of these foraging excursions. Formerly enslaved Jeffrey Brace, an infantryman with Captain Borker's company of the Connecticut Line, recounted his service with the Connecticut regulars in his autobiography. Brace detailed an excursion taken by himself and squad members to obtain food. As he described, a raid or "soldier-frollick" was made against the farm of a loyalist. A pig was stolen by Brace and his company mates and brought back to camp by the foraging soldiers. However, the owner of the pig came to the camp to recover it. Brace, being ever articulate, persuaded his commander that their intentions were honorable. He informed his commander that "the owner had brought it for sale, but that from his manner of conversation (knowing him to have been a tory) we unanimously suspected him to have come as a spy and were determined to keep the Shoat until the officers might have an opportunity of being acquainted with his designs." The result of this excursion was that Brace and his comrades kept the pig, and its loyalist owner was severely reprimanded by the American commanding officer.[17]

Shelter and housing for the common soldier, whether Black or white, varied with the time of the year and location of camps. During winter months, soldiers built wooden huts that held six to ten men each. Most of the wood for these huts came from nearby sawmills and farm fences. Gaps between the logs were filled with clay, moss, and straw. Fireplaces made of rock and mud provided heat and a place to cook. During warm weather, the army provided tents made domestically or procured from the British or French. The tents were designed to house six men, but because of shortages, they housed ten or more. The tents were transported on supply wagons and unavailable to the soldiers during marches.[18]

Congress authorized privates like William and Ben Frank to receive $6.67 per month as infantrymen. Higher pay went to the more specialized positions in the cavalry, artillery, and military police.[19] Given the fact that most Black soldiers were assigned to infantry units, they were at the lower end of the pay scale. But payment for all soldiers was affected by the depreciation of money during the war. The Franks' command officer, Colonel Angell of the Second Rhode Island, complained about the issue of pay in 1780. He reported that "news from Congress this day that was disagreeable they having reduced the officers wages 50 percent, and to pay them in a new omition [sic] of paper Money."[20] It is easy to understand Angell's frustration. In January 1777, 105 Continental dollars were equal to 100 Spanish milled dollars. By January 1780, 2,934 Continental dollars were equal to 100 Spanish milled dollars.[21]

Black soldiers like Jeffrey Brace and the Frank brothers were treated like white comrades in the distribution of food and in discipline. On the issue of pay, as stated earlier, Black soldiers were constrained by their assignment to the lower paid job of infantrymen. Most data provided on the war notes the overall shortages of pay, uniforms, footwear, and food rations for everyone.[22] Most first-hand accounts do not indicate any difference of treatment between white and Black soldiers. However, some biased statements have been attributed to members of the command ranks. A captain in the Fourth Pennsylvania Battalion informed his wife that "Negroes, Indians and whites, with old men and mere children . . . make a most shocking spectacle . . . sufficient to make one sick of the service."[23] What is interesting about this comment is the captain's disparaging description of some white soldiers who served alongside Blacks and Native Americans. His uncomplimentary remarks about some white soldiers may have been in reference to the members of the poor, dependent, or transient class that now filled the private ranks of the Continental regiments.[24] General Philip Schuyler of a wealthy and influential New York family owned and used enslaved labor at his mansion and mills. Regarding the use of Black soldiers, Schuyler announced that "Negroes disgrace our arms." General William Heath wrote to Samuel Adams of his unease at having "negroes" mixed with white soldiers. But more pragmatic leaders, like General Schuyler's son-in-law Alexander Hamilton, understood the need to disregard race due to manpower shortages.[25]

If these biased reactions and attitudes held by Continental command officers reflected the beliefs held by their white subordinates, they did not appear to translate into racist practices and behavior in camp. If the regular white soldiers of the Continental Line harbored ill will against African American soldiers, these negative attitudes did not make their way onto the page. Accounts of the day-to-day activities of Revolutionary War soldiers are uncommon, and rarely differentiate between the experiences of Black and white soldiers. Martin does recount incidents where he interacted with Blacks in a civilian capacity—some as enslaved fugitives as Martin related the case of General Cornwallis' disposal of ill slaves that had flocked to his lines. The diaries and journals from members of the First and Second Rhode Island regiments follow this pattern. The lack of recorded incidences of racist treatment might be attributed to the overall low percentages of Black soldiers in these regiments. Brace does not speak about a significant number of other Blacks in his company. Jeremiah Greenman as a private and eventual sergeant of the Second Rhode Island Regiment had experience serving with Black soldiers. But he makes little note of the Blacks assigned to his battalion.[26]

One instance of discriminatory treatment involved regiments of the Connecticut Brigade and may be attributed to the fact that the regiment had a significant number of Black soldiers. Colonel Samuel Parsons of the

Connecticut Brigade complained that his units had not received their fair share of clothing supplies. In the spring of 1779, he threatened to resign over this unfair treatment. Although Parsons did not specify the reasons why he suspected this unfair treatment, he was in command of a large segment of Black soldiers. The Third, Fourth, Sixth, and Eighth Connecticut regiments had the largest number of Black soldiers in the Continental army. According to the adjutant general's report of August 1778, these regiments had a total of 148 African American soldiers. The large contingent of Black soldiers may have prompted this unequal treatment. Colonel Parsons seemed to think that was the case. In contrast, a study of twelve African American soldiers in a Massachusetts brigade exhibited no evidence of discrimination against those soldiers in the areas of punishments, rewards, wages, provisions, or pensions.[27]

The condition of the Second Rhode Island Regiment at the time of the Franks' enlistment was not the best. Sergeant Jeremiah Greenman described their encampment in New Jersey as hot, humid, and sickly. His description of their camp as a "very unwholesum time" and "very sickly" refers to the outbreak of smallpox which infected the camp.[28] Disease was the cause of more casualties among Revolutionary War soldiers than battlefield injuries. Smallpox, typhus, dysentery, measles, mumps, and scurvy often swept through the camps. John Adams once wrote that "Disease has destroyed ten men for us where the sword of the enemy had killed one."[29] At any given time, one soldier in five was struck down due to illness. At the height of the epidemics, one-half of the army was too ill to fight. African American soldiers like Ben and William Frank were not immune to these diseases; however, the formerly enslaved had more resistance to some illnesses than many white soldiers. As the Franks and their fellow recruits dealt with the heat and sickness of camp life, they also were learning to deal with the lack of supplies and equipment.[30]

The command staff tried to ease the amount of sickness and suffering that occurred in camp. Strict rules were promulgated, regulating behavior deemed detrimental to the good health of the regulars. For instance, officers and their subordinates engaged in the practice of bathing in streams and rivers more than twice a week and spent more than eight minutes in the water cleansing themselves. The general command issued revised orders, stating that soldiers injured their health by bathing too often and that bathing should be less often and for a shorter duration. The commander-in-chief, concerned about putrid fever running rampant through camp, warned that bathing in the heat of the day was at least one cause of the disease.[31]

The daily grind of military life could have a negative effect on the morale of the Continental regular. The daily life of the regular started when reveille sounded one hour before sunrise and ended at 10 p.m. with the sounds of syncopated drumbeats. While in camp, soldiers drilled or paraded once in the morning and a second time in the afternoon hours. This was basically the only exercise for the encamped troops, including members of the Second Rhode Island Regiment.[32] The general orders for their Peekskill camp in July 1777 illustrate the monotonous life in camp: "General expects ye Troops . . . will be employ'd in military exercise & directs that every Company shall be exercised from Reveillee-beating to six oclock in ye Morning ye time for relieving ye Guard & from 8 o'Clock to 10 in ye forenoon & from 4 oclock in ye Afternoon till 7 & that each Regimt Shall have two Field Days in a Week for regimental exercise."[33]

Boredom, lack of equipment, foraging for food, and staving off sickness were all components that could affect the soldier in a negative manner. Religion played an integral role in countering the monotony and negativity of camp life. George Washington believed that to win the war, he needed at least an ethical army if not a religious army. While they were encamped at Morristown in May 1777, the order was given that "all the Troops In and about Morristown to attend Divine Service to Morrow. No excuse will be admitted." Washington further believed that the use of chaplains was a method to accomplish that goal. Washington wanted chaplains to be religious leaders, and he charged chaplains to give sermons of a patriotic nature to keep the soldiers from deserting. Chaplains were also responsible for counseling soldiers on the dangers of alcohol consumption, to not cheat at games, and to not gamble away the sporadic pay that they received. Washington also admonished chaplains who were not available at winter encampment, noting "that the Chaplains have frequently been almost all absent, at the same time, under the idea that their presence could be of any utility . . . in the future no furloughs will be granted to Chaplains except in consequence of permission from Headquarter."[34]

Despair and religion collided at Camp Peekskill during the summer of 1777, culminating in the suicide of Abiel Leonard, chaplain to the Regiment of Artillery, under the command of Colonel Henry Knox. The chaplain, driven by what he saw as resistance by the rank and file to godly guidance from their committed chaplains, cut his own throat with a razor at Judge Coe's tavern in Kakiate, New York. Ebenezer David, chaplain to the Second Rhode Island Regiment, wrote home to friends describing the terrible fate of Abiel Leonard and his concern that Leonard's actions would be used as propaganda by British forces:

I suppose you have heard the shocking news of Parson Leonards making an attack upon his own Life with a Razor the Gash was deep and his life despaired of some time but hopes are now entertained of his recovery—What are men when left to themselves—this awful accident gives me great concern not only as it respects himself and his immediate connections but on account of the use which the Enemies of our Religion and country will make of it—People here are pretty generally satisfied what disappointments lead him to so dreadful an act.[35]

Reverend Abiel Leonard died from his self-inflicted wounds on August 14, 1777. Since Leonard's actions may have been known and understood throughout the encampment, the notion that a chaplain attempted to end his own life and eventually succeeded must have cast a pall over the community of soldiers at Peekskill.

Colonel Angell tried to improve the conditions of his camp by issuing orders requiring subordinates to better police their equipment and appearance. At Camp Peekskill in July 1777, Angell observed that:

Men appear on parade for Guard &c: with their Arms in bad Order, their cloathing extreamly Dirty, & Slovenly in their Dress: for preventing these Evils, & this unsoldier like practice, tis most earnestly recommended to ye Capt. & Commanding Officers to have their respective Companies divided into Messes of six Men each, & appoint a Sergt. & Corp. to each Mess or more Messes as ye Case may require who are to be responsible to their Capt. Or other Officer for neglect in their respective Messes.[36]

Angell's orders and actions reflected his concern and anger at the lack of readiness of his troops. He displayed those emotions to his civilian superiors as well in the letter, describing his regiment being called the "Ragged, Lousy, Naked regiment."[37]

To hear the negative comments of various civilians while marching to their encampment must have been a trying experience for new soldiers like William and Ben Frank. If they thought that enlistment with the Continentals would result in respect and support from the community at large, they were mistaken. This lack of support from the community could result in the type of behavior exhibited by Rhode Islanders, which included theft of services and goods without feelings of guilt and remorse. Historian James Kirby Martin describes this type of action on the part of the common soldier as a direct result of the lack of material and psychological support from the civilian sector. He goes on to state that these actions were a form of protest and defiance on the part of soldiers in response to obvious ingratitude on the part of their government and their fellow countrymen.[38]

Disciplinary problems in the ranks normally occurred in the confines of camp, where strict regulations were enforced to temper the behavior of Continental regulars. Constant drilling not only prepared Continental regulars for battle and to follow orders quickly and correctly; it also helped to increase morale. Consequently, behavioral problems usually occurred during downtime at camp. Members of the Second Rhode Island were not immune to behavioral issues. These problems and crimes ranged from forgery to assault.[39] Lesser offenses of improper care of equipment garnered the offending soldier extra duty of cleaning latrines, guard duty, or time on the wooden horse. Mather Bryant of Captain William Allen's company absented "himself from the fatigue party" and got drunk. Bryant was sentenced to "ride the Woden horse" for twenty minutes with a gun attached to his feet.[40] More serious offenses, such as theft and assault, earned more serious discipline. The usual form of punishment for serious offenses was lashing or flogging. The guilty party was stripped to the waist and tied to a fixed object. He was then lashed with a whip made of several small cords for the prescribed number of lashes. Members of the Rhode Island regiments received lashes for major and minor infractions during the spring of 1777. Sergeant Greenman recorded that three to four men were flogged daily. James Duggins committed one of the most serious offenses when he shot at another soldier, whom Duggins claimed threatened his wife. The protective husband was constrained to hang from the gallows for fifty minutes and then flogged with fifty lashes.[41]

Angell also tried to rein in the instances of theft that occurred throughout the regiment. As he was pleading for better supplies and equipment for his men, he was alarmed to learn that some were in the habit of destroying and selling issued supplies. He was surprised to hear that "sum of the soldiers have had their blankets cut up to Make Great coats." He ordered that anyone caught in this practice be severely punished. Private Tobias Briggs was punished for selling his blanket. His pay was temporarily suspended, and he received fifteen lashes.[42]

If caught and convicted of desertion, the soldier usually received the punishment of lashing, carried out in front of the regiments. In July 1777, Sergeant Jon Smith and Private William White were tried and found guilty of desertion. Both were attempting to resort to the enemy with stolen cartridges. Smith was reduced in rank, and both received one hundred lashes on their naked backs.[43] Some deserters received the death penalty and were publicly hanged or shot. Thomas Persil (Powell) was a repeat offender. By July, however, his chances finally ran out. He was tried and convicted for "deserting to enemy, returning and deserting again and persuading other to desert with him."[44] He was sentenced to be shot to death. A member of the First Pennsylvania, upon his conviction for desertion, was shot and beheaded. His head was placed upon a pole as a deterrent for other deserters. The severity of punishment varied from regiment to regiment.[45]

There were cases of protest and discipline in the First Rhode Island Regiment. Sergeant John Smith described an incident of protest during his first days of encampment at Peekskill. On August 28, 1777, soldiers assigned to Colonel Greene's regiment had "Laid Down their Arms & Refused to Do any Duty on acct. of their Clothing that they had not Received according to Promise made them when they enlisted."[46] As a result of this action, a total of fourteen soldiers were placed under arrest: seven sergeants, five corporals, one drummer, and one private. After a court-martial held by Colonel Israel Angell of the Second Rhode Island, the seven sergeants were suspended for forty-nine days at the "pleasure of" the commanding officer, and the remaining soldiers were reprimanded and released.[47]

It appears that Colonel Angell, although not condoning the behavior of the officers, did feel sympathetic toward their plight. This would be consistent with his diatribe to the governor, detailing his feelings of disgust toward the government regarding its inability to properly equip its soldiers. This act of protest by members of the First Rhode Island was just a small portion of a larger, more complex aspect of life in Continental service that would remain a reality throughout the war. Common soldiers in the regular army, whether Black or white, would continue to exhibit their feelings of anger and dissatisfaction by committing various acts of protest and defiance. Generally, it was the recruit who, after becoming disillusioned with the realities of camp life, struck out against established rules and order. Their protests could take the form of cursing, excessive drinking, assaulting officers, deserting, or bounty jumping. Private John Martin attacked Sergeant Jeremiah Greenman with a club. It is unknown what provoked the attack. But Martin received one hundred lashes for his insubordination.[48]

Protests were induced by the brutal nature of camp life, broken promises regarding pay, food, and clothing or the fact that the civilian population held the soldiers in disdain.[49] William and Ben Frank experienced all these protest-inducing aspects of military life early in their careers. Their camps were filled with smallpox and sick soldiers. The commander of their regiment described his troops as "Ragged, Lousy, Naked."[50] The civilian population had regarded the troops with disdain as they marched through their towns. Historian James Kirby Martin asserts that the first days and weeks were those in which new regulars asked themselves if the sacrifice of service was worth the promises of rewards after service was concluded. Many new recruits concluded that it was not and fled.[51]

Neither William nor Ben deserted at this time in their careers. They made it through the first harrowing months of service and camp life and would eventually participate in major battles throughout the war. Neither brother received punishment for infractions. Their reasons for serving must have outweighed any desire to desert early in their military careers. They still saw military service as a means to reap the rewards of pay, land, and community recognition.

Their desire to serve would be severely tested at Red Bank in New Jersey—the first major battle that the Franks fought as members of the Second Rhode Island Regiment. The American forts situated along the Delaware River allowed American forces to control access to the waterway and prevented the British from establishing adequate supply and communication lines by sea from Philadelphia. General Howe, upon his capture of Philadelphia in October 1777, planned to remove the American presence from the important waterway by taking over two strategic forts along the Delaware—Fort Mifflin and Fort Mercer. Fort Mifflin on Mud Island and Fort Mercer at Red Bank, with *chevaux de fries* at Billings Island and Mud Island, and a redoubt at Billingsport, were the main obstructions to British control of the Delaware. The plan was to shell Fort Mifflin into submission and attack Fort Mercer by land. As British forces moved to the forts along the Delaware, Washington countered the move by sending the First and Second Rhode Island Regiments to repel their efforts. During the latter months of 1777, manpower totals for units under the immediate command of General Washington looked promising and allowed for more aggressive action on his part. The First Rhode Island, under the command of Colonel Greene, numbered 359, with 254 fit for duty. The Second Rhode Island had 233 fit for duty.[52]

After receiving their orders on October 7, 1777, both regiments marched to Red Bank. On October 10, 1777, the regiments parted ways when the Second Rhode Island was commanded back to Peekskill. The regiment paused in Bucks County for a few days, waiting for confirmation for their return to the main camp. They would eventually rejoin the First Rhode Island at Fort Mercer on October 18, 1777.[53] By October 10, 1777, Fort Mercer was already under heavy attack from British forces under the command of Colonel Sterling, who had taken control of the fortification at Billingsport. The First Rhode Islanders arrived to defend the fort on October 11. They were worn out by the long march. Sergeant John Smith of the First Rhode Island stated that the troops were very fatigued after marching. He stated: "we marchd again for the Red Bank—we march'd 6 miles & made another halt & Drew half Gill of Rum Pr. man—then marched into the fort [Fort Mercer] about 4 miles farther & Pitched our tents & Loged Quiet this night—their hath bin a Continuel fire of Cannon all Day Between the Enemy & our Galleys in the River."[54] As described by Smith, the First Rhode Island was thrown into an immediate battle to defend the fort. Chaplain Ebenezer described their situation as dire. The fort and its defenses were in great disrepair, badly designed and in need of a force of 3,000 men.[55] The fort was in "no state of defence."[56] But defend it they would under the overall command of Colonel Greene.

Maryland and Connecticut troops, under the command of Lieutenant Colonel Samuel Smith, were stationed at Fort Mifflin. Both units were low in numbers. On October 18, 1777, the Franks and the rest of the Second Rhode Island arrived at Fort Mercer after a two-day march of sixty miles without sleep. The arrival of the Second Rhode Island was fortuitous since a detachment of Second Rhode Islanders was promptly dispatched to reinforce troops at Fort Mifflin.[57]

While preparing to defend the forts at all costs and withstanding a constant barrage of fire from British forces, some members of the Rhode Island regiments and affiliated forces succumbed to their fears. Sergeant Smith described two such instances in his chronicle of the battles at Fort Mercer and Fort Mifflin: "[On October 12] Capt. Elijah Lewis Return'd back from his Expidition having one searjt. wounded Namely wardel Green belonging to Colo. Greene's Regemt. & one belonging to the fort on the other side [i.e., Fort Mifflin] & 4 or 5 Disirted to the Enemy being fritened at their Numbers as they were much Superiour for Numbers."[58] In the second case, Smith described the desertion of an entire boat crew: "Yesterday [October 17] a Boats Crew Deserted to the Enemy with the Boat from fort Mifflin

Overleaf: "The course of Delaware River from Philadelphia to Chester, exhibiting the several works erected by the rebels to defend its passage, with the attacks made upon them by His Majesty's land & sea forces," William Faden, 1777. Fort Mercer on Red Bank is along the Jersey shore at right. The route of Colonel Carl von Donop's forces is shown travelling from Gloucester to Fort Mercer. (*Library of Congress*)

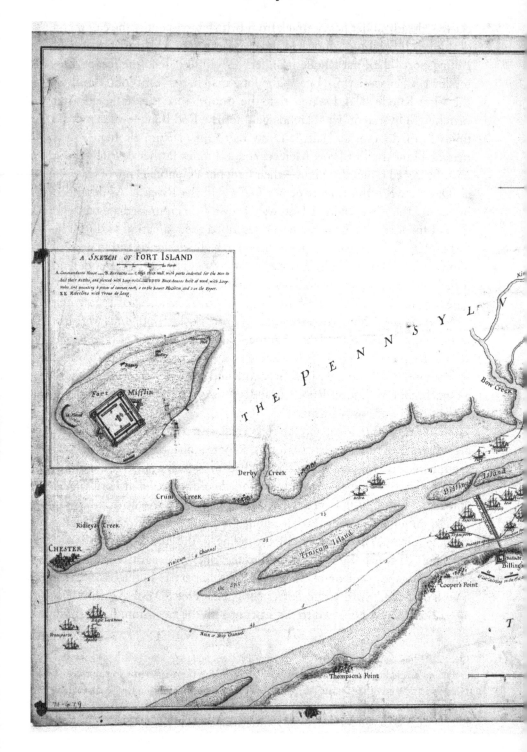

PHILADELPHIA

NIA S H O R E

Province Island

Carpenters Island

Hog Island

Mud Island

FORT ISLAND

Red Bank Island

Hollanders Creek

Hay Creek

League Island

GLOUCESTER

Timber Creeks

Eagle Point

RED BANK

Fort Mercer

New Redoubt

Billingport

Manto Creek

J E R S E Y S H O R E

Profile

and

Plan

of the Junk Frames, or Chevaux de Frise, which formed the Stockados in the River

G 3792
.D4S3
1777
F3

where they Landed their Officer & put off immeadialty to the Enemy—several shot was fired at them from a Blockhouse but Did them no Dammage."[59]

For the Frank brothers and other Rhode Island troops, the fiercest battle occurred on October 22, 1777. Colonel Carl von Donop and his regiments of Hessian grenadiers, auxiliaries to British forces, had crossed the Delaware at Cooper's Ferry and arrived at the doorstep of Fort Mercer, demanding surrender of the garrison. As a result of the Hessians' arrival, the detachment originally dispatched to Fort Mifflin returned to reinforce Fort Mercer.[60] Jeremiah Greenman described Colonel Greene's response as defiant: "Colo. Green answered with disdain, that he would defend it 'till the last drop of his Blood."[61] Colonel Greene's refusal to surrender prompted Donop to order two simultaneous assaults upon the fort, one from the north and one from the south. Since the garrison was too few to oppose the Hessian forces and since the fort's exterior works were unfinished, Greene and Angell ordered the Franks and their fellow soldiers to the interior defenses of Fort Mercer. The Hessians mistook this withdrawal for capitulation. The simultaneous assaults were made with great zeal on the part of the Hessians but met with great force on the part of the Americans. Sergeant Greenman described the retreat to the interior defenses of the fort and subsequent battle with a small group of men fighting around him: "we had a small place big enough for eight men to fight in which overlooked all the ground round the Fort which was surrounded with double abattis / Both of the attacks where such as was expected / they advanced as far as the abbatis, but they could not remove it (tho sum few got over) being repulsed with great loss."[62]

Colonel von Donop and Lieutenant-Colonel Minnigerode were both mortally wounded. Hessian soldiers' casualties exceeded 400. The American casualties were 14 killed and 21 wounded. In less than an hour after the first assault, the Hessians were in retreat. The Rhode Island troops held against the Hessian assault.[63]

The troops stationed at Fort Mifflin were not as successful. During the assault on Fort Mercer, the British batteries at the mouth of the Schuylkill River fired upon Fort Mifflin with little result. However, on November 10, 1777, a renewed assault upon the fort resulted in its capture. Reinforcement batteries by British forces on nearby Province Island had been installed and began to pummel the fort. Six large British frigates, along with several smaller vessels, also participated in the attack. Rhode Island troops stationed at Fort Mercer attempted to help the beleaguered soldiers at Fort Mifflin.

Major Simon Thayer of the Second Rhode Island volunteered to lead a contingent of Second Rhode Islanders to try to save the fort. And the group rowed to Fort Mifflin, but to no avail. On the evening of November 15, 1777, after a loss of over 250 men, killed or wounded, the survivors of the garrison retreated to Fort Mercer. When the British forces turned their combined weight of attack against the American forces, now all situated at Fort Mercer, the Rhode Island troops were forced to retreat and leave Fort Mercer, giving up control of the Delaware River to the British.[64]

The human toll of the battle at Red Bank is evidenced in the loss of life. Major Samuel Ward described the losses in a letter to the commander-in-chief. "Colo. Greens Regt has 2 Serjts—1 fife & 4 Privates Killd—1 Serjt & 3 Privates wounded and one Captain (who was reconnoitering) taken prisoner—Colo. Angel has 1 Capt. killed—3 Serjts 3 Rank & file—& one Ensign 1 Serjt & 15 R. & file wounded."[65] One of the fatalities was Private William Kirks. He enlisted in the spring of 1777, the same time as the Frank brothers. The practical side of military life is illustrated in the inventory of his clothing and equipment after the battle, in preparation for reassigning his clothing to surviving soldiers.

One uniform coat
One Blue outside Jacket
One Double Breasted Jacket all wool
One Black Waistcoat worsted
One Coarse Linnen Shirt
One white ditto (Linnen Shirt) with Ruffles
Two pairs of Linnen overalls
One pair of coarse worsted stockings
Two knapsacks
One Red Broad Cloth jacket without sleeves[66]

As a result of their actions at Red Bank, both regiments were commended. Colonel Greene received special commendation and a sword from Congress for his actions at Fort Mercer. The surviving Rhode Island troops would celebrate October 22 as an anniversary for years to come. The sense of early success and subsequent defeat must have been an education to the Frank brothers in the quickly changing fortunes of war—the movement from a hard fought victory to a hard fought defeat. Pride in their worth and fighting ability as Rhode Islanders would have been roused because of their actions at Fort Mercer. They had beaten back the Hessians and survived, while troops at Fort Mifflin met defeat and loss of life.[67]

The Franks endured their first year as members of an integrated regiment composed of former common laborers attempting to make a living in revolutionary America. Along with other free men of color, they were long-serving and long-suffering in their length and breadth of service. As men of color, they may have shared a sense of pride and well-being in knowing that they were part of a group of soldiers that had conducted themselves well during the tough and fierce defense at the Battle of Red Bank. Additionally, as Black men, there may have been a need to prove their fighting abilities to prove their masculinity. To the poor, immigrants, or other marginalized groups, fighting well provided a chance to gain respect. This sense of pride and well-being felt by the Franks after their survival at Red Bank would be challenged by the toughness of winter camp at Valley Forge and a change in the composition of their respective regiments as they would be forced to leave the known environment of the Second Rhode Island Regiment to an unknown environment defined by racial segregation.[68]

Integrating Free and Enslaved: The Creation of Rhode Island's Revolutionary "Black Regiment"

T HE ROAD TO SEGREGATION started at Valley Forge. The foundation of that road was laid by George Washington's early policies against the enlistment of Blacks and other free men of color. The impetus for Washington's reversal can be traced to the persistent shortage of fighting men in the Continental army. The enlistment and service of William and Ben Frank after their first year of service provide an opportunity to understand military practices and policies regarding the assignment and use of Black soldiers as discerned by upper-level command and carried out by field officers. Particular to the free Black soldiers of the First and Second Rhode Island Regiments were the results of the winter encampment at Valley Forge, including the enlistment of enslaved men and the segregation of Rhode Island troops, which I argue changed the experiences of the Franks and other free men of color. The free men of color of the Rhode Island regiments initially had the opportunity to prove themselves in integrated units without the matter of race being an identifying factor. The recruitment and enlistment of slaves changed the circumstances of their service.

After the battles at Red Bank in the autumn of 1777, Colonels Greene and Angell were able to safely retreat from the forts along the Delaware

River and march their troops to the American winter encampment at Valley Forge. The trek to Valley Forge was a march delayed by weather and confrontations with enemy forces. The beleaguered soldiers also withstood the cold and snow despite lacking proper clothing and equipment. Many were without appropriate clothing except for what they had gathered from dead Hessians at Red Bank. At night many slept on the frozen ground without covering or blankets. Their progress on the march could be tracked in the snow by the bloody residue left by unprotected and injured feet. Soldiers without proper footwear wrapped scraps from their blankets around their feet to provide relief from the cold and tough roads.[1]

The bitter and harsh winter encampment at Valley Forge has been well documented. William and Ben Frank experienced the harshness firsthand. They arrived with the rest of the retreating Rhode Island troops from the Battle of Red Bank. The winter camp was located south of the Schuylkill River with entrenchments located from Valley Creek to the river. The Rhode Island regiments were stationed near the junction of the Schuylkill and Valley Creek. Upon their arrival at camp, they found that the conditions of the encampment were dreadful. Washington described his army at winter encampment as "litterally reduced to a starving Condition."[2] The food rations were in such short supply that many of the army regulars threatened to revolt. Continental surgeon Albigence Waldo recalled the chants of "No meat! No meat!" from the disenchanted soldiers as he walked about the encampment.[3] Washington understood the gravity of the situation at camp. He assessed it as "The spirit of desertion among the soldery never before rose to such a threatening height, as at the present time—The murmurs on account of Provisions are become universal, and what may ensue, if a better prospect does not speedily open, I dread to conjecture."[4]

Lieutenant William Barton of New Jersey captured the desolation of Valley Forge in a letter to his father in Allentown, New Jersey. He wrote often of trying to obtain leave to return home, but to no avail. He also spoke of the shortages of food and clothing and was appreciative of his parents sending clothing to him at camp. In February 1778, Barton became so ill that he requested that his parents send a wagon to retrieve him, since he was too incapacitated to come home on horseback. But the wagon did not come, and Barton remained in camp until the late spring of 1778. Given Barton's status as a commissioned officer, his experience at Valley Forge— as miserable as it was—was better than that of the Frank brothers.[5]

The first days at camp for the Franks and other members of the Rhode Island regiments were especially harsh. Commander Varnum, in charge of

the Rhode Island regiments as well as two Connecticut regiments, complained to General Washington about the lack of bread and meat. The lack
of sustenance only made it more difficult for the Franks and others to set
up their winter encampment. Shelters had to be hurriedly constructed in
the first days after their arrival.[6]

The Frank brothers, along with other Rhode Island troops, were housed
with the Fourth and Eighth Connecticut regiments. As stated earlier, these
regiments of the Connecticut line were populated with Black soldiers. Upon
his arrival at Valley Forge in December 1777, Sergeant Jeremiah Greenman
wrote, "we drawed axes to build huts for ye winter . . . order'd to build them
with logs 14 feet one way & 16 ye other."[7] Twelve men were to be assigned
to each hut.[8] The completion of these huts was of the utmost importance
to Washington and his staff. The general pushed his command to have their
huts completed as quickly as possible so that the "Troops may get comfort-
ably Lodged."[9] The lodgings would be of great importance since the winter
of 1777–1778 turned out to be extremely severe. Washington issued very
specific directives regarding the building of the huts. Command officers
were instructed to closely follow the construction of the huts and precisely
mark the location of each hut under their control. The dimensions of each
hut were also specified. Each hut was to be fourteen by sixteen feet with
side walls of 6½ feet high, constructed with logs. The sides and roof were
to be fortified with clay. A fireplace was to be placed at the rear of the hut
with one door constructed of oak slats, if available. Washington also directed that each hut should house a maximum of twelve soldiers. However,
archaeological findings show that Washington's directives were not followed
exactly to the dimensions set in the general orders. An excavation of the
huts built and utilized by Virginia troops show that the dimensions of the
huts were smaller than Washington intended. The excavated huts' propor-
tions ranged from 6½ by 7½ feet to 12 by 12½ feet. Tent canvas was used
in place of clay to keep out the cold. The substandard conditions of the
huts were just one of the unacceptable parts of the camp conditions at Valley Forge.[10]

After construction of the huts, some soldiers were granted furloughs to
visit loved ones at home. The remaining soldiers were tasked with the mun-
dane and tedious obligations of camp life. They stood guard. They drilled.
They cut firewood and foraged for food. They were also dispatched from
camp "on command" to perform a variety of duties such as guarding prisoners or commissaries. William and Ben Frank remained at camp during
the early months of the winter encampment.[11]

Sadly, the Frank brothers did not escape the dire situation at Valley Forge. In December 1777, William Frank was deemed unfit for duty—indicating he could not perform his duties due to a lack of proper clothing or equipment. The shortages were so severe that soldiers stole the clothing and equipment of invalid soldiers. It appeared that "many men who go into the Hospitals well clad are in a manner naked when they get well and cannot return to their Regiments till new Cloathed."[12] The practice became so prevalent that orders were given that "No Man . . . be sent to the Hospitals without a List of the Regiment and Company they belong to and of every Article of their Cloathing."[13] Troops went for days without food, prompting General Varnum, the commander of the combined Rhode Island and Connecticut troops, to describe "Three Days successively, we have been destitute of Bread. Two Days we have been intirely without Meat . . . . The Men must be supplied, or they cannot be commanded."[14] These conditions led the Continental army to suffer debilitating losses from death and desertion. Out of 11,000 troops who initially went into winter quarters in December 1777, 3,000 had deserted by March 1778.[15] At the end of 1777, Washington notified Congress that:

> at the same time as a further proof of the inability of an Army under the circumstances of this, to perform the common duties of Soldiers (besides a number of Men confind to Hospitals for want of Shoes, and others in farmers Houses on the same Acct.) we have, by a field return this day made no less than 2898 Men now in Camp unfit for duty because they are bare foot and otherwise naked and by the same return it appears that our whole strength in continental Troops (Including the Eastern Brigades which have joined us since the surrender of Genl. Burgoyne) exclusive of the Maryland Troops sent to Wilmington amount to no more than 8200 In Camp fit for duty.[16]

A week later, an additional 1,000 were on the sick roll.[17]

The Rhode Island regiments were decimated as well, and these severe losses left them with barely enough soldiers to form one regiment. Colonel Angell wrote: "I am sorry to inform you that a very great sickness and mortality prevail among the Rhode Island troops which is judged to proceed in some measure from the badness of there Cloaths."[18] General Varnum was also concerned about the state of the Rhode Island troops: "the two Rhode Island Battalions have been sickly. They have lost a considerable Number. This is owing to their immense Fatigues in the Summer past."[19] The mortality described by Angell and Varnum was clearly demonstrated among the ranks of Black and Native American soldiers. Henery Pisquish and Quam Cook, members of the original cohort of fifty-four, died early during the encampment in January and February, respectively. Ceasar Cook died in April. Jack Allen lost his life later that spring, in May. At least nine soldiers of color did not survive the winter encampment, including a member of William's company, Francis Tifft—who had gained his freedom to serve with the Rhode Island regiments. And the rate of desertion also concerned Angell: "Desertion is what we may ever expect so long as the Soldiers see that the Publick faith is not to be depended upon."[20]

But the group of over fifty soldiers of color who then served with the Rhode Island regiments barely contributed to these losses from desertion. There is only one documented incident of desertion from this group. Robert Allen left the winter encampment in March 1778 . He later rejoined the Rhode Island battalions in August of the same year. Some desertions occurred before the brutal winter encampment and may be examples of young soldiers who left early in their careers, unable to cope with military life. John Daniels and Toby Coys left in February 1777. Both reenlisted for the duration of the war in the spring of 1777 and both survived the winter at Valley Forge.[21]

To solve the problem of depleted manpower, General Varnum, the commander of the Rhode Island regiments, recommended the creation of a battalion of slaves. In a letter to General Washington, dated January 2, 1778, Varnum argued that the recruitment and enlistment of enslaved men would enable Rhode Island to form two battalions.[22] In the letter he argued that:

> The two battalions from the state of Rhode Island being small, and there being a necessity of the state's furnishing an additional number to make up their proportion in the Continental army; the field officers have represented to me the propriety of making one temporary battalion from the two so that one entire corps of officers may repair to Rhode Island, in order to receive and prepare the recruits from the freed. It is imagined that a battalion of negroes can be easily raised there. Should that measure be adopted or recruits obtained from any other principle the service will be advanced. The field officers who go upon this command are Colonel Green, Lieutenant Colonel Olney, and Major Ward; 7 captains, 12 lieutenants, six ensigns, one paymaster, one surgeon and mates one adjutant, and one chaplain.[23]

Washington approved Varnum's proposal and forwarded the request with his endorsement to Rhode Island Governor Cooke. Cooke referred the proposal to the General Assembly, where after a heated debate, Varnum's request was approved with the passage of a law in February 1778 authorizing the formation of a battalion composed of former slaves. The Slave Enlistment Act of February 14, 1778, stipulated:

> every able-bodied negro, mulatto, Indian man slave, in this State may enlist into either of the said two battalions to serve during the continuance of the preset war with Great Britain; that every slave so enlisting shall be entitled to and receive all bounties, wages, and encouragements allowed by the Continental congress to any soldier enlisting into their service. It is further voted and resolved, that every slave so enlisting shall, upon passing muster before Colonel Christopher Greene, be immediately discharged from the service of his master or mistress, and be absolutely free.[24]

As stated, the act required that the new recruits receive the same bounties and wages given to any soldier enlisting with the Continental army. And, in return for their service for the duration of the war and after passing muster with their commanding officers, the enlisted slaves would receive their freedom. The act also provided compensation to slave owners for their losses. The new law did not, however, mention the need for Black enlistees to meet critical manpower shortages. It instead stressed the integrity of the assembly's action by stating: "History affords us frequent precedents of the wisest, freest, and bravest nations having liberated their slaves, and enlisted them as soldiers to fight in defense of their country."[25] A more accurate assessment might have been that the enslaved were liberated to fight in place of their so-called liberators.[26]

Colonel Christopher Greene was given command of the reconfigured First Rhode Island Regiment. Greene, a Rhode Island native and cousin of Major General Nathanael Greene, made a very comfortable living operating sawmills and forges before the war. There is little indication from military records as to why Greene was selected for this role. He started his military career as a lieutenant in the early skirmishes of the war and later joined the Rhode Island army as a major. In 1775, he was part of Benedict Arnold's failed Quebec expedition. His assignment with Arnold's force gained him a promotion to lieutenant colonel. He afforded himself well during the campaign but became a prisoner of war upon the failed assault upon Quebec City. By 1777, he was released and given command of the First Rhode Island. Greene and his staff of captains, who remained in their positions as company commanders, were tasked with recruiting, enlisting,

Colonel Christopher Greene of the Rhode Island Brigade, engraving by J. C. Buttre, 1865. (*Anne S. K. Brown Military Collection, Brown University Library*)

and training the new soldiers. Greene returned to his home state along with his staff to carry out his new mission.

During the period of open enlistment for enslaved men, Rhode Island officers searched the state for new recruits. Colonel Greene and his staff recruited soldiers for the new regiment primarily from the towns of North and South Kingstown in Narragansett country because of the high concentration of Blacks and enslaved men. As early as 1749, the Black population of South Kingstown was higher than the Black population of Providence, a much larger town. In 1755, one of every three residents of South Kingstown was an enslaved Black. By 1774, free and enslaved Blacks were well represented in the population in both North and South Kingstown. Of the seventy-four enslaved persons who enlisted from February to October 1777, twenty came from South Kingstown and eleven came from North Kingstown; only three came from Providence and four from Newport.[27]

The captains chosen to lead the recruitment effort had Black soldiers already assigned to their respective companies. For example, Captain Elijah Lewis recruited in the South Kingstown area. A meeting held by Lewis on March 19, 1778, in South Kingstown attracted many African Americans willing to enlist with the Rhode Island Continental regiments. However, prominent slaveholder Hazard Potter voiced the concerns of other slaveholders when he tried to prevent enslaved men from enlisting by using in-flammatory rhetoric claiming that the government would only employ Blacks as common laborers—constructing fortifications—and would even-tually allow any Blacks taken as prisoners to be sold off to the Caribbean as slaves.[28]

Despite the efforts of Potter and other slaveholders, Captain Lewis and other members of the recruitment unit were successful in their quest to en-list enslaved men for service with the Rhode Island Continentals. Among the first enslaved men to enlist were Cuff Greene and Jack Champlin. The state paid their white enslavers a promissory note in the amount of £120 for each. Jack Champlin was owned by Stephen Champlin of South Kingstown and enlisted on February 25, 1778. Jack, sometimes referred to as John, was eighteen years old upon his enlistment. Prime Babcock of Hopkinton, Cato Greene of Providence, London Hall and Peter Hazard of South Kingstown, and Pero Mowry of Smithfield all signed up for serv-ice and their freedom. Mingo Rodman and Richard Rhodes were recruited off the plantations of South Kingstown and would go on to serve for the duration of the war. Priamus Brown was the sole enlistee from Johnston—the hometown of the Frank brothers. All served with the permission of their owners who were reimbursed by the state.

The obvious motivation for these men's enlistment and service was free-dom from a lifetime of involuntary servitude. But did the opportunity to serve for freedom induce a grateful nature in the previously enslaved? Their actual service provides insight into their commitment to the patriot cause. Jack Champlin served for the duration of the war but not without incident. Approximately two years after his enlistment, Jack, along with York Cham-plin, left for almost one month before being retaken into service. Prime Babcock, London Hall, and Pero Morey served for the duration of the war, and each received one honorary badge during their tenure.[29]

After his service, Cato Greene was able to accumulate one acre of land and a house, eleven chairs, some knives and forks, and a table. Peter Haz-ard's tenure with the First Rhode Island was rocky. He was court-martialed for plundering residents of money and other offenses, for which he received fifty lashes. He also went absent without leave during his time with the First Rhode Island. Like the Champlins, his time away from the regiment was short, and Hazard would serve until the end of the war. Mingo Rod-man received his freedom and land after his service. Richard Rhodes be-came a mariner at war's end but also coped with a physical disability caused by a combat wound to his arm. But Rhodes did not begrudge his service with the Continentals.[30] Former slave Jeffrey Brace understood the irony of his enlistment and service: "Alas! Poor African Slave, to liberate freemen, my tyrants."[31] Brace's service with Connecticut regiments was spent mostly in integrated companies where he toiled alongside white hardcore regulars also serving to liberate themselves from "tyrants."[32]

There was resistance to the Slave Enlistment Act. Forces in opposition argued that other nations would look down upon the use of slaves as troops. They felt that Rhode Island troops would not get the same credit afforded to white troops. And they felt that raising this regiment would be more expensive than raising white troops, given the additional costs of purchasing the slaves, which averaged at $400 in Continental money. The opposition to the Slave Enlistment Act would eventually win. The state's white citizenry did not accept the notion of slaves as soldiers and voted out half of the assemblymen who passed the act. The new assembly promptly voided the act and refused to allow the enlistment of any "negro, mulatto or Indian slave" after June 1778. But this did not end the enlistment of enslaved men. At least sixteen additional men enlisted to serve in lieu of their freedom.[33]

It is ironic that the Rhode Island legislature was so diligent in limiting the opportunity for enslaved men to serve in return for their freedom. John Wood Sweet has argued that over one-third of the men sold to the state for military service had already served in the military in one capacity or another. An extended review of Rhode Island Continentals' records shows at least six Black soldiers who enlisted prior to the Slave Enlistment Act of 1778 but are not listed on the "Return of Freemen." This can mean one of three things. There may be an additional document not found in the military records, listing these soldiers. Or these soldiers were accidentally left off the listing of freemen, or they were enslaved—not free—but recruited and enlisted prior to the enactment of the Slave Enlistment Act. These soldiers—Ebenezer Caesar, Ceasor Cole, Ceasar Cook, Richard Pomp, Ceaser Sabins, and Pomp Watson—carry enlistment dates of May 1777 and are on muster rolls for the brutal Valley Forge encampment of 1777–1778. An indication of their legal status may be found in their names. Slave owners renamed slaves as to disconnect them from their African roots and to indoctrinate them into a slave mentality. Many of the names used by the masters included classical names, such as Caesar, Pompey, Venus, and Juno.

Some of these owners would misrepresent their slaves as freemen to appear to follow regulations that forbade the enslaved from bearing arms. If the above listed soldiers were indeed enslaved men, then they were recruited and enlisted prior to the passage of the Slave Enlistment Act and in conflict with Washington's prohibition to the arming of slaves. If they were free, they were enlisted in accordance with the official policy of the day, but that does not appear to be the case.[34]

Free Blacks and Native Americans also enlisted during this period. Seven freemen whose status would be captured on the "Return of Freemen" enlisted during this period. Simon Barton and Peter Dailey enlisted on March 1, 1778, at Warwick, Rhode Island. Ceasar Finch enlisted on the same day but in the town of East Greenwich. Another resident of East Greenwich, Prince Limas, followed suit on March 16, 1778. Cuff Roberts enlisted at Westerly on March 18, 1778. Joseph Boyer enlisted on May 4, 1778, at North Kingstown—one of the primary locations for recruiting slaves. However, Boyer became the only listed freeman to come from North Kingstown in this period. Regardless of their status, these new recruits would eventually join their veteran brethren.[35]

The new recruits, formerly enslaved and free, caused a major reorganization among Rhode Island troops—the segregation of the Rhode Island Continentals. Why did the Rhode Island military establishment segregate their Continental regiments? The segregation was possibly the byproduct of the Slave Enlistment Act, but why? Records do not indicate why segregation took place, only that it did.[36] There are clues in the wording and terminology of the texts that served to form the "Black Regiment," which offer an understanding of what occurred. The act states: "And whereas his Excellency General Washington hath enclosed to this State the Proposal made to him by Brigadier-General Varnum to enlist *into the two Battalions*, raising by this State, such Slaves as should be willing to enter into the Service."[37] In this wording, there is no indication nor stipulation that former slaves should serve in one battalion. Yet the original appeal made by General Varnum to Washington and then forwarded to Governor Nicholas Cooke is different in its connotation. Varnum wrote: "The two Battalions from the State of Rhode Island being small, & there being a Necessity of the State's furnishing an additional Number to make up their Proportion in the continental Army; The Field Officers have represented to me the Propriety of making one temporary Battalion from the two, so that one intire Core of Officers may repair to Rhode Island, in order to receive & prepare the Recruits for the Field. It is imagined that *a Battalion of Negroes* can be easily raised there."[38]

A policy passed and enacted at the legislative level can look different as it is carried out at the battlefront by a command staff struggling with logistics and resources. Did Rhode Island command find it more feasible to make one major wave of reassignments, and then funnel the new recruits into the battalion supervised by their recruiting officers and relying on the ability of veteran troops, like the Frank brothers, to provide leadership and guidance to the new troops? Or did Rhode Island command find it more feasible to create a regiment defined by the race of its soldiers? Whatever the reasoning, it appears that the military administration interpreted Varnum's request and the act as permission to segregate the Rhode Island troops. Was this an indication that the current alignment of the Rhode Island troops was faulty? That conclusion cannot be proven, given the troops' success in the field, particularly at Red Bank.

For whatever reason and purpose, the Franks and other experienced soldiers of color lost the opportunity to prove themselves in integrated companies without race as an identifying factor. Rhode Island's experiment in segregation—the merger of former slaves, freeborn Blacks, and Native Americans into one singular regiment—was the direct result of the Rhode Island Slave Enlistment Act and caused the racialization of the Rhode Island Continental regiments. Up to this point, the Franks and other Rhode Island soldiers of color were the epitome of hardcore regulars who came to military service for adventure and opportunity, served for longer terms under harsh and often bleak circumstances, and served in interracial companies. However, the "experiment" changed things.[39]

Of course, the change affected white troops as well. An analysis of the Rhode Island troops stationed at Valley Forge shows more than one hundred soldiers transferred from the First Rhode Island to the Second Rhode Island Regiment. Among the transferees were noncommissioned officers as well as company musicians. The white command officers, those at or above the rank of lieutenant, remained with their original regiment. The white privates, even though transferred, remained together, staying in the same companies. If those soldiers harbored ill will against African American soldiers, their negative attitudes did not make their way onto the page. The diaries and journals of members of the First and Second Rhode Island Regiments follow this pattern. Jeremiah Greenman, as a private and eventual sergeant of the Second Rhode Island Regiment, had experience serving with Black soldiers and made little note of the Blacks assigned to his battalion. For the white privates who had similar socioeconomic backgrounds and had formed a "soldierly fellowship" with their former Black regimental mates, race now trumped class. One of those white soldiers, Private William Champlin, a member of the integrated First Rhode Island Regiment, recalled his reassignment to the Second Rhode Island Regiment in quite simple terms, "Colonel Greene's regiment being greatly reduced by those killed in Battle and death by sickness this depondent and the white men in Greene's Regiment were transferred to Colonel Israel Angell's Regiment."[40]

At least fifteen other soldiers of color were reassigned from the Second Rhode Island to the First Rhode Island, along with William and Ben Frank. In December 1777, Ben served in the company led by Captain Thomas Hughes with at least ten other soldiers of color, serving alongside over thirty white soldiers. Those soldiers—Edward Anthony, Jonathan Charles, William Coopin, Toby Coys, Gideon Harry, Simeon Niles, Joseph Nocake, Cuff Peckham, Richard Pomp, and Fortune Sailes—all became members of the battalion during the early months of 1777. All were free men before their enlistments. In January 1778, William served in the company led by Captain William Potter, which included at least five other men of color (John Daniels, Francis Tifft, Henry Hazzard, Noah Sisco, and Ceasar Cook) who served alongside white privates.[41]

While Greene and his company commanders continued their recruitment and enlistment efforts in their home state, Ben Frank and other soldiers of color (Edward Anthony, John Daniels, James Daley, and Prince Jackson) were detailed for a temporary assignment at Radnor in Delaware County, Pennsylvania, in April 1778. Ben remained in that assignment for the month of May, as well. Radnor was an important strategic outpost located approximately five miles from the Valley Forge encampment. The small agricultural community sat on a major roadway leading from Philadelphia and was an ideal location for Continental troops to surveil and keep track of British troops' activities near Philadelphia. At the time of Ben's deployment, the Radnor picquet was commanded by Colonel Henry Beekman Livingston of New York and tasked with continuing their patrol activities against foraging parties dispatched from Philadelphia by the British and surveillance of British troop movement. By June, Ben was back in camp with the rest of his battalion.[42]

At the time of his temporary deployment to Radnor, Ben and other veteran soldiers of color were placed in a temporary detachment under the command of Captain Thomas Arnold, who began his service with the Continentals early in the war. Arnold was assigned to the short-lived regiment of Colonel Christopher Lippett from May 1776 to February 1777. As a member of that regiment, Arnold led a company in the ill-fated Battle at White Plains, which ended in the defeat of Continental forces, and a more successful fight at the Second Battle at Trenton in January 1777—resulting in a victory for the Continentals. So, Arnold brought with him a wealth of combat experience and understanding of the vicissitudes of war.[43]

Arnold's segregated detachment or company was composed of over sixty Black and Native American privates and organizationally belonged to the First Rhode Island Regiment. Ben's return to camp coincided with significant events which affected the end of the encampment. First, the much sought after alliance with France was secured. Second, British troops evacuated Philadelphia on June 18, 1778. In response, Washington and his troops marched out of Valley Forge in pursuit of the British army marching north to New York City. It was during this hot pursuit that Arnold's detachment along with Varnum's brigade and the Second Rhode Island Regiment were dispatched by Washington under the command of Major-General Charles Lee to engage with British forces en route to New York, where the Franks and others fought in one of the most contentious battles of the war.[44]

The longest battle of the war ensued when Lee's force of 5,000 troops eventually caught up with British troops led by Generals Charles Cornwallis and Henry Clinton at Monmouth Courthouse nineteen miles southwest of Sandy Hook, New Jersey. The battle would take place on a three-mile stretch of land filled with ridges and swamp-like morasses. Temperatures of near one hundred degrees made fighting difficult. As part of the advance force, Arnold's detachment was in the initial attack; however, as Lee's forces were overwhelmed, due to being outnumbered by a British force of approximately 6,000 troops, they fell into a controlled retreat—looking for reinforcement from the main body of the army led by Washington five miles to their rear. During their retreat, the Franks and others assigned to Arnold's detachment became involved in a heated battle at a hedgerow and fence line position in which several members of their company were injured, including Captain Arnold, who took a musket ball to the leg. The detachment fought successfully in maintaining their position until the arrival of the main force, which shored up the retreat and led to an hours-long battle resulting in many deaths due to heatstroke and injury. With nightfall, British forces left the field of battle—seeking and gaining respite in New York City within the week. The retreat of British forces allowed Washington to claim victory at Monmouth Courthouse. However, initial actions conducted by Lee led to his court-martial, by his own demand, to determine whether he failed to follow Washington's commands during the battle. Lee was found guilty on all counts. The court-martial and Lee's perceived disrespect of his commander-in-chief led to his eventual termination from the military.[45]

The Frank brothers' reassignment from the Second Rhode Island to the new First Rhode Island battalion allowed for their first opportunity to serve together in the same company. It was also their first experience serving in segregated regiments. As members of Arnold's detachment, they marched alongside Colonel Angell's regiment back to Rhode Island, to join up with their new regiment mates. Approximately fifty documented freemen of color and approximately one hundred formerly enslaved men were assigned to the new regiment, which became known as the "Black Regiment." Christopher Booker argues that prior to emancipation, Black masculinity was defined by enslavement and an "impenetrable web of oppression plaguing free blacks,"[46] which dictated their treatment as second-class citizens. For the first year of their service, William and Ben had escaped that web by serving alongside white soldiers in integrated companies—receiving the same pay, assignments, and discipline. Now, these troops had to become acclimated to new command and regiment mates. Any comradeship felt for former battalion mates was now expected to be transferred to new comrades. As members of the Second Rhode Island Regiment, the Franks had already tested their fortitude during the fierce fighting at Red Bank. They joined a group of former slaves—new recruits—who were literally fighting for their freedom.[47]

Other states formed all-Black units during the Revolutionary War but to a lesser degree than Rhode Island. No other state integrated freeborn and former slaves to form an entire regiment of fighting men. Thomas Kench of Massachusetts made an appeal to his state's leaders early in the war effort to raise a company of Black soldiers. His reasoning was that Black soldiers would try to outdo white soldiers in an attempt to prove their superiority. State officials paid heed to Kench's advice. Massachusetts designated two all-Black units. The Bucks of America, an all-Black unit, never saw action outside their home state or against the British and were used as a local police auxiliary to protect against loyalist sabotage. The unit received recognition after the war from then Governor John Hancock with a special, ceremonial banner carrying their emblem. Massachusetts also assigned an all-Black company to the Continental army that did participate in actual battles. The Sixth Massachusetts Regiment deployed "the black company," commanded by Captain Matthew Chambers.[48]

Connecticut also attempted to pass legislation allowing slaves to serve in return for freedom. The lower house of the state assembly approved the practice; however, it was rejected by the upper house. However, the assembly did pass a statute that allowed owners to substitute slaves for their own service. This legislation increased the number of Blacks among the Connecticut regulars. For the most part, Connecticut's Black soldiers—free and former slaves—served alongside their white counterparts. However, in June 1780, the Connecticut military command did form an all-Black unit—the Second Company of the Fourth Connecticut Regiment, segregating fifty-two formerly enslaved men and free men from other Connecticut units. Colonel David Humphrey, General Washington's aide-de-camp, became the titular commander of the company. His assignment at headquarters kept him from performing frontline supervision. This task was left to the all-white command and noncommissioned officers of the Second Company. The Black soldiers of the Second Company received equal treatment in terms of pay and provisions when compared with white soldiers of the Connecticut line.[49]

Regardless of the reasons or motivations behind the move, the Frank brothers were now assigned to a segregated unit—created by the integration of free Blacks and the formerly enslaved. The first test of the new fighting unit took place on their home soil. If battles prove to be the defining moments for military men, then for the Frank brothers and their comrades of the First Rhode Island, the Battle of Rhode Island of August 29, 1778, was their ultimate moment. The battle was the culmination of an elaborate expedition with the primary purpose of driving the British from Aquidneck Island and the important seaport of Newport. It was also the first major military action seen by the newly restructured First Rhode Island Regiment. It was the second major battle for the Franks—the first on their home turf. Any comradeship felt for former members of their regiment was now expected to be transferred to new untested comrades. The battle would be another personal trial for the brothers.[50]

The Rhode Island expedition was the first joint effort between American and French forces and fell under the command of Major General John Sullivan, the commander of the Rhode Island department. The Franks and their comrades were slated to fight alongside their new French allies. There appears to have been two major incentives for the American push to recapture Newport. The first was the strong feeling on the part of Rhode Island citizens and General Washington to drive British troops out of the extremely important and strategic island. The second was the entry of the French into the war along with the arrival of the French fleet under Charles Hector Théodat, Comte d'Estaing. This combination of emotions and French military strength convinced the Americans that an invasion of the Aquidneck Island was not only feasible but had every opportunity to succeed.[51]

The objective of Sullivan's expedition was to drive over 6,550 enemy troops off Aquidneck Island. The removal of the combined forces of British,

Hessian, and loyalist infantry, along with Hessian chasseurs, artillery, and marines would prove to be a formidable task. Fortifications, armed with numerous cannons, had been constructed to protect Newport against attack. The Franks and their comrades would face fierce opposition from enemy troops wishing to defend their positions and remain on the island. To accomplish this task, Sullivan developed an elaborate plan of action: On August 8, the French fleet would enter Narragansett Bay, home of Newport and Aquidneck Island. On the nights of August 9–10, American troops would ferry and land on the east shore of Aquidneck Island; French soldiers and marines would ferry and land on the west shore. Sullivan's troops would subdue British troops on the northern part of the island. The combined French and American forces would move south to attack British troops at Newport with the support of guns from the French fleet.

Against the British, the Americans amassed a fighting force of over 11,000 troops. Ten regiments of the Continental army, including the Rhode Island regiments, six regiments of the state's militia, and militia from Massachusetts, Connecticut, and New Hampshire rounded out the American side. An additional force of 1,000 French regular soldiers, 1,600 marines, and 1,400 sailors were expected to join the American side in the expedition. The French fleet arrived on July 29, 1778, and anchored in the open waters to the south of Aquidneck Island.[52]

The plan and resources were set for an American victory. Military leaders were eager and optimistic about the outcome of the expedition. Quartermaster General Nathanael Greene, Washington's trusted advisor and a native son of Rhode Island, was thrilled to begin the battle to rid Newport of British occupation. He wrote to Sullivan from the American encampment at White Plains, New York, on July 23, 1778: "You are the most happy man in the World. What a child of fortune. The expedition you are going on against Newport I think cannot fail of success. . . . I wish you success with all my Soul and intend if possible to come home to put things in a proper train in my department and to take a command of part of the Troops under you. I wish most ardently to be with you."[53] Greene's ardent wishes and optimistic outlook would eventually give way to the reality of bad weather, unforeseen British activity, and French abandonment.

Before Sullivan could implement his plan, British Commanders Robert Pigot and Richard Prescott ordered a withdrawal of troops from the northern part of the island to the heavily fortified town of Newport. In their wake, they herded livestock and enslaved Blacks into the town proper, destroyed carriages and wagons, and laid waste to houses and orchards in the firing line of their cannons. In light of the British retreat into Newport, Sullivan assembled his troops, crossed from Tiverton, and landed on the now vacant northern shore of Aquidneck Island on August 9. Sullivan hoped that the French troops would follow his lead and land on the southern part of the island. And d'Estaing did land troops on Conanicut Island in Narragansett Bay later on the ninth. However, newly arriving British warships scared off the French and the landed troops returned to their ships.[54]

With the arrival of the British fleet under the command of Admiral Howe, d'Estaing and his fleet sailed out to meet them south of Newport. This maneuver would lead to a series of naval actions between the French and British fleets. However, a major storm engulfed the region from August 11–13 affecting battle on land and sea. By August 22, d'Estaing and his fleet, in disrepair due to the storm, left Newport and sailed away to Boston to refit, leaving American forces on land without naval support. The Franks were part of the American force left in the wake of the French departure. The American force initially made camp on the high ground south of Butts Hill, twelve miles from the town of Newport, to await the return of the French fleet. However, on the night of August 11, 1778, Sullivan and his command decided to advance to Newport and lay siege to the town. No assault would be made, however, without reinforcements from the French.[55]

While waiting for the return of the French fleet, foot soldiers like William and Ben Frank kept busy dodging enemy cannon fire and marching toward Newport. They kept themselves ready for battle by cleaning and maintaining their weapons and building batteries for defensive purposes. The buoyant mood of the Rhode Island troops as they began their campaign to regain control of their island now gave way to the dreariness of camp life and the anxiety of waiting for reinforcements. Sergeant Jeremiah Greenman of the Second Rhode Island described the days of waiting as a constant trial of avoiding and returning enemy fire, dealing with inclement weather, and worrying about the return of the French fleet. William and Ben Frank, attached to Captain Jonathan Wallen's company of the First Rhode Island since July of that year, would be, in Greenman's words, "holding our Selvs in readiness for an attack." The soldiers built fortifications, served on picket duty, and maintained provisions, all in preparation for an attack on Newport.[56]

The Franks, along with the other Continental troops, waited for reinforcements from the French fleet. But reinforcements never came. On August 24, Sullivan learned in a dispatch from the American headquarters at White Plains that additional British fleets were heading for Newport. Sullivan decided to retreat to the fortifications at Butts Hill. On August 28, the American forces began to withdraw from the island, but the British, with their ships positioned to bombard the American lines, attacked. Colonel Israel Angell, commanding officer of the Second Rhode Island Regiment, described the Americans' initial flight to safer refuge on Butts Hill, as a race away from pursuing British troops to the northern end of the island. According to Angell, as positions became clear, the enemy troops formed on Quaker Hill to the south of the American fortification on Butts Hill. In the early morning hours of August 29, the American forces quickly refortified their positions. At 7 a.m. the British and Hessian troops attacked, beginning the battle that would last into the very hot and humid afternoon. William and Ben Frank, along with other members of the First Rhode Island, were now positioned to defend Durfee's Hill just to the west of Butts Hill. The British and Hessian forces drew up in line of battle from Quaker Hill to Turkey Hill, about a mile from their position.[57]

Major-General Nathanael Greene, who had arrived to take part in the battle, commanded the right wing of the American forces. The soldiers of the First Rhode Island, commanded by Major Samuel Ward, held one of the positions that would be assaulted throughout the day by British-Hessian forces and artillery. They were assigned to hold a redoubt on the far right. Ben and William Frank waited, along with their fellow soldiers, as the day grew hot and muggy. As Hessian forces made their move to strike against the American position at Durfee's Hill, Generals Greene and Varnum dispatched the Second Rhode Island Regiment to reinforce the troops stationed there. Angell described their advance: "I was ordered with my regiment to a redoubt on a small hill, which the enemy was a trying for, and it was with difficulty that we got there before."[58] The first strike occurred in the morning when two Hessian regiments advanced from their position in the valley below, in straight lines with muskets extended toward the regiment's position between Turkey Hill and Butts Hill. The Hessians, led by Captain von der Malsberg, had intelligence that the regiment consisted of Black men, some of whom had little or no battle experience. But the regiment of veteran and novice soldiers held and repelled the Hessian advance. Malsberg reported: "obstinate resistance, and bodies of troops behind the work and at its sides, chiefly wild looking men in their shirtsleeves, and among them many negroes."[59]

Prior to the second assault, British ships in the harbor and Hessian artillery on the ground showered the regiment's position with shell fire and cannon balls. About 2 p.m., the Hessians launched a second attack into the wooded position of the American forces. Rhode Island command officers refrained from giving the order to fire until the Hessians were almost into the woods. Upon that order, the Hessians retreated again. In their last effort, British and Hessians troops attempted to drive the Americans out of their position by using bayonets. This attempt was stymied not only by the aggressive defense of the Americans but also by the sweltering heat. In heavy uniforms and packs, the British-Hessian troops were weakened by thirst and heat exhaustion. The Hessians again retreated.[60]

All in all, the British-Hessian forces made three charges against the American right wing. The First Rhode Island Regiment, led by Major Samuel Ward, held the ground in its sector. After four hours of fighting, the enemy's advances had been halted.[61] Major Ward described the day's activities in the following manner:

> Early yesterday morning [August 29, 1778], the enemy moved out after us, expecting that we were leaving the island, and took possession of the Heights in our front. They sent out parties in their front, and we made detachments to drive them back again. After a skirmish of three or four hours, with various success, in which each party gave way three or four times, and were reinforced, we drove them quite back to the ground they first took in the morning, and have continued there ever since. Two ships and a couple of small vessels beat up opposite our lines, and fired several shots; but, being pretty briskly fired upon from our heavy pieces, they fell down, and now lay opposite the enemy's lines.[62]

Throughout the evening of August 29, 1778, the two armies exchanged long-range artillery fire. British-Hessian troops were stopped from any advance upon the American position, thus allowing the eventual retreat of the Americans to the mainland during the evening of August 30. The Battle of Rhode Island was a draw. Although the fight to retreat off Aquidneck Island was successful, the Rhode Island expedition was unsuccessful. The British continued to hold Newport.[63]

Military historian Michael Lanning concludes that the total American losses numbered thirty killed, 137 wounded, and forty-four missing. The Frank brothers were among the survivors.[64]

The activities of the "Black Regiment" were the subject of controversy after the American defeat at Newport. Rumors spread among white troops that the Black troops had not fared well. This misapprehension may have been caused by an omission on the part of General Sullivan in an early re-

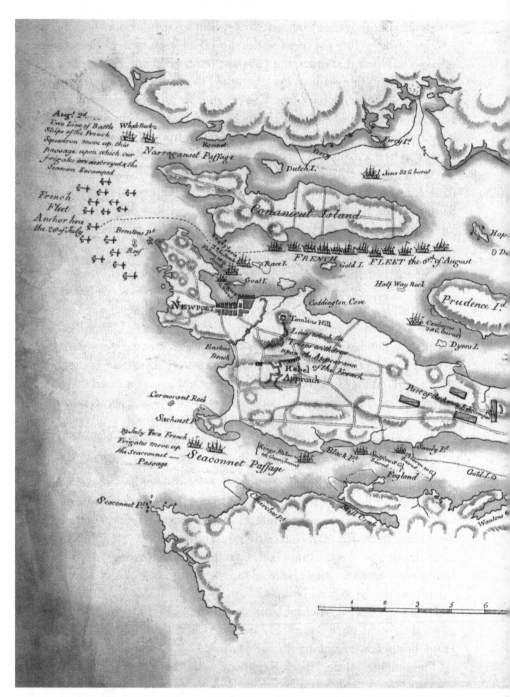

"Attacks upon Rhode Island August 1778." Newport is to the left on Aquidneck Island; Turkey Hill and Butts Hill, although unnamed, are located farther to the right along the island, below Prudence Island at the center of the map. (*Library of Congress*)

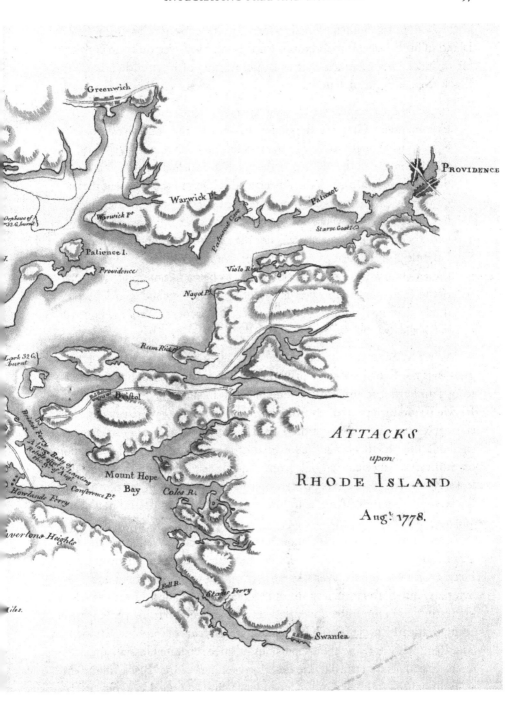

port to Congress. Sullivan failed to mention the actions of the First Rhode Island in his list of commendations for the day. However, Sullivan corrected his mistake. In a memo meant to dispel rumors of ineptitude among the Black troops, Sullivan stated:

> It having been represented by some persons that the conduct of Col. Commandant Greene's Regiment was not in the action yesterday equal to what ought to have been expected, and also that Major Ward, who commanded the regiment, was much dissatisfied with their conduct, the General assures the officers and soldiers of the regiment that no person has undertaken to censure their conduct to him, and that upon inquiry from Major Ward and sundry other officers who were with them in the action, there is not the least foundation for censure. Doubtless in the heat of action, Major Ward might have said something to hurry the troops in action which by being misinterpreted gave rise to the report, but by best information the Commander-in-Chief thinks that the Regiment will be entitled to a proper share of the honors of the day.[65]

Walter K. Schroeder offers an objective assessment of the battle. He argues that the five-week siege of Newport was unsuccessful, but American troops under the command of General Sullivan succeeded at the Battle of Rhode Island by repeatedly turning back charges made by British and Hessian attackers. The actions of the First Rhode Island and other soldiers assigned to the expedition force allowed for the safe and successful evacuation of Sullivan's American troops from Aquidneck Island without further losses. Schroeder's assessment identifies the battle as an important part of the strategy to remove American forces from Aquidneck Island in a timely and safe fashion.[66]

A more impassioned account of the battle is given in William Nell's *Colored Patriots of the American Revolution*. Nell cites a testimonial given by Dr. Harris, a Revolutionary War veteran, before the Congregational and Presbyterian Anti-Slavery Society at Francestown, New Hampshire, in 1842. In his testimony before the convention, Harris spoke about his participation at the Battle of Rhode Island. He recounted the feats of the First Rhode Island Regiment, stressing their repulsions of three separate Hessian attacks— repulsions that saved the day. He described soldiers of the "Black Regiment" as "fighting for our liberty and independence" and stationed in a "responsible position."[67] He went on to state that "had they [black soldiers] been unfaithful, or given way before the enemy, all would have been lost."[68]

Regardless of who was credited with valor and bravery during the battle, the disappointment felt by the Rhode Island troops in their inability to rid their home completely of the enemy threat was felt throughout the ranks and not lost on General Washington. He assigned the Rhode Island Continental regiments to duty in their home state for the remainder of the year and throughout the winter season. The Second Rhode Island was assigned between the towns of Warren and Bristol. The First Rhode Island was assigned between the towns of East Greenwich and Warwick.[69]

How did the defeat at Rhode Island affect the Frank brothers? The effects of the battle upon the brothers might be determined by addressing their possible physical and mental state after another difficult defeat. Additionally, the reorganization of the First Rhode Island Regiment may have had an impact on their later behavior. How would they regard themselves and their fellow comrades after their first battle as the so-called "Black Regiment"? And finally, were there any positive outcomes garnered by the brothers?

William and Ben did survive the Battle of Rhode Island; however, there is little documentation regarding their injury status after the battle. If either brother received injury, it was not severe enough to sideline the brothers for any lengthy period of time. Both brothers appeared on payrolls for the months following the battle. As privates in Captain Thomas Cole's company, William and Ben mustered and received pay for the months of September, October, November, and December 1778. However, Ben was listed as sick, but present on the muster roll for October 1778. Whether his sickness was a result of the battle is hard to determine. A deadly disease had stricken the camp shortly before the battle. Among the listed sick during this period were members of the previously free cohort. Jonathan Charles was listed in the record as sick at the hospital from August to September. Two members of Captain Dexter's company, James Daley and Peter Dailey, were also listed as sick in August—a possible indication that they came to some harm during the Battle at Rhode Island or were stricken with disease prior to the battle.[70]

Outside of any physical injury, emotional stress and turmoil may have had a greater impact on the young men. Disappointment and failure, however strongly felt, could not have been the only negative emotions experienced by William and Ben Frank and their brother soldiers. This was the second loss experienced in battle by the brothers. They were forced to leave Fort Mercer in New Jersey after fighting valiantly. And now they were forced to leave Newport after another round of fierce fighting. They had lost comrades in the most recent fighting during the retreat from Aquidneck Island. One wonders if the young brothers had become desensitized to the loss of life and other consequences of war, after suffering through the Battle of Red Bank, the cold, bitter winter at Valley Forge, and the loss at Newport. Were the negative aspects of war beginning to have a detrimental impact on their mental attitudes? If the spirit of the Frank brothers was adversely affected, it did not show in their actions. Both brothers continued to serve. Neither brother is on record for requesting a furlough. Neither brother is listed as leaving his post or deserting after the battle.

The issue of race now played a more fundamental part in their lives as soldiers. As members of the "Black Regiment," how did William and Ben perceive themselves as men and soldiers, especially after another defeat? This question is hard to answer; however, the actions and words of their commanding officers shed light on the subject. In his recollection of the battle, Major Ward appeared more concerned with the status of his command officers than the Blacks serving under his command. He stated: "I am so happy as to have only one captain slightly wounded in the hand. I believe that a couple of the blacks were killed and four or five wounded, but none badly."[71] It is difficult to believe that Ward did not have a better understanding of how many Black soldiers were killed during the battle. His attitude toward their loss appeared to be indifferent at best. And rumors spread among the troops regarding the alleged incompetence of the Black Regiment. However, Sullivan, the commander of the expedition, did acknowledge the role of the Black Regiment in the defense of Durfee's Hill. As members of Colonels Greene and Angell's integrated Rhode Island regiments, Black soldiers received high praise upon their defense and subsequent withdrawal from Fort Mercer. Now, as members of the Black Regiment, they were placed in a position of defending their honor after their very first endeavor as a group. Did this negativity affect their actions and attitudes, or did they feel a more solid bond with soldiers from their own race? Possible answers may be found by reexamining the reasons behind the Frank brothers' enlistment to serve.[72]

Peter Voelz argues that self-interest was a motivating factor for free Blacks to serve in the military. A part of that self-interest, he states, was their identification with white society and their disdain for slaves. Some free African American males were embarrassed by the lack of manliness displayed by their enslaved brethren. They attempted to counteract any association with slaves by emphasizing their physical and mental toughness. Subordination, timidity, or weakness did not have a place in their ideal vision of Black manhood. The ability to serve in the military gave them an avenue to prove their manhood. The free men of color of the Rhode Island regiments initially had this opportunity to prove themselves in integrated units without the burden of race as an identifying factor. The recruitment and enlistment of slaves changed the environment of their service.[73]

Since William and Ben Frank came out of a free Black household in Rhode Island with a history of military service, they may have felt lessened by reassignment based on their race. Or they may have welcomed the former slaves as members to a growing free Black population in Rhode Island. If self-interest was the key as argued by Voelz, then both William and Ben would have felt separate from and superior to the formerly enslaved. If their intentions were to obtain land, status, and opportunity because of their military service, then the Franks would be compelled to identify with their white counterparts as long-standing members of the free Black population and whose first year of service reflected their class status as opposed to their race. However, if after fierce battles and racial segregation, self-preservation became the key, then the brothers more than likely felt a type of survival bond with their new regimental mates. Additionally, the Frank brothers may have felt solidarity with their Black brethren based upon their own family's pride in their African heritage. Another thought on the brothers' mental state is offered by James Kirby Martin, who suggests that long-term regulars were more professional in their military demeanor. This sometimes translated into bonds of "unit cohesion." The personal needs of individual soldiers, whether recruited, dragooned, or pressed into service, became secondary to the needs of their company or regiment. This development among the soldiers was nothing more than comradeship in arms. Any threat or insult became an attack upon the group, especially if that threat or insult was directed toward all group members. An early pivotal battle and defeat, a singular racial identity, and the need to defend themselves against attacks on their valor quickly forced the Frank brothers and their new comrades into solid bonds of unit cohesion and solidarity.[74]

The positive impacts of the battle were physical and mental in nature as well. First, both Frank brothers survived without death or serious injury. The actual experience of battle, although tough, was crucial in their growth as soldiers and men. They continued to receive some semblance of pay—a very important aspect in a soldier's life. They were acknowledged, albeit belatedly, as contributing to the safe evacuation of American troops from Aquidneck Island. And finally, they would not serve their winter in the hell of another tough winter encampment like Valley Forge, but would be stationed on home turf, close to family and loved ones.

Benjamin Cowell described the state of Rhode Island at the close of 1778 as "in statue quo, many important events had taken place within her borders, conflagrations, battles, frightful storms and shipwrecks, camp-fevers, and other pestilences among the troop."[75] The end of 1778 would also find the Rhode Island units of the Continental Line ensconced within the borders of the state, guarding the shoreline against British raids. The assignment of guard duty in Rhode Island did not lessen the general duties and responsibilities of the soldiers. Soldiers like William and Ben Frank began their day at sunrise, defined as when the sentry could clearly see a thousand yards. They ended their day when it became too dark to work. Their duties varied. Clothing, arms, and other supplies required constant upkeep. Soldiers were required to make cartridges, repair huts or tents, and tend horses or livestock. Additionally, the soldiers of the First and Second Rhode Island Regiments, including the Franks, were now able to visit their families and attend to personal business. The officers of these regiments were able to deal with issues of poor discipline, ragged clothing, less pay, and fewer recruits.[76]

On October 25, 1779, the British finally evacuated Newport. All the Continental units in Rhode Island were ordered to march. However, at the last minute, the First Rhode Island was ordered to stay in the state and guard the wharves and streets of Newport. The First Rhode Island would remain home until 1780. Even with their guard and other miscellaneous duties and responsibilities, the soldiers were able to make time for private affairs. Ben Frank experienced a significant change in his private life, specifically his marital status, during this period. Military records indicate that several members of the First Rhode Island were married men. Eighty noncommissioned officers and privates were married men as of December 1782. Both freeborn Blacks and former slaves were among the married men. Ben Frank became one of them.[77]

CHAPTER SIX

The Poor Soldier's Marriage of Sarah Willbour and Ben Frank

ON JANUARY 31, 1779, Ben Frank was "Lawfully Joyned together in the Honnourable State of Marriage in the Town of Worwick," Rhode Island, to Sarah Willbour of Johnston, Rhode Island.[1] Elder John Gorton of the Sixth Principle Baptist Church of East Greenwich in Kent County performed the ceremony. The marriage of Ben and Sarah ended abruptly in 1780 when Ben left. The few existing documents that pertain to their marriage show a relationship besieged by issues of class and wartime upheaval. Hardcore Continental soldiers like Ben Frank spent long months away from home and family, and the Continental army did not provide adequate pay and support for its soldiers and their dependents. A close look at the relationship between Ben and Sarah reveals how war affected the private lives of soldiers and their wives and reveals how marriage affected the military service of soldiers like Ben Frank.[2]

Ben's marriage to Sarah Willbour was the second step in Ben's progression to adulthood—first finding work as a soldier, and second finding a wife. His marriage was atypical by some standards. Ben Frank was much younger than the typical New England groom. For most male New Englanders of the period, the average age of marriage was in the mid-to late twenties, and for women it was in the early twenties. A study of 192 soldiers married during the war showed the average age of marriage at twenty-four years. Ben Frank was well below the average age in both cases since he was eighteen years of age at the time of his marriage. The age of Sarah Willbour is not documented, but if she were the typical age, she would have been the same age as or older than Ben upon their marriage. The marriage did exhibit the characteristics of most marriages of poor Continental regulars—economic hardships, transient lifestyles, and forced separations. Ben Frank's marriage came to an unfortunate end when Ben fled his service with the Continental army and abandoned his wife, leaving her to provide for herself and a young child with little or no means. She became one of many women who petitioned town councils throughout New England for assistance and relief.[3]

Elder John Gorton's marriage records constitute the best evidence about the marriage of Ben and Sarah Frank. Gorton began his pastoral duties as the lead minister of the Sixth Principle Baptist Church in 1753 and served until his death in 1792. He preached and ministered throughout Rhode Island and nearby Bristol County, Massachusetts. He recorded various aspects of his ministerial life which included officiating at marriages and funerals, as well as documenting his sermons and self-authored sacred verse. Gorton took great care documenting the marriages he performed between 1754 and 1792 in his "Book of Marriages." His attention to detail originated in an early lesson he received in recordkeeping from Giles Pearce, town clerk of East Greenwich. In 1760 Pearce reminded Gorton to capture specific information about the couples he married: race, father's name, place of residence, father's place of residence if different, bride's previous husband, if appropriate, and the date and place of the marriage. Pearce pointed out that marriages of people of color required less documentation—record keepers often did not mention race or information about parents. The marriage records regarding the Black soldiers of the First Rhode Island Regiment follow this pattern. Gorton performed marriage ceremonies for several members of this regiment during and after the war. These marriage records do not include parental information and offers few details in the way of racial and ethnic identity. However, Gorton is careful to list the military status of the grooms. He listed Ben Frank as a "negro soldier." Gorton did not record the race and parental information for Sarah Willbour—an indication that she was a person of color.[4]

Who was Sarah Willbour? The scant records documenting Sarah's existence are not conclusive regarding her race. She married a "Negro"

Marriage license of Ben Franck and Sarah Willbour, January 31, 1779. (*Elder John Gorton's Book of Marriages, East Greenwich, Rhode Island, Collections of the Church of the Latter-Day Saints*)

soldier during the war, and she had a child. Rhode Island law and extant marriage records suggest that she was a person of color. Rhode Island statute, first enacted in 1701, in the Act to Prevent Clandestine Marriages, prohibited interracial marriages. The statute dictated that "no person . . . shall join in marriage any white person with any Negro, Indian or mulatto, on the penalty of two hundred dollars." And since Elder Gorton appeared to be a pedant for process and procedure, it is highly unlikely that he performed an interracial marriage.[5]

As indicated in Providence Town Council records, Sarah was originally from the town of Middleborough, Massachusetts. An extended Wilbur family lived throughout the Massachusetts Bay Colony, but primarily in the counties of Plymouth and Bristol. The town of Middleborough was in Plymouth County, near Rhode Island and Providence. By some accounts—primarily census and marriage records—these Wilburs were white. The 1790 Federal Census lists several Wilbur/Wilbore families in the counties of Bristol and Plymouth. Two households carried an additional "other free person," not identified as "Negro." The remaining members of these households are designated as white. Records also indicate a free Black presence in Sandwich, Massachusetts, in the early 1800s. The village of Sandwich, located on Cape Cod, neighbored Bristol County—both located

in southeastern Massachusetts. The Vital Records of Massachusetts confirmed the death of Daniel Wilbur, a man of color, age 60–70 of Sandwich,
Massachusetts, in 1809.[6]

Sarah Willbour was more than likely a person of color; however, no
records exist listing Sarah Willbour as a free Black, residing in Middleborough before or during the war. Sarah may have been formerly
enslaved as a servant in a Wilbur household before or during the war and
made her way to Providence due to being sold, after being freed, or having
escaped. If that were the case, she could have encountered other Black
Wilbours that populated southeastern New England and the Rhode Island
regiments. Boston Wilbour enlisted with the First Rhode Island Regiment
on April 14, 1778, because of the Slave Enlistment Act. A slave of John
Wilbour of Little Compton, Rhode Island, Boston was possibly the "bm"
(Black male) over the age of sixteen in the Wilbour household, as
enumerated in the 1774 Rhode Island Colonial census. His worth at the
time of his enlistment was £110. If Sarah was indeed Black or a person of
color, then her life before marriage could have been more like Boston's—
enslaved then freed—than her husband who was born free.[7]

As a woman of color, Sarah would have been a member of the domestic
workforce, free and unfree, that took care of households and families that
lived in much better conditions than their own. She saw firsthand the
growing gap between the haves and have-nots. To make a livelihood, Sarah
could have also sold her wares at the local market in Providence. In many
seaports, Black women were actively involved in the sale of fish and other
seafood. And, she also faced a racial double standard and did not receive
the protection or attention that was generally given to white women by
their fathers and husbands. Even so, a form of coverture governed the lives
of free and enslaved Black women. Laws based upon the concept of
coverture dictated the rights of enslaved married women to sue for their
freedom. Single women could do so. Free married Black women could not
bring lawsuits on their own behalf, nor did they have their own right of
residency. Their rights were subordinate to the Black head of household,
and those Black fathers and husbands were limited in their roles to protect
their wives and daughters.[8]

Records indicate that Sarah was a member of the lower class, dependent
upon others for her livelihood. She may have been a part of the day labor
workforce that slowly replaced indentured servitude with compensated day
labor. Poor women had few options available to them and were often forced
to work as domestic workers or washerwomen because of their lack of

education and class status.[9] Receiving wages for their daily work helped women gain some control over their lives; however, low wages and poor working conditions resulted in working women becoming part of a "growing marginalized class of the poor."[10] Joan Gundersen uses the phrase "emerging domestic ideology" to describe the labor relations developing at this time.[11] Middle- and upper-class women maintained their status by hiring domestic workers to perform household work for them. As a young woman, Sarah probably labored as a live-in worker. These workers often received room and board along with wages. However, as a young mother with the responsibility of raising a young child, she had few options. She may have lived away from her workplace with other women in similar conditions or she may have actively sought employers who would take both her and her child, so she could earn wages as a live-in domestic.[12]

By January 1779, Sarah had a child, named Abraham, born in the town of Middleborough. Even though premarital sex and pregnancy was not seen as a failing during the revolutionary period, a couple could redeem their respectability if they married soon after the pregnancy became known. It is unclear why she left her home in Middleborough. If Sarah conceived the child in her hometown, then an argument could be made that Ben Frank was not the biological father of Abraham. That being the case, Sarah may have been pushed by her parents to leave the household due to her pregnancy and the additional expense of having an extra mouth to feed. At some point, she relocated from her hometown. She claimed Johnston, Rhode Island, as her place of residence upon her marriage to Ben Frank.[13]

Sarah and Ben's initial meeting and decision to marry is not documented. Sarah probably relocated to Johnston to find a way to support herself and her child. However, Johnston was primarily a farming community and would not afford Sarah the domestic employment opportunities of larger towns like Boston or Providence. If she relocated to Providence after leaving Middleborough, she may have met Ben there. Ben was familiar with Providence since his father, Rufus, had ties to the town. Also, the town of Johnston, partitioned from the western part of Providence in 1759, was nearby and Ben did enlist at Providence in 1777. If Ben and Sarah met in Providence, they likely met at the workplace or at public facilities frequented by poor or working-class people. Blacks, free and enslaved, and working-class whites labored in the same types of occupations. In New England, they worked at menial professions such as farmhands, craftsmen's assistants, and house servants. They also congregated together at public places like the town water pump or tavern. It is possible that Ben and Sarah met at a common workplace or at a social gathering prior to Ben's enlistment with the Continental army.[14]

Sarah and Ben were not the first members of the Johnston-based Franks to take matrimonial vows, nor was Ben Frank the only Frank married by Elder John Gorton in 1779. Ben's younger sister, Hannah Frank, also took her marriage vows in front of the Baptist minister. She married Solomon Wanton of Tiverton, Rhode Island, on January 14, 1779.

This was the second marriage for Solomon. A decade earlier, he married Patience Dennis in his hometown. The marriage performed by Justice of the Peace John Bowen in October 1769 was an interethnic affair, explaining the demographics of the Wanton household in 1774. Patience, a member of a New England Native American group, possibly met her husband where they worked or at a variety of social functions, like religious meetings and Negro election festivals that attracted their share of both Blacks and Native Americans. So, by 1774, Solomon maintained a household of four Native Americans and one "Negro." A second Wanton household in Tiverton contained similar ethnic demographics. William Wanton headed a household of six Native Americans and one "Negro." Solomon and William Wanton were the Black heads of homes occupied predominantly by Native Americans. Military, census, and marriage records identify Solomon and William as Black. The relationships between the Wantons and their Native American household members were driven by a legal, economic, and cultural environment dominated by white Americans. Discrimination and prejudice produced segregation in some manner, forcing people of color to congregate at the same locations—taverns, jobs, and neighborhoods. These interactions sometimes resulted in cohabitation and marriage, which was the case in the households of Solomon and William Wanton.[15]

There is another explanation for the racial demographics of the Wanton households. William and Solomon Wanton may have been of Native descent, but census takers and other records keepers turned them into African Americans—a tactic used by many officials during the revolutionary era. Town officials throughout Rhode Island started to designate Native Americans as "black" or "Negro" in the written records to remove Native Americans from the written records. Is it possible that the census takers of 1774 felt the need to subjugate the Native Americans of Tiverton even more by making the heads of the Wanton families, dominated by Native Americans, Black? Regardless of the true demographics of his household, by 1779 Solomon was again in need of a wife and married for a second time, to Hannah Frank.[16]

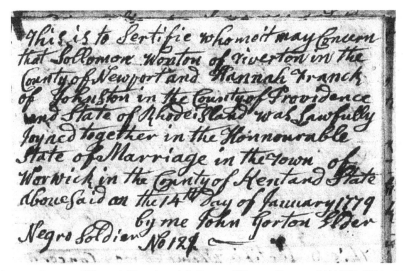

Marriage license of Hannah Franck and Sollomon Wonton, January 14, 1779. (*Elder John Gorton's Book of Marriages, East Greenwich, Rhode Island, Collections of the Church of the Latter-Day Saints*)

What would marriage mean to women like Sarah Willbour and Hannah Frank? Joan R. Gundersen argues that "marriage 'gave a complexion' to a woman's life."[17] What type of complexion was afforded Sarah and Hannah as they became wives of Continental regulars? One option was attachment to the Continental army. Throughout the war, Continental regiments were augmented by civilian women who followed the army for a variety of reasons. The number of female camp followers was different for each regiment, with estimates ranging from a total of 20,000 camp followers to a more conservative total of approximately 3 percent of the Continental army as a whole. For the most part, women ran to the camps of the Continental army to avoid poverty, loneliness, starvation, and other ravages caused by the war—and these numbers included women of color. These women became part of what Holly A. Mayer calls the "Continental Community." The community included Continental regulars, civilian personnel, and their dependents. The civilians served for the same reasons as the regulars—to fight for America's independence or their own survival.[18]

Women of the regiment, also known as army women, were official members of the regiments and performed regular support functions. Army officials expected women of the regiment to be of good character and hardworking. Female camp workers also performed an important function at camp. In their roles as washerwomen, women of the army helped to maintain camp hygiene. Dirty uniforms and clothing contributed to poor camp sanitation which resulted in diseases such as typhus and dysentery. Camp followers performed other functions as well. They sewed, mended, and washed uniforms and other pieces of clothing. They herded sheep and cattle. Any services provided by these women were regulated by set fees.[19] For instance, Washington ordered that laundry services should be only two shillings. "A dozen for all articles which they wash . . . provided they find their own soape, or one and sixpence per dozen if the soape be found them."[20] Washington also ordered regimental commanders to ensure that these fees were strictly followed and that "positively forbids Officers or Soldiers giving more than ye Rates for any Articles—disobedience will bee treat'd with no kind of Lenity."[21] In September 1777, the washing and ironing of clothing cost the following:

A Shirt & Stock 16 Lawful Money
Woollen Westcoats or Breeches 15
Stockings pair 13
Handkerchiefs 11
Blanketts 16[22]

Commanders worried about their inability to control the unofficial female masses following their armies. Given the lack of provisions and the neediness of the followers, these women often participated in acts of foraging and plundering of the battlefield dead. Colonel Greene of the First Rhode Island Regiment attempted to regulate the number of followers assigned to his companies by prohibiting "all women following the soldiers in camp" from ever returning, except for those recommended by company command officers. However, it was an accepted principle of eighteenth-century warfare that armies performed at a higher level if women were present. Washington resisted the request by the Secretary of War to limit the number of camp followers. Washington feared that the loss of female refugees would prompt desertions on the part of Continental regulars.[23]

Most of the women following the Continental armies were from the poorest levels of society. Like Sarah Frank and Hannah Wanton, many were the wives of common soldiers, too poor to take care of themselves or their children alone. They relied on the army for their sustenance. As camp followers, these women and their children were fed and infrequently housed. Female camp followers received half rations of food and their children received quarter rations. Housing was generally not offered, so women and children found shelter where they could. However, during the bitter winter of Valley Forge, separate huts were provided.[24]

As civilians attached to the military, women were bound by military rules and regulations. They were subject to court-martial and forms of discipline and punishment. Punishments for female camp followers usually involved whipping or ducking. Often, they were drummed out of the service.[25] The wife of Private Thomas of the Second Rhode Island Regiment suffered such banishment. Mrs. Thomas was caught in an act of thievery by a unit sergeant, who in turn notified Colonel Angell. Colonel Angell promptly rectified the situation; he "took the Gound [gown] in order to Send it to the owner. And ordered all the Drums and fifes to parade and Drum her out of the Regt. With a paper pind [pinned] to her back, with these words in Cappital letter, /A THIEF/ thus She went off with Musick."[26]

The Rhode Island regiments had their fair share of female camp followers. One Black woman trying to find her way through the war was Nancy Hill. Hill was born in New York City to free parents. At the age of fourteen she became an apprentice to Colonel Hutchings who also lived in New York City. After reaching the age of eighteen, Nancy left her position with Colonel Hutchings to follow the Continental army. She began a relationship with Briton Saltonstall, a Black soldier with the First Rhode Island Regiment. Briton enlisted after the passage of the Slave Enlistment Act in March 1778 and served with Captain Flagg's company. Hill's relationship with Saltonstall and the Continental community did not afford her economic stability. In July 1784, she requested assistance from the Providence Town Council. She returned for assistance in August 1786, this time with a three-year-old daughter named Sally Saltonstall. The town council ordered Nancy and her daughter's removal to her hometown of New York. Nancy Hill's experiences mirrored Sarah Willbour's— relationship with a Rhode Island soldier, mother of a young child, and poverty caused by war and racial and class status.[27]

If Sarah Willbour had been put out on her own to make a living for herself and her son, she may have sought employment with the Continental army, but she was also putting herself in a position to meet eligible males. Chaplain Ebenezer David officiated at marriage ceremonies between camp followers and soldiers. He concluded one of his letters in the following manner: "must wind up as it is late have been called off to marry a Couple of Camp Genius's we proceeded by vertue of Majr Gen Sullivan's Lisence," an indication that command staff understood and condoned marriages between soldiers and camp followers.[28]

Sarah Willbour may have been a camp follower when she found a husband; however, her role as the wife of a soldier meant more responsibilities and burdens. Increasingly during the revolutionary era, married women served as deputy husbands, handling the business affairs of the family. If married to a Continental soldier, a wife assumed the role of head of household when her husband was absent, and she made important decisions about family affairs. Farm wives during the war kept busy with the regular chores of housekeeping, gardening, and tending livestock and poultry. They also performed additional duties such as hoeing and plowing if the husband was away with the military. Wives sold produce and other goods from their farms and gardens. The war had expanded the market for surplus foodstuffs, so this was a good way to support the family, especially with a husband serving with the Continental army. Married women found other methods to support their families. Many took in boarders. Some produced and sold homespun cloth and clothing. Still others found employment in a variety of trades such as nursing, dressmaking, chair-caning, baking, and weaving. In these circumstances, it was difficult for Sarah to eke out a living on her own. The state of Rhode Island's economy suffered during the war due to the loss of important ports like Newport to British occupation. The options available to women like Sarah and Hannah were limited.[29]

The spouses of members of the command ranks also suffered during the war. Approximately fifty officers assigned to General Nathanael Greene's division "resigned their commissions" to return to their homes and take care of distressed family members. Command wages did not allow for the officers to purchase necessities at camp and provide for their families at home. They, unlike their subordinates, could not rely on public assistance to help their families to purchase those necessities that were overpriced due to the war.[30]

Ben's marital status was not unique among the group of men that composed the First Rhode Island Regiment. During the war, eighty non-commissioned officers and privates were married.[31] Some, like Ben Frank, took their vows in front of Elder John Gorton. These Black members of the First Rhode Island were a part of three groups that held ties to Gorton—the Kentish Guards, members of the Order of Cincinnati, and First Rhode Islanders. Like Ben, these Black soldiers also became married men at Warwick—Pero Morey, Prince Brown, David Greene, Prince

Limas, Abraham Pearce, and Ben's brother-in-law, Solomon Wanton. Other married members of the regiment included Simon Barton, Cuff Greene, Cato Greene, Dick Couzens, and Pomp Reaves. Simon Barton, like Ben Frank, was free before his service with the Rhode Island regulars. He was also a married man during his service. Born and raised in Warwick, Simon served for the duration of the war. He was absent with leave for a brief period in the spring of 1779. It was not unusual for married soldiers to request and receive leaves. Solomon Wanton, Ben Frank's brother-in-law, was also absent with leave during the summer of 1778. Many like Simon and Solomon sought out furloughs and leaves to visit wives and other family members at home. If they did not become camp followers, many of their wives were burdened with the sole responsibility of childrearing and taking care of a household. If Barton and Wanton did use their leaves to visit wives and families, there may have been pressure on them to stay at home. However, Barton did return from his short leave after a month's time—returning to his duty as a Continental regular. Wanton did as well.[32]

Formerly enslaved men of the First Rhode Island also married. Cato Greene, formerly enslaved by William Greene of Warwick, gained his freedom by signing up to serve with the First Rhode Island in 1778. Cato not only had to deal with the pressures of his newly found freedom but also had to maneuver the difficulties incurred by being a poor married soldier. However, he like Simon Barton, served for the duration of the war.[33]

One married soldier of the First Rhode Island Regiment did not survive the war. Ben's brother-in-law Solomon Wanton died December 28, 1781, at Wilmington, Delaware. Wanton's tenure with the First Rhode Island was littered with absences caused by illness. Whether defending the forts at Red Bank, wintering at Valley Forge, or working as a butcher at camp, Wanton did not experience long periods of good health. After enlisting in April 1777, he spent time in the camp hospital in August of the same year. He was carried as "sick absent" during the winter encampment at Valley Forge during the early months of 1778. Unsanitary camp conditions like those at Valley Forge led to a plethora of diseases and illnesses. Dysentery, otherwise known as "putrid diarrhea," ran rapidly throughout camps littered with poorly maintained latrines and rotting animal carcasses. Wanton could have also suffered from typhus, otherwise known as "camp fever," which was carried by lice. He suffered from another illness and was in the hospital again later that year. However, he managed to make muster and work a specialized assignment as a butcher in 1779 and 1780. His health took a turn for the worse in 1781, and by the end of the year he was on Colonel Greene's "Return of Casualties" for the year. Wanton was one of the more than 10,000 Continental soldiers who died of disease during the war.[34]

How did his death affect the circumstances for his wife? Hannah became part of a larger group of widows and single mothers deemed dependent and needy by Rhode Island town officials. Due to the heavy loss of husbands and fathers to the war effort, these officials carried out their tasks of determining rightful recipients of town aid in a very meticulous manner. If Hannah was forced to leave Tiverton after her husband's death, she was also joining an increasing number of Black transients in Rhode Island caused by emancipation and the war effort. The records are silent about the circumstances of Hannah Wanton after the death of her husband. Hannah Frank Wanton does not appear in the Providence, Johnston, or Tiverton town records as a person seeking public assistance. Such was not the case for her sister-in-law, Sarah Frank.[35]

By November 1779, the marriage between Ben and Sarah Frank had fallen on desperate economic times. By this time, Sarah and her son were living in Providence, having left Johnston after her marriage to Ben. On November 12, 1779, Sarah and her child, Abraham Frank, were deemed unworthy to receive aid and rejected as "true" inhabitants by the Providence Town Council. The councilmen ordered the removal of Sarah and her child to their proper residence of Johnston. It was an accepted practice by civic leaders to "warn out" of their towns individuals who were judged incapable of self-sufficiency if those individuals were not born in that town. Providence town leaders did not want the expense of supporting Sarah and her child. In warning her out of town, they were following established procedures for dealing with poor transients. Many transient women like Sarah Frank migrated to larger cities like Providence, looking for work and support. The presence of these poor individuals forced town and state officials throughout Rhode Island to establish and follow strict regulations regarding the issuance of aid and support to these poor transients. Local officials paid close attention to the plight of mothers, single or otherwise, left to fend for the needs of themselves and their children without the assistance of husbands or fathers. Sarah Frank now fell into this category—a struggling mother and wife of a poor Continental soldier. As such, she could be brought in front of the town council and made to prove her legal residency and ability to take care of herself and her child.[36]

Sarah Frank became part of a growing number of poor women trying to survive the Revolutionary War. The war increased the ranks of the impoverished, composed of refugees, poor widows, and needy wives of Continental soldiers. Poor transient women like Sarah Frank became problematic for Providence officials during the revolutionary era. In their attempts to monitor public funds, town leaders tried to distinguish the deserving from the nondeserving—those who brought on their own misfortune by laziness or immorality. From 1750 to 1800, approximately half of the transient heads of households investigated by town officials for public assistance were women; their average age was twenty-eight and they typically had several children. Most of these women held jobs but were unable to handle the expenses of maintaining their own households; instead, they sometimes formed households with other single, adult women. There are no records revealing the living arrangements of Sarah Frank and her child when they were brought before the Providence Town Council. It is obvious that she could not rely on assistance from her Johnston in-laws, since she was living in Providence at the time of her request. It is also unclear if she was employed. She probably made her way to Providence because of the opportunities afforded by the city's growing markets and population.[37]

Sometimes residents came to the aid of wives in need. In South Kingstown, a vulnerable wife was much more fortunate than Sarah Frank:

> Thomas Potter appeared in Council and agreed to Lett Dorcas Congdon wife of Robt Congdon a soldier in ye Continental Service live in his House where she now lives untill ye 13: day October next & also let her have 1/8 of an Acre of Land to plant for 48/ & Keep her Cow at grass for /18 pr weak from this Time [until] Foddering is past to which ye Council ye Council agree. Council Records from 1778.[38]

By 1780 the year of Ben's desertion, the situation for the Congdon family had not improved. "Voted that Mr George Babcock hire of Benjamin Saunders part of a House for Robert Congdon's Family & that he engage to pay the Rent in behalf of this Town."[39] South Kingstown officials also fed poor soldiers' families. "Voted that George Babcock be appointed by this Council to provide four Bushels of Corn for Jemima Thomas her Husband being a Soldier in the Continental Army."[40] However, not all women residing in South Kingstown in 1781 were as fortunate as Dorcas Congdon or Jemima Thomas. In 1781, town officials "Voted that the Clerk Issue a Warrant to the town Sergeant or either of the Constables to bring Penilope Godfrey a transient Person before the next town Council to be examined and sent out of the town."[41]

It is not surprising that the family of Ben Frank and others suffered from harsh economic conditions. The Continental army's practice of irregular pay and rations took away the ability for Continental regulars to support their families and thus, jeopardized their status as good men in the community, since good men provided for their families. The conditions that most soldiers' families found themselves in became a constant source of discontent within the ranks and increased the stress of soldiers already burdened with the responsibilities of war. Since eighty First Rhode Islanders were married, their inability to support their families would cause the regiment additional strain.[42] A letter to the editor of the *Connecticut Courant* illustrated the condition of women like Sarah Frank and her son— "How is it that the poor soldier's wives in many of our towns go from door to door, begging a supply of the necessaries of life at the stipulated prices, and are turned away, notwithstanding the solemn agreements of the towns to supply such?"[43] Sarah Frank had begged for help from the Providence Town Council but was turned away.

The situation for Sarah and her son did not improve after her initial appearance in front of the Providence Town Council. She likely came to the attention of town officials due to the testimony of observant neighbors who did not wish to see Sarah and her son on the town's dole.[44] By July 1780, Sarah and her son were granted aid in the form of traveling money from the Providence Town Council. Additionally, there was a significant change in the way the council described young Abraham. He was documented as Abraham Wildbur, instead of Abraham Frank, and was designated as a bastard child. This change could indicate several things. Town officials may have obtained information disproving Ben Frank as Abraham's natural or legal father during an interrogation of Sarah Frank during a council meeting. The purpose of this interview was twofold: "to determine whether a transient family should be warned out; and to determine where the family should be sent."[45] The use of the term "bastard" could also indicate that Ben Frank was unwilling or unable to provide financial support for the child.[46] Either way, the Providence Town Council assigned responsibility of Abraham Wildbur to his place of birth. The aid, granted by the town council, was used to cover traveling expenses for Sarah and Abraham to return to his hometown of Middleborough, Massachusetts:

> It is thereupon adjudged by this Council that the place of the Law-
> ful Settlement of said Abraham Wildbur is in the said Town of Mid-
> dleborough and as he has become Chargeable to this Town: It is
> ordered That . . . Warrant for the Removal of said Abraham according

to Law . . . It is ordered that Eighteen Pounds Lawful Money be paid and Delivered out of the Town Treasury to the said Sarah Frank alias Sarah Wildbur to defrey her Travelling Expenses to Middleborough: as she proposes to leave this Town.[47]

It is interesting to note that the removal warrant was issued for Abraham Wildbur, not his adult mother, Sarah. Why? Were Providence town officials unable to determine the legal residency of Sarah Frank? Why not? She obviously supplied enough information to town officials to determine the legal residency of her son. Town officials originally believed that Sarah and her son were legal residents of Johnston and were willing and ready to remove her to that town because of her marriage to Ben Frank. Did Johnston town officials refuse to accept her? Sarah does not appear in extant Johnston town records as a resident or recipient of aid. For whatever reasons, the Providence officials determined that Abraham's place of residency was his place of birth and they considered him chargeable to that town's treasury.

The warning out of Sarah and her son from Providence provides more information about the life of Sarah in Providence during the war. Providence town officials did not consider Sarah or Abraham legal residents of their town. Granted, those officials felt the need to lessen the numbers of poor living in their town, but individuals could obtain legal residence in a number of ways: being a servant of a master who lived there; buying a freehold; or marrying a man who was a legal resident of the town. How did Sarah measure up to these requirements? She was not married to a legal resident of Providence—Ben's hometown and place of residence was Johnston, Rhode Island. There are no records of her ownership of land. And there was not a master or former master willing to vouch for her.[48]

What recourse did Sarah and others like her have? Some women fought being warned out or removed from a town. They refused to appear in front of town officials when called to determine their status in town. They also hid or locked themselves away from officials looking to remove them from their homes. Others left town, only to return once town officials forgot about them. The record does not state what action Sarah took in response to the warrant—whether she initially fought the warrant or immediately acquiesced to the will of the town council.[49]

Evidence regarding Sarah's life after her removal from Providence is sparse. She is not listed as a resident of Providence or Johnston after the war. There are, however, listings of Sarah Wilburs throughout Massachusetts after the war. It is equally difficult to ascertain the circumstances of her son

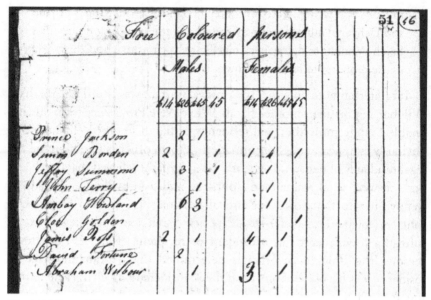

The 1820 Federal Census for Nantucket, Massachusetts, with Abraham Wilbour listed at the bottom. (*National Archives, Census Record for Massachusetts*)

after the war. However, there is one listing for Abraham Wilbour in the 1820 federal census. He is documented as a "free coloured person" living in Nantucket, Massachusetts—the head of a household of five, including himself and four females. Whether this Abraham Wilbour was the adult personage of the child thrown out of Providence, Rhode Island, is hard to ascertain. It would be a satisfying epilogue—knowing that the child survived to adulthood. Abraham's mother Sarah was forced to leave Providence because of her inability to support herself and child, due to a lack of family and other financial support. The most pivotal reason for her dilemma lay with the actions of her husband, Ben Frank.[50]

CHAPTER SEVEN

The Winter of Discontent
and the
Self-Furlough of Ben Frank

THE WINTER OF 1779–1780 was one of the harshest winters in Rhode
Island history. In January, the Providence Town Council had declared
a winter emergency because "the Snow has blocked up the Avenues to the
Town" and "many of the Inhabitants are in Deplorable Distress for want of
Wood" and other "Necessaries." The council called for every "able inhabi-
tant" to bring their shovels to "open the Roads so that they may be passable
for Teams."[1] Thirty miles south of Providence, camped near Newport in
the void left by retreating British forces, Ben Frank, his brother William,
and the other soldiers of the First Rhode Island Regiment foraged desper-
ately for food and other supplies. Two years earlier, Ben and William had
survived the legendary winter at Valley Forge. Perhaps this was one bad
winter too many for Ben. On a bleak winter day in February 1780, Ben
Frank left his service with the Continental army.

Bad weather and shortage of supplies were not the only reasons Ben
Frank left the army that winter. Ben's leaving was near the three-year anniversary of his original enlistment. He, like many other young men recruited into the Continental army with contracts that specified three years
or duration of the conflict, probably considered that he had fulfilled his

military obligation, whether or not the war was over. An American victory was nowhere in sight in February 1780, and Ben acted like many other discouraged soldiers in opting not to muster with their battalions that winter. He also had personal reasons to leave his soldiering life. The eighteen-year-old had gotten married the year before; he now had to support a wife and child on the meager or the mostly nonexistent pay he earned as a soldier—an impossible feat, as many soldiers discovered. So, when Ben deserted, he left behind not only his brother but also his own young family.[2]

An estimated 20–25 percent of Continental troops deserted during the American Revolution. Solid statistics are difficult to determine since many muster rolls listed absentees as "sick absent," "on furlough," or "on command" instead of "deserted." It was often difficult for command officers to capture accurate incidences of desertions since soldiers tended to be absent from camp for a variety of reasons, mostly foraging for food and other supplies or just to take a break from the military—returning to duty after a brief period.[3]

On February 10, 1780, Ben Frank mustered with fellow soldiers of the First Rhode Island, stationed at Providence. By March, the company rolls carried him as a "deserter." If the reasons for his departure are unclear, the circumstances are not. His self-furlough was not driven solely by the harshness of army life or the brutality of war. He did not leave after the tough winter at Valley Forge. He did not leave after the tough battles at Red Bank and Turkey Hill. He and others were unique in their leaving. He was a part of the small percentage of Black soldiers who left their service. His decision to leave was a complex mix of personal and professional factors that would eventually overwhelm the eighteen-year-old soldier.[4]

Motivating factors for most desertions, like Ben Frank's, can be placed into two general categories: professional and personal. Professional factors were diverse and complex and included life within the military ranks and condition of that service. Many desertions were the result of poor administration on the part of the military. Others were the result of the brutal nature of colonial warfare. And others were caused by the soldiers' own mentality due to their own negative perceptions of war and lack of support from the civilian populace. Sometimes soldiers were driven to leave due to bad conditions at camp, within their regiments or companies. Personal reasons included individual needs, and personal status in the ranks, illnesses, and conditions at home. Sometimes soldiers were driven to leave because of problems in camp or on the home front. Oftentimes professional and personal factors would merge to create an intolerable existence for the Con-

Muster roll of the fourth company, First Rhode Island Regiment, February–July 1780. Dots have been added to identify the listings for William Frank ("On Command, Rhode Island") and Benjamin Frank ([Deserted] D[itt]o March 1). (*National Archives, Revolutionary War Military Records, 1775–1783*)

tinental regulars. Professional and personal factors could affect all Continental regulars, and they did affect William and Ben Frank and the regulars of the Rhode Island regiments.

The problem of desertion showed itself early in the American ranks, stemming from a combination of "rage militaire" and the soldiers' own perceptions of service. As described by Benjamin Cowell, citizen-soldiers flocked to the ranks to lend support to their fellow citizens under siege in Boston. This "rage militaire," a passionate call to arms, was short-lived and expired in the reality of long-term warfare. Soldiers of the Continental army during the period prior to 1776 maintained the mentality of the militia or minutemen, thus this "first" army had the qualities and staying power of colonial militias. These soldiers were committed to the high-minded ideals of the founding fathers and responded to their calls to protect "our wives and children, with everything that is dear to us, [being] subjected to the merciless rage of uncontrolled despotism."[5] However, even though committed to a cause of liberty and freedom, these soldiers did not have the qualities needed for members of a long-standing army: discipline and training. They also lacked the ability to serve for long periods of time. The army of 1775–76 consisted primarily of land-owning farmers who were protecting hearth and home. They served for what they thought would be a short period of time, during which their ideals of freedom and equality would win the day against the British, whom they considered no more than paid mercenaries. When the contest did not follow the expected pattern of warfare, these militia regulars left the frontlines in droves or failed to renew their enlistments. Ben Frank's enlistment in the spring of 1777 was not prompted by the patriotic fervor ignited by the Battles at Lexington and Concord. He was not a member of militia groups that stormed toward Boston. Ben joined a more professional force that expected its soldiers to serve longer and harder.[6]

The brutality of war was also a leading cause for departures. Ben Frank saw this brutality firsthand as a member of the Rhode Island regiments. Those regiments suffered casualties at both the Battle at Red Bank and the Battle of Rhode Island. Sergeant Smith of the First Rhode Island Regiment chronicled the desertions of some Continental regulars during the month-long battle at Red Bank. The Rhode Island regiments also suffered losses at camp due to illness and starvation at Valley Forge, and many soldiers left as a result. The Rhode Island regiments suffered traumatic losses during that harsh winter, enough losses to force the recruitment of enslaved men and the formation of a battalion composed of freeborn men of color and the formerly enslaved and the segregation of Rhode Island Continental troops.[7]

Ben Frank and his fellow soldiers also had to deal with indifference to their condition on the part of the military administration and the civilian population. The Continental army had consistently failed to supply the material rewards of service that were promised to the enlisted soldiers, such as food, clothing, and pay. Historians have identified a link between the lack of material and psychological support and the amount of protest and defiance within the ranks. William and Ben Frank had both suffered from the lack of material support as members of the First and Second Rhode Island regiments. Both regiments had been reduced to constantly foraging for food and other rations. As a result, soldiers of the First Rhode Island had laid down their weapons and refused to fight in response to not receiving promised clothing. Sergeants assigned to the Second Rhode Island refused to wear their hats in the proper manner and sent a "mutinous" letter to their commander. They later relented. Another incident involved members of the Second Rhode Island taking up arms to remove a fellow soldier from his imprisonment for mutiny. They turned back before forcing the release of the prisoner. The mutinous behavior was the result of disagreement over terms of enlistment, amount of pay in depreciated Continental currency, and lack of supplies, clothing, and other provisions. The ever-growing anger and frustration felt by Continental regulars was based on what they perceived as a lack of support from the military administration and the public. One of the ultimate forms of protest was leaving the army.[8]

These acts of protest and defiance provoked the military administration to enact a harsher disciplinary code. Washington revised the disciplinary code after only one year of war in response to the mutinous behavior of his troops and to instill more discipline in the ranks. Many of the crimes committed by soldiers included being absent without leave, being insubordinate toward officers, and plundering the citizenry, all of which were acts of protest and defiance, as well as acts of criminal intent. Charles Patrick Niemeyer reviewed 3,315 Revolutionary War courts-martial and found that more than 80 percent involved desertion or mutiny. His analysis shows that the number of capital offenses increased because of Washington's dictate, and punishment for most offenses increased from thirty-nine to one hundred lashes. Connecticut soldier Joseph Plumb Martin reported that plunderers could receive up to five hundred lashes. The new code stipulated that "all officers and soldiers who having received pay . . . in the service of the United States and convicted of having deserted, shall suffer death or such other punishment as by a courts-martial shall be inflicted."[9] Soldiers reacted to the harsher code in one of three ways: they committed crimes, they mutinied, or they deserted.[10]

Personal reasons also affected desertion rates. Soldiers were motivated to leave or not return from furlough due to family hardships and responsibilities, personal injury or illness, or homesickness. Ben Frank and other members of the First Rhode Island suffered with physical ailments and injuries during their terms of service. Ben contracted some ailment in the fall of 1778 as he was listed "sick but present" in camp. The records do not state the nature of his sickness, but it was very likely the result of camp life, which was rife with illness and disease. A soldier's health was constantly endangered by camp sanitation. Human fecal and animal remains littered the camp. When regiments were encamped for long periods of time, like the First Rhode Island near Providence in 1780, the camp was covered with a haze of fumes rising from green wood campfires, gunpowder smoke, urine, feces, and butchered animal remains. Soldiers frequently suffered from the "Itch," a result of poor hygiene and sleeping on the ground. It could become severe enough to cover a soldier with scars or strip off his skin. Soldiers afflicted with the "Itch" were barely fit for duty. Others also suffered from outbreaks of measles, smallpox, and dysentery. Soldiers protested the conditions at camp by making themselves unfit for duty. "Barrel fever" was the practice of getting drunk daily, thus rendering a soldier incapable of performing his duty. Such practices were soldiers' revenge for broken promises from the military and the public.[11]

Military doctors eventually discovered that homesickness was a real illness that affected soldiers. Symptoms included loss of appetite, restlessness, and melancholy. Many soldiers from New England had never been far from their homes. William Frank had traveled to Tiverton, approximately thirty miles from his home, to enlist. Ben, however, enlisted in Providence, near his hometown. The Frank brothers and their fellow soldiers were not used to prolonged absences from home. Many had never lived with large groups of men in new and very uncomfortable settings. If granted furloughs to visit home and family, many soldiers were slow to return or did not return at all. Joseph Plumb Martin was issued a furlough to visit his grandparents, in part to apprehend and return others on furlough who had failed to return to camp. In the year of Ben's departure, Plumb Martin was sent "into Connecticut after two men belonging to our corps who had been furloughed but had stayed beyond the time allowed them."[12] Martin stayed home for ten days and returned to camp. However, many others had a more difficult time adjusting to long periods of time away from home, family, and friends. A soldier's strong affinity to his hometown came not only from attachments to family and friends but also from shared experiences with others from the same locale. Before the war, William and Ben had both resided in Johnston, a small farming community. Ben did enlist at Providence and both brothers probably visited the larger town, but they were raised in a smaller community and were very young when they enlisted. They did not have the maturity necessary to handle prolonged absences from the only life that they had known. The effects of homesickness were not just disappointment and temporary low spirits at being away from hearth and home. The effects of homesickness were long lasting. During 1776–1777, newspaper advertisements often described deserters as having a "dejected" or "down" look.[13]

With his marriage to Sarah Willbour, Ben became a member of an overburdened group of Continentals—soldier husbands. Some wives, like Sarah Frank, were unable to support their families in the absence of the husband and father. Ben Frank and other soldier husbands felt the increased burden of their families' hunger and homelessness, and some felt the increased need to return home to take care of their families. If state and local authorities failed to meet their responsibility to assist these families, the financial burden fell upon the soldier-husband's shoulders. Washington understood the power that tough family circumstances had over his soldiers and attempted to solve this problem. He allowed wives and families of soldiers to follow them at camp to lift soldiers' morale. He believed that "the lives of these Women; the suffering of their children, and the complaints of the Husbands would admit of no alternative. If pay is withheld from us, and Provisions from our Wives and Children we must all starve together; or commit Acts which may involve us in ruin. . . . In a word, I was obliged to give Provisions to the extra Women in these Regiments, or loose by Desertion, perhaps to the Enemy, some of the oldest and best Soldiers in the Service."[14]

Ben and William's early tenure with the Second Rhode Island allowed them, as new recruits, to witness how unauthorized departures affected the ranks. Since the beginning of the war, desertion was a problem among the Continental army as a whole and the Rhode Island Continentals in particular. Colonel Angell of the Second Rhode Island repeatedly dealt with this predicament. The colonel lamented to the Governor of Rhode Island how poor conditions and lack of support affected the morale and loyalty of his troops and appeared not to change three years later. In that letter dated August 1777, Angell claimed that: "Not one half of them can not be termed fit for duty on any immergency; of those, who of them went with me on a late expedition . . . many were barefoot . . . 5 of them there deserted to ye enemy which I have reason to believe was principles owing to ye non fulfillment of engagements on ye part of ye state."[15]

Even though Angell was sympathetic toward the horrible conditions experienced by the common soldier, his reactions to the incidences of desertion were consistent with Continental army protocols. He deemed deserters as villains and made every effort to track them down and return them to the ranks for punishment. His diary contains many succinct descriptions of soldiers leaving the regiment without permission: "This morning Ensign Roggers Come to my house going in Search of benoni Bishop and Robert Gilley two Deserters"; "there came another Express with four Deserters from beadford"; "also sent a Serjt and a file of men to pawtuxet and Cranston after some Deserters."[16] In his diary, he gave little explanation for those desertions.

As a hardcore Continental regular, Ben Frank had to be aware of the varying penalties and punishments meted out by military superiors. He also had personal knowledge of deserters and felt the impact of their departure on the regiment. Men left the military in every season and at every location. They left by themselves, and they left in groups. They slipped away under cover of darkness. They dodged into the woods while on the march. Many were captured and returned to camp. Many were not. Of those captured, all were brought to trial; if they were convicted, they were punished. The usual punishment was imprisonment or lashing. The harshest punishment was execution, especially for repeat offenders. The Continental Congress passed Articles of War which allowed for the execution of deserters in 1776. General Washington did offer pardons if deserters turned themselves in, and he issued wholesale pardons when there were unusually high desertion rates or when there were special events to celebrate. At those times, Washington made public notification in newspapers of his intention to grant full pardons to those who returned on their own. If absentees failed to do so, then, if caught, they might receive the harshest punishment.[17]

Even though Ben Frank spent most of his military career as a member of the First Rhode Island, his experience with the Second Rhode Island made him acutely aware of desertion and its consequences. Greenman's account of the Second Rhode Island's march to Red Bank during the summer of 1777 chronicles several incidents of desertion—"two or thre men desarted," "Sum men desarted, took off three horses with them," "came to Haverstraw where we flogged a Man 30 lashes for Desertion."[18] These desertions may have resulted from the march. Even though some food provisions and shoes were supplied to the troops throughout the march, clothing and other equipment were in limited supply. The camp was plagued with an outbreak of the measles. Additionally, a minor disturbance occurred "conserning thair wages."[19] During this period, several men "deserted," some taking camp provisions and horses with them.[20]

The actions of soldiers of the First Rhode Island paralleled their compatriots. Some soldiers left while on march and others during encampments. However, Sergeant John Smith of the First Rhode Island Regiment linked that battalion's desertions with conditions of battle, as opposed to conditions at camp or on the march. He recounted how soldiers deserted during and just prior to the Battle of Red Bank. Some deserted to the enemy and became spies for the British. Others were recaptured and given harsh punishments of imprisonment, lashings, or, in extreme cases, execution by hanging.[21]

Understanding their motivation to serve is instrumental to understanding why Ben Frank and other free men of the First Rhode Island chose to depart. We need a broader context to make sense of the desertion rates for the Black members of the Rhode Island regiments. This context includes the important reality that not all Black soldiers were former slaves, recently freed. In this context any analysis of desertion rates among these Black soldiers should consider three things. First, not all African American soldiers were former slaves who gained freedom by entering the army. Former slaves may have had less reason to leave the army than white soldiers, but freeborn men of color came into the military for very different reasons than the formerly enslaved. Second, Black soldiers overall endured longer terms of service than white soldiers. And third, a sense of unit cohesion and/or solidarity may have been stronger among Black troops, who were segregated because of military policy.[22]

The Frank brothers had a variety of economic and social reasons for joining the military, but they were also motivated by the military tradition set by their father, Rufus Frank, and the direct link between military service and masculine reputation. The Revolutionary War became an outlet for them to prove their manliness. Their father's experiences were living proof that military service gave a man the ability to earn a living, raise and support a family, and live in his own home. As the Frank brothers entered their third year in the military, they must have compared their initial motivation with the reality of service. Regardless of how patriotic or practical their initial desire to serve, actual service turned out to be a tangle of brutal battles, hard marches, and unhealthy camp life. The brothers had participated in two major battles that resulted in significant losses. They were torn away from their original regiment by military policy. And they had lost several regimental mates in battle and at camp. Those losses may well have dimmed their desire to continue in the military.[23]

If Ben Frank and the other members of the First Rhode Island were motivated by practical needs, then service with the military offered them the chance to get out of physical, social, and economic bondage. As stated in earlier chapters, the situation for most African Americans was dismal prior to the war. Most were enslaved, and even those who were free faced a struggle. Few owned land or property, and most worked as common laborers, like the Frank brothers, competing against whites in a sometimes depressed job market. Successful Blacks, such as Anthony Kinnicutt of Providence, who owned their own land and businesses, were not afforded the rights and privileges granted to their white counterparts. They could not vote and did not have a voice in the governance of their immediate communities.[24]

It must have been obvious to Ben Frank and his compatriots that military realities did not live up to recruitment promises. Their pay did not even match that of day laborers in the civilian population. Neimeyer's survey of fifty African American soldiers' pension records showed that one-fifth listed laborer or servant as their occupation after leaving the army; their military service had not led to better occupations. Others listed semi-skilled occupations, such as weavers or waggoners. A survey of the service and pension records for members of the First Rhode Island shows similar results. Of the thirty-five soldiers listed on the "Return of Freemen," occupations or trades at time of enlistment are stated for fourteen. Ten are listed as common laborers, including William and Ben Frank. Two made their living on the seas as mariners. One was a waggoner and another worked as a butcher during his military service. Many of these men had been part of a general labor force that had struggled to maintain some type of economic competency. The cash bonuses and bounties offered by recruiting officers would have been particularly appealing. The appeal of steady pay for steady work was very strong for common laborers like the freemen of the First Rhode Island, even though the reality of military service with its irregular pay and supplies proved to be no better than their earnings as common laborers.[25]

Ben Frank and his fellow soldiers may have been motivated to serve for the same reasons as their poor white counterparts—"opportunity, hope and excitement."[26] For the Franks and other free men of color, this meant a hope for a better life and standing in their communities, opportunity for economic competency, and excitement for young men whose experiences were stunted by stifling Black Codes which regulated their behavior. As soldiers, the Franks and their fellow soldiers of color enlisted for the same pay and bounties as white soldiers. However, the regularity of that pay was always in question. Did their sporadic employment in civilian life prepare the freemen of the First Rhode Island for the erratic pay schedule of the

Continental army? Or were they, like the mutinous members of the Second
Rhode Island, willing to mutiny and/or desert because of insufficient provisions and pay? If the freemen of the First Rhode Island looked to military
service to further their ambitions, then the reality of that service must have
come up wanting by early 1780—the year of Ben's departure.

Another motivation for service was the chance at steady food and other
provisions. Did they eat better as soldiers or civilians? The diaries, journals,
and memoirs of Revolutionary War soldiers are rife with complaints of little
or no food during service with the Continental army. Early in the war,
Colonel Israel Angell, commander of the Second Rhode Island, wrote to
his superiors regarding his concerns about his poorly maintained troops.
Since food provisions were usually in short supply, Continental soldiers
were often forced to forage or acquire their own daily rations. The average
soldier spent most of his day in a search for food or performing guard duty.
African American soldier Boyrereau Brinch, aka Jeffrey Brace, remembers
incidents of foraging during his military career with the Connecticut regiments.[27] The practice of foraging and plundering became so prevalent that
army officials took steps to prevent the practice. Sergeant Greenman was
charged to "take up all Soldiers . . . and if suspected to have been a plundering the Inhabitance they was to receive from one hundred to 500 Lashes
on ther back at the Descretion of the officers Commanding the Guards."[28]
When soldiers could not appropriate or plunder the countryside, they
sometimes stole from the military stores. Winsor Fry, a freeman of the First
Rhode Island, was found guilty of robbing the regimental commissary of
beef, rum, and meal. Fry was given the death sentence, which was eventually
overturned. The drastic measures and punishments given for plundering
are evidence that these acts had become problematic for the Continental
army. Given the continuous problems with pay, provisions, and equipment,
were the freemen of the First Rhode Island confident that a new independent country would fulfill promises of land ownership at war's end? If there
were concerns among the ranks of the Black soldiers, they were not appar-
ent in the length of their service.[29]

The professionalism of Black troops like Ben and William Frank can
be measured in a number of ways. Since they enlisted and served with the
Continental army, their length of service was longer than those in militia
forces, who on the average served for three to twelve months. Most African
American soldiers enlisted for three years or for the duration of the war.
By 1780, Ben Frank and other free men of color of the First Rhode Island
Regiment had served, on the average, three years. Granted that many Black

soldiers were exchanging their longer service for their freedom, a substantial number of free Blacks also served for the duration of the war. This increased term of service allowed African American soldiers to become more proficient at their craft.[30] The Marquis de Chastellux commented on the professionalism of the Black soldiers by stating: "At the ferry-crossing I met with a detachment of the Rhode Island regiment. . . . The majority of the enlisted men were Negroes or mulattoes; but they are strong, robust men, and those I saw made a very good appearance."[31] During the victorious review of American troops after Yorktown, Baron von Closen, aide-de-camp to General Rochambeau, remarked that: "Three-quarters of the Rhode Island regiment consists of Negroes, and that regiment is the most neatly dressed, the best under arms, and the most precise in its maneuvers."[32]

The professionalism of Ben Frank and other Black soldiers of the First Rhode Island Regiment was also driven by their desire for acceptance by their peers and society at large. Military service offered an opportunity for upward mobility and a chance to gain social and economic status. Most colonial Americans believed that one's social status was directly tied to one's work, and a soldier's work was more important than that of a common laborer, especially during a time of war. Since both Frank brothers and most Blacks of the First Rhode Island were common laborers before the war, military service provided one of the few ways for them to move upward.

William and Ben's path to the First Rhode Island Regiment differed from some of their fellow soldiers and may have shaped their commitment to the unit. Both were reassigned from an integrated regiment where they were familiar with the command staff and other soldiers. Both became part of a different regiment because of a reorganization scheme that segregated the regiment along racial lines. Unit cohesion and solidarity among soldiers also produced higher levels of professionalism. Since the First Rhode Island was reorganized into a primarily all Black unit, the soldiers now had the bond of racial identity and common life experiences to tie them together. Long-term assignment with a company or regiment tended to reduce the potential for desertion. As soldiers bonded with each other over battles and harsh camp life, they gained confidence in one another and felt personally responsible for the well-being of their group. This type of solidarity reduced the tendency to use desertion as a means of personal protest.[33]

What was the general profile of the previously free soldiers of color at this point in the Frank brothers' service? Thirty-three documented free men of color served alongside the Frank brothers at the reorganization of the Rhode Island regiments in the winter of 1778–1779. By the winter of

1779–1780, the average length of service for this cohort was two to three years—twice as long as the average of six months to one year. Members of this group had participated in major expeditions and two major battles of the war. They suffered with diseases and illnesses at camp. And they suffered casualties from battles. Some lost their lives. And others left.

In comparison, the men who enlisted as a result of the Slave Enlistment Act provide a different profile regarding the numbers who left but is comparable to when they left. Of the seventy documented formerly enslaved men, six left their service in 1780. This lower number corresponds with the analysis determined by Quarles and most recently by Robert A. Geake that the formerly enslaved proved to be steady and professional soldiers. Sharpo Gardner left in February 1782 but returned to service in May and then served until the end of the war. Peter Hazard left in April. James Clarke, Jack Fones, and Isaac Rodman left during the first week of July. Rodman's departure occurred one year after he was listed as a prisoner of war in 1779. Thomas Lefavour and William Greene departed on July 21 and July 23, 1779, respectively. As it was for the freemen of color, 1780 appears to have been a problematic year for these men. So, instead of a winter of discontent, summer was the time of year that occasioned their departures. Judith Van Buskirk stipulates that the arrival of General William Heath in June 1780 and the ensuing fractious relationship between Heath and Colonel Greene led to a tenuous situation at the encampment of the Rhode Island regiments which was a factor in the desertions of soldiers of the First Rhode Island.[34]

Of the thirty-five soldiers who appeared on the "Return of Freemen Inlisted," eighteen or about half left military service at one time in their careers. These eighteen soldiers were not running to something but running away from poor circumstances. A total of ten freemen from the original list of thirty-five freemen left during the winter encampment of 1779–1780, including Ben Frank. These ten young men chose to leave when encamped in their home state.[35]

Ben Frank was not the first to leave. Two free men of the First Rhode Island left prior to Ben Frank's departure in 1780. Toby Coys left in the winter of 1777 and may be an example of a young soldier who left early in his career, unable to cope with military life. At the time, Coys served in Captain Samuel Phillips' company of Colonel Richmond's Rhode Island State regiment.[36] Coys' desertion was carried in the *Providence Gazette*, dated April 26, 1777: "Deserted the 26th of February ... two Indians, viz. John Daniels, about 20 years of age, 5′7″, long hair, belongs to Charlestown.

Toby Coys, about 17 years of Age, 5'6", belongs to Charlestown."[37] Coys did return to duty—he enlisted for the duration of the war on May 20, 1777. However, his military career did not end well. Five years later, he was listed as dead. Asa Gardner/Gardiner met a similar fate. Gardner left the First Rhode Island on January 28, 1779. However, by the following March, he was again mustering with Captain Dexter's company of that regiment. Gardner may be an example of those soldiers who received furloughs and found it difficult to return to their military duties. He was listed as "on furlough" from Dexter's company in December 1778. His departure in January 1779 may have been an informal and unauthorized extension of his furlough. Gardner served steadily after the incident and was in camp during the winter of 1779–1780—the time of Ben Frank's departure. However, by the fall of 1780, Gardner's military career was over. He died October 26, 1780. The cause of his death is not documented.[38]

The winter leading up to Ben Frank's departure was brutal. Rivers froze deep, snow piled high, and the temperature remained low. The weather was so severe that the British could drive horse-drawn sleds across the frozen harbor from Manhattan to Staten Island. Wintering troops suffered from a lack of supplies due to impassable roads. As stated earlier, Providence town officials ordered able-bodied citizens to help clear the roads made impassable by snow.[39] Sgt. Greenman described the winter as "very cold and [we] almost Starved for Want of Provision and as the mens huts was near completed moved [them] up into one of the Serjeants Huts."[40] The atmosphere surrounding the winter campaign of 1779–1780 was fraught with concerns about weather, supplies, equipment, and pay. By 1780, Congress had charged each state with the responsibility of paying its own Continental Line. State governments hampered by low taxes and a depreciating currency had problems reimbursing their soldiers. This of course elicited resentment among the Continental regulars. Issues of problematic behavior spread among the rank and file throughout the encampment, resulting in courts-martial and subsequent punishments. The year started with a mutiny in the Massachusetts Line. At winter camp at West Point one hundred Massachusetts troops decided that their term of service ended on the first of January 1780 and left. They were returned to West Point. Some received punishments and the rest were pardoned.[41]

In the months leading up to Ben Frank's departure, the terms and degree of punishment for desertions had also been increased. Greenman reflected upon a new order issued by Washington in an entry dated January 18–28, 1779. The order stated that any soldier found moving about camp after reveille without a proper pass was to receive "one hundred Stripes on their Naked Back." If any soldier was suspected of "plundering" the citizenry, they were to receive "one hundred to 500 Lashes on ther back at the Descretion of the officers Commanding the Guards."[42]

Execution remained the ultimate penalty, but some commanders attempted to instill even more terror among the troops by making the circumstances of execution even more brutal. Colonel Henry "Light Horse Harry" Lee believed in terrorizing his troops to make them comply. He proposed the use of beheading to deter deserters. Washington denounced the proposed beheading to Lee in a letter dated July 9, 1779. In the correspondence, Washington stated: "The measure you propose of putting deserters from our Army to immediate death would probably tend to discourage the practice—But it ought to be executed with caution and only when the fact is very clear and unequivocal. I think that part of your proposal which respects cutting off their heads and sending them to the Light Troops had better be omitted."[43] Washington's disapproval did not arrive in time. Because, in July 1779, a few months before Ben's departure, after the capture of three deserters, Lee ordered the beheading of one. Afterward, Lee ordered the head carried back into camp by the two surviving deserters as a deterrent. General Washington immediately denounced the actions taken by Lee and ordered the end of the practice. But the damage to morale and incentive to conform was already done. Given the brutality and uniqueness of this punishment, it must have gained notoriety throughout the Continental rank and file—including among Rhode Islanders assigned to the Continental line.[44]

For Ben Frank and the First Rhode Island troops, the winter of discontent was characterized by isolation, relegation to manual labor, and harsh conditions at camp caused by lack of supplies and harsh weather. Ben and other members of the First Rhode Island Regiment were assigned to guard Newport and Providence during the winter of 1779–1780. British troops had recently evacuated Newport as their forces moved south. British officials believed they would find more material and psychological support in the southern states. As they departed Newport, British forces burned materials and resources of value, including the lighthouse on Conanicut Island. During the early part of the winter season, both Rhode Island regiments established camp on home soil. Greene and his man established a temporary base on Goat Island in Newport harbor, while Angell's regiment prepared to leave their temporary base in North Kingstown. By early December 1779, the Second Rhode Islanders were enroute to the Conti-

nental army's winter headquarters at Morristown, New Jersey, leaving the
First behind in Rhode Island, away from the main army.[45]

While stationed in isolation from the rest of the army, Washington ordered the Black regiment to construct fascines and other fortifications for
the rest of the Continental army. Did the Franks and other veterans of the
First Rhode Island perceive this change—being relegated to primarily manual labor—as a demotion in their assigned military roles? And did this
change, coupled with other poor conditions at camp, cause a tenuous and
unacceptable camp environment? In comparison, the soldiers of the Second
Rhode Island were also serving out a tough winter encampment at headquarters with Washington and the rest of the Continental army at Morristown, New Jersey. But, by June 1780 Angell and his battalion played a
serious role at the Battle of Springfield, New Jersey. The battle was pivotal
in driving the British out of that state, while the First Rhode Island was
busy constructing fortifications in their home state.[46]

A change from combat to support mode was a major shift for the Franks
and other veterans of the First Rhode Island. The reassignment and segregation of the troops allowed Rhode Island command to assign their activities
based on race. Philosopher William T. Fontaine has defined a segregated social
order as a "rigged experiment" and a method to divide whites and nonwhites
into different classifications of human beings—the nonwhite group being designated as a subclass to whites. The segregation of the Rhode Island regiments
forced soldiers of color into roles and conditions that General Washington
deemed best suited to their capabilities. They were kept in support roles close
to home even though they had already proven their capabilities on the battle-
fields at Red Bank, Turkey Hill, and Monmouth and their ability to survive
fierce winter encampments at Valley Forge and Rhode Island.[47]

The segregation also allowed military commanders to act on their own
personal biases. Washington dispatched Brigadier General William Heath
to Rhode Island in June 1780 to prepare for the arrival of the French fleet
at Newport. Washington also tasked Heath with recruiting new white enlistees from that state since Blacks were no longer allowed to enlist. Early
in the war, Heath's aversion to the use of Black soldiers was detailed in a
letter to Samuel Adams, stating that the mixing of Black and white troops
displeased him. During his time in Rhode Island, Heath argued that the
presence of Black soldiers hurt his recruitment efforts, since he believed
potential white recruits did not wish to serve in mixed race regiments. Believing that the removal of the First Rhode Island would enhance his
chances of recruiting whites and against the wishes of Colonel Greene,

Heath ordered the Black troops marched out of town to the main winter encampment. General Washington countermanded those orders and the troops returned to North Kingston.[48]

The change in the Frank brothers' conditions of service with the segregation of the Rhode Island regiments can also be seen in the reactions of white soldiers toward soldiers of the "Black Regiment." In March 1778, a Black soldier reported an assault on his person by Corporal William Cole of the Massachusetts militia regiment from Bristol County. Cole's fellow soldiers refused to allow him to be seized and punished for the offense. They were offended that a white soldier would be disciplined for an assault upon a Black man. Cole and another corporal were eventually placed in irons and their collaborators were confined. Both Cole and the second corporal were later discharged. In July 1779, a second incident involved the mutiny of members of the Second Rhode Island Regiment—the Frank brothers' former regiment. In response to a lack of pay, food, and other necessities, Second Rhode Islanders petitioned their command to rectify and improve their living conditions. Once it was perceived that assistance was not forthcoming, they proceeded to march without orders from their encampment at Warren. When informed that the "Black Regiment" was being dispatched to stop their mutinous march, a leader of the mutiny stated that "we do not fear you with all your black boys!"[49] The mutiny ended with the jailing of its leaders, the pardoning of most participants, and the receipt of back pay to the members of the Second Rhode Island.[50]

The 1779–1780 winter encampment of the First Rhode Island Regiment at Rhode Island Village was rife with difficulties. Of course, the First Rhode Island Regiment was also beset with the poor living conditions suffered by the Second Rhode Island Regiment. Another issue was driven by a lack of supplies and what Greene described as "detestable practices" committed by the men under his command. Colonel Greene described theft as the prevailing problem in camp. He wrote to headquarters:

> I have been very severe in punishment for stealing but almost to no purpose. There has hardly been a week, interval, during the winter, but more or less have been detected in Stealing, Breaking in to Shops, and Stores. I greatly fear they will not be broke of the detestable practice unless capital punishment takes place. . . . I should be very happy if companies of my Regt. was called from the State to join the Army, as I am very confident they would be of more Service to the Public when carried from their acquaintances and conections . . . and . . . Stealing would be less prevalent.[51]

Greene's description of the unacceptable attitudes existing at Rhode Island Village can be attributed to one of two factors: a complete breakdown of discipline and protocol on the part of the rank and file and/or complete malfeasance on the part of the military administration to supply its soldiers with food and other supplies. Whatever the reasons, the conditions at Rhode Island Village were distressing enough to warrant its commanding officer to call for the use of capital punishment to deter and control his subordinates. Additionally, the conditions were so unbearable that some members of the First Rhode Island left.

One soldier stood at the intersection of theft and desertion—Winsor Fry, a comrade of Ben Frank. Fry's actions at winter camp brought him to the attention of Colonel Greene as a member of the group wreaking havoc in the regiment. As stated earlier, Winsor Fry was found guilty of "plundering the commissary store and stealing a quantity of beef, candles, and rum; and breaking open two windmills and stealing a quantity of meal."[52] According to Greene's correspondence to Washington, Fry was "The one whose trial I have sent has been several times whipt for Stealing, so no purpose in reclaiming him. . . . I think him as a proper subject" for capital punishment. Fry deserted twice during this period—an initial court-martial was overruled by General Washington. A second trial sentenced him to death. Upon Fry's being retaken Colonel Greene interceded on his behalf calling for leniency—which saved Fry's life and military career. Fry served in good standing till the end of the war and received an honorable discharge.[53]

It was not unusual for command officers to intercede on their subordinates' behalf, including the Rhode Island commanders. The Franks' former commander, Israel Angell, understood how the morale and loyalty of his troops were affected by poor conditions and lack of support from public officials. Two years before the tough encampment at Rhode Island Village, Angell lamented to the governor of Rhode Island that "Not one half of them can not be termed fit for duty on any immergency; of those, who of them went with me on a late expedition . . . many were barefoot . . . 5 of them there deserted to ye enemy which I have reason to believe was principles owing to ye non fulfillment of engagements on ye part of ye state."[54] In a similar fashion, Greene's intercession on Fry's behalf may have been prompted by his understanding of why his troops were "acting out." Greene understood that the proximity to families and friends had a deleterious effect on his soldiers, but he may have also understood that being singularly isolated from the main body of the army also had a detrimental effect on his troops.[55]

Did the disruptive activities of disgruntled soldiers of the First Rhode Island originate from the "non fulfillment" of promises from the state? The reasons for the discontent may have started with the enactment of the Slave Enlistment Act. Prior to the act, as stated earlier, only two members of the fifty-four documented free soldiers of color, Toby Coys and John Daniels, deserted. Robert Allen's departure in March 1778 was the harbinger of things to come. Private Allen was a member of the original First Rhode Island Regiment and as such did not have to acclimate to new command. He served a seven-day stretch "on command" in January, two months before his leaving. But his departure took place after the passage of the Slave Enlistment Act. Of course, the conditions at the Valley Forge encampment also played a significant role in his departure. Allen would rejoin his comrades in August and served for a total of five years and eleven months. At war's end, he was granted an honorary badge for "long and faithful service."[56] Cuff Peckham left in August 1778, prior to the winter of discontent. Like Ben Frank, he enlisted in the spring of 1777 and initially served with the Second Rhode Island in Captain Hughes' company. Like Ben, he survived the winter at Valley Forge and had to adjust to new command and regiment mates. George Thompkins and Louden Thompson, also survivors of Valley Forge, both enlisted in 1777 and deserted in 1779. The departures of Allen, Peckham, Thompkins, and Thompson may have signaled the effects of the Slave Enlistment Act, which prompted the segregation of the regiments and/or signaled the growing frustration on the part of young men who joined the service looking for opportunity and equality.[57]

Up to the winter of discontent, Ben Frank and other soldiers of color who had transferred from the Second Rhode Island seemed willing to accept their reassignments, based on their rate of desertion and other behavior. Up to this point, they were given similar assignments as their counterparts in the Second Rhode Island Regiment. But for whatever reasons and purposes, General Washington and the Rhode Island military administration decided to assign Rhode Island soldiers based on race. This reassignment/realignment led to different treatment—assignment to support functions as opposed to more traditional camp life—culminating in the winter of discontent. But by the winter of 1779–1780, some of these soldiers were affected by the change and took action to leave it. Fifteen previously free members of the First Rhode Island left in 1780, more than half of the total number of documented deserters from the regiment during this period. And most left during the winter encampment of 1779–1780. Eleven deserted from March to June 1780; three more left in July. In comparison, a survey of 111 transferees from the First Rhode Island to the Second list twenty-three white soldiers who deserted after the realignment of the Rhode Island troops. Four deserted in 1780, the year of Ben Frank's departure. Five departed in 1778 and thirteen in 1779. By the winter of discontent, the average length of service for the men of color who enlisted before the Slave Enlistment Act was two and a half to three years—almost three times as long as the average of six months to one year for the Continental hardcore regular. The Frank brothers and other members of their regiment had participated in major expeditions and two major battles of the war. They suffered with diseases and illnesses at camp. And they suffered casualties from battles. Some members of the regiment lost their lives. But only three deserted before 1780.[58]

Others followed Ben Frank's departure. James Daley left in April from Captain Thomas Cole's company—Ben Frank's assigned company. Daley's service record is unblemished but for his desertion. Like the Frank brothers, Daley enlisted in early 1777. He served continuously from that time until his departure. He does not reappear on the muster rolls of the First Rhode Island Regiment after his departure from the winter encampment at Rhode Island Village. Like Ben, he did not return to service with the Rhode Island Continentals.[59] His desertion appeared in the *American Journal and General Advertiser,* dated Providence, April 11, 1780:

> DESERTED from Col. C. GREENE'S regiment, one JAMES DAILEY, an Indian, about 24 years of age, five feet nine inches high, was born at Warwick, in this State; has black hair; had on a red coat faced with white but as he took with him a light coloured coat he may perhaps change his dress. He is strait built. Whoever will take up said deserter, and send him to the regiment, at Providence, or secure him in any goal, shall receive fifty dollars reward, and all reasonable charges paid by, DAVID JOHNSON, Lieut.[60]

Solomon Wanton, the husband of Hannah Frank Wanton, deserted in May 1780. He enlisted for Continental service in April 1777—the same month and year as his brother-in-law William Frank. Both enlisted at Tiverton, where Solomon was a lifelong resident and member of a large Wanton family. Solomon's departure in the spring of 1780 came after three years of service strewn with various bouts of illness. He had already received one leave of absence in July 1778—during the period of reorganization of the Rhode Island troops after the implementation of the Slave Enlistment Act. Wanton fled his duty with Cole's company two months after the recorded desertion of his brother-in-law. However, unlike his brother-in-law, Solomon was "retaken" in December 1780. He died later at Wilmington, Delaware, on December 28, 1781.[61]

For months after Ben's departure, other men of color continued to leave their service. Richard Potter, Frances Gould, and Jonathan Charles all deserted in July. Potter enlisted in 1777 and left on July 3, 1780. There were no incidents of disciplinary action against Potter prior to his departure. However, in 1778, two years before his "desertion," Potter was sick in camp, at Valley Forge and then Camp Paramus in New Jersey. But he did not shy away from his service with the First Rhode Island Regiment in his sworn pension application. He highlighted his presence at the Battles of Red Bank and Rhode Island and his discharge from service at East Greenwich three years after his enlistment. Potter also received a pension.[62] Frank Gould left on the same date as Potter. He enlisted in January 1777 for the duration of the war. He served in the companies of Wallen and Cole. And at one point in November 1778, he was under guard for an unknown reason.[63] Gould did return to service. He "joined from desertion 1 November 1781."[64] Jonathan Charles enlisted in the spring of 1777 for the duration of the war. His desertion took place at the end of July 1780. He struggled with illness during his tenure with the First Rhode Islanders. During the summer campaign of 1778, he spent time in the hospital and was "sick present" the following summer of 1779. The desertion is Charles' last action as a Continental regular. His service record is quiet after July 1780.[65]

Gideon Harry of Charlestown also departed in the spring of 1780, the same period as Ben Frank. Harry had enlisted in 1777 and served continuously until his departure from Captain Cole's company. He rejoined his company in March of the following year. However, he did not stay long. He left again in May 1781. His second desertion did not last long. He returned to his regiment and served until the end of the war, serving as a member of Olney's regiment "at the capture of Cornwallis."[66] Harry received his monthly pension of eight dollars starting in November 1819.[67]

James Greene had deserted by June 1780. Greene served as a member of the Rhode Island militia during the *rage militaire* period in 1775. His length of service with Rhode Island troops was longer than most of his comrades except for Winsor Fry. After returning from his desertion, Greene served until he was honorably discharged in 1782.[68]

Injury and illness also affected some members of the First Rhode Island Regiment who left military service. Ben Frank had suffered some type of ailment in October 1778, while his regiment was wintering in Rhode Island. He was "sick, but present." Jonathan Charles was sick at Princeton in June 1778. He was ill in the hospital during the late summer of 1778 and was "sick present" approximately one year before his desertion. James Daley was also "sick present" in August 1778—a month that saw several members of the First Rhode Island ill or hospitalized. Winsor Fry was "sick present" in January and February 1778. Richard Potter suffered an illness at Camp Valley Forge during the winter encampment of 1777–1778. He had not recovered from his illness by June 1778 when reassigned to Camp Paramus, New Jersey. Ben also saw the suffering of other family members. His brother-in-law, Solomon Wanton, was sick a number of times throughout his service with the Rhode Island line. Wanton was "sick absent" in January and February 1778. He spent time in the hospital in August 1777 and 1778. These illnesses culminated in his death in December 1781.[69]

Solomon Wanton's death did not affect Ben Frank's decision to leave, since Solomon died a year after Ben's departure. However, the death of another comrade did occur a few short months before Ben's departure. William Coopin of Charlestown, Rhode Island, died in January 1780. His career with the Rhode Island regiments mirrored Ben Frank's. Both young men enlisted in the spring of 1777—Coopin in March and Ben in May. Both initially served with the Second Rhode Island Regiment, comrades in the company of Captain Thomas Hughes. Both transferred to the First Rhode Island upon the integration of the formerly enslaved into the Rhode Island regiments. As a member of Captain Cole's company, Coopin served in the same segregated unit as Ben Frank. But the similarities stop there. William Coopin dealt with persistent illnesses during his service, starting in March 1778. "Sick present" or "sick absent" defined his service from March 1778 until December 1779. For a brief period in August 1779, Coopin nursed his illness while under guard at East Greenwich, Rhode Island. The two months before his death, William was listed as "sick absent" from his assignment in Newport, Rhode Island—an indication that he may have been hospitalized at Providence, where he died in January 1780. The loss of Coopin as a comrade must have had an impact on Ben Frank. The two had served continuously together since the beginning of their careers with the Rhode Island Continentals. Coopin's death and Ben's departure seem connected.[70]

Ben Frank's self-furlough was a complex and complicated decision, reflecting the diverse factors and conditions that influenced other Revolutionary War soldiers to leave. A combination of professional and personal factors drove him to leave his brother and other colleagues and follow a path into unknown territory.

Specific conditions in Ben Frank's professional life may have caused his desertion. As stated before, the lack of food, equipment, and supplies was common throughout his career as a regular with the Rhode Island Line. Pay was insufficient and irregular. His early years with the Second Rhode Island were filled with disease-plagued encampments, poor clothing and equipment, and disdain from the public. His own brother was declared unfit for duty during the early part of his career with the Second Rhode Island Regiment. Ben had lived through one harsh winter. He had survived two brutal battles, where several battalion mates had been killed. He probably felt troubled when he was reassigned to an all-Black regiment and assigned to support services—a major change in the circumstances of his service.

Can Ben's departure be considered an act of protest and defiance? Yes. His desertion may have been the result of several factors: surviving deteriorating conditions at winter camp; battle fatigue after the fights at Red Bank and Turkey Hill; and the reorganization of the First Rhode Island and his subsequent transfer. Additionally, at the time of self-furlough, Ben's original term of service was coming to an end. He originally enlisted in May 1777. A three-year term of service was almost completed but not soon enough for Ben. Military documents note that Ben enlisted for the duration of the war, but he may have thought he had enlisted for three years, as his brother had.

Ambiguity regarding the actual length of promised service sometimes resulted in conflicts between enlisted men and their superiors, and some enlisted men left service at the end of three years in defiance of the expectations and demands of their superior officers. Members of the Rhode Island regiments were included in this ambiguity and defiance. The desertion of Josiah Sole is an example of how terms of enlistment may have been misunderstood by enlisted men. Josiah enlisted in March 1777 and records show that he enlisted for the duration of the war. He is carried as deserted in March 1780—three years after his initial enlistment. Was this desertion? Sometimes these absences resulted in unwarranted charges of desertion, sometimes not.[71] Colonel Israel Angell spoke to this issue in his journal: "some soldiers in the regiment who not having the good of the service in view are frequently complaining in a very unwarranted manner about their enlisted and even threatening to leave or desert the service after the expiration of three years, although their enlistments are during the war . . . all those who are the least dissatisfied or in doubt about the term for which he enlisted are assured there has been a fair and impartial examination of all the enlistments that are collect and that no non-commissioned officer or soldier is returned for any other term of service than what is expressly mentioned in his enlistment."[72] If Ben and Josiah, like the soldiers of the Massachusetts Line, believed they were being unfairly detained in military service with the Continentals, their acts of desertion could be seen as acts of protest or defiance.[73]

Homesickness cannot be used to explain Ben's flight from the Continental army. He, along with the rest of the First Rhode Island Regiment, were stationed in their home state in the first months of 1780. Ben had enlisted at Providence three years earlier. His family maintained their residence in Johnston, Rhode Island, a village created out of the northwest corner of Providence. His new wife and child lived in Providence. And he was serving alongside a family member, his brother.

Were there specific conditions that existed in Ben's personal life to cause his departure? Yes. In all likelihood, as a fifteen-year-old enlistee, he was not ready to follow in the footsteps of his father and older brother. He may have had a falling-out with his brother, although if that were the primary cause, he could simply have asked for reassignment to another company in the Black regiment. The pressure of family and married life was certainly one of the pivotal factors for Ben's leaving. As an eighteen-year-old, it is likely that he was not prepared mentally or emotionally to deal with the double stress of military and family responsibilities. His wife Sarah Frank petitioned the Providence Town Council for aid in the first year of their marriage. Additionally, she had a child that Ben had to provide for. Ben carried the burden of providing financial support for his family with inconsistent and insufficient pay from the army. Upholding the family name and maintaining his own family's well-being may have been too tough a burden for this eighteen-year-old young man.

Once the decision was made to leave, Ben must have realized that his options were severely limited. His brother could not help him. His father probably would not help him. And his wife did not have the resources to help him. William's continued service and loyalty to the First Rhode Island prevented him from helping his brother escape or giving him financial assistance. In all likelihood, Rufus was the primary example and reason for Ben's enlistment, so Ben would have been unlikely to request aid or run home to a father who may have disapproved of his actions. Rufus, a veteran of the French and Indian War, probably could not have understood one son's motivation for leaving military service while another son was still in harm's way. The Continental army had also initiated a campaign of shaming soldiers to keep them from deserting. This campaign proclaimed that deserters cheated their country, failed others who depended on them, and proved themselves to be cowards. Some "deserters" fought back by claiming that they had been fraudulently recruited, cheated, or legally discharged. Ben may have been able to make a legitimate claim of lack of pay and supplies, but the claims of bad enlistment or legal discharge would not hold with a father who had military experience.[74]

If Ben's plan had been to reunite with Sarah, the prospects of capture and shame may have been frightening enough to forestall any attempt to return to his wife. By March 1780 Sarah Frank had already requested aid from the Providence Town Council for herself and her child, indicating Ben was unable to provide support from his meager pay. If his departure was part of a plan to divorce his wife due to marital problems or overwhelming pressure to take care of his family, then a flight away from Rhode Island was Ben's original intent.

Once he left, Ben may have found it difficult to return to military service with the Continentals. Ben had firsthand information regarding the punishment given to deserters. He must have understood that any intention to join the enemy could be punished by death. Since the beginning of the war, the number of soldiers condemned to die had steadily increased. James Fergus, a member of the Pennsylvania militia, recounted an incident that occurred in May 1778. Four deserters—two white, one mulatto, and one Black—were captured and put to death on order of the governor who ordered: "hang them up to the beam of the gate."[75] In 1779, the year prior to Ben's desertion, the overall number of capital cases increased to twenty-nine—33 percent over the 1776 number. Thomas Dexter was one of the fortunate ones. A member of Colonel Israel Angell's regiment, he was court-martialed in 1780 for desertion to the enemy and received a penalty of one hundred lashes and was also forced to make up the time lost during his desertion. The fact that Dexter survived a desertion to the enemy may not have been proof enough for Ben to return to his unit. He knew from experience that others had been punished harshly. During Ben's first year of service with the Second Rhode Island Regiment, a member of Colonel Greene's battalion, his current commander, was shot for desertion. This incident must have made a disturbing impression on a young soldier.[76]

If Ben could not return home, then a viable option was flight to the British. The number of Blacks that fled to British forces numbered in the tens of thousands. Many Blacks, however, showed a reluctance to fight with British forces. A British officer assigned in Rhode Island in 1778 was surprised at the low number of Blacks that had joined British troops, even with the promise of pay and provisions. The British army continued to make appeals throughout the war to Continental regulars to desert to their cause. They offered money and other incentives to draw unhappy Continental soldiers from American regiments.[77]

In the case of African Americans, Dunmore's proclamation, promising freedom to enslaved men who fought for the British cause, was followed by General Clinton's proclamation at Philipsburg, New York on June 30, 1779 (the Philipsburg Proclamation). Granted that the proclamation primarily referred to slaves, both free and enslaved Blacks fled to the British. Clinton ordered that captured Black soldiers or "auxiliaries be purchased for the public service."[78] He also proclaimed that Blacks who deserted to the British cause would have "full security to follow any occupation he wished while in the British lines."[79] Land had also been promised to British regulars and could apply to Black "soldiers," as well. Ben Frank may have been skeptical that Americans would win and suspected that they would not be able to fulfill their promises of money and land. American forces had suffered a string of defeats, some of which he personally witnessed. Even with France's entry into war on the side of the Americans, Ben may have been unconvinced of their fidelity since he was a victim (witness) of French forces' lack of fortitude at the Battle of Rhode Island. Ben may have believed that the British had a greater likelihood of winning the war and thus fulfilling any promises made to their soldiers.

Ben Frank disappears from the military records after his departure. Family lore and records dictate that he reappears as Ben Franklin in Nova Scotia after the war. In October 1782 he was named on the passenger list of the brig *Elijah* bound for Nova Scotia. His lot was now cast with members of the loyalist exodus, leaving to make new lives in what is now present-day Canada. He was leaving behind his family and the only life that he had ever known. He was now separated from a brother at whose side he had fought for three years. This brother stayed behind to uphold the family name and military tradition in America. William Frank chose to continue his service with a fledgling army and country.[80]

CHAPTER EIGHT

Brothers Divided:
the Frank Brothers in the Final Years
of the Revolutionary War

B EN FRANK'S FAITH IN AN American victory was challenged by his professional and personal experiences during the war. The American government's inability to care for its servicemen and their families was a factor
in his departure. The losses on the battlefield and in camp probably caused
Ben to lose faith in the new country's ability to win and allow its soldiers
to reap the benefits of their service—compensation in money, land, and
honor. And the segregation of the Rhode Island regiments may have affected Ben's belief in the new country's ability to provide him a true sense
of equality. As Ben threw his lot in with the British cause, the now divided
wartime experiences of the Frank brothers allow for an examination of how
service for Blacks played out on the British as well as the American side.
Did the Frank brothers have parallel experiences or was one experience better than the other? What is noteworthy about their divided experiences is
the role that race played in their lives for the rest of the war. William's service and military experience came full circle from integrated to segregated
to some semblance of integration while Ben's experiences continued to be
affected by formerly enslaved individuals who had fled to the British lines
in search of freedom.

W ILLIAM F RANK probably felt compelled to remain with the Continental army for the entire duration of the war, to uphold the family name and to protect his own chance for land or money. Did William have a stronger belief that military service with the American forces would open the doors for better economic and occupational opportunities? William's continued service with the Rhode Island Continentals is evidence of his belief in America's ability to win the war. He reenlisted in February 1781 for the duration of the war and served with Rhode Island forces until the end of the conflict in fulfillment of his contract.

William's actions may have been influenced by a tradition of military service among Frank men in the colonial era. As stated earlier, his father served in various campaigns during the French and Indian War. Andrew Frank, a probable relative from Providence County, served as a member of the Rhode Island militia during the Revolutionary War. William's unblemished military record reflected his father's service during the French and Indian War. Additionally, the revolutionary era's vision of Black masculinity may not have allowed him to buckle under to the pressures and harshness of army life. Weakness of this sort did not have a place in this ideal of Black manhood. He prevailed even with the loss of his brother-in-law, Solomon Wanton, and other comrades. He suffered through the indignity of being "unfit for duty." He survived the ferocious winter encampment at Valley Forge and a turbulent winter season at Rhode Island Village. He was not influenced by the actions of his brother and other deserters from the Rhode Island regiments. He remained committed to his service with the Continental regulars regardless of harsh conditions and segregated service.[1]

William was not alone in his continued service. The departure of his brother and other free men of color did not seem to diminish the patriotic spirit of William Frank and the remaining Black soldiers of the Rhode Island regiments. He and others maintained their belief in what military service could mean to their adult lives. What were the sustaining motivations that kept William and others on the side of the patriots? Unit cohesion and solidarity among soldiers who served for long periods of time together was motivation to continue service. Since the First Rhode Island was reorganized into a primarily all-Black unit, the soldiers also had the bond of racial identity and common life experiences to tie them together. This was not enough for almost half of the freemen of the First Rhode Island who, like Ben Frank, left the patriot cause at one point or another, but the remaining soldiers stayed committed to the cause and to each other. Maurice O. Wallace argues that Black men sought to "link their manliness to the building of nationhood."[2] These feelings of solidarity, loyalty, and patriotism fortified the beliefs and actions of William and others. Whatever the reasons and motivations, the brothers would not serve together again. Even though he lost the companionship of his brother, William still served and fought alongside several members from the original group of over fifty free men of color, who enlisted prior to the Slave Enlistment Act. If William was affected by Ben's departure, it did not evidence itself in negative actions. There is no documented discipline or absence without leave on his record during this period. He and his fellow soldiers received pay from the State of Rhode Island on December 26, 1780, while continuing in their guard duty in their home state. They patrolled throughout the state from Providence to Newport, especially after the British evacuation of that port in late 1779.[3]

The First Rhode Islanders must have been disheartened upon their arrival at Newport. The city was "but a shadow of what it was before the war." The city was rendered into a "state of great depression." The state house was in ruins since British troops had turned the building into barracks. All the churches were "desecrated," and over four hundred buildings had been destroyed.[4] William and the First Rhode Islanders had returned to a ruined city, a city that they were unable to free two years before. The following July of 1780, the Comte de Rochambeau arrived in Newport with 4,000 French troops. An officer with Rochambeau's troops described a member of the First Rhode Island as wearing a cast-off French waistcoat with long sleeves and red cuffs, as well as the waved helmet with bluish plumes.[5] With the arrival of Rochambeau, the defense of Rhode Island was turned over to French troops. However, William and the First Rhode Island Regiment remained in the state throughout the summer.

In October 1780, Congress reorganized the army, reducing the number of infantry regiments from eighty to fifty. The two Rhode Island regiments were consolidated into one. With this consolidation, Colonel Israel Angell of the Second Rhode Island retired. Colonel Christopher Greene moved into the leadership of the consolidated battalion. Colonel Greene and his First Rhode Islanders were ordered to West Point to effect the merger with the Second Rhode Island.[6]

The consolidation of the two regiments did not affect at least two members of the First Rhode Island. Private Charles Henly is listed on the Return of Freemen muster roll and enlisted at the same time as the slave recruitment program of early 1778. Henly served in Captain Thomas Cole's company—the same company as the Franks. From March 1779 until April 1780, Henly suffered various bouts of illnesses and eventually died in May 1780 during encampment at Rhode Island Village. A second private, Asa Gardner, died on October 26, 1780, before the merger, while the regiment was still on patrol in its home state. There are no details regarding his demise in the military records, so the circumstances of his passing are hard to determine. His death is not attributed to injury or wounds and there is no indication of illness in his service record. He died of some type of illness in camp since the battalion was not involved in any meaningful skirmishes during this period.[7]

The service of Henly and Gardner was both similar and dissimilar to William Frank. All entered the service as free men. However, Gardner and Henly started and ended their tenure as members of the segregated "Black Regiment," unlike William Frank, who began his career as a member of an integrated battalion. Both enlisted in early 1778, while Colonel Greene and others diligently worked to recruit enslaved men as soldiers. Gardner, a free man, had served previously with Colonel Topham's regiment of the Rhode Island State Brigade in 1776. He left his service with the Rhode Island Continentals on January 28, 1779, but returned shortly thereafter, being put on guard duty for Captain Dexter's company in February 1779. He served without incident from that date until his death.[8]

William and his surviving comrades marched across frozen roads in December 1780 to meet the Second Rhode Island Regiment at West Point. Upon their arrival, the tale of the "Black Regiment" came to an end. William and the remaining African American soldiers of the First Rhode Island became members of the integrated and consolidated First and Second Rhode Island Regiment. Segregation remained, however. William and other soldiers of color served in two segregated companies within the new consolidated regiment. Many of them, William included, approached their fourth year of service, and became the more experienced soldiers in the consolidated battalion. William had come full circle in his service with the First Rhode Island Regiment. He began his service as a member of an integrated regiment and ended his military service as a member of the integrated and consolidated regiment. Of the thirty-five men of color originally listed on the "Return of Freemen," seventeen previously free Black and Native American soldiers remained on the rolls and included Edward Anthony Jr., Simon Barton, Joseph Boyer, Prince Childs, Toby Coys, Peter Dailey, Ceasar Finch, Winsor Fry, Pharaoh Hazzard, Prince Limas, Jacob Ned,

Toney Phillips, Thomas Reynolds, Cuff Roberts, George Rogers, Elijah Waggs, and Solomon Wanton.[9]

William Frank continued to witness losses to Rhode Island troops due to desertions. These departures did not stop after the winter encampment at Rhode Island Village. Several freemen also left in the aftermath of the consolidation of Rhode Island Continental regiments. For instance, Edward Anthony left in November 1780. He had served without blemish and interruption of service since April 1777. He began his service with the Second Rhode Island Regiment the same month as William Frank. At one point in their service, William Frank and Edward Anthony served together as members of Captain Thomas Cole's company. Anthony originally enlisted for a term of three years. Private Anthony received a furlough during the winter of Valley Forge and escaped the horrors of that encampment. He did not, however, escape the brutality of Rhode Island Village during the winter of 1779–1780. He continued his service after the expiration of his original term of service—after April 1780. He did not return nor was he retaken into service after his departure in November 1780. He, like Ben Frank, did not return to service with his comrades of the Rhode Island regiments.[10]

Three more members of the original group of freemen followed the example of Ben Frank and Edward Anthony in 1781. Cuff Roberts left in February 1781. Roberts had enlisted in March 1778 at Westerly, Rhode Island, as part of the recruitment effort initiated by the Slave Enlistment Act. Cuff's absence without leave in 1781 lasted for only a short duration. He was retaken in September of the same year. After his desertion and return to service, Private Roberts remained with his regiment until the end of the war.[11] Rueben Roberts ran off in June 1781. He had enlisted for the duration of the war three years earlier on February 20, 1778. Roberts returned to service and worked toward rehabilitating his reputation as a soldier. He earned an honorary badge with reputation in 1782. Elijah Waggs also felt the need to take a respite from his military tenure with the Rhode Island Continentals. He enlisted in May 1777. He left on January 6, 1781, and returned to service on March 1, 1782. He then served continuously until relieved of duty at the end of the war.[12]

The last soldiers on the list, Cuff Roberts, Rueben Roberts, and Elijah Waggs, returned to duty with the Rhode Island Continentals and continued in that service until the end of the war. They represent the typical profile of desertion exemplified by the free-born men of color who served with the "Black Regiment" and later the Rhode Island consolidated troops. What do the desertion records of these men say about their service? As stated in the previous chapter, it was difficult for command officers to accurately document deserters under their command. Most of the deserters (over half) returned to service, either by force or voluntarily. And many continued to serve with distinction or without further blemish to their records for the duration of the war. Most of these men had already served three years with the Rhode Island Continentals prior to their desertion. It is interesting to note that most left remarkably close to their three-year anniversary dates, suggesting that they believed their term of service ended at the three-year mark. However, they soon realized that others did not share their belief, since they voluntarily returned to their regiments or were retaken by force. Eight of the deserters experienced some type of sickness in camp prior to their desertion date. Three died after their return from desertion. The surviving free-born men of the "Black Regiment" endured the cruelties of war by leaving their military responsibilities—temporarily or permanently. But their use of desertion as a coping mechanism does not lessen their original commitment—as illustrated in their average length of service before desertion of three years and their continued service for the duration of the war, as evidenced by the more than half of the deserters who returned to duty. These men continued to serve with William Frank until the end of the war.[13]

In the spring of 1781, William and members of the Rhode Island consolidated regiment suffered another loss when their unit took up defensive positions in Westchester County, New York. The area was home to daily confrontations between loyalist and American troops, which continued in the region. The area was not heavily populated since most families were run off due to the foraging of loyalist troops to the south and Continental forces to the north. Major-General Heath ordered Colonel Greene and the consolidated regiment to guard Pines Bridge that spanned the Croton River against loyalist troops led by Colonel James Delancey—known as Delancey's Refugees, composed of American-born soldiers who resided in Westchester County and had chosen to remain loyal to the British cause.[14]

Sergeant Jeremiah Greenman, assigned to bridge duty, became a party to one of the most infamous incidents to occur in the history of the Rhode Island regiments. His guard was on duty the morning of May 14, 1781, when a group of loyalists crossed the river and surprised soldiers of the Rhode Island Regiment while in camp. Greenman's entry for that date is poignant:

> This morning was alarmed by the appearance of a party of Cavalry supported by Infantry, which proved to be Delancey's Corps of

Refugees/they soon surrounded me and being vastly surperiour in force—& having no prospect of escape, I thought it most adviseable to surrender myself and Guard prisoners of War—They informed me they had taken two officers from the Colo. Quarters, that he was Mortally Wounded & Major Flagg killed.[15]

Delancey and his troops had been acting as raiders in the area for some time. Their attack upon the Rhode Island Regiment's headquarters was typical of their tactics. On the occasion of the surprise attack, Delancey and his raiders attacked the headquarters at the Davenport House, near Pines Bridge, in the early morning hours. Some members of the regiment surrendered, but Colonel Greene and Major Ebenezer Flagg decided to fight. Flagg was killed immediately. Other members of the Rhode Island Regiment were killed or suffered injuries in an attempt to fight off the attacks. Their attempts were not successful. Greene's wounded and dying body was strapped to a horse and dragged about a mile toward British lines. Eventually, Delancey's troops left the colonel's body at the side of the road, and he was later buried, along with Flagg, at a site near their headquarters at Pines Bridge. This brutal attack by Delancey's loyalists deprived many of the Rhode Island Continentals of the only commander they had known.[16]

It also robbed the Rhode Island Regiment of several members, including one of the original thirty-five free men of color. Primus Childs enlisted in the spring of 1777, at the same time as William Frank. Childs served with William and Ben Frank in Captain Cole's company during the winter of change—when the Rhode Island regiments became segregated to incorporate enslaved men recruited because of the Slave Enlistment Act. Primus was one of the soldiers ambushed and killed during the attack. He died May 23, 1781, due to wounds received on the evening of the attack. Other Black soldiers also lost their lives in defense of themselves and their commander. The formerly enslaved Africa Burk, Cato Bannister, and Simon Whipple were also killed during the assault. The loss of Primus Childs probably had a greater personal impact on William Frank and other hardcore soldiers of color of the Rhode Island regiments than the loss of their colonel. William's relationship with Primus as a comrade-in-arms more than likely overshadowed any relationship with Colonel Greene.[17]

The death of Colonel Greene has provided fodder for quite different historical interpretations. Michael Lee Lanning asserts that the attack upon Greene was unusually violent. Greene's body was mutilated with swords and bayonets during his death ride toward the British lines. Lanning argues that this level of violence resulted from the loyalists' anger against the colonel for his leadership of the African American regiment.[18] While Lanning suggests that Greene was a victim of racism, Sidney Rider asserts that Greene was a victim of his own soldiers' ineptitude—a stereotype that had followed the "Black Regiment" since its inception. Rider claims that: "The attack on Colonel Greene was a surprise, by a few cavalry made in the night upon the rear of the battalion; had these 'faithful guard of blacks' been attending to their duty they would not have been surprised."[19] Rider's interpretation of the event does not factor in the loss of life on the part of the Rhode Island regulars and Greenman's description of the event. As a member of the "faithful guard of blacks," Private Primus Childs gave his life for the protection of his regiment. Sergeant Greenman's depiction of the raid does not agree with Rider's assessment. Greenman and his detail were equally surprised by Delancey's retreat from Pines Bridge. Greenman decided it was better to surrender than fight. As a result, he became a prisoner of the British for five months in Long Island.[20] And, he was not the only captive taken that night. Private Peter Dailey was also taken. Dailey's captivity lasted until September of that year.[21] William Frank must have known Private Peter Dailey, since he was a fellow member of the First Rhode Island and listed on the "Return of Freemen."[22]

William Frank's involvement in this affair is unclear. He was not killed, and he was not listed as sick or injured on muster rolls following the incident. He was not taken as a prisoner of war with Greenman and Dailey. He may have been one of the surrendering soldiers or he may have been fortunate enough to survive a fight with the raiding loyalists.

Lieutenant Colonel Jeremiah Olney took command of the regiment after the death of Colonel Greene. Olney had assisted in the recruitment of enslaved men for the reorganized "Black Regiment." The regiment became known as Olney's regiment. Jeremiah Olney's attitude about the Black soldiers under his command seemed to reflect the sensibilities of the time. The Rhode Island Assembly had already reversed the Slave Enlistment Act—forbidding the recruitment and enlistment of slaves for their regiments. Other state governments followed suit, restricting men of color from military service. By the end of the war, New England states excluded Blacks and Native Americans from militia service, which mirrored their exclusion from federal service as well. Olney's actions in 1781 and 1782 reflected this mindset to reduce the participation of men of color in military service. In January 1781, while mustering for troops in East Greenwich and Providence, Olney stipulated that Blacks would not be accepted. A year later in 1782, Olney reported the stereotypical notion that Blacks, Native Americans, and mulattoes failed as good soldiers and should not be recruited. The reality of command must have perplexed Olney because he commanded a group of soldiers of color whose skills he denigrated. But regardless of his assessment of his troops, Olney still commanded an integrated regiment not meeting its mandated numbers. The authorized strength of the regiment was 650 troops with nine musket companies. The actual strength of the regiment fluctuated between 400 and 450. After the promotion of Olney, William Frank remained assigned to the company of Captain Thomas Cole.[23]

Regardless of their commander's attitude toward them, William and other soldiers of the Rhode Island Regiment welcomed good news in the form of better clothing and supplies. Vendors came to the camps with goods to sell and were able to deal directly with commanding officers. Additionally, soldiers visited nearby towns to purchase much-needed supplies. For the first time since the beginning of the war, soldiers were properly clothed. William received his share of his regiment's good fortune. It now appeared that the government could and would supply their needs.[24]

In September 1781, William Frank and the rest of Olney's regiment marched south with Washington's main force to encircle Cornwallis and the British forces at Yorktown, Virginia. Washington chose 2,500 of his best troops to make this march. Olney's regiment was part of the group.[25] Private Samuel Smith described their arrival at Yorktown in the following manner:

> The next march we made was to Yorktown, where we encamped within half cannon shot of the British, and commenced a fortification by digging a trench, or rather by each man digging a hole deep enough to drop into. When this was accomplished, we stationed a man to watch the enemy's guns, at which every man dropped into his hole. But we soon left this ground, and in the night stormed two of their fortifications, and dug a trench all round the British encampment, completely yarding them in.[26]

The siege of Yorktown lasted from September 30 to October 18, 1781. Rhode Island regulars participated in a variety of attacks and counterattacks against the enemy, and they shared the task of digging and manning trenches, which were built increasingly closer to the British lines. As the Rhode Islanders dug and built, British forces returned heavy fire against their entrenchment attempts, resulting in injuries to soldiers assigned to the Rhode Island Regiment. Formerly enslaved Bristol Rhodes suffered the loss of an arm and a leg during the siege.[27]

Additionally, Rhode Island troops participated in the assault of redoubts surrounding Yorktown. The capture of Redoubts 9 and 10 would help American and French forces fire directly upon Yorktown. As part of this excursion, light infantry members of the Rhode Island Regiment, led by Captain Stephen Olney, a member of the extended Olney family, participated in the assault of Redoubt 10 and were successful. Olney described the results of the assault in the following manner: "My company, which consisted of about forty, suffered . . . only five or six wounded, all slightly, except Peter Barrows, who had a ball pass through the under jaw; I believe we had none killed." The performance of the Black soldiers of the Rhode Island regiments at Yorktown did not go unnoticed. Baron Ludwig von Closen, a German officer serving with French troops fighting with the Americans, noted that many members of the Rhode Island regiments were Black soldiers and that they were smartly dressed and precise in their maneuvers.[28]

The British surrender at Yorktown on October 19, 1781, did not mean the end of the war and service for Olney's regiment or William Frank. British forces in New York, Savannah, and Charleston did not surrender and continued the fight. At this point in its history, only three hundred soldiers carried muskets in Rhode Island's Continental regiment. An army inspector's report detailed that the regiment needed seven ensigns, nine sergeants, three musicians, and seventy-five privates. The Rhode Island Assembly voted to raise two hundred more recruits, offering up 100 Spanish milled dollars as a bounty. Its efforts were successful, bringing the regiment's strength up to 659.[29]

After the victory at Yorktown, Olney's battalion lost three more privates enumerated on the "Return of Freemen." Whether due to injuries sustained at Yorktown or illness acquired at camp, William's brother-in-law, Solomon Wanton, and Jacob Ned died at the end of the year. Solomon, succumbing to repeated bouts of illness, died on December 28, 1781, leaving William's sister, Hannah, a widow. Jacob Ned died on December 30, 1781. And the deaths continued. Toby Coys passed on January 14, 1782. Coys, a resident of Charlestown, had an uneven military experience. He deserted early in his career when he served in the Rhode Island State Regiment. He enlisted with the Second Rhode Island Regiment in May 1777—the same time as Ben Frank. Coys and Ben served together as members of Hughes' company before segregation took place. Coys' service as a member of the Rhode Island Continentals did not include desertion or discipline. He received a discharge in July 1780. He must have reenlisted, and this third stint of mil-

Watercolor by the French artist and officer Jean Baptiste Antoine de Verger sketched during the siege of Yorktown. From left to right, a soldier of the First Rhode Island Regiment, a New England militiaman, a frontier rifleman, and a French artillery officer. (*Anne S. K. Brown Military Collection, Brown University Library*)

itary service resulted in his death. His death, however, did not signal the end of fatalities for the freemen of the return.[30]

In February 1783, William Frank, along with the rest of Olney's battalion, was dispatched to New York to capture the British garrison and trading post at Oswego on Lake Ontario. General Washington called on Colonel Marinus Willett to lead a combined force of Rhode Island Continentals and Willett's New York troops to remove the British presence from the area. On the march to the post, the regiment went off course and many soldiers froze to death. Private Samuel Smith described their situation in the following manner, "a number of men having frozen to death, and a great part of the regiment being more or less frozen."[31] One of the Black soldiers meeting his demise during the trek was Toney Phillips, who died on February 22, 1783. At the time of his death, Phillips had served a total of six years—the same length of service as William Frank. He survived the winters of Valley Forge and the Rhode Island encampment of discontent. He experienced the segregation of Rhode Island troops. He deployed to Yorktown and survived the siege. But he could not survive the disastrous wintry Oswego expedition after the battle at Yorktown. William Frank survived the march. Olney's regiment would remain in New York until the summer of 1783.[32]

On June 13, 1783, in Saratoga, New York, the soldiers of Olney's regiment received their discharges. Many of the original thirty-five African American enlistees had served for more than five years before their discharge. William Frank served a total of six years, two months, and four days.[33] Upon dismissal of his troops, Olney expressed his admiration for their steadfast service throughout the war. Contrary to his previous assessment, he commended his troops for "faithfully persevering in the best of causes, in every stage of service, with unexampled fortitude and patience through all the dangers and toils of a long and severe war."[34] He also promised a "continuance of his interest in their favour, and shall be happy to be useful to them in the future in using his endeavors to obtain their just dues from the public and on every other proper occasion."[35] The discharged soldiers of Olney's battalion—hungry, penniless, some sick or injured—made their way back to their homes. There were no welcome home parades or "just due" from the public. Many of the soldiers had to fight to gain the rewards of back pay and land promised to them. Rhode Island legislators would eventually award farm lots and houses once belonging to loyalists to the veteran soldiers in lieu of money due. William Frank eventually received his back pay. He enlisted as a very young man but was a hardened veteran of the war upon his discharge.[36]

Ben Frank's desertion

AFTER HIS DESERTION in March 1780, Ben Frank disappears from all official military records and documents. He is not listed as being retaken or returning to service with the Continentals. After the war, the 1790 Federal Census for Rhode Island was populated with members of the Frank family, including William Frank. However, there is no listing for Ben Frank. The documentary trail had gone cold. But I believe he reappears in New York City in 1782 as Ben Frankham, stating he was a free man of Charlestown, South Carolina. This enigmatic man would eventually leave his native land in October 1782 aboard the brig *Elijah* bound for Nova Scotia.[37]

Ben Frankham had thrown in his lot with a group of loyalists that for a variety of reasons had decided to remain true to the king and their British roots. Most studies of the loyalist experience attest to the fact regarding the diversity of its members and their motivations and lend credence to a broad definition of loyalism. The insertion of Black loyalism into this scholarship allows for an even more intense examination of the motivating factors. Many white loyalists were convinced that there would be no security for their wealth and property under an American republic. Others held that there was no just cause to denounce their allegiance to the king and it was their responsibility to prevent rebellion against the king's rightful authority. Still others felt that allegiance to the king could not be dissolved since the king's authority was granted through divine providence and no human action could destroy it. The motivations for Blacks to remain loyal to the Crown were similar but also different than those of their white counterparts. Both shared a concern for security, but for different reasons—Black loyalists were looking for protection, security, equality, and freedom.[38]

There are instances of Black soldiers and civilian workers who fled to the British cause because they were assured of continued personal liberty and reward at the end of the war. Formerly enslaved John Twine earned his freedom working as a wagoner for American forces. However, he chose to throw his lot with the British due to the Patriots' inability to provide pay and proper clothing for its employees. Twine based his loyalty in part on which side could fulfill their promises. Black loyalists, like Twine, believed that the British were their only chance for a "secure and permanent release from the bonds of colour."[39]

The British based their policy regarding the use of Blacks in military service on their efforts to deny the American side a large pool of available manpower—enslaved labor. Early British policies sought to drive a wedge between the enslaved population and its owners. Lord Dunmore's Proclamation of 1775 offered freedom in exchange for military service. General Henry Clinton, British commander in chief, followed this policy with one of his own that sought to entice Blacks to the British cause. The Philipsburg Proclamation issued before the British invasion of South Carolina and eight months before the departure of Ben Frank stated that Blacks captured in service with the rebels would be sold for the benefit of the British, but those who sought refuge with the British would be protected. Additionally, Clinton promised "to every Negro who shall desert the Rebel Standard, full security to follow within these lines any occupation which he may think proper."[40]

If known to British officials, Ben's status as a "deserter" may have subjected him to extra scrutiny. British officials interrogated deserters from the Continental army to ascertain the circumstances surrounding their desertions and the situation at Continental army encampments. They were particularly interested in the status of Continental command structure and whether Continental regulars received enough pay and food. The type of information gathered from these deserters was varied. James Mitchell reported on the number of men who were fit for duty (effectives) when he stated that "men in his company . . . The whole Army now for 30,000 about 15,000 effectives."[41] Thomas Oakley deserted from New York or Second Artillery under the command of Colonel Lamb, stationed at West Point. He reported that "there are four brigades there . . . Starks, Clintons, Maxwells . . . says their provisions consisted of one pd Bread and . . . beef . . . says the reason of many others not deserting is the report that their present Army is reduced and a new one raised immediately." Oakley returned to Continental service on September 18, 1782.[42]

In the year of Ben's departure, statements from other deserters are telling regarding the conditions of service for the American army. Anthony Manual, described as a "foreigner" in the records, of Colonel Crane's artillery, also known as the Third Continental Artillery regiment, stated that Army clothing "was burnt at Boston" because it was so badly contaminated. He reported "26 officers going to give up their commissions in Genl. Patterson's Brigade. The reason of it is that a proper [request] made to disband the men enlisted for the War, Congress refused it [and] . . . that he heard them warning other officers in the Army do the same." Jacob Dilloe and Joseph Swatheridge, also members of Crane's Artillery, stipulated similar opinions. Dilloe stated that "there are very few men left of those enlisted for the War having mostly deserted," and Swatheridge reported that "only 4 men in this company enlisted for the War says he is certain all the men in the same situation will desert as he heard many of them say so."[43] John Porter, a sergeant in the Sixth Massachusetts Regiment reported that there were "no cloaths . . . except what the soldiers buy themselves . . . he told his Officer some time ago he would desert if he was not treated better, the Off[icer] made answer he can not blame him."[44] Soldiers Adam Happele and John Chesley of the New York regiments reported, "Cloathing very bad. Has not had pay these nine Months. . . . Soldiery very discontented many of them swear they will desert the first opportunity."[45] And these dire reports were not limited to soldiers fleeing from harsh conditions and harsh treatment. Joe, a Black servant and valet to Captain Arnold of the Militia Light Horse, fled from the Morristown, New Jersey, encampment and "was eight days has been concealed . . . in a barn." Joe reported the "Cloathing exceedingly bad. . . . The soldiery say they will not serve another year."[46]

Of specific relevance to Ben Frank's departure is Private William Ormsby, who left his regiment on April 20, 1781, a year after Ben's departure. Ormsby, previously assigned with the Second Rhode Island Regiment, detailed the circumstances of the newly consolidated regiment. He stated that "The regiment gets recruits very fast. They are inlisted chiefly for three years—has not had any pay for 14 months—he says the whole of his regiment are Determined to desert the first opportunity being so ill used—their cloathing very bad—They are fed with salt meat at present which is scanty."[47]

Like Ben Frankham, other deserters were "desirous" to continue in military service. On one occasion, General Cornwallis' aide-de-camp Alexander Ross provided passes for "four deserters from the Rebels" stating that the bearers of the passes "have leave from General Cornwallis to pass to Charles Town, being desirous to serve in His Majesty's Navy."[48] After the interviews and interrogations, deserters were approved to enlist. Most joined loyalist regiments or enlisted to serve on board a loyalist privateer.[49]

Black loyalists brought a variety of skills and knowledge with them as they ran to British lines. Many of them were not general laborers or field hands. They held specialized training as blacksmiths, coopers, carpenters, tailors, and bakers. Many Black loyalists served in the civil branches of the British army—barrack master general, quarter master, and the engineering departments. They held jobs as laborers, carpenters, valets, cooks, and blacksmiths.[50]

The wagon master general department also saw a significant number of Black loyalists on their rolls. The department provided the type of logistical support necessary to move large armies of men. The wagon master supervised the primary modes of transportation—horses, carts, boats, and drivers and arranged for the transportation of provisions and stores used by the army in the field. Most Black loyalists served as laborers, boatsmen, and wagon drivers—who moved supplies to the troops in the field.[51]

Overall, many Blacks served as cooks, orderlies, and waiters or as personal servants to officers in British regiments. Some British regiments had a Black drummer or fifer and several Blacks acted as guides or spies for invading British troops. Some Blacks saw active military service as regular soldiers with various Provincial units. This policy ended with the appointment of Alexander Innes as inspector general of the Provincial forces in January 1777. Innes advocated for the expulsion of Blacks and Native Americans from the Provincial forces which resulted in orders from General Sir William Howe to discharge them from the ranks. Still, others saw active duty as sailors and pilots in the Royal Navy. Others used their combat skills as members of the "followers of the flag," freelance guerilla units that served as raiding forces along the American lines. These units eventually became known as the Black Brigade. A survey of the Black loyalists who were part of the migration shows that approximately one-third had been in service with the British army.[52]

Another group of Black loyalists officially tied to the Provincial forces were the Black Pioneers. They became the only Black corps put on the Provincial rolls. General Henry Clinton commissioned the Black Pioneer company in May 1776. Sixty to seventy Black loyalists were placed under the command of a white lieutenant and ensign. As pioneers, they were used to clear land and perform other engineering duties.[53] The Black Pioneers continued their service throughout the war, and a year after Ben's departure from the Continentals, other "rebel deserters" were assigned to their ranks. In June 1781, James Bowles, Shappel (Sharpor) Gardner and John Burrows (Burris) joined the ranks of the Pioneers.[54] Gardner may be the same Sharpo Gardner who deserted in February 1780 from the First Rhode Island Regiment during the same month as Ben's desertion—another casualty of the winter of discontent. The formerly enslaved Gardner from South Kingstown enlisted on April 3, 1778, because of the Slave Enlistment Act.[55] After his desertion, he joined the Black Pioneers. The unit served under the auspices of General Clinton, who directed the commander of the unit, Captain Martin,

> as an encouragement to them [the Black Pioneers] to demean them-selves with diligence and fidelity in the Service it is my direction that they are acquainted that they are to be regularly supplied with Provisions and to be decently clothed, and that they are also to receive such pay as may be hereafter determined, from which the Expence of Cloathing and Provision will be deducted and further that at the ex-piration of the present Rebellion that [they] shall be intitled (as far as depends upon me) to their freedom-And from my knowledge of you I shall rely on you and desire that it may be particularly recommended to the rest of the officers to treat these people with tenderness and humanity.[56]

As a result of Clinton's direction, the lot of the Black Pioneers was much better than that of the other Black loyalists. Pioneers' pay was equal to the pay of white soldiers at a base pay of sixpence per day. Pay for skilled workers equaled eighteen pence per day, unskilled eight pence, with women receiving half pay for their labor. Officials deducted money from their pay for clothing and other provisions. Black Pioneers were issued one coat, one small jacket, one pair of woolen pants, one white shirt, and a hat. Local vendors provided other items such as shoes, socks, and waistcoats. As the war progressed, British command assigned Pioneers, usually one per company, to Provincial regiments throughout the British military.[57]

Clinton and the Black Pioneers made their way to Charleston, South Carolina, as the major theater of the war moved south. It is possible that Ben Frankham joined up with these troops after his departure in early 1780, as Clinton and his forces laid siege to and captured Charleston. It is unclear if Ben Frankham officially became a Pioneer at this time or at all. He is not identified as one in the muster rolls of the Black Pioneers.[58] Evidence of the Black Pioneers' role during the southern campaign is little discussed in correspondence and other official documents. They lost one Pioneer to death and none to desertion. Ten members were added to their company during the siege of Charleston. Twelve other recruits joined after the city fell. These twelve were given to the commissary general's department three weeks later. The Pioneers were assigned to aiding with the construction of the massive earthworks around the city, built in spring 1780. At war's end 5,000–6,000 Blacks evacuated with British forces when they left Charleston. Ben Frankham claimed to be one of these.[59]

It would be a dramatically climactic moment if the Frank brothers met during the siege and eventual British surrender at Yorktown, but there is no documentation to suggest that. William Frank was there as a member of the Consolidated Rhode Island Regiments under the command of Lieutenant Colonel Jeremiah Olney. But it is unlikely that Ben Frank's service with the British led him to Yorktown during that fateful moment in American history, especially since Ben claimed he was from South Carolina and probably evacuated with other loyalists from Charleston at war's end.[60]

At war's end, British commander in chief Sir Guy Carleton, who relieved General Clinton in 1782, ordered the commanders at Savannah and Charleston to evacuate all loyalists from those cities to St. Augustine, East Florida, Jamaica, and New York. Brigadier General Alexander Leslie, in charge at Charleston, established a commission of inquiry to determine the status of refugees. Leslie also worked out a deal to hear appeals of slave owners for the return of their fugitive slaves. The agreement ensured the liberty of enslaved persons who had served the British army or were motivated by the Philipsburg Proclamation, with their masters being compensated for their loss. Vessels with evacuating Loyalists were to be inspected before their departure. The plan broke down after a skirmish between American and British forces. The ships left with their Black loyalists on board.[61]

The experiences of other Black loyalists fleeing to the British, like Ben Frankham, help to mark their journey from American to loyalist. David George and Boston King were among the Black loyalists fleeing

Charleston. David George, a formerly enslaved Baptist preacher, made his way from Savannah with his family. In his memoir, he stated: "When the English were going to evacuate Charlestown, they advised me to go to Halifax, Nova Scotia, and gave the few Black people . . . their passage for nothing." George and a few other Black families left Charleston and eventually arrived at Halifax to start new lives there.[62] Formerly enslaved Boston King served as a carpenter and orderly for the British army. He also carried dispatches.[63] He "entered on board a rum [*sic*-man] of war. . . . We stayed in the bay [Chesapeake] two days, and they sailed for New-York where I went on shore."[64] Ben Frankham, Boston King, and other Black loyalists made their way to New York to wait out the negotiation process between Great Britain and the United States to learn their collective fates.[65]

New York City was the safe haven for Ben Frankham and other loyalists at war's end, while Carleton and George Washington negotiated the evacuation of loyalists from American shores. By the end of the war over 40,000 soldiers and civilians had made their way to New York. Ben Frankham and other Black loyalists brought a sense of community to their makeshift homes in New York. Not truly transient in nature, these communities took on the characteristics of maroon communities in the Caribbean. They recreated families and reestablished extended kinship relationships. Historian Cassandra Pybus argues that these Black refugees were brought together by their common African past and a common struggle to survive the aftermath of the war. They also told stories—sharing traditional tales about tricksters and other figures from West African culture and the exploits of Black fighters of the Revolutionary War. One wonders if Ben shared his exploits as a former Continental soldier during the nightly tale-swapping sessions.[66]

The population of Black loyalists in New York City grew from over 1,200 in 1779 to over 2,700 when 1,500 Blacks joined them after evacuating from Savannah and Charlestown. Ben Frankham arrived at the city in that latter wave. Most Black loyalists migrated to and lived in an area between Broadway and the Hudson River. A raging fire swept through the region in 1776 and the area was not repaired or rebuilt. The region supported crude, makeshift dwellings constructed from canvas and other found materials. These canvas tent communities housed many Black loyalists. British officers and members of the Loyalist gentry resided in the remaining houses of the area. Some Black loyalists formally employed by the civil branches of the army received housing in barracks across the East River in Brooklyn. Ben Frankham may have been one of the lucky residents of these barracks. Other Blacks attached to the Royal Artillery resided in barracks created out of rowhouses in lower Manhattan. They received rations, a lamp, and oil for lighting purposes.[67]

To survive and start anew, they worked together and played together. Because of the shortage of labor, Blacks had little trouble finding employment. Many contracted employment as temporary workers through third parties. Black skilled workers found work in the naval yards and rebuilding projects. Others worked as teamsters, nurses, orderlies, pilots, and laundry workers. Many plied their trade in the entertainment districts. Fiddlers and banjo players worked at taverns. Black jockeys rode for rich patrons. For the most part, all workers were paid for their services, without the burden of paying taxes. For Ben Frankham and others, employment was not an issue during their stay as refugees in New York.[68]

While negotiations were taking place in Paris between American and British officials to officially end the war, loyalists in New York began to make plans for their future. White leaders created loyalist associations that negotiated with General Carleton for safe passage and settlement away from their former homes in America. Their proposals to the general included transportation to Nova Scotia for themselves and their families, provisions, rations for one year, tools, and most importantly, land. Carleton assured these loyalists that British authorities would fulfill their requests.[69]

Ben and other Black loyalists were also concerned about their future and their safe passage from a country that saw them as traitors. They waited with their white counterparts for the results of the ongoing peace talks in Paris. Of major concern to most Black loyalists was the issue of what would happen to the thousands of former slaves that fled to British lines in search of freedom. A provisional peace treaty was signed in December 1782. An armistice followed and the terms of the treaty were finally published in New York in March 1783. Article VII was of most interest to the Black loyalists. It promised the return of all confiscated property by British to the rightful American owners. This included the enslaved. Boston King remembered the despair felt by many due to this clause in the treaty:

> the horrors and devastation of war happily terminated and peace was restored between America and Great Britain, which diffused universal joy among all parties; except us, who had escaped from slavery and taken refuge in the English army; for a report prevailed at New-York that all the slaves, in number 2000, were to be delivered up to their masters altho' some of them had been three or four years among the English. . . . For some days we lost our appetite for food, and sleep

departed from our eyes. The English had compassion upon us in the day of distress, and issued out a Proclamation, importing, That all slaves should be free.[70]

General Carleton felt that the article contradicted the promise of freedom made by the British to the refugees. He thus interpreted Article VII to apply only to those Blacks that were not free. He considered Blacks already within British lines before November 1782 as free and no longer American property. To deal with frustrated American slaveholders, Carleton formed a board of inquiry to deal with the claims of these slaveowners. He added that the British would make fair compensation to the owners of the enslaved not returned. To ensure that compensation was made, Carleton directed command staff to inventory Blacks behind British lines.[71]

Brigadier General Samuel Birch, British commander of New York City, was charged with creating a process to determine which Black refugees met the standards promulgated by General Carleton. Birch also had to adjudicate the petitions brought by American slaveowners attempting to reclaim their enslaved property. Birch decided to issue "certificates of freedom" to those refugees who had served with British forces prior to the peace treaty. There were restrictions, however. Birch and his commission excluded Blacks who were imprisoned for crimes, ranging from arson to murder. Those who did receive a certificate were guaranteed their freedom and passage aboard a British ship.[72]

Carleton informed all Blacks who had been with the British forces before the established date to present themselves to the Birch commission, who in turn would issue certificates attesting to their freedom. These certificates of freedom became the passports for Black loyalists to leave the United States. Between April and November 1783, over 3,000 Blacks presented themselves to this panel of judges. The commission met every Wednesday afternoon at Fraunces Tavern, owned by Samuel Fraunces, who had previously owned one of the finest taverns in New York City. As part of the process at Fraunces Tavern, Blacks had to provide their names, details of escape or other claim to freedom, military records, and name of former owner. This listing became known as the *Book of Negroes*. It contained the names of 3,000 Black loyalists, among them 1,336 men, 914 women, and 750 children, who met the requirements stipulated by General Carleton and were granted certificates of freedom. Also included was the name of the commander and destination of the vessel in which each was to be evacuated. Fourteen percent of these petitioners—like Ben Frankham—claimed to have been born free or freed by their former masters.[73]

Ben Frankham recorded in the *Book of Negroes*. Top, verso page detail with Ben's name written second from the bottom. Bottom, the corresponding recto page with the comments
about his free status written second from the bottom. (*Nova Scotia Archives. Book of Negroes.
Guy Carleton, First Baron Dorchester Papers*)

Ben Frankham was now forced to prove his freedom to Carleton's board
of inquiry. He stood in line with other Black loyalists at Fraunces Tavern
and presented himself to the commission now headed by General Thomas
Musgrave. General Birch departed in late 1783 after issuing over 878 certificates. Musgrave followed in his wake by issuing 278 passports to freedom.[74] How does Ben Frank fare in the detailed listing provided in the

Book of Negroes? Ben forges a new persona and consequently a new life as he presented himself to General Musgrave and his fellow commissioners. He introduced himself as "Ben Frankham, 21, ordinary [fellow]. Says he was born free in Charlestown, South Carolina."[75]

This change in his surname may have been prompted by an incorrect listing by the recorder of Ben's name. Or Ben, concerned about his status as a deserter, may have decided to provide a different name to the Musgrave commission. Regardless of the reasons behind the change, he left New York aboard the brig *Elijah* on October 31, 1783, bound for Nova Scotia. He was free from the burdens of military and familial obligations and duties. However, he now faced starting a new life in an unknown world without the backing of family and lifelong friends. He had been given the opportunity to live the life that he chose, a free man, albeit with the hardships he knew to expect.

Ben and William Frank survived the final years of the American Revolution in different places and different stages in their lives. Their divided experiences during the final stages of the war illustrated the varied role that race played in their military lives. Ben's flight to the British probably caused him to lose his status as a combat soldier. British policy diminished the opportunity for Blacks to serve as official soldiers of the Crown. Ben more than likely served as a general laborer for the British military—a step down from his position with the Continentals. If he served as a Black Pioneer, Ben would have received compensatory pay as an official member on British payrolls. However, race played a major role in that Ben was required to prove his freedom as a requirement to obtain refuge after the war. In contrast, William's military experience came full circle from assignment to integrated units to segregated regiments to an integrated battalion—just as American military policy started to prohibit the military service of Blacks. On the personal side, Ben was embarking on an unknown journey with new companions and compatriots. William was returning to his childhood home and family. Both would lean on the skills honed during a difficult military career to survive and thrive in postwar North America.

CHAPTER NINE

William Frank,
African American

As Ben set sail for Nova Scotia, his brother William embarked upon a new life as a free Black man in a country officially built upon the principles of freedom and equality. William and his fellow Black veterans of the First Rhode Island Regiment would discover that life in postwar America was a continuing battle to obtain their promised rewards and equality. After the American Revolution, marginalized peoples, who had obtained an increased measure of equality during the war, sought to maintain those levels of achievement. James and Lois Horton have identified the "voice of black America" as beginning in the postwar period as the "voice of America's conscience." This voice called on all Americans to remember those, like the veterans of the "Black Regiment," who helped to build the nation. These veteran Black soldiers built families and communities in a new nation still struggling with the uncomfortable and ill-fated coexistence of liberty and slavery. Additionally, the promised benefits of military service did not guarantee that veterans would have a better life and position in the community than nonveterans.[1]

William was part of a cluster of free Black men who returned to Rhode Island after the war, often to the very place where they lived when the war started. Of the thirty-five men of color registered on the "Return of Freemen," seven left the military and did not return and eight died from war injuries or illnesses. Fifteen (less than half) survived the war, received documented honorable discharges, and returned to civilian life. For these fifteen men, the average length of service was five years. Some of these men were recognized for their "long and faithful" service when awarded honorary badges. These badges were created by General Washington in General Orders dated August 7, 1782, in the following manner:[2]

> Honorary Badges of distinction are to be conferred on the veteran Non commissioned officers and soldiers of the army, who have served more than three years with bravery, fidelity, and good conduct, for this purpose a narrow piece of white cloath of an angular form is to be fixed to the left arm on the uniform Coats. Non commissioned officers and soldiers who have served with equal reputation more than six years are to be distinguished by two pieces of cloth set on parallel to each other in a simular form.[3]

Among the honorees were members of the "Black Regiment," including Joseph Boyer, Caesar Finch (with reputation), Rueben Roberts (with reputation), Peter Dailey, Cato Varnum, London Hall, Caesar Updike, and Mingo Rodman. Even though William Frank had served up to five years faithfully by the time of the award designation, he and others with similar time served were not selected to receive this decoration. What is particularly interesting about the nonselection of William is that there is only one blemish on his record—being deemed "unfit for duty" during the winter encampment at Valley Forge 1777–1778. His performance and service illustrated the appropriate amount of time served and documented his "fidelity and good conduct."[4]

Most survivors of the Black Regiment returned to their homes in Rhode Island. The state was hardly a bastion of African American liberty, given its intensive involvement in the transatlantic slave trade, but Rhode Island officials tried to honor commitments to African American veterans. In October 1782, the state legislature voted to pay veterans their back wages. Members of the Black Regiment identified as free prior to their enlistment received their back pay. In April 1784, William Frank received $200 in back wages, the same amount as most of the survivors, including Joseph Boyer, Simon Barton, Peter Dailey, Caesar Finch, Winsor Fry, Prince Limas, Rueben Roberts, and Plato Vandorum. Others like Pharaoh Hazzard and Elijah Waggs received less. Hazzard was paid $53.50, due to his earlier discharge from service and Waggs was paid $174. Frank Gould does not appear on the register of payments and may have returned to his place of birth, New York City. Private Toney Phillips does appear on this list even though he lost his life in February of the previous year during the fateful march to Fort Oswego. His entitled payment of $80 was captured in the records with no indication as to whom the payment was made. These men of color received less than noncommissioned officers like Jeremiah Greenman. Sergeant Greenman, one of the few soldiers to sign with his signature for his back payments, received the amount of $2,158.[5]

William Frank returned to Johnston, Rhode Island, after the war. In his study celebrating the 250th anniversary of the founding of Providence, local historian Welcome Arnold Greene described the town of Johnston as acting "nobly" during the Revolutionary War by "sending freely of her sons and of her money to carry on the great contest."[6] These sons of Johnston looked forward to returning to their homes and the honor that awaited them. If William and other veterans did not possess land to farm, there were opportunities for them to work in nonagricultural enterprises in the small town. Cotton manufacturers started to spring up. By the turn of the century, there were four cotton mills in operation. However, such jobs may have been too late in coming for war veterans like William Frank. He and others would have found better opportunities in the principal commercial center of nearby Providence.[7]

For Blacks looking for better opportunities, Providence became the primary destination. By 1790, over four hundred free Blacks lived in the city compared to forty-eight enslaved persons. The existence of a strong, established African American community also pulled Blacks to the city and they arrived from nearby towns and villages like Johnston. But William Frank did not follow this trend. He remained in Johnston until the 1790s, choosing to remain where his father had established a homestead and not return to his father's first place of residence.[8]

The service of William Frank and his compatriots did not have much influence on how officials and policymakers perceived their status in a new American society built on freedom, liberty, and equality for all. State and local officials placed a variety of restrictions on free Blacks so that their status in the community was much the same as it had been before the war. Joanne Pope Melish has argued that the emergence of a growing class of free people of color in southern New England in the postwar era prompted nervous officials to construct laws and regulations to control these "others" in their midst. To deal with the perceived threats to the public welfare by free Blacks, town officials ordered police officials to "detain, question, and incarcerate" people involved in disorderly conduct. This kind of early American racial profiling occurred in Providence. The town council directed its night watch to restrict the activities of persons engaging in disorderly behavior in public. Even though the law did not target a particular group, most of the arrests involved people of color. The enforcement of restrictive legislation was intended to control the lives of free Blacks and cement their low social and legal status.[9] Charles Pinckney, a delegate from South Carolina to the Constitutional Convention, summed up this thinking in 1789 when he wrote: "There did not then exist such a thing in the Union as a Black or colored citizen, nor could I have conceived it possible such a thing could ever have existed in it."[10] Pinckney and many others chose to disregard the Revolutionary War service provided by William Frank and other members of the First Rhode Island Regiment.

Another obstacle for free Blacks was the concept that "the right of settlement rested with the town not the individual."[11] Local officials had the power to warn out and remove unwanted residents from their towns. Since Blacks found it difficult to satisfy the most common means of establishing residency by land ownership or the completion of a skilled apprenticeship, many were subjected to the scrutiny of town officials looking to evict the potential poor. After the war, town authorities feared disruptive behavior more than they feared poverty, which led to the removal of Blacks, including Black veterans, from their towns. Consequently, they broadened their list of reasons to interrogate and remove residents. Owning a dance hall, violating curfew ordinances, maintaining a disorderly household, and even making a rash comment could result in a court inquiry. This led to an adversarial relationship between free Blacks and the towns in which they lived. An illustrative example of this is the experiences of Private Cuff Roberts in Providence after the war.[12]

Historian Gabriel J. Loiacono tracked veteran soldier Roberts and his efforts to prove his right of settlement and freedom to live in his chosen place of residence—Providence. After the war, Cuff married Elizabeth Grummick and initially settled in West Greenwich, Rhode Island. Cuff and his family relocated and settled for a time in Providence in 1801. Elizabeth died shortly thereafter. By 1806, Cuff and his second wife, Jenny, and their family of six were warned out of Providence. Town officials compiled a list of approximately eighty individuals who were to be forced out of Providence and returned to their native towns. Cuff Roberts was born free in Coventry, Rhode Island, and lived in that city until relocating to Providence in 1801. After his warning out, Roberts was able to purchase an acre and a half of land in his hometown of Coventry in 1811 and 1813—exhibiting an ability to work and save enough money on a general laborer's salary to purchase land. He sold the land in 1813 and returned to Providence in 1816, only to be warned out again in 1819 and 1829, but at least in those incidences he had applied for and received veterans' benefits from the federal government. After his third warning out, Roberts had had his fill of Providence and left the town for good. He married for a third time in November 1829 and relocated to Boston and arranged to have his pension transferred to that city. Cuff Roberts died at the age of seventy in Boston in May 1831, listed as a member of the "city poor."[13]

During and after the Revolutionary War, the presence of African American veterans helped to stabilize the Black population in New England, which remained static between 1776 and 1790. In the first census of the United States, African Americans totaled 16,822 in New England out of a total population of 1,099,206. The white population had grown by more than 50 percent since 1776, but the Black population had only increased by 4 percent. The slow growth can be attributed to several factors. The Revolutionary War ruined the slave trade and prevented increase by slave importation. By 1790 all New England states had started the abolition of slavery by enacting gradual emancipation legislation. The flight of Black loyalists also helped to diminish the population figures, as in the case of Ben Frank. By 1790, there were 4,442 African Americans residing in Rhode Island. Of that number, 3,484 or 78 percent were free and 958 remained in bondage.[14]

The presence of Black veterans like William Frank also helped to establish free Black communities throughout Rhode Island. William established a home in Johnston that included an adult female—an indication that he married or set up a household with a surrogate wife after the war. Other Franks also resided in Johnston after the war. Andrew Frank of Troy, Massachusetts, served as a member of the Rhode Island militia during the Revolutionary War. He settled in Johnston after the war and headed a household of eight persons. And he received a pension for his service, starting in 1831 when he was eighty years old. The cluster of households that surrounded William Frank's small family was composed of racially diverse individuals. William's home was located near the households of Andrew Frank and Prince Lewis, free men of color. William's former battalion mate Peter Dailey also resided in the vicinity, living next door to another free man of color, Cesar Harris. Johnston's Black community followed the same pattern as Providence, where Black homes and other dwellings sprang up in the residential areas of Olney Street, Benevolent Street, and Snowtown. Forty-three percent of free persons of color lived near other Black households in the larger town.[15]

The men of the Black Regiment settled throughout the state of Rhode Island after the war. Many of William's former comrades married and started families. Prince Limas, one of the original thirty-five free men of the Black Regiment, married after the war. Like other First Rhode Islanders, Limas was married by Elder John Gorton. "Prince Limas a Negro man and Mercy Austin an Indian woman Both of East Greenwich . . . was lawfully Joyned together in the Honorable Estate of Marriage in said Greenwich on the 30th day of Novem AD 1783/by me John Gorton."[16] Peter Dailey settled in Johnston, as well, and by 1790 was the head of a household of five free persons. Simon Barton moved from Warwick to settle in West Greenwich with his family of five. Winsor Fry settled his large family of seven in North Kingstown after the war. The formerly enslaved members of the First Rhode Island also married and started families. Richard Rhodes was married in 1786 by a Baptist clergyman. Prince Robinson and his wife had three children; the eldest at fourteen worked as a housekeeper in the home of Jesse Gore. Henry Tabor also married in the Baptist church had three children. Families of color settled near each other in towns and villages throughout Rhode Island.[17]

Former members of the Black Regiment appear periodically in vital and census records in the late 1700s and early 1800s. These records show men who lived quiet, uneventful lives—striving to maintain households during difficult economic times during the waning years of the revolutionary era. A postwar depression, along with an unstable monetary system, made economic stability difficult for Black war veterans to achieve. These veterans also had to deal with an American public who sought to ignore them and their wartime accomplishments. Veteran African American soldiers, like William Frank, continued fighting after the war to guarantee that their military service would be commemorated with political and economic gains.[18]

William Frank was finally issued a land bounty in June 1795. The land bounty program was part of a recruitment system approved and established by Congress in the early years of the war. A Congressional resolution passed in 1777 stated that privates who served in the war were entitled to one hundred acres of free land in the Military District of Ohio. This enticement lured many young men, like the Frank brothers, to serve in the Continental

William Frank received a land bounty

army. William must not have had the motivation or resources to develop
his allotment, since he immediately signed over his plot to a man named
Samuel Emery. Many soldiers gave up their land as William did, primarily
because they did not have the capital to move to their land in the western
areas of the country, nor did they have the resources to live on the land,
sow crops, and wait for a harvest. Many sold their land warrants to others,
usually land speculators. These speculators made a practice of buying the
deeds, merging their holdings, and then reselling these consolidated holdings to make a profit.

Franklin oral tradition stipulates that William and his family migrated
to New Orleans in the period after the war. He is not listed in the federal
censuses of 1800 or 1810 as a resident of Rhode Island. A move to New
Orleans after 1795 or subsequent death of William may explain the fact
that he did not apply for a pension under the 1818 or 1820 pension legislation.[19]

Pension records indicate that applications were approved, and land
bounties were indeed offered to former members of the Black Regiment.
After an application was approved, a veteran received a warrant that entitled
him to select a plot of land in the designated military district of Ohio. The
veteran advised the federal government of his selection and was then issued
a patent for the land. Simon Barton, Peter Dailey, Winsor Fry, and Rueben
Roberts all received land warrants in the amount of one hundred acres each.
But these men, like William Frank, did not settle on their allotted land—
which is ironic since the possibility of land ownership lured many Black
veterans to serve with the Rhode Island Continentals. Many saw land ownership as a means to improve their lives, and to gain economic competency.[20] Veteran Jeffrey Brace captured the importance of land ownership
in his memoir: "Finding I could not get the land contemplated I removed
in the spring of 1804, to Georgia [Vermont], a pleasant situated town on
the banks of Lake Champlain, where I purchased with my son-in-law sixty
acres of land of Esq . . . and where I contemplated spending my days. Here
I settled down in the peaceful sunshine of anticipated delight. Industry
caused prosperity to hover round my cot."[21]

Some of these veterans did acquire town lots and they did possess their
own homes. Formerly enslaved veteran Cato Greene obtained one acre of
land in Cranston, Rhode Island. Greene, brought from Guinea as a slave,
was owned by William Greene of Warwick, Rhode Island, before the war.
Cato's holdings, after the war, included an old house, a table, four chairs,
and other miscellaneous household goods. He received a pension starting

in 1818 and lived to the age of 102. Formerly enslaved Richard Rhodes served for five years with the Rhode Island Continentals. After the war, Rhodes lived on one acre of land, in a very old house. He owned 3,000 shingles, one axe, four old chairs, and other miscellaneous property.[22]

The survivors also sought and received rewards in the form of pension allowances. Extant pension records detail the allowances given to the former soldiers of the Black Regiment. Congress passed a series of pension laws to reward Revolutionary War veterans, starting as early as 1776 and ending in June 1832. The initial law of 1776 authorized temporary pensions for disabled soldiers and sailors in the amount of half the normal service pay for the length of the disability. The 1778 resolution authorized half-pay for all officers who stayed in the Continental Army until the end of the war. Enlisted men were eligible for a lump sum payment of $80. The intervening laws until 1818 dealt with disabled soldiers. The Congressional resolution of 1818 was a lifeline for the survivors of the Black Regiment. The law rewarded soldiers who had served nine months or more in the Continental army with pension allowances of eight dollars per month. Pension applicants did not have to prove a disability or financial need until the 1820 supplemental legislation. At that point, pensioners had to provide an inventory of their property, including household goods. The integrity of the records depended on the honesty of the veterans and their ability to re-call and relate their experiences; it also depended on the integrity of the transcriber, who had to understand and record the memories of veterans in their senior years. Since most veterans lacked the ability to write their own narratives and applications, they had to depend on court reporters and clerks to record their experiences. Under the 1832 law, applicants were re-quired to have two or more character witnesses, including a clergyman, en-dorse their applications. These pension records provide much insight into the lives of the Black Regiment in the decades after the war.[23]

The rewards of service would prove to be essential for the veterans of the Black Regiment. They had to compete and survive in a postwar eco-nomic depression. Additionally, since many of them lacked specialized trade skills, they became members of a large pool of common laborers seeking steady employment. The lot of the common laborer or day laborer was not easy. Finding permanent positions as an unskilled laborer was extremely difficult—the goal was often simply finding a day's work. Bristol Rhodes, a veteran of the Revolutionary War and the First Rhode Island Regiment, secured permanent employment at a foundry. Unlike Rhodes, other veter-ans struggled to obtain jobs that lasted for a few weeks or months. Many found intermittent employment on local construction crews, working on road and bridge projects.[24]

The Rhode Island veterans' navigation through these rough postwar economic waters was complicated by a wheat famine in 1789. Veteran Jeff Brace commented, "But at the close of this period, there came one of the most distressing famines I ever knew. Many people were in danger of starving and others were obliged to live weeks without bread."[25]

The survivors of the Black Regiment managed to survive employment difficulties and the famine. They created lives for themselves in postwar America under challenging conditions. Richard Potter, for example, made his home in Charlestown after the war. After serving over three years with the Rhode Island regiments, Potter worked as a common laborer. The postwar years were not kind to Potter. By 1822, he had "no property no family nor no trade and almost past Labour from Age and Infirmity."[26] However, he did earn and receive a monthly pension allowance commencing in 1818.[27]

Prince Limas settled in East Greenwich with his Native American wife, Mercy Austin. Limas and his wife became members of Elder Gorton's Six Principle Baptist Church. Limas' occupation as a mariner afforded him the opportunity to purchase land for "Eighty Good Spanish Milled Dollars" from fellow church member Nicholas Goddard. Limas purchased a "Quarter of an acre of land" with a "Dwellling House there on standing." The sale was registered on March 27, 1784. It is ironic that six years later Limas' bounty land warrant was issued on March 27, 1790. However, Limas was no longer alive to accept the bounty. The warrant was issued to his wife, Mercy Limas as his heir. It is unknown whether she settled on the allotted land.[28]

As discussed earlier in the chapter, Cuff Roberts and his family moved from their home in West Greenwich and settled for a time in Providence. His time in Providence was fraught with difficulties. He received a pension allowance of $89 a year, commencing in 1818. His wife and three children depended on his work as a common laborer to make ends meet. By 1820, the Roberts family had accumulated the following property: one scythe, one hoe, two axes, one rake, eight old chairs, two teakettles, and one Bible. Ten years later, Roberts and his family moved to Massachusetts—where he lived out the remainder of his life.[29]

Winsor Fry has the most documented life among the members of the original thirty-five free men of color. Clerks have labeled him variously as "mustee," "Indian," "man of colour," and "Negro" throughout the records. However, he might have identified himself racially, Fry was a key member of the Black Regiment. His wartime service and his postwar life have become emblematic of the regiment. He enlisted during the first year of the war and served the longest—seven years. While William Frank's service can be described as deliberate and steady, Fry could be considered to embody the collective experiences of the Black Regiment. His service is long but not unblemished. He received the death penalty for theft but survived that sentence by fleeing temporarily from the army. He left but returned to duty and stayed for the duration of the war. He suffered from illness and poor health during the war. However, he proudly boasted about his length and tenure of service: "I continued during the whole war between this Country and Great Britain—and think I may say without, during all that time having been absent but once."[30] This self-confidence helped him weather the tough times of his postwar years. Like many of his former comrades, he moved from one place to another within a limited geographic radius. He lived for periods in North Kingstown, Newport, and East Greenwich to find steady work. By 1820, Fry was destitute, without much property and unable to depend on his own labor to earn a living. Like many Revolutionary War veterans, Fry remained a common laborer, but by 1820 he was "much out of health and broken down with infirmities—and without his pension he must depend on Charity." He was placed on the pension rolls in 1818 at the rate of eight dollars per month. After reapplying in 1820, Fry was deemed worthy to continue on the pension rolls. He died on February 1, 1823.[31]

William Frank and other Black veterans did gain status within their own communities and neighborhoods because of their military service. Black leaders pointed to the exploits of Black veterans to enhance their calls for liberty and equality. Black leaders were not the only segment of the African American community that marked their gratitude to the Black veterans. As the veterans began to die off, their graves became the sites of memorials that drew attention to the deceased heroes and marked their graves as war relics. African Americans in New York City held their "Pinkster" holidays near a military graveyard that held the graves of African American soldiers of the Revolutionary War.[32] There is evidence that members of the white community also recognized the sacrifice of Black war veterans. George Middleton commanded the Bucks of America, a Black quasi-military unit which may have operated in Massachusetts during the war. Their actual service has received little historic recognition. However, years after the war, Middleton resided in Boston as a respected member of the Black community and was paid "public respect by Boston whites."[33]

The acquisition of land and pension did not eliminate problems for Black veterans. Free Blacks still had to endure problems brought about by racial conflicts. Veteran Jeffrey Brace related his problems with one of his neighbors: "The first season [in Poultney] I cleared about 7 acres and sowed it with wheat, enclosed the same with an excellent pole and log fence. But one Jery Goram who wanted my land and to whom I refused to sell it, pulled down my fence and let in cattle. The same year I had a crop of good corn, which land I had cleared off early in the spring, he also turned his cattle into that and destroyed it, so that I did not get 5 bushels from 8 acres, which otherwise would have produced me more than one hundred bushels."[34] Brace's neighbor was relentless in his attack on the family. Goram asked the town's selectmen to bind out Brace's two sons. Brace argued: "that as I had suffered so much by bondage myself, my children should never be under the direction of any other person whilst I lived. That if they would keep Goram from destroying my property, I could support my family as well as Goram could his, and they never wanted for wholesome food or clean linens, neither were they backward in education."[35] The situation between the neighbors came to a head when Brace was arrested and tried for making a menacing statement regarding Goram: "I said to one of my neighbors, if Goram pulled down my fence and destroyed my crops that year, I should be tempted to burn his barn. For this I was arrested and tried by 2 justices, who, on a fair and full examination of the matter, honorably acquitted me."[36] Brace's service during the Revolutionary War may have swayed the justices to his cause.

These types of problems and disputes did not dissuade Venture Smith from his embrace of American capitalism. The formerly enslaved man, whose son served as a Continental regular with the Connecticut regiments, believed in action over rhetoric, and he prized self-sufficiency in terms of land ownership, home ownership, and steady employment as a general laborer and entrepreneur. Venture Smith believed that land ownership was paramount. However, this acceptance of capitalism—the notion of freedom through hard work—did not erase what Smith perceived as racism in the postwar era. The young veterans of the Black Regiment survived in an American society that often blunted and blocked the efforts of free Blacks to move out of the ranks of the unpropertied lower sort. Yet their existence and endurance motivated others.[37]

The presence of young men like William Frank in the Black community also served another important function—as motivation for abolition efforts. American principles, ideals, and way of life changed drastically after the

war. Slavery became a central issue in the new nation. Gradual emancipation legislation in the North showed how gratitude for African American
military service could affect the larger Black community. The American
Revolution and the ideals of freedom and liberty that fueled it had a major
impact on the continued existence of slavery in the North. However, many
white Northerners objected to gradual emancipation and did not wish to
end slavery; they had to be convinced that slavery had a corrosive effect on
their society and that emancipation was the fair and correct thing to do.
Given this environment, gradual emancipation legislation barely passed in
some northern assemblies. The State of Rhode Island passed and used a
gradual emancipation law to end slavery there. The 1784 statute freed children of slaves born after March 1, 1784, when they reached adulthood and
declared that masters could free any slaves aged twenty-one to forty without
obligations for their future support.[38]

Activists used the achievements of William Frank and fellow Black soldiers as ammunition in the war for freedom for those African Americans
still enslaved. The activities of the Black soldiers of the First Rhode Island
were constantly repeated by the abolitionist activists to build up the reputation of the Black Regiment, in particular, and all African Americans in
general. Governor Eustis of Massachusetts extolled the actions of the First
Rhode Island at the Battle of Red Bank even though he implied that the
then-integrated First Rhode Island was an all-Black unit during the battle.
The Battle of Rhode Island became the defining moment for the regiment
and a symbol of Black gallantry and bravery. This battle was used by abolitionists to elicit sympathy and support for their cause. Historian William
Cooper Nell's account of the testimony of a white veteran soldier from
Massachusetts, in particular, demonstrates how abolitionists used tales of
valiant deeds performed by Black troops to electrify audiences and to rally
them against the unfair treatment of Black veterans and the continued enslavement of other Blacks.[39] As stated in a previous chapter, Dr. Harris, a
participant at the Battle of Rhode Island, spoke about the valor of the soldiers of color during that battle. This longer excerpt from his speech at an
antislavery convention in Francestown, New Hampshire, is an excellent example of how deeds of valor were used to call for the freedom of all Blacks:

> Yes, a regiment of negroes, fighting for our liberty and independ-
> ence,—not a white man among them but the officers,—stationed in
> this same dangerous and responsible position. Had they been un-
> faithful, or given way before the enemy, all would have been lost. Three
> times in succession were they attacked, with most desperate valor and

fury, by well disciplined and veteran troops, and three times did they successfully repel the assault, and thus preserve our army from capture. They fought through the war. They were brave, hardy troops. They helped to gain our liberty and independence.

Now, the war is over, our freedom is gained—what is to be done with these colored soldiers, who have shed their best blood in its defence? Must they be sent off out of the country, because they are black? or must they be sent back into slavery, now they have risked their lives and shed their blood to secure the freedom of their masters? I ask, what became of these noble colored soldiers?[40]

African American leaders in the 1780s and 1790s stressed the national gratitude owed to Black veterans and urged that these men should be repaid in the form of freedom for all Blacks. They used gratitude for the veterans' actions and memories of the war to push for an end to slavery. Sermons by Black leaders reflected their determination to use the exploits of the Black veterans for these purposes. A sermon by the anonymous "Black Whig" led citizens of South Carolina to demand that the "blood of the innocent"[41] shed in the war required the emancipation of all Blacks. Another African American orator known as "Æthiopian" made a connection between Black military service and freedom. He placed African American men among the group of military heroes worthy of gratitude and admiration. He wrote that "the fair fields of Boston stand as eternal monuments . . . the blood of an Attucks and a Maverick can tell."[42] These sermons and writings expressed gratitude for Black veterans and called for action that would "ennoble" the country, calling for the freedom of the enslaved.

William Frank and fellow Black veterans were part of a growing free Black population, enlarged by a wave of manumissions and gradual emancipation laws enacted after the war. Their lot was not an easy one. Those soldiers who had been enslaved became free, but the everyday circumstances for most veterans of the Black Regiment did not change. They maintained their position on the lower edge of the socioeconomic ladder. Many veterans continued in occupations that did not generate much wealth or prestige. Overall, most of the former First Rhode Islanders had acquired only minimal household furnishings and very little money. Many relied on government pensions to supplement their own labor. Some did own small town lots with small homes. Most did not accept nor settle the bounty land offered by the federal government. They were governed by a rash of Black Codes—enacted to limit their social, political, and economic status. All these disadvantages, however, did not stop the veterans from marrying and

starting their own families. More than half married and started families of
their own. Even though Black veterans had less than full citizenship, their
shared wartime experiences with white veteran soldiers gave them an avenue to push for gratitude and acceptance from a white citizenry that benefitted from these veterans' hard labor during the war. These African
American veterans found a collective voice of protest and demanded their
just rewards for their service in the war.

Community and family pride concerning Black service in the War for
Independence carried on through the generations. The tombstone of
Charles Haskell in Providence's North Burial Ground simply reads: "man
of color. A soldier of the Revolution."[43] An article concerning the service of
Blacks during the Revolutionary War appeared in the *Army and Navy Journal* in September 1863. As a means to validate the service of Blacks during
the Civil War, the article announced "that from the beginning to the conclusion of the war of the Revolution, Negroes served in the Continental
armies with intelligence, courage, and steadfastness; and that important results in several instances are directly traceable to their good conduct."[44]
William Frank and other members of the Black Regiment did show intelligence in dealing with military rules and regulations. They exhibited courage
at the Battles of Red Bank and Rhode Island. And they illustrated their
steadfastness in their long-term commitment to Continental service.

William Cooper Nell's tribute to Black soldiers of the Revolutionary
War, initially published in 1855, was antislavery literature at its finest, using
their service as reason for the liberation and freedom of all Blacks. In her
introduction to the work, Harriet Beecher Stowe wrote:

> In considering the services of the Colored Patriots of the Revolu-
> tion, we are to reflect upon them as far more magnanimous, because
> rendered to a nation which did not acknowledge them as citizens and
> equals, and in whose interests and prosperity they had less at stake. It
> was not for their own land they fought, not even for a land which had
> adopted them, but for a land which had enslaved them, and whose
> laws, even in freedom, oftener oppressed than protected. Bravery,
> under such circumstances, has a peculiar beauty and merit.[45]

Nell used his study of Black veterans as a vehicle to push for the emancipation of all Black persons still enslaved in a country whose liberty was
gained partially with the toil of Black soldiers.

The Battle of Rhode Island serves as a touchstone for the remembrance
of the Black Regiment soldiers, both formerly enslaved and freeborn. A mon-

Detail from the 1790 Federal Census for Johnston, Rhode Island, listing William Frank (Negro). (*National Archives*)

ument to their service is in Portsmouth, Rhode Island, at the junction of Routes 114 and 24, near the site of the Battle of Rhode Island. The National Park Service recognized the location originally in 1975. In 1976, the Newport branch of the National Association for the Advancement of Colored People (NAACP) erected a simple plaque commemorating the battle. It states: "In honor of the first Black slaves and freemen who fought in the Battle of Rhode Island As Members of the First Rhode Island Regiment The Black Regiment." A larger memorial was dedicated in 2005. The new monument lists the names of over one hundred soldiers of color who served with the Black Regiment. Services are held annually at the monument— attended by reenactors as well as descendants of the Black Regiment. The names of the soldiers engraved on the monument came from a listing compiled by Louis Wilson, professor of history at Smith College. The names of Andrew, Ben, and William Frank appear on the monument. Ben's inclusion on this wall of remembrance raises an essential question. Does his name belong on the monument? Yes. Ben served with the Rhode Island regiments for a total of three years. He served at the major battles encountered by those regiments. He survived the winter at Valley Forge. And he served at the battle for which the monument was erected. His commitment and service up to the Battle of Rhode Island was unblemished and steady. His brother's service is less complicated.[46]

By 1790, William Frank headed his own household of two in his hometown of Johnston, Rhode Island. He more than likely shared his household with a wife.[47] Before that, in April 1784, he received a settlement for back wages in the amount of over $200. He sold his land bounty of one hundred acres to Samuel Emery in June 1795. There is a lack of documentary evidence detailing William's life after 1790. As stated earlier, he is not listed in the 1818 or 1835 pension rolls. This may be an indication that he died soon after the bounty land transaction or moved away from Rhode Island. Franklin oral tradition states that William and his family moved to New Orleans during the postwar years. Limited opportunities and restrictive codes in Rhode Island may have led William to leave the confines of his native home for Louisiana—mirroring the transient nature of his brother's postwar existence. The appearance of Franks in the Louisiana censuses for 1870 and 1880 may be reason enough to believe that William did make the transition to the Bayou State, even though a direct link to those Franks and William has not been established. But one cannot help but speculate if the household of Ben Frank in 1870 Napoleonville, Louisiana, or the household of William Frank in 1870 St. Mary Parish somehow have a link to the diligent and tenacious veteran.[48]

CHAPTER TEN

Ben Franklin,
Black Loyalist

B EN FRANK LOOKED UPON the retreating shores of Long Island, New York, as he stood aboard the brig *Elijah* as it made its way to Nova Scotia. He was leaving behind his family, his name, and his allegiance to his native land. However, he was not leaving behind family tradition and his sense of community and what it meant to be a man. He would carry on the Frank family's story in North America even as he carried a different name. He was no longer known as Ben Frank. He was now Ben Frankham, a Black loyalist described as an "ordinary fellow." It was the start of a strange and difficult journey.

Ben Frankham and his fellow Black loyalists were part of a much larger loyalist migration composed of refugees fleeing the American port cities of Charleston and New York looking for security and freedom in Great Britain, the Caribbean, and British North America. Ben's departure to Nova Scotia initiated a journey of continual struggle and migration as a member of a larger community of free Blacks trying to maintain their hard-fought freedom and gain equality in terms of economic competency and independence. Previous studies of Black loyalists and Black loyalism focus on former slaves and free Black leaders like Stephen Blucke. Most studies begin with the flight of enslaved Blacks to British lines during the American Revolution and end with the mass migration of Black loyalists to Sierra Leone. These studies provide limited analysis of those free Black loyalists who fled to the British cause and who remained in Nova Scotia after the movement of many Blacks to Sierra Leone. The experiences of Ben Frankham, who remained in Nova Scotia, allow an understanding of those free Blacks who stayed.[1]

For Ben, this was also the beginning of a more personal journey to re-define and reconstitute his life as a free man of color. He shed his prior life as he had shed his name. As Ben Frankham, he was now being given the opportunity to start anew by forming new familial and community ties. His journey was also a physical one as he traversed the Nova Scotian peninsula, seeking the best place to restart his life. Ben and other Black loyalists would continually attempt to gain economic independence for themselves and their families through the quick acquisition of enough land and other resources to provide a sustaining livelihood. These Black Nova Scotians would also build and foster institutions that reflected what they valued and enabled them to survive in an often hostile environment. Church, school, and family became the founding blocks and survival mechanisms for Black loyalist communities in Nova Scotia.[2]

Black loyalists like Ben were also caught up in the debate concerning true loyalism. They may have been aware of the statements offered by the Board of Associated Loyalists, headquartered in New York, which established its own definition of loyalism. Board members divided loyalists into two distinct groups. The ultraloyalists supported the Crown from the start of the conflict. "Faux" loyalists included anyone who had ever supported the Americans and only came to the British cause due to promises of free land and provisions. Board members may have placed Ben Frankham in the latter category of fake loyalism—an artificial supporter of the king, only trying to obtain personal gain.[3]

Ben and other Black loyalists were part of a larger multiracial migration that started as early as 1776 with the mass evacuation of British citizens and soldiers from Boston during the early years of the war, concluding with the last wave of refugees evacuating Long Island at the end of the war. An estimated 200,000 to 500,000 Americans of European, African, or Native descent left their homes in America. A significant portion of loyalists, over 40,000, made their way to the Canadian colonies of British North America. Over 20,000 eventually settled in Nova Scotia, tripling the population of that British province. Ben Frankham and other Black loyalists bound for

Nova Scotia totaled over 3,000 members and included those who were born free, those who purchased their freedom, recently freed slaves, and the enslaved and indentured servants of white loyalists. The fate of these loyalists in their new homes was based in part on their needs and the government's ability to fulfill those needs. They formed new settlements and societies based upon common bonds forged during wartime and evacuation, along with shared ideas concerning race, race relations, and slavery.[4]

Ben and his fellow Black loyalists made up three separate migration waves to Nova Scotia during the revolutionary era. The first occurred in 1776 with the Company of Negroes, a British fighting unit that evacuated with British citizens and soldiers. The second group of 4,000 Black loyalists and 6,000 enslaved persons migrated after the British defeat and evacuation at Charleston, South Carolina, which was finally evacuated in December 1782 to three separate destinations: the Caribbean, England, or New York. About five hundred were immediately dispatched to Halifax. The last group left New York, after the signing of the Paris peace treaty in 1783.[5]

The loyalist migration to Nova Scotia included eighty-one ships in three main waves over a period of ten months. These ships carried racially mixed groups of loyalists. However, as the massive migration progressed and military units started to move out, the ships' passenger lists grew more segregated. The brig *Elijah* and its passengers were part of a racially segregated fall fleet that departed from New York between September and November 1783. Most of the ships transporting Black loyalists were dispatched to Port Roseway and Annapolis Royal and the growing loyalist communities there. However, Ben and his fellow passengers were part of a smaller group of Black loyalists, aboard four ships, who were destined for the settlement at Port Mouton in the fall of 1783. The voyage from Long Island to Nova Scotia took one to two weeks. The conditions of the voyage were rough and treacherous. Food supplies were limited, sickness prevailed on all the ships, and the threat of shipwrecks loomed large due to the rough waters of the northern Atlantic and rugged coastline of Atlantic Canada.[6]

Ben was a member of this last group of loyalists embarking on October 31, 1783. The overall group of 3,000 Blacks who departed for Nova Scotia included 1,336 men, 914 women, 339 boys, 335 girls, and 76 other juveniles of unspecified gender. They traveled alone, as married couples, and as extended families. The greatest majority—like Ben Frankham—traveled alone. These solo passengers included 1,119 men, 492 women, 215 boys, and 174 girls. However, many families were able to remain intact during a period of disorder and disruption. Over eighty-six couples without children were among the Black loyalists that migrated to Nova Scotia, and seventy-four additional families had at least one child and other extended family members.[7]

The passengers of the brig *Elijah* were not members of the better known Black Pioneers, but they were representative of many Black loyalists sailing to Nova Scotia. They reflected the general characteristics of the typical Black loyalist. They were American born. They were formerly enslaved. And they were mostly from the South. Ben Frankham, however, regardless of his alleged residency in South Carolina, was not the typical Black loyalist on board the *Elijah*. He was American born but not from the South, and he did not claim the status of being formerly enslaved.

Historians have argued that members of the loyalist establishment did not look out for the best interests of Black loyalists. Ruma Chopra contends that employees in the British administration sought to make profits from the sale of refugees seeking safe haven in New York City. James St. G. Walker argued that provincial officers and other loyalists were active participants in the sale of some fugitive slaves. In particular, he wrote that forty-three refugees were transported to Montreal and sold there for approximately £33 each. Michael McDonnell asserts that authorities sometimes used runaways as payment for services rendered. Sylvia Frey argued that some British and loyalist officials also failed to properly feed and clothe Black loyalists under their supervision. Overall, such behavior may have prompted Black loyalists to be circumspect when presenting themselves to the commissioners responsible for adjudging their right to evacuate. Regardless of their motivations and actions to ensure their evacuation, they still had to pass all stages of a process designed to allow only "legitimate" refugees to embark.[8]

Prior to actual embarkation, Black loyalists had to endure one final screening. An inspection team of British and American officials met them on the decks of their designated transport ships to validate their status as legitimate loyalist refugees. The embarkation commissioners/inspectors who approved the embarkation of the brig *Elijah* on October 31, 1783, were Thomas Gilfillan and William Armstrong on behalf of the British, and William Stephen Smith and Samuel Jones on behalf of the United States. The commissioners made sure that Ben and his fellow passengers possessed legitimate certificates of freedom, signed by either General Samuel Birch or General Thomas Musgrave. General Birch signed most of the certificates possessed by passengers of the brig *Elijah*; however, General Musgrave certified others like Ben Frankham as free men. The inspection team cross-checked each of the names listed on the ship's official passenger manifest against the names registered in General Carleton's *Book of Negroes*.[9]

If a passenger did not pass this final inspection, he or she was not permitted to evacuate, and the case was referred to the board of inquiry. General Carleton created the board to deal with American slaveholders who claimed that people of color belonged to them. Board commissioners met twice weekly to determine the status of fugitive slaves who sought freedom from angry and distraught former owners. The board made their determinations based on Carleton's decision to give certificates of freedom only to those slaves that had fled to British lines by November 1782. However, this decision-making was inconsistent. On the one hand, the board returned some fugitive slaves to their owners, sometimes precipitating the separation of family members. In one case, Samuel Dobson "stole away" his two children, Peter and Elizabeth, from their master, only to have the children returned to the slaveholder by order of the board, based upon their finding that the children were "too young" to respond to offers of freedom from the British. In another case, the board ruled that a wife and her three children had to remain in the United States, while her husband, a fugitive slave, was allowed to evacuate due to his service with the British military. However, the board did uphold the testimony of some formerly enslaved individuals against the claims of their former owners, and American military officials found their claims undercut when slaveholders refused to travel to Long Island for hearings. In general, American slaveholders used the board as a last ditch effort to retrieve their runaway slaves. British officials also used the board and its decisions to follow the directives contained in the Paris Peace Treaty. As a final check, every ship captain carrying passengers of color to Nova Scotia was warned "that he would not be permitted to Land any other Negroes than those mention'd in the List, and that if any other Negroes were found on board his vessel he would be severely punished."[10]

As the Black loyalists received their final approval, obtained supplies, and set sail for Nova Scotia, some must have experienced a wealth of emotions over the sensation of leaving lives of perpetual servitude and moving on to lives of self-determination. Like the formerly enslaved, Ben was also running away from his former life and toward what he must have perceived as a better life. Unlike the formerly enslaved, Ben was not leaving a life of institutionalized slavery, but a life of self-selected responsibilities that began to overwhelm him—serving with the Continental army and becoming the head of a fledgling family. He was not leaving to seek freedom from enslavement. He was leaving to seek freedom of another type. His military service with the Continentals, his self-furlough, his marriage, and his estrangement from his family were almost certainly the precipitating factors in his flight to a new life in Nova Scotia.[11]

So, in the fall of 1783, Ben's new life started as a member of one of the "Black Companies" under the leadership of individuals with honorary command status. Blacks as well as whites were organized into various companies to facilitate the distribution of government provisions. Many members of these companies traveled on ships comprised solely of Black passengers. Many were enslaved, indentured servants, or apprentices to white loyalists. Many traveled "on his (or her) bottom," a term used by members of the Birch Commission, meaning that some Black loyalists gained their freedom in return for their service to the Crown. The Black loyalists on board the brig *Elijah* comprised one such company under the leadership of Captain Robert Bridges, an "ordinary fellow" but lame by the age of forty-three. Bridges, a blacksmith employed by the Wagon Master General's Department, traveled with his wife and daughter. The remainder of Ben's fellow passengers was a diverse group. Thirteen passengers were carried under the banner of the Wagon Master General's Department. Thirty-five passengers were listed in some form or fashion as "free." Of that number, twenty-one were listed as being born free or listed as infants born within British lines. Ironically, two of those passengers, Lucy Johnson and Patience Jackson, claimed Rhode Island, Ben's home state, as their place of birth. Ten passengers proved to be free as certified by a commission officer or by producing a bill of sale. Four others stipulated that they had either earned their freedom or lived as free people before the war. Some traveled with infirmities and major disabilities. For instance, James Rea was listed as an "ordinary fellow without legs." And Hannah Linning, a formerly enslaved woman, was listed as being "blind of an eye."[12]

Ben's passage to Nova Scotia with other members of the Wagon Master General's Department may indicate his role with the British after his departure from the Continental army. Blacks in these branches served throughout the theater of war in large numbers, serving oftentimes in integrated companies, which felt familiar to Ben given his experience early on in his military career. Blacks served as general laborers, sawyers, blacksmiths, and wagon drivers. The Wagon Master General's Department was charged with the maintenance of horses, carts, and drivers. The department was also tasked with transporting provisions and other equipment to troops in the field. If Ben served as a wagon driver, his new job did not protect him from the hazardous conditions of the battlefront.[13]

Fifty-two of Ben's shipmates were formerly enslaved, and the records often captured when they left their owners and ran to British lines. Ten members of Bridges' company left in 1776, early in the conflict. This may have been in response to Dunmore's Proclamation issued in December 1775, calling upon slaves to leave their masters to fight for the British cause in exchange for their freedom. Five in this group fled from owners in Virginia, the location of Dunmore's Proclamation. Most of the former slaves fled from 1778 to 1779, the highest flight year being 1779.[14] British policy as directed by military high command may have contributed to these higher numbers. General Henry Clinton, British commander in chief, followed Dunmore's Proclamation with one of his own that sought to protect the rights of Blacks who had fled to British lines. The Philipsburg Proclamation, issued in June 1779, stated that Blacks captured in service with the rebels would be sold for the benefit of the British, but those who sought refuge with the British would be protected. Additionally, Clinton promised that these "volunteers" would be allowed the opportunity to practice any occupation that they felt was "proper."[15] Only six of the formerly enslaved indicated a time of flight near the time of Ben Frankham's desertion. But of those six, three—George Price, Hannah Linning, and Dinah—fled from South Carolina, Ben Frankham's self-proclaimed place of residence. All the formerly enslaved who arrived at Port Mouton aboard the brig *Elijah* fell well within General Carleton's interpretation of the provisions included in the Paris peace treaty regarding the return of slaves to American owners. He believed that Article VII of the treaty applied only to those Blacks who were not free. He considered Blacks already within British lines before November 1782 as free and no longer property. The formerly enslaved who sailed with Ben Frankham to Nova Scotia were not latecomers to the British cause. They fled during the early and middle years of the war at a time when American military officials were still grappling with the issue of recruiting the enslaved as soldiers.[16]

The loyalist associations and British officials selected Nova Scotia as a destination for a variety of reasons. First, it was nearby. The southern tip of its peninsula was approximately one hundred miles from the coast of Maine. Its naval base at Halifax was six hundred miles from New York City. The voyage from Long Island to Nova Scotia took only one to two weeks. Second, approximately five million hectares of land were available for allocation to the loyalist refugees. The Canadian peninsula attracted the loyalist associations and British officials because of its strong British commercial and military presence. Additionally, Nova Scotia was a destination for New

Englanders in the decades before the American Revolution. There was already a Yankee presence in the province. They were attracted by the fertile lands, vacated by the forced Acadian expulsion. In 1759, British policy encouraged migration of English-speaking immigrants to Nova Scotia by offering large tracts of former Acadian lands to New Englanders. From 1760 to 1774, some 8,000 former New Englanders settled throughout the region. Finally, reports of Nova Scotia's picturesque harbors, forests of spruce, pine, and maple, and its bountiful cod fishery made it seem a good place to settle loyalist refugees. The negative aspects of the Nova Scotian landscape—its rocky soil and impenetrable forests and swamps—did not deter those choosing a place for the fleeing loyalists.[17]

Ben Frankham and other Black loyalists made up approximately 10 percent of the total loyalist population. They joined approximately five hundred Blacks already living in Nova Scotia. The Black presence in Nova Scotia began at Port-Royal, present-day Annapolis Royal, in the early 1600s when Mathieu Costa accompanied French explorers Pierre Du Gua, Sieur de Monts, and Samuel de Champlain to the region. A free Black person known as "La Liberte" was counted in the 1686 census as a resident of Cape Sable Island. A 1767 census of Nova Scotia recorded 104 people of African descent residing in twelve of the thirty townships enumerated. Additionally, early Black settlement occurred in the pre-loyalist era with a wave of transplanted New England farmers and former military personnel looking for land and other economic opportunities. By 1750, fifteen Blacks received rations in Halifax. By 1760, the government opened new lands confiscated from the exiled Acadians. Blacks also seized this opportunity and took up residence in Halifax, Liverpool, Bridgetown, Annapolis, and Onslow. With the arrival of several waves of Black loyalists, the province would gain over 4,500 Blacks by 1783.[18]

Ben Frankham's early experiences in Nova Scotia were filled with the difficulties faced by poor men and women attempting to start a new life in a new land. These settlers not only were dependent upon their own devices but also relied on the support of their government. As new settlers, the loyalists arrived at their new homes with both trepidation and expectation. The loyalist associations' negotiations and agreements with the British government held out the promise of land for farming. The loyalist emigrants would try to hold provincial officials to agreements and promises made before they set sail to Nova Scotia.

British officials did attempt to ease the burden of resettlement by providing land and assistance to the loyalist refugees. Negotiations between loyalist associations and the British government, represented by General Carleton, took place during the Paris peace treaty talks. The initial planning meetings held by members of the associations concentrated on determining the destination of each group and naming agents to represent their concerns in Nova Scotia. These agents would travel in advance to Canada and arrange for the acquisition and allocation of land. The members of the associations then turned their attention to other concerns. They drafted proposals to General Carleton requesting first and foremost land: land free of title, land in parcels of 300 to 500 acres for each family, and land that was "well situated." The associations also requested transportation, livestock, farming tools, and a year's worth of food rations and other supplies. General Carleton countered with an offer that was tempered by his need to supply not only civilian loyalists but also members of the disbanded provincial troops migrating to Canada. The land allocation for the 30,000 loyalists that settled in Nova Scotia between 1782 and 1784 gave priority to those who had suffered the greatest losses. They received land equivalent to what they had lost during the war. Military personnel and ordinary loyalists were to be granted plots of land ranging from 1,000 acres for ranking officers to one hundred acres for privates, with an additional allowance of 100 acres for family members, and 100 acres for the heads of families of ordinary loyalists and fifty acres for each member. The list for land was long, and Black loyalists were placed at the end of it. Carleton also promised civilian loyalists transportation to Nova Scotia and provisions for six months, including full military rations for men and boys over thirteen, half rations for adult women, and one quarter rations for children. Black loyalists were to be given the same provisions, supplies, and land as other loyalists.[19]

The sheer number of loyalist emigrants overwhelmed the small, underdeveloped colony of Nova Scotia. Its officials struggled to deal with the incessant and very real needs of its new residents. Those residents believed that their hardship was exacerbated by the ineptness of local and provincial officials like Governor John Parr. A tense, frustrating, and conflicting relationship consequently developed between and among the arriving loyalists and government officials. According to previous agreements, Governor Parr's responsibility toward the incoming loyalist force was threefold: preparation for actual settlement; placement on their own land; and assurance of their survival. By the spring of 1783, Parr made some progress in accomplishing these tasks, as he dealt with the waves of loyalists being channeled into Port Roseway, later renamed Shelburne after the British prime minister, and the region surrounding the Bay of Fundy. Building supplies were transported to the areas. Parr also assigned provincial surveyors to lay out towns and allocate land grants to individual loyalists. Regardless of British promises and assurances, however, the first-year experience in Nova Scotia for most loyalists was characterized by minimal supplies, overcrowded housing, and stingy governmental support. Loyalists complained of tardy surveys that slowed their settlement on allocated land and the ineptness of government officials who cared little about their dire circumstances.[20]

For Ben Frankham and other Blacks who arrived in the fall of 1783, race further complicated these already existing difficulties. Upon arrival in Nova Scotia, Ben and other refugees became the responsibility of Governor John Parr. However, Parr did not receive any specific notification or instructions regarding the influx of a large Black contingent. Carleton did not offer or recommend any special considerations to assist the group of the formerly enslaved or freeborn men like Ben Frankham. He repeatedly reminded the governor of the promises made to all loyalist refugees. Carleton reiterated that the British government, in the personage of Governor John Parr, had agreed to supply free land and food rations while the new loyalist settlers became self-sufficient on their own land.[21] Early in the evacuation, General Carleton instructed Parr to be ready for the refugees and provide them with resources, especially land. Parr replied in October 1782 that land could be made available but "there is not any Houses or Cover to put them under Shelter . . . this Town is already so crouded . . . that army recruits had to be hutted in the Woods . . . and when I add the Scarcity and difficulty of providing fuel, and lumber for building which is still greater, the many inconveniences and great distress these people must suffer, if any of them come into this Province this Winter, will sufficiently appear."[22] Governor Parr's response to Carleton foreshadowed the problems that would plague and haunt Black loyalists for the first ten years of their existence in Nova Scotia.

As one of the last groups of loyalists to arrive, Ben Frankham and his shipmates were entering a very tenuous environment. They disembarked at Port Mouton in late 1783. Soldiers of the Southern campaign during the war from Banastre Tarleton's Legion and their families already inhabited the settlement, located at the southern tip of the peninsula. With land, resources, and supplies stretched to their limits, Tarleton's soldiers and their families lived in the worst of conditions. They tried to survive the winter in tents or huts made of sod and logs. Their clothing was too limited and blankets too thin to withstand the harsh Nova Scotian environment. The arrival of the fall fleet with its Black loyalist passengers only caused greater consternation among the inhabitants of the settlement and officials tasked to provide shelter and subsistence to them.[23]

Ben Frankham's first and only winter at Port Mouton was bleak, with lumber needed to build shelters arriving too late to protect many from the harsh elements of winter. Refugees like Ben had to depend on government officials for supplies and food rations. Additionally, the British navy had standing orders to support and supply the loyalists when necessary. The ship *Bonita,* anchored at Port Mouton, served this purpose for the struggling settlers. Because of limited supplies, bad weather, and an overwhelming influx of refugees, Ben and other Black members of Captain Bridges' company had to wait longer for housing and other provisions than white refugees. During their first winter at Port Mouton, they lived in either tents, shelters made of bark, transport vessels, or huts built of sod, like Tarleton's Legion before them. The combined factors of cold, hunger, and frustration resulted in violence, with fights and other unruly behavior occurring throughout Port Mouton. A fire the following spring destroyed shelters and warehouses that stored most of the provisions for the settlement. The destruction caused by the fire and the loss of provisions forced many of the townspeople, including many Black loyalists, to other settlements. Many Black loyalists migrated to an area near Chedabucto Bay on the northeast shore of mainland Nova Scotia. This group would eventually create the all-Black settlement of Little Tracadie. Others migrated to the all-Black settlement of Birchtown, near Shelburne, just southwest of the ruins of Port Mouton on the southwest coast of the peninsula. Ben Frankham was among this latter group.[24]

Shelburne was the domain of the Port Roseway Loyalist Association, composed of over four hundred families. Prior to the evacuation, leaders of this group had negotiated with General Carleton in New York for land, supplies, and transportation to the sparsely populated rural region. Upon their arrival, the Port Roseway settlers found a very unsettled place. There was no town. There was a forest filled with pines, hemlock, oak, and thick brush covering the site selected for their new community. Town lots, streets, or roads did not miraculously spring out of the forested landscape to welcome the new settlers. White and Black refugees immediately set about the task of clearing the forest and brush to construct housing and the foundation of a town. Out of this initial wilderness, a large, thriving loyalist community developed. The Shelburne loyalists were driven by their desire to create a mercantile capital in British North America as the premier trading post between the British Caribbean and Great Britain. Governor Parr boasted that "I have not a doubt of its being, one day or other, the first Port in this part of America."[25]

By the time Ben moved to the area in the spring of 1784, Shelburne had a population of over 10,000 inhabitants, making it the largest community in Nova Scotia. It boasted two newspapers, two churches, a coffeehouse, and several taverns. It was led by members of a small but ambitious commercial class that seemed hell-bent on replicating an upper-class lifestyle in impressive homes and business establishments. These members of the upper class, comprised of field officers and civilian loyalists of the same stature, were eligible for land grants of 1,000 acres, but they did not constitute the larger percentage of Shelburne loyalists. Most loyalists at Shelburne did not come from the upper classes. And most members of the loyalist elite returned to England or migrated to Halifax. Members of the working classes populated Shelburne. They were farmers, merchants, mariners, and artisans. They were primarily city folks and, according to loyalist deputy surveyor Benjamin Marston, they lacked education and qualities of leadership. Marston also felt that they were unsuited to the harsh life and hard work necessary to create a new community. Additionally, the creation and development of Birchtown as a satellite community of Shelburne illustrated an emerging pattern of segregation based on ethnic and regional ties. Former colonial and state identities remained important to loyalists as they searched for new homes and communities in Nova Scotia. Immigrants from the same region felt a strong sense of cohesiveness and tended to settle together. Loyalists also tended to settle with members of their own ethnic group. The arrival of free Black loyalists intensified this impulse to segregate.[26]

The large number of Blacks, over 1,500, arriving at Port Roseway in the late summer and early fall of 1783 facilitated the creation of Birchtown. In comparison, only 558 Black loyalists disembarked at Port Mouton—the site of Ben Frankham's arrival. By the summer of 1783, Shelburne was dealing with a burgeoning population. The Black passengers arriving aboard the ship *L'Abondance* that had left New York City on July 31, 1783, were instructed to start a new settlement near Shelburne. Many of the passengers aboard *L'Abondance* were formerly enslaved from various locations in Virginia. The contingent also included several families with small children and infants born "within British lines," an indication that families were able to maintain their integrity during the war. Also on board were Blacks that claimed to be born free. Individuals like Elizabeth Hutchens, Rose Williams, Margaret Wallus, and Stephen Blucke were among the few on board *L'Abondance* that claimed that status. Blucke became an influential figure in the history of Birchtown. He is listed in the *Book of Negroes* as a "stout fellow. Says he was born free in the Island of Barbadoes."[27] Blucke is sometimes identified as a Black Pioneer. However, his military record is vague, and he is not listed in any of the records for the Black Pioneers. Contemporaries such as Captain William Booth of the British Royal Engineers described him as a "man of surprising address, being perfectly polite and I believe has had a superior education."[28] Since he had experience as a leader of the Black loyalists during their stay in New York City, Blucke was again given the responsibility of leadership in developing the settlement of Birchtown. He emerged as one of the first Black leaders in Nova Scotia. Governor Parr appointed him lieutenant-colonel of the Black militia stationed in the Shelburne district upon his arrival there. This position allowed Blucke to become the de facto mayor of the settlement with the authority to speak on behalf of Birchtown Blacks.[29]

Orders to Governor Parr preceded the arrival of the Black loyalists, directing their eventual placement on land on the northwest harbor of the small bay formed by the Jordan River. The government's lead deputy surveyor, Benjamin Marston, received the responsibility of mapping out the allocation of land in the Shelburne area to the incoming loyalists. He captured his feelings of frustration in his diary and in letters to his supervisor as he tried to satisfy loyalist refugees and their demands for land. Marston wrote that the development of Shelburne was moving along quite nicely, regardless of the complaints from many white loyalists. In contrast, Marston appreciated the response received from the Black loyalists of Shelburne when they were shown the land upon which their new settlement would be built. On August 28, 1783, Marston met with Colonel Stephen Blucke, the leader of the Shelburne Blacks, "to show him the ground allotted for his people. They are well satisfied with it."[30] Marston and his subordinates immediately began to survey the property, breaking it up into single town lots. By early September 1783, the new Birchtown residents were hurriedly building huts on their lots to survive the upcoming winter, while Marston's subordinates continued to survey the remaining parcels of their allocated land.[31]

The new settlement was located on the northwest portion of a heart-shaped bay on the Atlantic coast and several miles northwest of the city of Shelburne, along the Jordan River. Initial survey maps, compiled by Marston's crew, indicated a landmass insufficient for its occupants. One map showed Birchtown located near a marsh on a block of land measuring

1,350 feet by 1,160 feet with a land base of 1,056 feet. A second map showed Birchtown with thirty-five ten-acre lots along the banks of the West Birchtown Brook that flowed through the settlement. Household lots were intended to provide enough room for growing fruits and vegetables and Birchtown residents were also in line to receive larger plots of land for farming purposes. However, considering the acreage available to the residents, the land granted to the Birchtown Blacks was not large enough to sufficiently accommodate the needs of its residents or the promises made by the British government. This initial outlay of land did not provide economic competency for Black loyalists.[32]

The distance between the larger city of Shelburne and the Black settlement could be covered by a short ferry ride or a walk of approximately six miles. The strip of land between the two contained an army barracks, built to house over three hundred soldiers. Additionally, a road linking the two settlements allowed the soldiers to march to church in Shelburne and provided better communication between the two communities. By September 3, 1783, six Black companies with almost five hundred members under the overall leadership of Blucke made their residence at the new site, named after Brigadier General Samuel Birch, who had signed many certificates of freedom for the freed Blacks now living at Birchtown. The members of these six companies became the founders of the largest Black settlement in North America.[33]

Ben Frankham, still a member of Captain Robert Bridges' company, was part of five companies of free Blacks that relocated to Birchtown on the last day of April 1784. The movement caused an influx of over three hundred free Blacks into the growing settlement. Captain Bridges' company was the second largest and included seventy-two persons with twenty-eight adult males, twenty-four adult females, and twenty children. All claimed their right to receive "the King's Bounty"—food rations and other provisions supplied by government officials. None were rejected.[34]

There was an obvious change in Bridges' company after its arrival at Port Mouton and then resettlement at Birchtown. Many individuals who embarked at New York with Ben Frankham's group were no longer listed with the company. Of the eighty-four loyalists that set sail with Ben Frankham, approximately one-half arrived at Birchtown with other transplanted settlers from Port Mouton. Several new family members had joined the group. It appears that Patience Jackson, who claimed to have been born free in Rhode Island, became Patience Warrington—the spouse of fellow brig *Elijah* passenger Joseph Warrington. Solomon and Chloe Lawson wel-

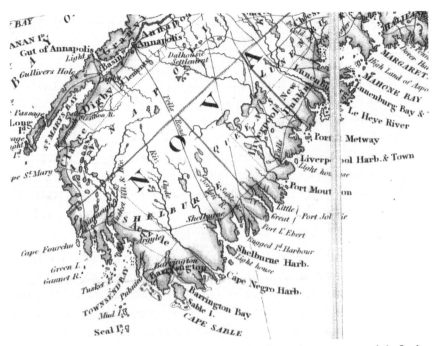

Detail from an 1827 map of Nova Scotia showing Shelburne, lower center, and the Jordan River just to its right. "Map of the United States and the provinces of upper & lower Canada, New Brunswick, and Nova Scotia. London," published by J. & A. Walker, June 1st, 1827. (*Library of Congress*)

comed daughter Jane into their family. George and Peggy Wise also added a new daughter to their family. Both daughters were six months of age at the time of the Birchtown inventory. With the addition of Ben Frankham and other displaced Black loyalists, Birchtown's population rose to a total of 1,521 free Blacks in 686 households.[35]

The first winter at Birchtown was as daunting and miserable as the bleak winter survived by Ben Frankham and his fellow shipmates at Port Mouton. Some residents were lucky enough to live in very rudimentary huts, built on town lots during the waning days of the preceding fall.[36] Boston King described the situation in Birchtown in the following manner: "We arrived at Burch Town in the month of August where we all safely landed. Every family had a lot of land, and we exerted all our strength in order to build comfortable huts before the cold weather set in."[37] For some, the "comfortable" huts were no more than cave-like dwellings constructed to stave off the harsh winter elements. Native Nova Scotian Clara Dennis described the remains of these "comfortable" huts in her essay detailing her visit to the province in the 1930s:

> Later I wandered through the woods where the earlier pioneer black men had had their habitations. "Surely human beings could never have lived in this place," I said. "They are only holes in the ground!" "That's all they were," said the present owner of the land. . . . "The government gave the negroes land here, but they had no houses, not even log cabins. They just dug a hole in the ground and put a little peaked roof over it. They chose a hill for their purpose because the ground was drier. The peaked roof would shed the water when it rained. There was a small trapdoor in one side of the roof and the negroes entered the house by dropping right down through."[38]

Archaeological data reinforces Clara Dennis' description of the Black loyalists' homesteads at Birchtown. An excavation conducted in 1993 by archaeologist Laird Niven examined the remains of a habitat with its main living quarters occupying a depression measuring five feet by five feet and approximately twenty inches deep. These pit houses were built as temporary shelters to survive the winter, but archaeological evidence shows that these structures were used for more than one season.[39]

Ben Frankham had seen this type of rudimentary housing before. "Hutting" was a principal occupation of Continental troops during the harsh winter months. During his tenure with the Continental army, the Rhode Island regulars lived in huts during their encampment at Valley Forge in the winter of 1777–1778. There were standard orders regarding the building of huts. Each hut was to be fourteen feet wide and sixteen feet long, with walls six and one-half feet high. The walls and roof were constructed of wood and fortified with clay. The reality of life in camp and at war may have altered the actual construction of huts occupied at Valley Forge. Archaeological data indicates that some huts did not meet the standard. Many soldiers dug a hole, in the shape of a hut, into the ground, reinforcing the hole with lumber and covering the hut with tent canvas. Ben was more than likely reminded of the harsh circumstances of his wartime service, but because of those experiences, he was equipped to deal with these harsh conditions.[40]

Many of the Black loyalists at Birchtown faced the first winter without the support of a farm and turned to employment as sharecroppers for more prosperous white farm owners or as laborers in a Black militia group led by Colonel Stephen Blucke. Enrollment with the latter ensured their housing

Reconstructed Birchtown huts, Nova Scotia. (*Author*)

in barracks or tents. Given Ben's service with the Continentals and experience with military life, it is possible that he served with the militia and
afforded himself the opportunity to endure the harsh winter in housing
supplied for the group. Food provisions and other supplies were still distributed by government officials, who had at their disposal a stockpile of
provisions—mostly salted foodstuffs and biscuits—for loyalist refugees. In
early 1784, commissary officer Ed Brinley supplied daily rations to over
8,600 individuals in the Shelburne district, including civilian loyalists, soldiers, freed Blacks, and their families. Brinley's responsibility to feed and
clothe loyalist refugees did not end at the original six-month cutoff date.
Later in 1784, Brinley distributed over 2,500 pounds of bread, over 200,000

pounds of flour, 3,900 pounds of beef, 3,200 gallons of rum, and 7,600 gallons of molasses. Refugees were entitled to an assortment of other supplies and clothing. Allocations included an axe, shoes, mittens, woolen cloth, and linen. Carleton's promise to supply food and other provisions for six months was adjusted in the following manner: refugees were entitled to full rations for one whole year; two-thirds rations for the second year; and one-third ration for the third year. Carleton and other officials expected the new settlers to be self-sufficient by the end of the third year.[41]

Ben and his companions became part of a growing community of free Blacks who were trying to establish a thriving, stable settlement. The prospects for Black loyalists living at Birchtown looked encouraging at first glance. Even though most settlers like Ben Frankham were general laborers, the settlement did have its share of industrious skilled laborers. Carpenters, sawyers, coopers, and sailors also inhabited the settlement. Members of Captain Bridges' company brought with them a diversity of talents and skills. Company leader Robert Bridges and George Johnson were black-smiths. Richard Bush and Jacob Watson were sawyers. John Bellamy was a sailor, Nate Martins was a sail maker, and single men Pompey Donaldson and Thomas Francis were farmers. Another important characteristic among the residents was education. Some Birchtown inhabitants were literate and brought their experiences as free people with them. Birchtown also had a strong-willed and charismatic leader, Stephen Blucke. However, for all its strengths, Birchtown would not become the strong and independent community desired by its inhabitants. Above all else, Black loyalists wished to obtain economic independence through land ownership. This notion of competency drove their concerns about the rapid acquisition of land and other resources. Their hopes for economic self-sufficiency and the success of Birchtown would dim as the realities of life in Nova Scotia took hold. Their community deteriorated quickly due to a series of unfortunate man-made and natural events.[42]

A major problem preventing the self-sufficiency of the Birchtown community was its lack of commerce. No commercial stores dotted its landscape. One peddler lived in the settlement, but no shopkeeper was listed among the residents in the 1784 census. As stated earlier, members of Captain Bridges' company brought with them marketable skills and abilities. However, these men were forced by the limited opportunities in Birchtown to sell their services in the larger town of Shelburne. Birchtown residents similarly purchased what they needed from white business owners of Shelburne.[43]

The most important issue preventing the self-sufficiency of Birchtown was the limited and delayed distribution of land to its residents. As stated earlier, the geography of Birchtown also made it a poor location for large farming enterprises. It was remote, swampy, and rocky. Many of the Birchtown inhabitants were formerly enslaved and worked primarily in a plantation economy that cultivated tobacco and rice. They were ill prepared to eke out a living cultivating the native cereal crops of Nova Scotia. Ben and other new residents of Birchtown were allocated town lots like those already granted to earlier settlers. However, greater parcels of land for farming were limited to a minority of residents. Survey maps of the region indicate the problem of land availability for all Birchtown residents. The block of land given to the Black loyalists at Birchtown was entirely too small to accommodate the numbers needing plots of land for farming purposes. The farm lots promised to ordinary civilian loyalists--100 acres for the heads of families and fifty acres for each member—were not available to all the Black residents of Birchtown. The average land grant given to white loyalists—a small town lot and fifty acres for farming—was also not available to the Black loyalists at Birchtown. Most white loyalists acquired their lots within three years, many years before Black loyalists.[44]

The steps to acquire land were cumbersome and time-consuming. There were ten steps and six legal papers to be filed before a grant was processed. The process involved the grantee petitioning the government for the land, the surveyor-general viewing the land in question and clearing the land for title, and the governor approving the legal title to the land. Also, there were other conditions stipulated for land ownership. Survey costs were not to be paid by grantees and an annual quitrent of two shillings per one hundred acres was suspended for the first ten years. However, grantees were expected to make improvements on their property within a timely manner and take an oath of allegiance to the mother country.[45]

Only thirty-one residents were listed as farmers on the 1784 Birchtown census. By 1785, of the 649 free Black men at Birchtown, only 184 or 28 percent were able to complete the process and receive farm lots, averaging about thirty-four acres each—an amount sorely insufficient to provide economic competency. Colonel Blucke possessed the largest land grant at two hundred acres. The lots were located about ten miles west of Birchtown near an inland lake on very rocky and acidic soil. The lots near Beaver Dam were covered with large rock outcroppings and not conducive to growing significant farm crops. The allocated land, with its unsuitable soil, did not provide the necessary means for the Birchtown residents to take care of themselves or their families. The situation forced the Blacks at Birchtown to rely more upon the King's Bounty (rations from government officials) and the labor needs of white Shelburnians as opposed to establishing their own economic independence and sense of competency, which had initially driven many of them to the British cause.

The fifty-two adult members of Captain Bridges' company who moved to Birchtown from Port Mouton along with Ben Frankham in the spring of 1784 were recipients of limited opportunities due to inadequate land procurement. Ben, listed as Ben Frankum on the Birchtown muster roll, is not documented as receiving land in the Birchtown settlement. However, others in the Bridges' company did—in the form of town lots described by loyalist Jas Courtney as "just large enough for a Good House and Small Garden."[46] George Johnson and William Deane received legal titles to individual town lots of about one acre each, providing some sort of self-sufficiency in the form of a home and garden. For Johnson, a single thirty-year-old and skilled blacksmith, the lot may have provided the location for a small blacksmithing business. For Deane, a sixty-year-old married laborer, the grant allowed him to provide a home for himself and his wife, Flora. Also at the age of sixty, Richard Bush built a home on his town lot, providing shelter for his small family including his wife Lilly and daughter Jenny. A much younger husband and father, twenty-four-year-old Ishmael York, established a household on his town lot with his wife Elizabeth and young daughter Indiana. No members of Bridges' group received enough acreage for farming purposes.[47]

Even though some Birchtown residents did receive their land grants, land ownership did not necessarily provide self-sufficiency. Much-needed capital or credit was not available to Birchtown farmers. As war refugees and (for the most part) formerly enslaved, Birchtown farmers came empty-handed to their new settlement. They did not possess the basic resources needed to carve farmsteads out of the wilderness. These prospective farmers had no tools, no livestock, no seed, and no capital or credit to purchase them. They did not have the manpower resources available to white loyalists. There were no servants, and fewer children lived in their households. The 1784 Birchtown muster showed that a typical household had 2.3 persons compared to the average five persons in white households.[48]

To provide for themselves and their families, Black loyalists sought employment in Shelburne. Very few became small time entrepreneurs. Boston King, who arrived at Port Roseway on board *L'Abondance*, made chests and sold them for cornmeal. He later supplemented his income by working on

salmon and herring boats. Many worked at menial jobs. Some became day
laborers or servants. Some, like Boston King, augmented their income by
inshore fishing, and others joined ships' crews.⁴⁹ Many took up land clear-
ance and wood lotting as an occupation, described by Captain William
Booth in the following manner: "they do for eight dollars, cutting firewood
for fires."⁵⁰ Black artisans worked as carpenters, masons, blacksmiths, bakers, and other occupations, but not at the wages paid to white workers.
Most earned wages lower than their white counterparts.⁵¹

Some Birchtown residents even resorted to indenturing themselves
under one year contracts for an average of $60, from which the costs of
food and clothing were deducted. Some indentures provided only food and
clothing but no wages. White employers often mistreated and exploited
Black indentured servants, who were caught in a spiral of poverty and despair. Employers often used their prospective servants' lack of education
against them. Lydia Jackson signed an indenture contract, which stipulated
a term of thirty-nine years, but she believed her service would only last for
the customary one year. Her owner later sold her to an abusive master who
beat her when she was eight months pregnant. Other Black loyalists had
the misfortune of working for Alphea Palmer. One several occasions,
Palmer failed to meet the requirements of the indenture contracts. He did
not pay Henry McGregor, who labored as Palmer's servant for eight
months without receiving any wages. Palmer collected and withheld most
government food rations designated for his servant Thomas London for
nine months in 1784, giving London only two and a half months' rations.
And instead of paying Cyrus Williams his rightful wages at the end of one
year, Palmer charged Williams twelve shillings a week to obtain food provisions. Palmer's actions are illustrative of how indentured servants were
abused and victimized. Mistreatment also included harsh and violent punishments. Servants could receive whippings of ten stripes or less when neg-
ligent in the performance of their duties.⁵²

Many Blacks were forced into sharecropping as a means of survival and
as an alternative to actual land ownership. Black sharecroppers worked on
land owned by white proprietors and received half of the resulting crop in
payment. The sharecropper needed to save enough funds for seed costs
from his half of the profits. Many complained that their share was not
enough to accumulate sufficient capital to buy enough seed and other necessities to cultivate and harvest their own crops. This arrangement, however, worked well for the white landowner who gained free labor to improve
and cultivate his land—a requirement to maintain title to the land.⁵³

Regardless of their work status, Blacks were always in competition with white veterans. The former soldiers came to Nova Scotia with little or no money and few skills to market. These veterans resented Black loyalists, who were used to living on little and were willing to work for less, sometimes one-quarter of the wages of white veterans. Former soldiers were also dealing with the problems caused by the lack of provisions and the slow distribution of land. Depressing poverty, the harsh environs, and their belief that they were being pushed aside by British authorities led to a volatile climate. This resentment finally reached a boiling point. Starting on Monday, July 26, 1784, and continuing for almost a week, groups of white armed veterans rampaged through the Black section of Shelburne, driving all the Blacks from their town into Birchtown. They attacked several individuals and destroyed more than twenty homes of Black loyalists.[54] Surveyor Benjamin Marston was even fearful for his own safety during the riot. He made note of his concern:

> Tuesday, 27. Riot continues. The soldiers force the free negroes to quit the Town—pulled down about 20 of their houses. This morning I went over to the Barracks by advice of my friends, who find I am threatened by the Rioters, and in the afternoon took passage for Halifax. By further advice from Town, find I have been sought after. Arrived in Halifax Thursday, 29th.[55]

Provincial troops, dispatched to the area, put down the riot after several days. But Birchtown now dealt with an influx of Black refugees displaced by the Shelburne riot. After the riot, the process of land distribution was also revised. Governor Parr turned over the responsibility of land distribution in the Shelburne district to the Port Roseway Associates. They, in turn, worked to ensure that landless white settlers received their land claims. Two years after the riots, most white loyalists had received their farm lots. Those lots would eventually encompass and surround Birchtown, leaving only the least arable and most distant lands available for distribution to landless Black settlers for farming purposes. Oftentimes, Black land grantees were unable to work their land, thus forfeiting their claims and losing their lands to auction.[56]

A wheat famine hit the region in 1789 and residents were forced to import their food from outside of their community. This came at a particularly bad time for loyalist settlements since the provincial government had ceased distribution of the King's Bounty the year before. A wheat parasite, known as the Hessian fly, diminished the fall harvest of 1788 and a cold spell in the following spring contributed to the food shortage. People's fears exaggerated the effects of the famine in New England and Nova Scotia. An increased demand for wheat in European markets had prompted many Nova Scotian farmers to plant only wheat crops, which were not resistant to the Hessian fly. Additionally, as the famine settled in, overstated press reports caused an increase in grain prices and hoarding of grain supplies. Worries about a protracted famine prevented the distribution of grain to those few communities that were severely affected by the shortage.[57]

The famine was particularly hard on the struggling settlements of Nova Scotia as they were still trying to grow fledgling communities in the harsh environment of that province. Reports of hunger spread throughout loyalist settlements. William Clark of Digby stated that "the Dearness of Provisions and Scarcity of many things, not to be had for money, the Poverty of the People, and apprehensions of an approaching famine, have induced Some Gentlemen to put forward a petition to his majesty, praying . . . for some immediate Relief, or Numbers of the people must actually starve."[58] Birchtown residents also felt the ravages of the famine. John Marrant, an itinerant Black minister, came across two women "who had been over to Shelbourne to beg something to eat," but they "had no strength to reach home with it."[59] He also wrote about the desperation felt by many Birchtown residents as the famine took hold. He tried to aid the many "distressing objects" that came to his door, but he was unable to offer or provide much assistance since the home office of his church, the Huntingdon's Connexion, failed to respond to his call for help.[60] Birchtown entrepreneur and Methodist pastor Boston King described the situation in Birchtown in distressing terms. He wrote:

> Many of the poor people were compelled to sell their best gowns for five pounds of flour, in order to support life. When they had parted with all their clothes, even to their blankets, several of them fell down dead in the streets, thro' hunger. Some killed and eat their dogs and cats and poverty and distress prevailed on every side so that to my great grief I was obliged to leave Birchtown because I could get no employment.[61]

Adding to this misery was the outbreak of smallpox in the settlement. Pastor Marrant, while attending his congregants throughout the region, was struck by the disease. Marrant reported in his journal that he "did spit blood for eight days continually."[62] He remained housebound for the duration of his illness.[63]

By 1789, Birchtown was a difficult place to live. Birchtown residents no longer received government subsidies. It was difficult to eke out a living on the small town lots, nonarable farmland, and short growing seasons. Most, like Ben Frankham, had not received their promised land grants and were surviving on the low wages paid by Shelburnian merchants and farmers. The harsh swamps, almost impenetrable woods, and cold winters added to the problems for Blacks trying to forge a livelihood from their natural environs. William Booth, a captain of the Royal Engineers in nearby Shelburne, described the town as a settlement in wretched shape. His descriptions of Birchtown and its leader Stephen Blucke indicate the problems that had beset the community by 1789: "His [Colonel Blucke] neighbours, who, were at first 800 or thereabouts, are now reduced to a third of that number; very poorly Lodged indeed. . . . Land at this moment is too cheap here, for him to make his market of it— and to go to market somewhere else."[64]

Birchtown was also affected by the conditions of the Shelburnian community, because its economic fortunes were tied closely to the larger port city. In 1788, the government finally discontinued the King's Bounty. This action had disastrous effects since residents of Shelburne and its surrounding area were unable to produce enough food to feed themselves. Additionally, Shelburnians suffered in the famine of 1789, and they blamed their woes on the government. During the famine, Shelburnian merchants dispatched a petition to London, detailing their problems and listing their beliefs as to what caused their problems—elimination of King's Bounty, trade restrictions with the United States, and the lack of necessary roads to make Shelburne a thriving trade port. By the late 1780s, Shelburne had shrunk from a loyalist settlement of 10,000 to a struggling pioneer settlement continually losing its population to death, frustration, and despair. The first winter, famine and a smallpox outbreak caused some deaths. The delay of land distribution and poor economic opportunities caused many to seek better prospects elsewhere. Because of this bleak situation, Shelburne lost most of its population to the United States, Great Britain, and Nova Scotia's capital city of Halifax.[65]

Shelburne declined for many reasons. The expectations were too great. The work ethic of its inhabitants was too weak. Government fulfillment of provisions and land was too little and too late. Cohesion among loyalists' groups was too fragmented.[66] Regardless of the causes of the decline, Shelburne did not become the thriving port city envisioned by the Port Roseway Associates. In 1789—the year of the wheat famine—Boston King summed up what he believed caused the decline of the city:

The circumstances of the white inhabitants were likewise very distressing owing to their great imprudence in building large homes and striving to excel one another in this piece of vanity. When their money was almost expended, they began to build small fishing vessels but, alas, it was too late to repair their error. Had they been wise enough at first to have turned their attention to the fishery instead of fine houses, the place would soon have been in a flourishing condition whereas it was reduced in a short time to a heap of ruins and its inhabitants were compelled to flee to other parts of the continent for sustenance.[67]

As loyalist settlements expanded throughout Nova Scotia, most communities of Blacks sprang up in areas segregated from their white counterparts. The establishment of all-Black settlements was characteristic of the province. Waves of loyalist newcomers populated the peninsula, settling as religious or ethnic groups. The primary Black settlements that developed during this period were satellites of mostly larger white towns and cities. The Shelburne-Birchtown area had the highest concentration of Black loyalists. Other Black communities also sprang up, principally Brinley Town (a satellite of Digby), Little Tracadie, and Preston.[68]

All these settlements dealt with the hardships experienced by Black pioneers as they fought to build better lives for themselves and their families. The early years at Birchtown showed how difficult it was for Black loyalists to achieve a sense of competency and equality in a system and climate that was either unable or unwilling to allow its Black constituents to access economic independence. To deal with the legal and social constraints established by the white establishment and to survive socially and economically, Ben Frankham and other Black Nova Scotians had to develop separate institutions—family, schools, and churches. These three institutions were pivotal to the salvation of Black loyalists in Nova Scotia.[69]

Black Nova Scotians suffered from the same legal restrictions as their counterparts in the United States. Black residents of Birchtown and Shelburne did not have the right to vote even if they met the requirement of land ownership. Additionally, white loyalists asserted control over the free Black population at Birchtown as a warning to the significant contingent of enslaved persons living in Shelburne. During this period, Birchtown became a refuge for fugitives from throughout the province, and their owners looked for ways to prevent their enslaved servants from running to free Blacks for assistance. The social activities of all Blacks, free and enslaved, were also regulated. Local statutes often prohibited events such as frolics and dances. As early as May 1785, handbills appeared in the city of Shelburne forbidding "Negro" dances. Law enforcement officials were put on notice to arrest frolickers, partygoers, and gamblers. Shelburne Blacks were warned that "riotous behavior" would result in imprisonment or other forms of punishment. Frolickers were ordered to the house of corrections, and keepers of disorderly houses were reprimanded by officials for allowing Blacks to party and dance at their domiciles. Blacks caught indulging in public partying were arrested and/or brought before the court. This restrictive policy stood in stark contrast to the actions of white Shelburnians concerning their own social lives. The white loyalists of Shelburne engaged in various forms of community sociability, whether for special occasions or as part of their daily activities, with visits to parlors and taverns sprinkled throughout the town. The practice of community social gathering ended at the borders of white Shelburne. They were unaccustomed to free Blacks and uncomfortable with their enslaved population regularly socializing with their free counterparts. Thus, whites considered it of utmost importance that the Blacks of Shelburne and Birchtown be controlled, and one method was the elimination of dances and other communal gatherings among Black loyalists.[70]

Whites also controlled Blacks through the criminal justice system. In 1784, the Shelburne court system was established and charged with a variety of responsibilities. Among their legislated duties were the maintenance of public order, the enforcement of local laws, and the operation of local jails. The court system wielded its power over all residents of Shelburne County and strict laws and penalties were used against Black loyalists as one method to control their lives. Some Blacks received leniency due to their perceived status in the community. John Hamilton, identified in court records as a Black captain, appeared before the court on charges of fraudulent practices. Hamilton was initially jailed for defrauding his company of part of their rations. However, after he appeared before the magistrate for a reexamination of the charges, he was released from his imprisonment. The court records stated the following regarding the disposition of the charges against the captain: "They dismiss him by reason no proof was adduced against him; but as he, himself, confessed to have defrauded his Company of a part of their Rations, under his care, The Court order he be liberated on paying the Sheriff, and Goalers Fees. This they think Just, from his own confession of Fraud."[71]

Other Blacks received harsher penalties for minor offenses. Prince Frederick received seventy-eight lashes and a month of hard labor for stealing a pair of shoes. Diana was convicted on two cases of petty larceny and received two hundred lashes for the first offense, 150 for the second act. Alicia Wiggins received thirty-nine lashes for theft and was hanged for a second act. One Black man in Halifax was hanged for stealing a bag of potatoes. Patty Brown was given ten lashes on her bare back for the theft of a calico gown to wear to church. She was also banished from Shelburne.[72] It appears that Ben Frankham did not come to the attention of law enforcement officials. However, fellow members of his company felt the sting of the criminal justice system. A court entry for August 25, 1785, detailed the circumstances that brought Birchtown resident and Bridges' company member Pompey Donaldson to the attention of the Shelburne court system and a subsequent whipping:

> Thursday 25th August 1785—Pompey Donaldson and Thomas Gould, Negroes, were brought into Court in Custody of the Keeper of the House of Corrections. They were charged before Nicholas Ogden, and Valentine Nutter, Esquires, on the 20th Instant of having stolen sundry articles belonging to Mr Samuel Burling. They received a corporal punishment as Vagrants, Rouges by order of the said magistrates. The Court order them to be discharged and advise the said Pompey and Thomas to goe to Birchtown and not to be seen in Shelburne.[73]

Banishment to Birchtown was a regular punishment meted out by the magistrates in Shelburne and indicated their desires to purge their village of Blacks who were not enslaved, servants, or laborers.[74]

Even though they had to deal with political, economic, and social restrictions, Black loyalists created opportunities for themselves. To increase their chances for economic competency, parents and guardians sought out education for their children. Between 1785 and 1791, over three hundred children of Black loyalists attended schools in the major Black loyalist settlements. Petitions for schools and education came closely after petitions for rations and land. British Anglican charitable organizations like the Associates of the late Dr. Bray and the Society for the Propagation of the Gospel (SPG) established free schools for Blacks throughout Nova Scotia. Schools were established in Halifax, Digby, and Birchtown. They hired only Black Anglicans to positions of leadership in their schools. William Furmage, an assistant of John Marrant, was hired as the headmaster for the school in Halifax. Joseph Leonard was hired to head the school for the Digby and Brinley Town Blacks. And Stephen Blucke became the headmaster for the school in Birchtown, established in 1785. The Associates and SPG provided the books and payroll for teachers, and Black loyalists provided a school building. The curriculum of these schools was designed to produce workers, not scholars. For instance, female students learned practical skills, such as knitting and sewing. But these schools were the best opportunity for the children of Black loyalists to read and write. They also instructed their students in the doctrine of the Anglican Church.[75]

Without the burdens and responsibilities of raising children, Ben did not have to worry about the educational opportunities available to the settlement's children. But for those with children in Birchtown, the free school was particularly important. Approximately thirty-eight students attended the Birchtown school by 1787, ranging in age from five to eleven years. Their reading materials included primers, the Bible, and the Psalter. Blucke's letters for assistance to the SPG home office in London depicted the poor conditions under which his students were being educated. He begged for clothing and other essentials, stating that his students were "almost naked . . . at this inclement season."[76]

Loyalists brought with them a diverse mix of religious beliefs and practices. For the most part, loyalists were overwhelmingly adherents of the Church of England. However, other denominations such as the Methodists and Baptists also claimed the refugees as congregants. Regardless of their beliefs, loyalists and their religious practices came into an environment affected by the work of Henry Alline, a charismatic itinerant preacher who brought the spirit of the Great Awakening into the Nova Scotian wilderness. Born in Rhode Island into a Puritan household, Alline migrated to Nova Scotia with his family as part of the early migration of New Englanders to Nova Scotia in the 1760s. By 1776, he had embraced the teachings of the Great Awakening and found his calling in the evangelical style of proselytizing associated with that religious phenomenon. However, Alline's religious philosophy reflected the turbulent and difficult times of the American Revolution and the economic difficulties incurred by rural Nova Scotians because of the war. He advocated the rejection of the secular world and a greater concern for one's own salvation. His message to Nova Scotians was to ignore the secular influences of both the British and Americans since both endangered the soul. Alline preached throughout Nova Scotia, especially in the Annapolis Valley, from 1776 until his departure to the United States in 1783. However, his teachings lingered in the Nova Scotian landscape and may have influenced the creation of dissenting Black churches.[77]

The Black church became a dominant feature in the Black communities of Nova Scotia, as it did in the United States. Within one or two years of their arrival, Black refugees created churches in every Black settlement. Ben Frankham and other Black loyalists had four viable options when determining the role of religion in their lives—Anglican, Huntingdonian, Methodist, and Baptist. Regardless of denominations, church membership was high among Black loyalists, and church services had an evangelical flavor, which helped to foster a sense of community among the congregants. The church became the center of communal activities for the betterment of each settlement. Black religious life in Birchtown was vibrant and intense, driven by charismatic leaders and a need for Birchtown residents to become active participants in their religious lives.[78]

Ben eventually affiliated with the Anglican Church. Birchtown residents were initially attracted to the state religion of their white allies, the Church of England. Early reports showed that Blacks sought out the church to sanctify and bless important family events. Between December 1783 and August 1784, Reverend George Panton baptized forty-four children and eighty-one adults and married forty-four couples among the Black residents of both Shelburne and Birchtown. Anglican churches in Shelburne welcomed Blacks to their services and communion, but not as equal congregants. Blacks were relegated to separate pews and excluded from services altogether when white parishioners packed the church. Furthermore, active participation among Black loyalists was restricted by a yearly pew fee of twenty shillings. Only Black schoolmaster and Birchtown leader Stephen Blucke could afford to pay the yearly fee. As outreach, Anglican pastors were dispatched by church officials to Birchtown to minister to the needs of their Black congregants. Reverend Panton found the Birchtown residents very responsive to the call of the Anglican Church. As a way to reach out to more Blacks, Reverend John Breynton of St. Paul's Anglican Church in Halifax appointed and authorized several Black loyalists to instruct other Blacks in the Anglican tenets. This practice on the part of Breynton led to the formation of a Black Anglican leadership in Birchtown, most notably Isaac Limerick, who officiated as a preacher and catechist for many Birchtown religious ceremonies. Overall, Black Anglicans adhered to the policies and practices of white officials. So, they were not the leading spokesmen for Birchtown Blacks when lodging their dissatisfaction with British policies, especially regarding land distribution.[79]

Some Blacks, disenchanted with the Anglican Church, looked for other options. The Huntingdonian sect provided one of those alternatives. An offshoot of the Anglican Church, the Huntingdon Connexion was part of a reform movement started by Selena Hastings, the Countess of Hunting-don. Her beliefs mirrored those of Henry Alline—personal salvation, along with daily prayer meetings and enthusiastic revivals. She attracted a group of Methodist ministers who shared her ideology and formed several churches under her sponsorship by 1783. An enthusiastic preacher of the Huntingdon Connexion was John Marrant, a free Black born in New York City who migrated to London after the war. He was drawn to Birchtown by the letters of his brother, a Birchtown resident. His brother praised the religious fervor of the settlement but lamented the lack of Black religious leadership.[80]

David George was the leading Baptist minister in Nova Scotia. In 1773, he was one of the original founders of the first Black church in America—the Silver Bluff Baptist Church in South Carolina. George arrived in Hal-ifax in 1782 and migrated to Shelburne a year later. George first held religious camp meetings in the borderland between Birchtown and Shel-burne. His meetings drew both white and Black congregants. But he was driven out of Birchtown after the riots in 1784 and eventually went on a preaching tour of the peninsula that took him to Liverpool, Saint John, and Fredericton. His message of the Baptist Church as a self-originating and self-governing body resonated with many Black loyalists. With this message, George helped to start churches in Shelburne, Birchtown, Preston, and Halifax.[81]

Black Methodists looked to Boston King and Moses Wilkinson for leadership. Wilkinson, blind and lame, recruited many Blacks to the Methodist church. His disabilities earned him a certain amount of fame in Birchtown, where his efforts resulted in the Methodists having the largest Black congregation. Among his earliest converts were Boston and Violet King. Boston King eventually became pastor of his own congregation in Birchtown. These Black Methodists developed their own rituals which were unique to their own culture and included ecstatic "lovefeasts."[82] These re-ligious leaders, regardless of ideology and denomination, sought to provide guidance, stability, and direction to their Black congregants inundated with the burdens of making new lives in an unforgiving environment.

As a single man, unburdened by family responsibilities, Ben would have found it easy to relocate and move throughout the province—Port Mouton to Birchtown to the Annapolis region. However, by the late 1780s, Ben de-cided to start a family—again. He married a second time to Margaret Jack-son, the daughter of Black loyalists Edward and Isabella Jackson. Margaret and her family resided in Granville in the Annapolis region on the western side of the Nova Scotian peninsula.

The Jacksons' migration to Canada did not parallel Ben's. Edward Jackson and his family probably came to Nova Scotia with British or Provincial regiments or with earlier refugees from Boston at the beginning of the war. Jackson was more than likely attached to a regiment as auxiliary personnel, or as a free Black loyalist.[83] By 1784 Jackson is listed as "a free negro living on Mr. Benjamin James Farm in Annapolis County, 2 adults, 2 children and one other. Possibly under the command [?] of Dickson's."[84] A year later, Edward and Isabella welcomed a third child, while still residing on the James farm in Granville with their two older children, Thomas and Margaret.

In July 1785, Edward Jackson acquired property in the form of fish lots from his landlord, Benjamin James: "Benjamin James, Gentleman of Granville to Edward Jackson, a free Negro man of Granville. Price = 5 shillings on 18 July 1785. A Fish Lott in Granville known by no. 16 and being part of the town lott bought by Peleg Little known by the name of no. 58 approximately 100 acres. Witnesses: Elizabeth Sinclair, F. Sinclair, Captain Fifth Regiment."[85] Two years later, Jackson acquired additional property in land: "Abigail Letch, widow, to Edward Jackson of Granville, carpenter, for 5 pounds 16 shillings and 8 pence on May 5, 1787. Lot of land in Granville, a basin lot #17."[86] Abigail and her husband, John Letch (Litch) owned several acres of land from the Annapolis River across the North Mountain to the Bay of Fundy.[87] Jackson's transition from carpenter to fisherman was a shrewd move according to Royal Engineer and surveyor William Booth. A diary entry captured his assessment of Black economic opportunity in the region: "Fishing is the chief and most profitable employment for these Poor, but really spirited People;—and, which they follow, as far as their circumstances will admit; for it must be known, that even a Fisherman requires a little yellow and white earth to commence his business."[88]

Jackson's purchases may have been the beginnings of the small Black settlement at Thorne's Cove in present-day Karsdale. Another Black settlement at nearby Delap's Cove would provide much needed communal support for the Jackson family. Even though fish lots did not equal the farm lots promised to Black loyalists by government officials, these lots did provide an opportunity for their owners to make a living—one of the few opportunities afforded to poor Blacks. Jackson possessed the shoreland and had fishing rights to the lots that he owned. Owners of these lots used strategically placed netting to capture fish for market. Jackson's ownership of these lots and the basin lots and his occupation as a carpenter would give him the ability to provide a livelihood for his family.[89]

Edward Jackson appeared to have fostered a relationship with Benjamin James, a leading figure in Annapolis County. James held the title of assistant commissary in Granville in 1784 and served in the same position with the British army. James was elected as a township official in 1785. James and his wife, Elizabeth, had six children. The James household also included four servants or slaves. Two of these servants were under the age of ten. It appears that the James farm, located in central Granville, became more populated with the addition of Edward Jackson and his family of free persons. Existing records do not indicate whether Edward Jackson was a former servant or formerly enslaved to Benjamin James. Records do indicate that James did hold servants or enslaved persons with the surname of Jackson, including two young boys named Edward and James Jackson, ages fourteen and twelve. They arrived aboard the ship *Apollo* at Port Roseway (Shelburne) in the summer of 1783. Both young men held certificates of freedom from Benjamin James indicating that they were free. He signed over the indentures of two young Black males to Edward Green to learn the trade of shoemaker until they were both twenty-one years of age. The relationship of these two young boys to Edward Jackson, Ben's father-in-law, is unclear. It is probable these young men were the teenaged sons of Edward. Their relationship to Benjamin James, however, is not unclear. Benjamin James obviously, at one point, held some form of ownership over the two young men. If Edward Jackson's relationship to Benjamin James was the result of previous servitude, then his former attachment to James proved to be beneficial to him and his family—due to James' position in the Annapolis community.[90]

By 1789, Ben Frankham, now known as Ben Franklin, had moved away from the deteriorating conditions at Birchtown and settled in the Annapolis region. The county of Annapolis was established in 1759 before the loyalist migration. Annapolis County was repeatedly described as possessing fertile land and the loyalists residing there had made good improvements to their environment. So, it was an accepted notion that loyalists in this region were better off than in places like Shelburne/Birchtown. And Ben sought to improve his own life and standing by moving to the Annapolis region which included the towns and townships of Wilmot, Granville, Annapolis Royal, and the newly created Digby.[91]

Ben's short stint as a husband and father in Rhode Island during the war did not prepare him for the stress and practicalities of raising a young family in tenuous times. By 1792, Ben and Margaret were the parents of three children. Daughter Isabella, named after her maternal grandmother, was born in 1789 and baptized at All Saints Anglican in Granville the following year. Her brother, Peter, followed shortly thereafter in 1790 and was baptized as well in 1792. A third child, Hannah, named after Ben's own sister, was born a year later in 1791. Ben and his young family struggled in their daily existence in Granville. Ben's experience as a soldier did not guarantee him work in postwar Nova Scotia. He and other Black loyalists did not receive the employment opportunities promised in Clinton's Philipsburg Proclamation nor the farmland promised to white loyalists. Given his former life in Rhode Island, Ben was well informed about the occupation of fishing. Maybe Ben used that knowledge to work alongside his new father-in-law. It is likely that Ben, Margaret, and their three children resided with his in-laws. That situation could only be temporary at best, and Ben continued to seek those things promised him and others.[92]

By the late 1780s, Ben started to look south for opportunities to provide for his growing family. As evidenced in the twelve baptismal records of his children, Ben's search for economic competency caused him to relocate from Granville south to nearby Digby Township. Ben's oldest three children were baptized at the Anglican churches located in Granville and Annapolis Royal. Starting in 1800, his remaining children received baptism at the Digby Trinity Anglican Church—an indication that Ben uprooted his family and moved to nearby Digby County to acquire a better life.[93]

Ben and his family moved to a Black settlement near the town of Digby. Surveyor Ben Marston's description of Digby did not match the overall positive description of the region. He described Digby as "a sad grog drinking place."[94] Digby, originally called Conway, received its first wave of over 1,200 loyalists in the fall of 1783. By the summer of 1784, over 200 Black loyalists lived in or around Digby, of which sixty-nine were veterans of the Black Pioneers, along with their families. This Black population established their own community at Brinley Town approximately one mile from Digby—and would become the second largest Black loyalist settlement in Nova Scotia.[95]

Ben and his family were not alone in their travels. Another member of Captain Bridges' Company, thirty-one-year-old Thomas Francis also moved to the Brinley Town settlement. Francis was a farmer but could not engage in his chosen profession because he did not receive his allotment of land near the Birchtown settlement. Both he and Ben were drawn to the Brinley Town settlement by officials' promises of land. The trip to Digby could have been difficult. A short trip down the basin by boat was the easier voyage. If Ben and his family and others could not arrange for passage on one of the boats heading to the new community, then a trek through a heavily wooded area filled with rocky terrain was not easy, especially with a young family. But the trek was worth it if promised land and supplies were gained. These promises were brought about by the activities of Digby's and Brinley Town's tenacious and vocal Black leaders, Thomas Peters and Joseph Leonard.[96]

The Black residents of Digby and Brinley Town looked to Joseph Leonard for religious guidance. Digby became an Anglican parish in 1786 under the supervision of Reverend Roger Viets, who founded a group of forty-nine regular communicants—thirty-one were Black. Brinley Town residents did not attend services at Digby, unless for special occasions. For his part, Viets only visited the settlement a few times a year to preach and perform other rituals. The needs of the Black Anglicans at Brinley Town were accorded, by the townspeople, to Joseph Leonard. Leonard was literate, a schoolteacher, and now minister and became recognized as a lay minister in the Anglican Church. He was given permission by the church to lead services, read the Bible, and lead his congregants in prayer. However, Leonard went against the wishes of his Anglican superiors when he administered communion, baptized, and performed marriages for Black parishioners. Leonard wanted to be ordained and independent from the white Anglican Church.[97]

Leonard was also pivotal to the operation of another important institution of the Black loyalist community—schools. As stated earlier, the Society for the Propagation of the Gospel in Foreign Parts began to found schools for Black loyalists throughout the province. Before the formation of the SPG-sponsored school, an earlier attempt at schooling had attracted at least fifty students who were obliged to work on the instructor's farm for tuition. Lieutenant Colonel Joseph Barton was tasked with proposing the new school to the parents at Brinley Town. After accepting his proposal, the parents pushed for Leonard as the headmaster of the Brinley Town school. The first group of thirty-four students met in Leonard's home, where they received instruction in spelling, reading, and religion. Leonard also conducted education classes for adults.[98]

Leonard's fellow leader in the community, Thomas Peters, brought his military experience to dealings with British officials and became the spokesperson to petition the government for land. Peters and some of his followers served as members of the Black Pioneers, the only such company mustered under the auspices of British military command. Formed in 1776, the company served in several campaigns as auxiliary and support units. At the end of the war, Peters and sixty-eight other Black Pioneers migrated to Nova Scotia. The residents of Brinley Town received one-acre town lots, granted to them in 1785, where they cleared land, built huts, and planted garden plots. Like their counterparts in other Black settlements, they petitioned the governor for farm lots. In 1785, Governor Parr granted and assigned twenty-acre plots of land across the river from Brinley Town to twenty-three veterans, including Thomas Peters. The settlers started to clear this land, but the land was given to an Anglican school and the settlers remained on their small town lots.[99]

Peters and his followers did not give up in their quest for land—a quest that involved Ben Franklin by 1788. In that year, Governor Parr, after receiving yet another petition from Peters, instructed Charles Morris, the head surveyor, to find land in the area near Digby and Brinley Town for Black veterans. Ben Franklin was included in this group and received a land warrant of fifty acres. Morris, without approval from Parr, conducted a survey of 147 lots of fifty acres each in Clements Township. The property had been abandoned by whites who had returned to the United States. In September 1789, the Black veterans signed for those plots of land, but no final grant was given. Issuance of a final grant depended on the payment of surveying fees, which the veterans were unable to provide. They did, however, clear a road to the property, but they never obtained a legal title to the tract of land and never moved onto it. Ben Franklin remained without farmland.[100]

Ben and other Black loyalists lived with the anger and disappointment brought on by British officials' broken promises of land. Because of these unfulfilled promises, some dissatisfied Black Nova Scotians decided to leave Nova Scotia and immigrate to Sierra Leone, establishing a colony there. The lack of land acquisition was paramount to their dissatisfaction. Of more than 3,500 Black loyalists who migrated to Nova Scotia, only 385 received legal title to land. Of those, 184 received over 6,000 acres in Birchtown; seventy-six received one-acre town lots in Brinley Town; seventy-four received a total of 3,000 acres in Little Tracadie, and fifty-one received over 2,000 acres in Preston. Overall, the Black loyalists received less land and the land granted was rocky and acidic. And they rarely received clear title to the land granted to them. They started to look toward immigration to Africa to settle their grievances against the Crown. Unlike some of their white counterparts, Black loyalists did not see a return to the United States as a viable option.[101]

Black Pioneer Thomas Peters personified this back-to-Africa movement as he was affected by the nonpossession of the Clements Township lots in 1789. Peters traveled to Great Britain in 1791 to present his land petitions to the Crown, in particular, to the Secretary of State. While there, he met abolitionist Granville Sharp and came to the attention of the Sierra Leone Company. The company was seeking to establish a free Black settlement in Sierra Leone and needed new settlers. The company offered Peters and his followers the opportunity to have their own land, community, and autonomy in Africa. Peters excitedly took this offer back to Nova Scotia. He, along with John Clarkson, a representative of the Sierra Leone Company and brother of abolitionist Thomas Clarkson, worked diligently to recruit Black loyalists for their settlement.[102] Their efforts were successful.

The emergence and subsequent strength of the Black church in Nova Scotia was part of a community consciousness that was illustrated in the mass exodus of these Black settlers. Over one-third of the surviving Black loyalists would eventually leave for Sierra Leone. The entire population of the Preston Black settlement left for Africa. Six hundred left from Shelburne-Birchtown, 200 from Preston, 200 from New Brunswick, and approximately 180 from the Annapolis-Digby region, most coming from Brinley Town. Religious affiliation was a major factor in the Nova Scotian exodus. Excitement and willingness to emigrate depended on where Blacks lived and their religious affiliation. Most of the Black ministers and religious leaders took part in the exodus. They were joined by the members of their congregations who were not restricted by debt or indenture and who agreed with their move to Sierra Leone. From the Shelburne-Birchtown region, Baptists led by David George and Moses Wilkinson and members of the Huntingdon Church under the guidance of Cato Perkins (John Marrant's replacement) left in the exodus. Gideon White, a white leader in the Shelburne community, bemoaned the loss of Black loyalists to Sierra Leone by writing, "the 800 Negroes carried to Serea Leone was a serious loss but more so to me than any One—I had Eight Negro Families Tenants which had each a quantity of my Land and allow'd me rent—each had His House &c. those are all gone."[103] Joseph Leonard led most of his Anglican congregation, along with the Brinley Town Methodists, to Sierra Leone. Methodist Boston King led the Halifax group.[104]

Why did Ben stay? Ben Franklin's experience as a previously free person who decided to remain in Nova Scotia provides us an opportunity to examine and understand why some Blacks decided to stay. As with his decision to leave the Rhode Island Regiment, Ben probably stayed in Nova Scotia for a variety of reasons. The Black loyalist community in the Annapolis-Digby region had the smallest number of individuals willing and able to migrate to Sierra Leone. Since most emigrants left as community groups, Ben, his in-laws, and others probably decided as a community not to leave Nova Scotia. Did personal connections and relationships to leading white figures in the Annapolis region convince them to stay? As evidenced by Edward Jackson, there was a pathway to economic sufficiency for Blacks in Annapolis County. Many Blacks leaving Nova Scotia had strong ties to their religious leaders. Ben's religious affiliation was tied to the Anglican institutions of Annapolis Royal and Granville. His children were baptized in the Anglican faith and more than likely baptized by Joseph Leonard in their home. However, he was not convinced by the minister to emigrate from Nova Scotia to the Sierra Leone settlement.[105]

James St. G. Walker argues that the Blacks left behind were of poor character and were "slaves, indentured servants and sharecroppers, by definition excluded from the free labour pool, and the weak, the aged, the indebted and the unskilled . . . neither free to choose their employment nor capable of bargaining an equitable share in Nova Scotia's economy."[106] This was not the case for Ben's father-in-law, Edward Jackson. And this was not the case for Ben. He was not aged nor infirmed. He was married with children and affiliated with the state church. There are no extant records listing him as an indentured servant. It appeared that he was not willing to give up on the promises made by British officials. He also was not prepared, yet again, to leave his family. Edward Jackson and his family remained in Nova Scotia. Jackson's oldest two children were now married with families of their own. Ben, probably prompted by his wife, was unwilling to leave his newly acquired extended family.[107]

Many white loyalists did not wish to see Blacks leave because they were taking cheap labor from the community. White merchants and farmers spread rumors that Black refugees would not receive land once they arrived at Sierra Leone and would remain tenant farmers.[108] Stephen Blucke, the leader at Birchtown, also tried to convince Blacks to stay. He presented a petition to officials, signed by twenty-two petitioners. George Wise, who sailed with Ben Franklin to Nova Scotia aboard the brig *Elijah*, signed as a resident of Birchtown. The petition called for "the prayer of this our Petition to the Throne that our most Gracious Sovereign of his Great goodness will grant to us som much as may enable us to purchase a Cow and two Sheep, which (if obtained) will make us comfortable on our little farms."[109] The provincial government did not honor their requests. The petitioners did not receive their cows or sheep and received no new land grants.[110]

Ben, however, was more fortunate in his endeavors. By 1796, he was in possession of 100 acres of farmland in Digby County bordered on the south by Saint Mary's Bay Road. Like Frank Nigro before him, he used his property as collateral to obtain needed cash for his ever-growing family—which by 1796 included himself, his spouse, and three children. The holding of the land provided some form of economic competency since Ben was able to parlay that ownership into cash. However, he may not have been able to survive off the items cultivated from land and soil that was too rocky, too acidic, and too infertile. Ben mortgaged off one-half of his lot to George Wood for the "Sum of thirteen Pounds one Shilling and six pence Lawful Money."[111] The mortgage stipulated that Ben repay the mortgage by 1799. And like Frank Nigro before him, Ben made good on his debt. He repaid the loan to Francis Wood, the executor of George Wood's estate and regained control of his land.[112]

Like Ben Franklin, the Black loyalists who stayed behind in Nova Scotia had to fend for themselves. They would become the first of the permanent Black settlers in the region and continued to struggle in Nova Scotia. The loss of leading ministers and teachers disrupted their ability to maintain separate institutions under the distinct control of Blacks. The educational opportunities that remained for Blacks forced many young people to migrate to Halifax looking for apprenticeships. The loss of over one thousand of their residents severely depopulated Black settlements. There remained scattered Black populations who worked as agricultural laborers or as servants in the homes and businesses of whites. Those who received land remained on small town lots or farmland in barren and remote areas. Many still served as indentured servants or as tenant farmers—sharecroppers—on lands controlled by large white landholders. Many migrated to the larger city of Halifax to find work as general laborers with merchants starting to reengage the American and Caribbean markets.[113]

By the 1810s and 1820s, the situation started to improve economically. Indenture terms were fulfilled and those young men who fled to Halifax for apprentice opportunities started to see the results of their training. They filled the void in a province always short of labor. During the War of 1812, they received wages ranging from five to seven shillings per day. The war also provided opportunities for Black Nova Scotians to confirm their loyalty to Great Britain. For the remaining Black loyalists this would be an affirmation of their continuing loyalty to the Crown. A Black militia company recruited over 120 volunteers in Halifax and was described as equal to their white counterparts.[114] In the Annapolis region, there were signs of economic advancement, as well. James Jackson, the probable son of Edward Jackson and the former indentured servant of Edward Green, registered his earmark symbol with the town's clerk—an indication that he owned livestock. "James Jackson (Black Man) earmark is a slit on each ear entered the 31 of May 1803." Henry Jackson owned livestock as well. "Henry Jackson (Black Man) his earmark for cattle and sheep is a square crop of the left ear and two half pennies out the top of the right ear."[115]

As one of the few Blacks who owned land, Ben had the stability of land ownership to buttress against the shaky economic and social conditions for Blacks in Nova Scotia at the turn of the century. And he needed that stability because his family continued to grow. Starting in 1800 and ending in 1813, Ben and Margaret had ten more children. All were baptized at Trinity Anglican Church in Digby. A year before the baptism of their last child, the couple sold one-half of their farm lot to Richard Marshall for the sum of "Forty five Lawful money of Nova Scotia."[116]

The paramount concern for Black loyalist families in Nova Scotia remained the acquisition of land, even after the departure of so many for Sierra Leone. Ben Franklin and the other remaining heads of household needed property to provide a livelihood for their families and to protect their families from falling into economic dependency on the provincial government.[117] Ben and others did not give up their dreams to own enough land to acquire economic competency. They continued efforts throughout the first decades of the nineteenth century to acquire lands substantial enough to sustain a livelihood. In 1809, Ben and others again petitioned the provincial government for their rightful entitlement of land:

> Petitioners are colored men of Annapolis County who had lands laid out for them in the regime of Governor Parr between Moose and Bear River, Township of Clements, in the rear of the Hessian settlement in 50 acres lots. Some of them left for Sierre Leone and they had the land laid off for those left in 100 acre lots. Meanwhile Jonathan Milner and others of the Hessian settlement applied for the lands, of this was laid out to them by Mr. Harris whose former surveys appeared incorrect. Request that they (Jordan and et al?) be granted lots of no. 1 to 11 as marked on the plan. And they also request that the lands laid out to Milner and others can be granted consistent with justice they may have them:
>   To Abedingo Jordan 500 acres; John Ervin 150 acres; Francis Harrison 100 acres; Philip Marble 100 acres; Henry Reddock, Jr. 150 acres; Thomas Francis 200 acres; Benjamin Franklin 400 acres;

William Barton 200 acres; Isaac Jordan 150 acres; John Williams 100 acres; Abraham Bush 100 acres; Robert Johnston 150 acres; John Sheppard 100 acres; Henry Nutis 150 acres; Henry Woodow 100 acres. Voted the quantity prayed for if not interfering with land located to Milner and others.[118]

Ben and his fellow petitioners did not receive their land. They tried again in 1814 and 1817. These attempts were stymied by bureaucratic red tape or pressure from the Anglican Church. The latter attempt in 1817 included Ben's oldest son, who is listed as receiving a grant of thirteen acres. Peter had reached the age of twenty years by this time. But the Crown Grant of the Marsh Land at Digby did not result in the petitioners holding title to the land. An introductory paragraph prefaces a listing of the individuals who have sold their rights to the property to the Anglican Church:

> People of Colour, to say Negroes & Mulattos who have subscribed to the Digby Marsh Grant and having for the most part sold their claims . . . the purchaser have become guarantees to make their subscription undertaking good. . . . Know ye that of our special grace, certain knowledge have given and granted, and by these presents, for use, our heirs, and successors, do give and grant unto vesting of Trinity Church in the parish of Digby and County of Annapolis and to their successors forever for the user of said Church.[119]

At the time of the transfer of rights to the Digby parish, Ben and his family were still residing on their homestead on St. Mary's Bay Road because Ben and Peter are listed as "settled within the District or Parish of Weymouth ie on St. Mary's Bay Road and Sissibo River"—which is the same location designated in the aforementioned mortgage and sale records.[120]

That was not the only property transaction that Ben was engaged in for the year. Ben and Margaret inherited fish lots #16 and #17 from Margaret's father, Edward Jackson. Margaret's brother Thomas and his wife Ann also inherited the lots. As stated earlier, Edward had purchased these lots, which eventually led to the origins of the Black community at Thorne's Cove. Both couples eventually sold the lots to John Croscup in March 1817.[121]

The sale of one-half of his farm lot in Digby and the fish lots at Thorne's Cove, near Granville, may be an indication of Ben's immediate need for funds and the fact that his properties did not or could not afford him and his family a stable livelihood. Early on, Black settlers had the freedom to produce foodstuffs from their town and fish lots and sell them in makeshift marketplaces, but they lost that ability due to restrictions on owning arable land and food laws which governed their abilities as vendors.[122]

As stated earlier, the allotment of land did not equate to the ability for Black settlers to make a livelihood because they were allocated less arable plots of farmland. Added to this inability was a shift in marketplace patterns and regulations. Laws and statutes passed in Shelburne and Birchtown provide examples of how these restrictions affected Black loyalists—legislating the Black loyalists out of making a good living on their farms and fish lots. A court decree of February 1785 ordered that bakers in Shelburne sell bread loaves that weighed one pound thirteen ounces and made of "good sound inspected wheat and flour." This stipulation hindered Black bakers, who often used cornmeal or rye flours because of their reduced costs.[123] Later in the year, the court ordered that bread must be shaped into "single or double Loaves."[124] The court also regulated the pricing of these loaves. Coupled with these types of laws were the restrictions made concerning what constituted a marketplace. In May 1785, the court passed regulations which prevented vendors from selling meat, vegetables, and other products "from being sold in any St Lane or on the strand or shore of this town other than in the market or places established by orders of sessions."[125] So, Black vendors were required to go through the process of obtaining market stalls. These laws prevented free Black bakers and vendors from selling their products at market and limited their participation in the market economy that became established in the Annapolis region and set the tone for Black participation in the rest of the province.[126]

Most significantly, food laws governing fishing would impact Blacks involved with the fishing enterprise like the Jacksons and the Franklins. Another set of laws passed on April 10, 1786, limited fishing activities—one of the few ways in which people without lands supplemented their food income. The laws prevented the use of fishing nets and seines (vertically hung nets) extending more than one-third of the way into the river or bay. The laws also banned fishing from Saturday to Monday. This proved problematic for Black fishermen who were day laborers during the week, working on the farms of white loyalists. These laws gave whites the advantage in the fish trade. Overall, the laws and regulations severely limited Black loyalists' ability to maintain any semblance of economic competency. Ben Franklin and his family needed to overcome these odds if they were to survive in these tough conditions.[127]

The records are scant regarding Ben's life between 1817 and 1838. However, his children married into families who became part of the founding members of Nova Scotia's early Black communities. Nine of Ben's children grew to adulthood as evidenced by vital records—Isabella, Peter, Hannah, Thomas, James, Margaret, John, Celia, and Hester. Marriage records have been discovered for six. Five of their marriage partners can be identified. Four of the Franklin siblings married into the families of other identified Black loyalists. All resided in the Annapolis region and shunned migration to the larger city of Halifax in this period.

Ben's eldest child, Isabella, married Henry Brothers around 1811. Henry was the second child of Samuel and Elizabeth Brothers. Samuel and his family arrived in Annapolis County as part of the loyalist migration in 1784. During the war, Brothers and his family fled slavery, possibly because of Dunmore's Proclamation, from Willis Wilkinson of Virginia. Samuel and his wife, like the Franklins, became affiliated with the Anglican Church. Both were listed as persons "desirous of receiving confirmation at St. Luke's Church," in September 1791. Both were later confirmed as members of the Anglican Church. Samuel and Elizabeth eventually had nine children. As Samuel constructed a life for his family in Nova Scotia, he, like Edward Jackson, fostered a relationship with an influential white loyalist. An incident that occurred in 1815 is illustrative of that relationship. On March 21, Brothers participated in a duel as a second to prominent landowner Francis Story. Story had challenged J. G. Strive to a duel that occurred at 6 p.m. Thomas H. Bailey, the son of Reverend Jacob Bailey, served as Strive's second. This incident was captured in court records because Story was charged with accepting the challenge and for the assault upon Bailey, possibly because of an errant shot. Of interest in this incident is Story's selection of a man of color as his second—the position being one grounded in trust and loyalty.[128]

Ben's second child and eldest son, Peter, married Abella Kelly on October 26, 1826, "by banns," at the Digby Trinity Anglican Church. It is possible that Abella was related to one of two different Kelley families that migrated from Port Mouton to Birchtown at the same time of Ben's relocation to the larger settlement. Moses and Jenny Kelley arrived at Port Mouton aboard the ship *Ranger* and suffered through the first rough winter there. They are listed as members of Captain Read's company as a couple. There was no listing of a child at that time. A second Moses Kelley, sometimes spelled Morris, also resettled at Birchtown at the same time as Ben. As a single man of twenty years, he sailed to Nova Scotia aboard *L'Abondance* with other members of the Black Brigade. By 1838 Peter and his wife headed a household of eight—three female children and three males. Peter worked as a laborer, still living in the Township of Digby where he and his father had previously held and sold land.[129]

Ben's third child, Hannah, married William Pomp on March 7, 1818, at St. Luke's Anglican Church. At the time of this marriage, the Franklin family resided in the parish of Annapolis, as captured in the marriage record: "William Pomp, a Black man of the parish of Granville and Hannah Franklin of the parish of Annapolis were married by publication of Banns with consent of parents this 7th day of March in the year 1818 By me John Millidge, Missionary at Annapolis—This marriage was solemnized between us In the presence of William Walker and Peter DeLancey."[130] William was the eldest child of John Pomp, a former Black Pioneer, and Amy Pomp. John Pomp fled from his slaveholder, John Morris of Portsmouth, Virginia, in 1779. As part of the loyalist migration, the family disembarked at Annapolis Royal in 1784. The elder Pomps had seven other children besides William.[131]

The marriage records for James, John, Celia, and Hester Franklin are scant. James married Elizabeth Barton on January 7, 1823, at Bridgetown-Wilmot Anglican Church. His father-in-law, William Barton, although not listed in the *Book of Negroes*, received a land grant of fifty acres in Clements Township—the same acreage offered to Ben Franklin. This is an indication that William Barton was part of the Black loyalist migration. Barton was also influential in the Black loyalist settlement at Brinley Town—an indication he was a member of the Black Pioneers. John married Ann Johnson in 1826 in Bridgetown. There were over fifty individuals with the surname of Johnson who made the passage to Nova Scotia, as listed in the *Book of Negroes*. It is more than likely that Ann was born into one of these families. Hester married Aaron Butler in 1832 at Granville. There are two Butler families listed in the *Book of Negroes*. It is possible that Aaron was the son of Anthony Buttler, who arrived at Annapolis Royal aboard the ship *Lord Townsend* at the age of eighteen. According to the *Book of Negroes*, Anthony claimed that he was formerly enslaved by a Captain Carter of the Virginia regiments. Anthony also received a land grant at Clements Township. Or Aaron may have been the child of George Butler and his spouse Sukey who arrived at Nova Scotia aboard the ship *Mary*.[132]

By the time of the 1838 Nova Scotia census, Ben is listed as a "poor pauper," residing in Granville, in a household of six, including two children under the age of fourteen and three females above the age of fourteen. Now in his late seventies and with no other adult male in the household, his fortunes and more than likely his health had failed, leaving Ben and his family

to rely on government assistance. And the Franklin family was not unique
in these circumstances. The largest group designated as "paupers" in Nova
Scotia in this era were Black. Black Nova Scotians represented about 3 percent of the population but made up to 4.5 percent of the inmates in the
Poor House during that period. This may be attributed to the fact that
"paupers" could be "purchased" and their free labor used to offset the cost
of their upkeep at poor houses or the homes of their "owners." Ben and his
family did not meet the criteria for the poor house. However, the acquisition of land and fish lots did not provide the type of economic competence
necessary for Ben and his family to survive without government assistance.
It is probable that Ben sold off his remaining land leading him to require
government assistance. This type of assistance followed a system of state
relief where local public officials enacted poor laws to deal with the needy
who lived in their jurisdictions. Additionally, the type of assistance depended on the need of the persons involved. If the poverty was caused by
temporary unemployment, then those individuals could qualify for "outdoor
relief"—meaning the recipients did not require residency at the poor house.
Individuals identified as paupers who lived in their own homes could receive assistance in the form of coal, clothing, and money. Additionally, living
in his own home, Ben and his family were able to live close to family members, like the Jacksons, who worked as farmers and laborers. As a Black
man, it was not unusual for Ben to have fallen onto desperate times. The
largest percentage of those identified as "paupers" were Black, caused by
the tragedies that befell poor families in pre-Confederation Nova Scotia
but also caused by racism in the society in which they lived as evidenced
by the lack of land acquisition and restrictive food and vendor laws.[133]

Ben passed away sometime after 1838, living behind a legacy of military
service and the ability to create his own household in turbulent times and
conditions. This legacy was memorialized by the Franklin oral tradition,
passed along from generation to generation, which tied the story of Ben
Franklin's Canadian family to a greater narrative that crossed national and
international boundaries—the story of two young men from Rhode Island
who fought for their country's independence.

Ben Franklin, like his father before him, forged a family in the wake of
a major war and during difficult times for people of color. He had difficulty
obtaining and retaining property in the form of land. But he did parlay his
service with the British to identify himself and his family as Black loyalists
and founding members of the Black community in Nova Scotia. W. Bryan
Rommel-Ruiz explains the mindset of Black loyalists in the following man-

ner: "they forged a counterculture to this modern ideology [liberal impulse], they pursued a more traditional and communitarian idea of competency that valued their family's material well-being."[134] Rommel-Ruiz attributes these characteristics to those Black loyalists who migrated to Sierra Leone. However, the desires of Ben Franklin and the remaining parents to protect and serve their children in the Black loyalist communities of Nova Scotia cannot be denied. Perhaps this is where Ben Franklin's idea of manhood, family, and loyalty finally rested.

Thomas Henry Franklin, landscaper. (*Author*)

Epilogue
My Grandfather Came from Canada

My GREAT-GRANDFATHER, Thomas Henry Franklin, carried on the legacy
of the Frank/Franklin family by passing down the long history of his family
in America to his sons. He resided in a homestead located in Lequille in
western Nova Scotia, very near the town of Annapolis Royal (formerly
known as Port Royal), the provincial seat of government for Annapolis
County. As in all the Atlantic provinces, water influenced people's lives.
Thomas's home sat on the banks of the Annapolis River, which flowed near
and parallel to the Bay of Fundy. The river also separated Lequille and Annapolis Royal from the towns of Granville, Granville Ferry, and
Bridgetown. Thomas, while well known for his landscaping prowess, also
operated a transport service that carried passengers who ferried across the
Annapolis River to their destinations on the south side of the river.[1]

Thomas Henry Franklin knew and understood the importance of his
family's history in North America. He understood how he came to live in
Nova Scotia. He imparted that part of his family's heritage to his son John
William before his passing in 1929. Thomas' loss was felt by his family and
his community. An obituary, printed in the *Annapolis Spectator*, hailed the
life of the talented landscaper:

> There passed away at his home in Lequille early Sunday morning
> after a year or more of gradually failing health one of the best known
> and most highly esteemed of the colored population of this commu-
> nity in the person of Thomas Henry Franklyn, who was nearing the
> four score mark as to age, but always as faithful and enterprising in
> his work, as long as he was able to work as when a younger man. . . .

About 35 years ago he ran the first bus conveyance in this town, with a one-horse trap, charging five cents from the Mile Corner to the Ferry or fifty cents a week. . . . Besides his widow he leaves two sons and one daughter surviving.[2]

What did it mean to Thomas Henry to understand his family's origins and history in early America? Genealogist Dee Palmer Woodtor raises an important question to ask; "Is there generational continuity in your family?" Thomas Henry knew about the origins of the Franklin oral tradition—that two brothers served together in the Revolutionary War. Thomas Henry was part of the generational continuity of that tradition which resulted in military service among generations of Franklin men. Thomas Henry's understanding of that continuity obviously gave him a sense of pride and belonging, which is evident in his telling of his family origins to local historian William Inglis Morse, who captured his meeting with the landscaper during his investigation of ancient cemeteries of Nova Scotia. Franklin explained to Morse that his ancestors came from Africa, and he also displayed pride in understanding the local origins of his surname. Did this sense of self-awareness, family history, and self-pride result in his own standing in his Nova Scotian community as a "highly esteemed" member of this community? Genealogist Tony Burroughs argues that knowledge of one's family history fosters a sense of pride and self-esteem. The knowledge of his own family's history affected Thomas Henry and translated to the way he conducted himself in his dealings and standing in his community.[3]

Thomas Henry Franklin's life provides a living contradiction to the prevailing arguments regarding the feelings and beliefs of those Black loyalists who decided to stay in Nova Scotia. James St. G. Walker argues, "the Black loyalists who stayed in Nova Scotia, though they too remained distinct from the greater society surrounding them, did not bequeath the same heritage of pride and superiority to their descendants."[4] In direct contradiction of Walker, Thomas Henry Franklin honored his own family's heritage through his dignified and respectful retelling of the story. Gene Smith captures a different understanding of the legacy passed along to the descendants of Black loyalists: "The Revolutionary War and the War of 1812 landed most of them here, and their talked about and much probed generational inter-family connections and their growing up on streets named for ancestors, whose names they bear. They've been bonded together in these places, on owned lands handed down, along with facts, from their elders."[5]

Increased interest in rediscovering the story of Black loyalists has culminated in their creation of the Black Loyalist Heritage Society, founded in 1989. The society is dedicated to "discovering, interpreting, safeguarding, and promoting the history and heritage of the Black Loyalists" and oversees the Black Loyalist Heritage Centre, located in Shelburne, Nova Scotia (near the former settlement of Birchtown). The history and heritage of Black loyalists is commemorated in the Old School House, the Black Burial Grounds, and an exhibition gallery that displays a virtual copy of the *Book of Negroes,* listing the names of the over three thousand Black loyalists who made their way to Nova Scotia, including Ben Frank/Frankham/Franklin.[6]

Some descendants of Black loyalists made their way back to the United States. Even though they had been physically separated from families and former communities in the United States, Black Nova Scotians did not completely disavow their emotional and cultural identities developed in their former homeland. The Franklins and other descendants of the Black loyalist diaspora participated in the continuing connection and movement across national boundaries to maintain ties with their former communities but also to seek out better opportunities for themselves and their families. Harvey Amani Whitfield explains this movement across national boundaries as a "fluid frontier" which led to the formation of a transnational Black community held together by formal and informal institutions and practices.[7]

My maternal grandfather, John William Franklin, Sr. was one of those wandering descendants and carried the Franklin family heritage with him. He was born and raised in Nova Scotia, Canada. When he talked to me about Nova Scotia when I was a child, it seemed a mystical place—where my elderly grandfather lived before his immigration to the United States. His origins made me feel unique among my peers—having a grandparent who lived in a different state but was also born in a different country about which we knew very little. But I did come to an understanding that the Black experience in North America did not end at the boundaries of the United States. I learned at an early age that the narrative of Blacks in America was diverse and not monolithic. I also understood that my mother's origins in Massachusetts may have meant that my own family's story could be tied to the events of my country's founding. However, I did not know to what extent that would be and that it would involve the separation of the family along two lines, one in the United States and one in Canada.

John William Franklin, Sr. was an example of the fluidity and transnationality described by Whitfield. My grandfather's passage to America can be traced back to the whaling tradition of Atlantic Canada. His first job, as a young man, was on a whaling ship. As was the custom for young men in the Annapolis community, many obtained their first job on a whaler out of Weymouth, Nova Scotia. After one of those whaling trips, he landed in New York City and established residency there. He eventually obtained employment as a pressman for an established tailor in the Lower East Side of Manhattan.[8]

My grandfather was following a migration pattern already established by other members of the Black Annapolis community, starting in the 1830s. After the initial surge of Black loyalist settlements, additional communities started to spring up throughout Annapolis County. According to local historian Ian Lawrence, members of the Black communities at Delap's Cove, Granville Mountain, and Phinney's Cove in Nova Scotia, seeking to improve their economic conditions, began to immigrate to Maine and then Lynn, Massachusetts, as early as the 1830s. Two of the earliest Franklin descendants to return to the United States were Henry and Jacob Brothers, the sons of Ben's eldest daughter, Isabella. Henry and his family migrated across the Bay of Fundy and initially settled in Robbinston, Maine—the easternmost part of the United States—with Henry making a living there as a fisherman. By the end of the Civil War, in 1865, Henry resided in Lynn, Massachusetts. His younger brother, Jacob, followed suit—living for a brief period in Maine. But, by 1867, both brothers were living and working as laborers in Lynn.[9]

The Brothers siblings were part of a larger group of Black Nova Scotians that by 1880 had settled in Massachusetts—including the families of Andrew Camps, Thomas Smith, Charles Lanzey, Israel Esser, and Richard Fowler. Camps was one of the first documented Black Nova Scotians to settle in Lynn. Andrew and his spouse, Hannah (Middleton) Harris, migrated to Lynn about 1852. This was the second marriage for his spouse. Hannah was probably a descendant of Black loyalist Sarah Middleton, who migrated to Nova Scotia at the same time as the patriarchs of the Franklin and Brother families, during the loyalist exodus from Long Island after the war. Andrew was born in 1827 at Bridgetown—where a Black community was formed by the sons and daughters of the Black loyalist wave to Nova Scotia. Andrew's migration to Lynn set off a pattern of chain migration from his native Nova Scotia to the small city in Essex County, Massachusetts, which eventually included my grandfather, John.[10]

Even though he left his homeland, John William did not leave behind his heritage or sense of loyalty to nation and family tradition. Following the Frank/Franklin military tradition, John and his older brother, Peter, a

John William Franklin, Sr. (*Author*)

lifelong Canadian resident, served in World War I. They also experienced
a pattern of segregated service, since both Canadian and American military
forces segregated their troops during the conflict. And those Black troops
primarily served in a support capacity. That was the case for Peter's service.
He enlisted in July 1916 and served with Canadian Expeditionary Forces
as a member of the Second Construction Battalion in France and Belgium.
The service of John was different. As a noncitizen, to enlist in the U.S.
Army, he was required to be living permanently and legally in the United
States. John was among the many immigrants who served during the war.
Almost one in five draftees, and more than 18 percent of the total U.S.
Army, was foreign-born. By the time of his enlistment in June 1918, John
was still residing in New York City and became a member of the segre-
gated 372nd Infantry Regiment of the 93rd Division of the United States
Army. He served overseas, at the end of the war, from August 3, 1918, to
July 6, 1919. After his service in World War I and marriage, John returned
to his hometown in Annapolis County for a brief period, but eventually
settled in Lynn. He always displayed a Canadian flag in his American
household. He passed away in 1963 and never forfeited his Canadian citizenship.[11]

John's two sons, my uncles John William Franklin, Jr. and Benjamin Franklin, not only carried on the Frank/Franklin military tradition—they also carried the names of the first Frank brothers to serve. Both served in segregated units during World War II. John, Jr. served as a surveyor in the Philippine Islands. His younger brother, Benjamin, enlisted at the age of eighteen and served in France. They both served together during the Korean Conflict in integrated companies after the desegregation of American military troops in 1948. Like their namesake ancestors, they served in both segregated and integrated units.[12]

The oral tradition of the Canadian Franklin family is the foundation of this study. Thomas Henry Franklin captured the essence of the uniqueness of the Franklin family best when describing his surname as "an uncommon name in these parts." My grandfather, John William, did not provide the details of the Frank/Franklin oral tradition to his young granddaughter from Toledo who visited for many summers. But when asked why there was a Canadian flag in his dining room, he simply responded, "because that's where I'm from." He spoke with fond memories of his Nova Scotian childhood. But he did pass along the oral history of the Frank/Franklin family to his son, Ben Franklin, who luckily for me, related the fascinating story of the Frank brothers to his inquisitive niece. It is beyond ironic to me that my Uncle Ben, the keeper and purveyor of the story, is the namesake of the original Ben Frank/Frankham/Franklin.

Learning about the Franklin family background and origins has been a fascinating personal journey. Their struggle to gain standing in their communities and to fight on equal footing with their white counterparts in the Continental army has helped me to put my own life and career choices in perspective. Like the Frank brothers, I followed in my own father's footsteps when I became a police officer in Toledo, Ohio, in 1976—one of the first female officers on the department. My father, a well-respected police investigator and Civil War history buff, instilled a love of history in me and, like Rufus Frank to his own sons, was an inspiring figure in my life. But did the heritage from my maternal line instill an unconventional streak in me that allowed me to envision myself as someone equal in a male dominant workforce? It is possible that this nonconforming trait came from the Frank/Franklin line?

Learning about my family's history has also provided a heightened sense of belonging to the American story, especially having the privilege of learning about their role in the American Revolution. To hear that the Revolution tore apart families and their loyalties to country and each other is one

John William Franklin, Jr., left, and Benjamin Franklin, right. (*Author*)

thing. To know and understand the separation of brothers on a personal level and how that separation reverberated from the eighteenth century to twenty-first-century America is a fascinating thing. I have a much better understanding of the difficulties incurred by revolutionary era households as they tried to decide which side, if any, to commit their allegiance. As I am a professor of early American history, my family's personal story provides a very human aspect of the trials and tribulations faced by many families and usually prompts students to delve into their own family's history in America.

Throughout my research, I have often asked myself which of the brothers I identified with the most. And even though Ben's life and decisions provide a better framework to understand my own predilection to take the road less traveled, as the oldest sibling of my family, I tend to identify with William, the older brother who was persistent and steadfast in his service. But I am not judgmental or unsympathetic to Ben's actions and decisions. To the contrary, the combination of these two dichotomous personalities has found a home in this author and motivated me to not only continue their history of public service but to also write their story.

So, this study is complex, like the brothers it is based on. This story crosses boundaries of time, location, and subject matter. It is a complicated project because of its expansive examination of a group of individuals who lived during a period of extraordinary events. However, at the root of this project sits the Frank/Franklin family, in all its diversity and simplicity. The Frank/Franklins were uncommon in their breadth of experiences during the revolutionary era. They were exceptional due to the actions they took to survive and thrive during a time of conflict and change. And they were typical in their desires to gain standing in their communities and to create and maintain their families in early America.[13]

Notes

INTRODUCTION: THE MYSTERY OF THE LANDSCAPER

1. "Obituary for Henry Franklin," *Annapolis Spectator* (1929).

2. Thomas Henry Franklin died in 1929. William Inglis Morse, *Gravestones of Acadie and other Essays on Local History, Genealogy and Parish Records of Annapolis County, Nova Scotia* (London: A. Smith & Co., 1929), 2.

3. Morse, 2.

4. "Obituary for Henry Franklin"; Ian Lawrence, "The Franklin Family of Granville Township," Annapolis Heritage Society (AHS), n.d.

5. Nikki M. Taylor, PhD was a visiting professor with the History Department at the University of Toledo. At the time of this publication, she serves as a Professor of U.S. History at Howard University. Barbara Thompson Howell, *How to Trace Your African-American Roots* (Secaucus: Citadel Press, 1999), 61.

6. National Archives, "Compiled Service Records of Soldiers Who Served in the American Army during the Revolutionary War" (hereafter known as CSR and name of soldier) M881/Roll 843, RG 93, Chicago, IL, William Frank/Franck; CSR Benjamin Frank/Franck.

7. Judith Van Buskirk argues that Black soldiers of the Revolutionary War are "elusive" and "anonymous" actors who often get "lost" and receive little coverage in African American history. Judith Van Buskirk, *Standing in Their Own Light: African American Patriots in the American Revolution* (Norman: University of Oklahoma Press, 2017), 3–4.

8. Dee Parmer Woodtor, *Finding a Place Called Home: A Guide to African-American Genealogy and Historical Identity* (New York: Random House, 1999), 9.

9. *Finding Your Roots*, season 1, episode 9, "John Legend /Wanda Sykes /Margarett Cooper," PBS, May 13, 2012, written by Henry Louis Gates, directed by Hazel Gurland, Sabin Streeter, Jesse Sweet.

10. David E. Kyvig and Myron A. Marty, *Nearby History: Exploring The Past Around You*, 3rd Edition (Lanham: Rowman and Littlefield, 2010), 113. Carla L. Peterson uses her family history "as a point of departure" when telling an extensive story about the Black elite in nineteenth-century New York. Carla L. Peterson, *Black Gotham: A Family History of African Americans in Nineteenth-Century New York City* (New Haven: Yale University Press, 2011). While trying to solve the mystery of his family's name and how family lore obscured

the truth of its African origins, Joe Mozingo provides a fascinating tale of how an Anglo-American family traced its roots back to seventeenth-century Jamestown and an enslaved African warrior and in the process details the construction of racial identity in post-revolutionary America. Joe Mozingo, *The Fiddler on Pantico Run: An African Warrior, His White Descendants, a Search for Family* (New York: Free Press, 2012), 3. John F. Baker's discovery of a nineteenth-century photograph of his ancestors in his seventh-grade textbook led him on a lifelong journey of research which resulted in not only a family study but a greater understanding of the workings of the largest tobacco plantation in Tennessee. John F. Baker, Jr., *The Washingtons of Wessyngton Plantation: Stories of My Family's Journey to Freedom* (New York: Atria Books, 2009), 1–2.

11. Francesca Mari, "The Microhistorian," *Dissent,* Spring 2013, https://www.dissent magazine.org/article/the-microhistorian–2 (accessed August 19, 2016).

12. Mr. Benjamin R. Franklin is my uncle, and a direct descendant of Ben Frank/Franklin. His father, John William Franklin, Sr., a native of Nova Scotia, migrated to the United States by the 1920s. The Franklin oral tradition passed through the Canadian line of the family. A DNA test was performed on Benjamin R. Franklin. His sample matched an individual residing in the Dominican Republic, putting the Frank/Franklin ancestral line very close to its Haitian origins. His sample also matched an individual residing in Togo and a member of the Ewe Peoples. Benjamin R. Franklin, personal interview with writer, Lynn, Massachusetts, July 12, 2000. FamilyTree DNA, https://familytreedna.com (accessed November 11, 2010), "yDNA37 test results for Benjamin R. Franklin."

13. The 1810 and 1820 Federal Censuses for Massachusetts do list a Ben Frank, man of color, residing in Springfield, Massachusetts. However, since this Ben Frank is residing in Massachusetts at the same time that Ben Franklin is residing in Nova Scotia, I concluded they are two separate individuals. Letter to Mrs. Hattie Gilton from Finn Bower, Curator Shelburne County Museum, 24 June 2000; Graham Russell Hodges, *The Black Loyalist Directory: African Americans in Exile After the American Revolution* (New York: Garland, 1996), 170; Library and Archives of Canada (LAC), *Shelburne Town Records Collection,* "Muster Book of Free Black Settlement of Birchtown, 1784 Captain Bridges' Company who have drawn provisions at Port Mouton"; United States Federal Census, 1810, Massachusetts; United States Federal Census, 1820, Massachusetts.

14. Ian Lawrence, "The Franklin Family of Granville Township," Annapolis Royal: AHS, n.d.

15. Rhode Island State Archives (RISA), *Regimental Book Rhode Island Regiment for 1781,* 1–38; John R. Bartlett, ed., Census *of the inhabitants of the Colony of Rhode Island and Providence Plantations, 1774* (Baltimore: Genealogical Publishing Company, 1969), 228; RISA, *1774 Rhode Island Census.*

16. Military records indicate two additional soldiers of color with the surname of Frank. Neither served with the "Black Regiment." Andrew Frank served with Rhode Island militia troops and Nehemiah Frank served briefly in the First Rhode Island Regiment from June 1777 until December 1777 when he died. RISA, *Regimental Book Rhode Island Regiment for 1781*; Cherry Fletcher Bamberg, *Elder John Gorton and the Six Principle Baptist Church of East Greenwich, Rhode Island* (Greenville: Rhode Island Genealogical Society, 2001), 270; Library and Archives of Canada (LAC) *Shelburne Town Records Collection,* "Muster Book of Free Black Settlement of Birchtown, 1784 Captain Bridges' Company who have drawn provisions at Port Mouton."

17. Megan Smolenyak, *Who Do You Think You Are? The Essential Guide To Tracing Your Family History* (New York: Viking, 2009), 160; Buzzy Jackson, *Shaking the Family Tree: Blue*

Bloods, Black Sheep, and Other Obsessions of an Accidental Genealogist (New York: Touchstone, 2010), 129.

18. Jackson, *Shaking the Family Tree,* 119, 129.

19. FamilyTree DNA.

20. Joanne Pope Melish, "Recovering (from) Slavery: Four Struggles to Tell the Truth," in *Slavery and Public History: The Tough Stuff of American Memory,* ed. James Oliver Horton and Lois E. Horton (New York: The New Press, 2006), 126.

CHAPTER ONE: THE POSSIBLE ANCESTOR

1. Peter Kolchin, *American Slavery, 1619–1877* (New York: Hill & Wang, 2003), 45; Gerald Astor, *The Right to Fight: A History of African-Americans in the Military* (New York: Presidio Press, 1988), 8–9.

2. These five documents regarding Frank Nigro are unique since Black representation in colonial records was limited. Gretchen Holbrook Gerzina argues that New England record keepers were methodical in their recordkeeping but that did not include documentation of Blacks unless they were involved in court dealings. Gretchen Holbrook Gerzina, *Mr. and Mrs. Prince: How an Extraordinary Eighteenth Century Family Moved Out of Slavery into Legend* (New York: HarperCollins, 2008), 13; Catherine Adams and Elizabeth H. Pleck, *Love of Freedom: Black Women in Colonial and Revolutionary New England* (Oxford: Oxford University Press, 2010), 13.

3. John Hutchins Cady, *Rhode Island Boundaries, 1636–1936* (Providence: Rhode Island Tercentenary Commission, 1936), 13; Horatio Rogers, George Moulton Carpenter, and Edward Field, eds., *The Early Records of the Town of Providence Volume V Being Part of the Third Book of the Town of Providence Otherwise Called the Book with Brass Clasps* (Providence: Snow and Farnham City Printers, 1894), 278–279.

4. Ira Berlin, *Many Thousands Gone: The First Two Centuries Of Slavery In North America* (Cambridge: Belknap Press of Harvard University, 1998), 369; Rowena Stewart, *A Heritage Discovered: Blacks in Rhode Island* (Providence: Rhode Island Black Historical Society, 1975), 5; Lorenzo J. Greene, *The Negro in Colonial New England* (New York: Atheneum, 1968), 27–28; Richard Archer, *Jim Crow North: The Struggle for Equal Rights in Antebellum New England* (New York: Oxford University Press, 2017), 23.

5. For a more comprehensive analysis concerning the origins of slavery in the New England colonies, see Margaret Ellen Newell, *Brethren By Nature: New England Indians, Colonists, and the Origins of American Slavery* (Ithaca: Cornell University Press, 2015), 5–6; and Jared Ross Hardesty, *Black Lives, Native Lands, White Worlds: A History of Slavery in New England* (Amherst: Bright Leaf, an imprint of University of Massachusetts Press, 2019), 11–12.

6. Wendy Warren, *New England Bound: Slavery and Colonization in Early America* (New York: Liveright Publishing Corporation, A Division of W. W. Norton and Company, 2016), 10, 32; Kolchin, 16; Lorenzo J. Greene, "Slaveholding New England and Its Awakening," *Journal of Negro History* 13, no. 4 (October 1928), 495–496, 503; Edgar McManus, *Black Bondage in the North* (Syracuse: Syracuse University Press, 1973), 56, 61; Christy Clark-Pujara, *Dark Water: The Business of Slavery in Rhode Island* (New York: New York University Press, 2016), 30.

7. Warren, *New England Bound,* 113.

8. Christy Clark-Pujara details the progression of slavery in Rhode Island by tracking Rhode Island's General Assembly acknowledgment of enslaved Native Americans and Africans in 1703. Clark-Pujara, 11, 35; J. Stanley Lemons, "Rhode Island and the Slave Trade," *Rhode*

Island History 60, no. 4 (Fall 2002), 98; Lorenzo J. Greene, *The Negro in Colonial New England*, 32; Keith W. Stokes and Theresa Guzman Stokes, *A Matter of Truth: The Struggle for African Heritage and Indigenous People Equal Rights in Providence, Rhode Island (1620–2020)* (Middleton: Rhode Island Black Heritage Society, 2021), 18.

9. Lorenzo Johnston Greene, *The Negro in Colonial New England*, 135–136, 291–295; Robert J. Cottrol, *The Afro-Yankees: Providence's Black Community in the Antebellum Era* (Westport: Greenwood Press, 1982), 16; Clark-Pujara, 34–35.

10. Cottrol, 16; Joanne Pope Melish, "The Manumission of Nab," *Rhode Island History* 68, no. 1 (Winter/Spring 2010), 37; Charles Rappleye, *Sons of Providence: The Brown Brothers, the Slave Trade, and the American Revolution* (New York: Simon and Schuster Paperbacks, 2006), 29; Clark-Pujara, 28–29, 46; Adams and Pleck, 41; Glen A. Knoblock, *African American Historic Burial Grounds and Gravesites of New England* (Jefferson, NC: McFarland, 2016), 19–21.

11. Genealogist Tony Burroughs teaches that to understand the genealogy and experiences of an enslaved ancestor, one must understand the genealogy and history of the slaveholder. Tony Burroughs, *Black Roots: A Beginner's Guide to Tracing the African American Family Tree* (New York: A Fireside Book, 2001), 42; Daniel Hoogland Carpenter, *History and Genealogy of the Carpenter Family in America from the Settlement at Providence, RI, 1637–1901* (Jamaica, Queensborough, NY: Marion Press, 1901), 8–9, 30; William Richard Cutter, *Genealogical and Family History of Western New York: A Record of the Achievements of Her People in the Making of a Commonwealth and the Building of a Nation, Volume I* (New York: Lewis Historical Publishing Company, 1912), 274; C. S. Mangold, *Ten Hills Farm: The Forgotten History of Slavery in the North* (Princeton: Princeton University Press, 2010), 75.

12. The Carpenter and Arnold families were among the largest landholders and taxpayers in Pawtuxet. Donald A. D'Amato and Henry A.L. Brown, *Images in America: Pawtuxet, Rhode Island* (Dover, NH: Arcadia, 1997), 7; Daniel Hoogland Carpenter, *History and Genealogy of the Carpenter Family in America From Settlement at Providence Rhode Island 1637–1901* (New York: The Marion Press, 1901), 13–15, 17, 28; Clarence S. Brigham, compiler, *Seventeenth-Century Place Names of Providence Plantations, 1636–1700* (Providence: Rhode Island Historical Society, 1903), 18; Hazel Wade Kennedy, *Fragments of Time in Pawtuxet* (Cranston: Modern Press, 1986), 7.

13. Hoogland Carpenter, 18, 30; John R. Bartlett, editor, *Colonial Records of Rhode Island and Providence Plantations, Volume II 1664–1677* (Providence: A. Crawford Greene and Brother State Printers, 1857), 442, 457, 479, 509–510; Gail I. Winson, "Researching the Laws of the Colony of Rhode Island and Providence Plantations," Roger Williams University School of Law Faculty Papers. Paper 1. http://lsr.nellco.org/ rwu_fp, 8, 19–20.

14. *Rhode Island Land Evidence, Volume I 1648–1696 Abstracts* (Providence: Rhode Island Historical Society, 1921), 52.

15. John Smith was granted land on the Mooshassuc River at Wainscote meadow to erect a mill in March 1646. The location was off Charles Street above the Mill Bridge, which is present-day Mill Street, a short link connecting North Main and Charles Streets. Horatio Rogers and Edward Field, *The Early Records of the Town of Providence Volume XV Being the Providence Town Paper Volume I 1639–April 1682 Nos. 01-0367* (Providence: Snow & Farnham City Printers, 1899), 188; William Read Staples, *Annals of the Town of Providence From Its First Settlement to the Organization of the City Government in June 1832* (Providence: Knowles & Vose, 1843), 174; Welcome Arnold Greene, *The Providence Plantations for 250 Years: The People and Their Neighbors, Their Pursuits and Progress, 1636–1886* (Providence:

J. A. and R. A. Reid, 1886), 44; Gertrude Selwyn Kimball, *Providence in Colonial Times* (Boston: Houghton Mifflin, 1912), 275; Clark-Pujara, 22–23.

16. Hoogland Carpenter, 20–21, 23, 27; Horatio Rogers and Edward Field, *The Early Records of the Town of Providence Volume XVII Being the Providence Town Papers Volume 2, April 1682– March 1722 Nos. 0368-0717* (Providence: Snow & Farnham City Printers, 1903), 122.

17. Cottrol, 16; Clark-Pujara, 6, 45; Lorenzo J. Greene, *The Negro in Colonial New England*, 168; James Oliver Horton and Lois E. Horton, *In Hope of Liberty: Culture, Community and Protest Among Northern Free Blacks, 1700–1860* (New York: Oxford University Press, 1997), 6, 40; Rogers, Carpenter, and Field, *Early Records of Providence, Volume V*, 278–279; Hoogland Carpenter, 322; McManus, 56; Mangold, 46; Warren, 32.

18. Hoogland Carpenter, 19, 322; Lorenzo J. Greene, *The Negro in Colonial New England*, 100–101; Tapping Reeve, *The Law of Baron and Femme Of Parent and Child, Guardian and Ward, Master and Servant, and of the Powers of Courts of Chancery, with an Essay On The Terms Heir, Heirs, and Heirs of the Body Second Edition with Notes and References to English and American Cases* (Burlington: Chauncey Goodrich, 1846), 340; Berlin, *Many Thousands Gone*, 58–59; "Colonial America's Pre-Industrial Age of Wood and Water," Building Community Medieval Technology and American History Project of Penn State University and National Endowment of the Humanities, https://www.engr.psu.edu/mtah/articles/colonial_wood_water.htm; Ira Berlin, "Coming to Terms with Slavery in the 21st Century," in *Slavery and Public History: The Tough Stuff of American History*, edited by James Oliver Horton and Lois E. Horton (New York: The New Press, 2014), 9; Gwendolyn Midlo Hall, *Slavery and African Ethnicities in the Americas: Restoring the Links* (Chapel Hill: University of North Carolina Press, 2005), 14; Adams and Pleck, 15; Warren, 138.

19. Knoblock, 203–221; Lorenzo J. Greene, *The Negro in Colonial New England*, 111, 121–122, 177–178.

20. The Will of William Carpenter details one incident listing the gift of land to Ephraim identified by the Seven Mile Line. The record of the bequeathment reads as follows: "I give unto my Grandson Ephraim Carpenter & his heirs, all that Right of lands meadowes and Coming to me belonging on the west side of ye seven mile line ariseing to me by virtue of my owne Right in sayd towne." *Early Records of the Town of Providence, Volume V*, 278–279; Hoogland Carpenter, 23; Knoblock, 27; Lorenzo J. Greene, *The Negro in Colonial New England*, 177–178; Arthur Zilversmit, *The First Emancipation: The Abolition of Slavery in the North* (Chicago: University of Chicago Press, 1967), 19; Darlene Clark Hine, William C. Hine, and Stanley Harrold, *African Americans: A Concise History*, Third Edition (Upper Saddle River, NJ: Pearson, Prentice Hall, 2010), 67; Adams and Pleck, 12–13; Richard B. Morris, "The Emergence of the American Laborer," in *The History of the American Worker*, ed. Richard B. Morris (Princeton: Princeton University Press, 1983), 17; "Samuel Cranston, December 5, 1708, Newport, Rhode Island to the Board of Trade," *Records of the Colony of Rhode Island and Providence Plantations in New England, Volume IV, 1707–1740* (Providence: Knowles, Anthony & Co., 1859), 55, 60; John Hope Franklin and Evelyn Brooks Higginbotham, *From Slavery to Freedom: A History of African Americans, Ninth Edition* (New York: McGraw-Hill, 2011), 146–147; Horton and Horton, *In Hope of Liberty*, 1.

21. Adams and Pleck, 12; Lorenzo J. Greene, *The Negro in Colonial New England*, 309.

22. William E. Clarke, *The Early Records of the Town of Providence, Volume XX Being the First Part of the Second Book for the Recording of the Deeds and Called Deed Book No. 2* (Providence, Snow & Farnham Co., 1909), 128–129; Lorenzo J. Greene, *The Negro in Colonial New England*, 309.

23. It was the practice that enslaved "servants" appear among the listing of property filed with the local probate courts. Horatio Rogers, George Moulton Carpenter, and Edward Field, *The Early Records of the Town of Providence Volume VI Being Part of Will Book No. 1 Otherwise Called the First Booke for Providence Towne Councill Perticulior Vse* (Providence: Snow & Farnham, 1894), 156–159; Horatio Rogers, George Moulton Carpenter, Edward Field, *The Early Records of the Town of Providence Volume III Being Part of the Third Book of the Town of Providence Otherwise Called the Book With Brass Clasps* (Providence: Snow & Farnham, 1893), 115–116; Lorenzo J. Greene, *The Negro in Colonial New England*, 290–291; Pope Melish, "The Manumission of Nab," 37; Warren, 129; Bartlett, *Records of the Colony of Rhode Island and Providence Plantations in New England, Vol. IV 1707 to 1740* (Providence: Knowles, Anthony and Company, 1859), 59.

24. William E. Clarke, *The Early Records of the Town of Providence, Volume XX Being the First Part of the Second Book for the Recording of the Deeds and Called Deed Book No. 2* (Providence, Snow & Farnham Co., 1909), 128–129, 169–170; Zachary Garceau, "Making Sense of Money in Colonial America," *Vita Brevis: A Resource for Family History from AmericanAncestors.org*, Making Sense of Money in Colonial America | Vita Brevis (americanancestors.org), (accessed October 17, 2022); Eric Nye, "Pounds Sterling to Dollars: Historical Conversion of Currency," www.uwyo.edu/numimage/currency.htm; Lorenzo J. Greene, *The Negro in Colonial New England*, 309.

25. Horatio Rogers, George Moulton Carpenter, and Edward Field, *The Early Records of the Town of Providence Volume IX Being Part of the Book of Records of Town Meetings No. 3 1677 To 1750 And Other Papers* (Providence: Snow & Farnham, 1895), 181; Robert L. Walcott, "Husbandry in Colonial New England," *New England Quarterly* 9, no. 2 (June 1936): 244–245; Virginia DeJohn Anderson, *Creatures of Empire: How Domestic Animals Transformed Early America* (Oxford: Oxford University Press, 2004), 142–144, 146, 149, 164; Clark-Pujara, 39; Lorenzo J. Greene, *The Negro in Colonial New England*, 309; Hoogland Carpenter, 322; Adams and Pleck, 12.

26. Winson, 19–20; Amasa M. Eaton, "The Development of the Judicial System in Rhode Island," *Yale Law Journal* 14, no. 3 (January 1905): 150; Hoogland Carpenter, 18; Bartlett, *Colonial Records of Rhode Island and Providence Plantations, Volume II 1664–1677*, 509–510.

27. Rhode Island Historical Society, *Providence Town Papers*, MSS 214 Series 1, Volume 39A, no. 16751; Lorenzo J. Greene, *The Negro in Colonial New England*, 137, 299–300.

CHAPTER TWO: THE FRANK FAMILY BEFORE THE REVOLUTIONARY WAR

1. The records are not conclusive as to the identities of children of Frank Nigro. This could reflect changes in his surname or other difficulties with tracking and documenting the activities of free Blacks in colonial Rhode Island. Additionally, records are not conclusive regarding the age of Rufus Frank. He does not appear in the records after 1774, possibly an indication of his death after that date. Adams and Pleck, 157–158; Midlo Hall, 53; Gloria McCahon Whiting, "Power, Patriarchy, and Provision: African Families Negotiate Gender and Slavery in New England," *Journal of American History* 103, no. 3 (December 1, 2016): 583–605, 600.

2. James N. Arnold, editor, *Vital Records of Rhode Island 1636–1850. First Series: Births, Marriages and Deaths. A Family Register for the People Volume X Town and Church* (Providence: Narragansett Historical Publishing Company, 1898), 232.

3. Rhode Island town councils were directed by colonial law on how to deal with persons who died without making a will to "take and receive from any Administrator or

Administratrix of the Estate of any Person dying Intestate, . . . a good and sufficient Bond with two Sureties for his or her faithful Administration of said Estate." The administrator was also required to make an honest inventory of the estate and report back to the town council the results of that inventory. *Acts and laws, of His Majesty's colony of Rhode-Island, and Providence-Plantations, in New-England, in America*, "An Act empowering the Town Councils of the several Towns within this Government, to take Bonds from Administrators, for the Rendring of Accounts of their Administration on the Estates of Persons dying Intestate," Evans Early American Imprint Collection (Ann Arbor: Text Creation Partnership, 2011), 202; Providence Old City Hall Archives, "Administration Bond of the Estate of Phillip Frank, 1758," *Wills and Probate Records, 1582–1932*; John D. Cushing, editor, *The Earliest Acts and Laws of the Colony of Rhode Island and Providence Plantations, 1647–1719* (Wilmington, DE: Michael Glazler, 1977), 149; George L. Haskins, "The Beginnings of Partible Inheritance in the American Colonies," *Yale Law Journal* 51 (1942): 1285, available at: https://digitalcommons.law.yale.edu/ylj/vol51/iss8/5; Howard M. Chapin, *Rhode Island in the Colonial Wars: A List of Rhode Island Soldiers and Sailors in the Old French and Indian War, 1755–1762* (Providence: Printed for the Society, 1918), 68; Benjamin Quarles, "The Colonial Militia and Negro Manpower," *Mississippi Valley Historical Review*, 45, no. 4 (March 1959), 643–644; Edward Sandel, ed., *Black Soldiers in the Colonial Militia: Documents from 1639 to 1780* (Roseland: Tabor-Lucas Publications, 1994), 23; John Wood Sweet, *Bodies Politic: Negotiating Race in the American North, 1730–1830* (Baltimore: Johns Hopkins University Press, 2003), 199; Lorenzo J. Greene, *The Negro in Colonial New England*, 189.

4. Providence Old City Hall Archives, *Book of Marriages*, 96.

5. There is no documentary evidence that states the relationship between the two Andrew Franks. However, the younger Frank lived in the Providence region, one generation after the senior Frank. Arnold, *Vital Record of Rhode Island 1636–1850. First Series. Births, Marriages, Deaths: A Family Register for the People. Vol. 2, Providence County* (Providence: Narragansett Historical Publishing Company, 1892), 74; Lorenzo J. Greene, *The Negro in Colonial New England*, 309–310.

6. Samuel Frank is not listed as residing in Johnston, Rhode Island, in the 1790 census. 1800 United States Federal Census; 1810 United States Census.

7. Lorenzo J. Greene, *The Negro in Colonial New England*, 188; Sandel, 35.

8. Sandel, 23, 35. 38; Quarles, "The Colonial Militia and Negro Manpower," 643–652; John W. Shy, "A New Look at Colonial Militia," *William and Mary Quarterly*, 3rd series, 20, no. 2 (April 1963), 182.

9. Quarles, "The Colonial Militia and Negro Manpower," 643–644; Sandel, 23; Sweet, 199; Greene, *The Negro in Colonial New England*, 189; Philip Foner, *History of Black Americans From Africa to the Emergence of the Cotton Kingdom* (New York: Greenwood Press, 1975), 311.

10. Lorenzo J. Greene, *The Negro in Colonial New England* 187–188; Foner, 311; Quarles, "The Colonial Militia and Negro Manpower," 651–652.

11. Philip D. Morgan and Andrew Jackson O'Shaughnessy, "Arming Slaves in the American Revolution," in *Arming Slaves: From Classical Times to the Modern Age*, ed. Philip D. Morgan and Andrew Jackson O'Shaughnessy (New Haven: Yale University Press, 2006), 186; Chapin, *Rhode Island in the Colonial Wars*, 68; Chapin, *Nine Muster Rolls of Rhode Island Troops Enlisted During The Old French War To Which is added The Journal of Captain William Rice in The Expedition of 1746* (Providence: Printed for the Society by the Standard Printing Company from original MSS in the Library of the R.I. Historical Society, 1915), 19, 29, 34, 38.

12. Oscar Reiss, *Blacks in Colonial America* (Jefferson, NC: McFarland, 1997), 231.

13. Armand Francis Lucier, ed., *French and Indian War Notices Abstracted from Colonial Newspapers Volume 3: January 1, 1758–September 17, 1759* (Bowie: Heritage Books, 1999), 123–125.

14. Chapin, *Rhode Island in the Colonial Wars*, 14–15, 68.

15. Bruce Campbell MacGunnigle, transcriber, *Red Coats and Yellow Fever: Rhode Island Troops at the Siege of Havana, 1762* (Providence: Printed for the Society by Webster Press, 1991), 5–6, 19, 22.

16. Jeffrey Brace, *The Blind African Slave or Memoirs of Boyrereau Brinch, Nicknamed Jeffrey Brace, as told to Benjamin F. Prentiss, Esq.*, ed. Kari J. Winter (Madison: University of Wisconsin Press, 2004), 151.

17. Chapin, *Rhode Island in the Colonial Wars*, 15; MacGunnigle, *Red Coats and Yellow Fever*, 5, 19.

18. Shy, 182; Lisa Wilson, *Ye Heart of a Man: The Domestic Life of Men in Colonial New England* (New Haven: Yale University Press, 1999), 115; "Administration Bond on the Estate of Phillip Frank, 1758"; Rogers, Carpenter, and Field, *The Early Records of the Town of Providence, Volume V*, 278–279.

19. Darlene Clark Hine and Earnestine Jenkins, "Black Men's History: Toward a Gendered Perspective" in *A Question of Manhood, Volume 1: Manhood Rights: The Construction of Black Male History and Manhood, 1750–1870*, ed. Darlene Clark Hine and Earnestine Jenkins (Bloomington: Indiana University Press, 1999), 3–5.

20. Brace, 94–95.

21. Jack J. Cardoso, "The Black Man as a Soldier," in *The Negro Impact on Western Civilization*, ed. Joseph S. Roucek and Thomas Kiernan (New York: Philosophical Library, 1970), 337.

22. Bartlett, *Census of the Inhabitants of the Colony of Rhode Island and Providence Plantations, 1774*, 228; Welcome Arnold Greene, 400; Louis H. McGowan and the Johnston Historical Society, *Images in America: Johnston* (Dover, NH: Arcadia Publishing, 1997), 7; Judith C. Harbold, "The 1774 Census of Rhode Island: Johnston," *Rhode Island Roots* 32, no. 4 (Dec. 2006), 187; Theodore Coleman, "Camp Hill, Hardscrabble, and Addison's Hollow in Early Providence," *Small State Big History*, April 22, 2023. http://smallstatebighistory.com/camp-hill-hardscrabble-and-addisons-hollow-in-early-providence/; Jeremy L. Wolin, "Hard Scrabble and Snow Town," *Demolition and Amnesia: Roger Williams National Monument Online Project* (Providence: Brown University, 2017).

23. Gloria McCahon Whiting addresses this characteristic by arguing that "liberty was gendered in early New England" with enslaved men more likely to gain freedom, manage to liberate their families from servitude and establish households ("Power, Patriarchy and Provision," 583–605, 594, 597). Bartlett, *Census of the Inhabitants of the Colony of Rhode Island and Providence Plantations, 1774*, 38–53, 227–231; RISA, 1774 Rhode Island Census; "Johnston, Rhode Island," www.rihs.org/mssinv/Mss202.htm (accessed September 20, 2004); McGowan, 7; Harbold, 187; Lorenzo J. Greene, *The Negro in Colonial New England*, 85–86; Cottrol, 29; *Creative Survival: The Providence Black Community in 19th Century Providence*: The Rhode Island Black Heritage Society (RIBHS), 1985), 31; Adams and Pleck, 30; James N. Arnold, *Vital Record of Rhode Island 1636–1850. First Series. Births, Marriages, Deaths: A Family Register for the People. Vol. 2, Providence County*, 316; Chapin, *Rhode Island in the Colonial Wars*, 28.

24. McGowan, 7; Lorenzo J. Greene, *The Negro in Colonial New England*, 332–333; RISA, "1750, An Act to Prevent Persons Keeping House in this Colony from entertaining Indians, Negros or Molattos," accessed at http://sos.ri.gov/archon/index.php?p=digitallibrary/digitalcontent&id=448; Zilversmit, 16; Rhett S. Jones, "Plantation Slavery in the Narragansett Country of Rhode Island, 1690–1790: A Preliminary Study," *Plantation Society in the Americas* 2, no. 2 (1986), 165–166.

25. RIBHS, *Creative Survival*, 31; Lorenzo J. Greene, *The Negro in Colonial New England*, 299, 333.

26. Christy Clark-Pujara argues that court records indicate that the types of crimes committed by free Blacks, like theft of household items and livestock, were "a sign of economic insecurity and desperation." Clark-Pujara, 35, 39–40; Lorenzo J. Greene, *The Negro in Colonial New England*, 299–300, 333; Archer, 27.

27. Wanton family members have been classified as Native American and Black. See Chapter 3, "Brothers to War," for discussion regarding racial classification. Bartlett, *Census of the Inhabitants of the Colony of Rhode Island and Providence Plantations, 1774*, 184–191; Adams and Pleck, 16.

28. Donna Keith Baron, J. Edward Hood and Holly V. Izard, "They Were Here All Along: The Native American Presence in Lower-Central New England in the 18th and 19th Centuries," *William and Mary Quarterly*, 3rd series, 53, no. 3, Indians and Others in Early America (July 1996), 562–564.

29. Newport was one of the five largest cities in the American colonies on the eve of the American Revolution. Newport also played an instrumental role in the colonial slave trade. Newport merchants were heavily involved in the inter-colonial trade shipping products to the West Indies. Newport's second leading industry was distilling rum from molasses, with 22 percent of the liquor shipped to Africa on trade for slaves. As one of the seats of slavery in the American colonies, Newport was also the location of fervent antislavery activity led primarily by Quaker activists. The Quaker manumission movement affected the establishment of a free Black population in Newport. Benjamin L. Carp, *Rebels Rising: Cities and the American Revolution* (Oxford: Oxford University Press, 2007), 6, 10, 115; Rappleye, 138–140; Bartlett, *Census of the Inhabitants of the Colony of Rhode Island*, 1–37; Adams and Pleck, 31, 85, 90–91, 97; Christian McBurney, *Dark Voyage: An American Privateer's War on Britain's African Slave Trade* (Yardley: Westholme Publishing, 2022), 10.

CHAPTER THREE: BROTHERS TO WAR

1. Extant military records do not list the age of Ben Frank at the time of his initial service. The Muster Book for the free Black settlement of Birchtown, Nova Scotia, dated July 1784, listed Ben Frankum (Ben Frank) as twenty-two years of age. Using that date, Ben would have been fifteen-years-old upon enlistment. Additionally, other records list the brothers as general laborers. RISA, *Regimental Book Rhode Island Regiment for 1781*; CSR Benjamin Frank; Samuel Arnold Greene, *History of the State of Rhode Island and Providence Plantations: From the Settlement of the State, 1636 to the Adoption of the Federal Constitution, 1790* (Providence: Preston & Rounds, 1899), 399; RISA, Military Returns, Volume I; Joseph Jencks Smith, *Civil and Military Lists of Rhode Island, 1647–1800: A list of all officers elected by the General assembly from the organization of the legislative government of the colony to 1800* (Providence: Preston and Rounds, 1900), 340.

2. Michael Lee Lanning, *Defenders of Liberty: African-Americans in the Revolutionary War* (New York: Citadel Press Kensington Publishing, 2000), 44–45; Michael Stephenson, *Patriot Battles: How the War of Independence Was Fought* (New York: Harper Perennial, 2007), 21.

3. Monthly strength totals are separated into two main categories: Present, Fit for Duty and Grand totals, which include soldiers who were classified as sick, on command, or on furlough. The Present, Fit for Duty total indicates the number of soldiers readily available during the month in question. Charles H. Lesser, ed., *The Sinews of Independence: Monthly Strength Reports of the Continental Army* (Chicago: University of Chicago Press, 1976), 2–3; 12–13; Lanning, 44–45.

4. Bartlett, *Records of the Colony of Rhode Island and Providence Plantations in New England, Volume VII, 1770–1776* (Providence: A. Crawford Greene, State Printer, 1862), 310; Anthony Walker, *So Few the Brave: Rhode Island Continentals, 1775–1783* (Newport: Seafield, 1981), 1.

5. The actual monthly strength totals for each of these regiments did not exceed their authorized strength. In July 1775 their combined strength total was 1,268 officers and men. Their highest monthly totals occurred in August 1775 with Varnum's force at 483, Hitchcock's at 510, and Church's at 461. Lesser, 2–13; Walker, *So Few the Brave*, 98–103.

6. The monthly present and fit for duty totals for the 9th and 11th Continentals reached highs of 409 in May 1776 for the 11th Continentals and 387 for the 9th Continentals. Lanning, *Defenders of Liberty*, 44–45; Stephenson, 32; Lesser, 15–42; Walker, *So Few the Brave*, 98–103.

7. Astor, 7; *Massachusetts Soldiers and Sailors of the Revolutionary War*, 17 vols. (Boston: 1896–1908), 12: 520, 743, 788.

8. Quoted in Sarah Loring Bailey, *Historical Sketches of Andover* (Boston: Houghton, Mifflin, 1880), 324.

9. Benjamin Cowell authored this history of Rhode Island's involvement in the American Revolution after serving several years as the clerk for the U.S. District Court in Providence. As part of his employment, he processed pension applications of Revolutionary War veterans. He became personally aware of the service given by these veterans and because of his access and working relationships with these men and their families, Cowell became a staunch advocate on their behalf. Benjamin Cowell, *Spirit of '76 in Rhode Island or Sketches of the Efforts of the Government and People in the War of the Revolution* (Boston: A. J. Wright, Printer, 1850), 20.

10. National Archives, Revolutionary War Pension and Bounty Land Warrant Application Records (hereinafter known as RWPR) Andrew Frank.

11. RWPR Andrew Frank; RWPR Winsor Fry; Walker, *So Few the Brave*, 98.

12. Henry Wiencek, *An Imperfect God: George Washington, His Slaves, and the Creation of America* (New York: Farrar, Straus and Giroux, 2003), 198–199.

13. Washington was following the policy set in May 1775 by the Committee of Safety, also known as the Hancock and Warren Committee, when it allowed for the service of free Blacks already in uniform but determined that the service of slaves was detrimental to their fight for independence. "Instructions for the officers of several regiments of the Massachusetts-Bay forces, who are immediately to go upon the recruiting service. . . . Given at the headquarters at Cambridge, this 10th day of July. Horatio Gates, adjutant-general." Watertown, 1775. Pdf. https://www.loc.gov/item/rbpe.03802500/; Michael Lee Lanning, *The African American Soldier: From Crispus Attucks to Colin Powell*, updated edition (New York: Citadel Press, 2004), 8.

14. The George Washington Papers at the Library of Congress, 1741–1799, "General Washington to Continental Army General Officers, October 5, 1775," http://memory.loc.gov (accessed December, 2006).

15. Peter Force, ed., *American Archives, Fourth Series Containing a Documentary History of the English Colonies in North America From the King's Message of March 7, 1774 to the Declaration of Independence by the United States, Volume III* (Washington, DC: M. St. Clair Clarke and Peter Force, 1840), 1161.

16. George Washington Papers, "George Washington, October 31, 1775," General Orders; "George Washington, November 12, 1775," General Orders.

17. Lanning, *Defenders of Liberty*, 49.

18. Benjamin Quarles, *The Negro in the American Revolution* (Chapel Hill: University of North Carolina Press, 1961), 72–73.

19. Lord Dunmore Proclamation, http://blackloyalist.com/canadiandigitalcollection/documents/official/ (accessed October 10, 2006).

20. Quarles, *The Negro in the American Revolution*, 19.

21. James Corbett David, *Dunmore's New World: The Extraordinary Life of a Royal Governor in Revolutionary America—with Jacobites, Counterfeiters, Land Schemes, Shipwrecks, Scalping, Indian Politics, Runaway Slaves, and Two Illegal Royal Weddings* (Charlottesville: University press of Virginia, 2013), 104–106, 110–112, 122–124; Morgan and O'Shaughnessy, 189; Astor, *The Right to Fight*, 8; Quarles, *The Negro in the American Revolution*, 28–30; Douglas R. Egerton, *Death or Liberty: African Americans and Revolutionary America* (New York: Oxford University Press, 2009), 71; John B. Boles, *Black Southerners, 1619–1869* (Lexington: University Press of Kentucky, 1983), 54.

22. Peter Maslowski, "National Policy Toward the Use of Black Troops in the Revolutionary War," in *Slavery, Revolutionary America and the New Nation*, ed. Paul Finkelman (New York: Garland Publishing, 1990), 383; Foner, *History of Black Americans*, 316.

23. The George Washington Papers, "George Washington, December 30, 1775, General Orders."

24. *The Papers of George Washington, Revolutionary War Series, vol. 2, 16 September 1775–31 December 1775*, ed. Philander D. Chase (Charlottesville: University Press of Virginia, 1987), 622–626.

25. Joseph T. Wilson, *The Black Phalanx: African Americans in the War of Independence, The War of 1812, and the Civil War* (New York: DaCapo Press, 1994, Previously published Hartford: American Publishing Company, 1890), 40; Maurice O. Wallace, *Constructing the Black Masculine: Identity and Ideality in African American Men's Literature and Culture, 1775–1995* (Durham: Duke University Press, 2002), 55.

26. Wiencek, *An Imperfect God*, 196–197.

27. Horton and Horton, *In Hope of Liberty*, 10.

28. Wiencek, *An Imperfect God*, 199.

29. *The Papers of James Madison*, vol. 2, *20 March 1780–23 February 1781*, ed. William T. Hutchinson and William M. E. Rachal (Chicago: University of Chicago Press, 1962), 209–211.

30. Quarles, *The Negro in the American Revolution*, 15–16.

31. *Journal of the proceedings of Congress, held at Philadelphia, from September 5, 1775, to April 30, 1776* (Philadelphia: United States Continental Congress, 1778), 105.

32. The George Washington Papers, "George Washington to Continental Army Captains, January 13, 1777"; Lorenzo J. Greene, "Some Observations on the Black Regiment of Rhode Island in the American Revolution," *Journal of Negro History*, 37, no. 2 (April 1952), 150.

33. Recruitment districts and pay were set by Congress in July 1777. Daniel Littlefield, *Revolutionary Citizen: African-Americans, 1776–1804* (New York: Oxford University Press, 1997), 37; Quarles, *The Negro in the American Revolution,* 52; Lanning, *Defenders of Liberty,* 64; Glenn A. Knoblock, *"Strong and Brave Fellows": New Hampshire's Black Soldiers and Sailors of the American Revolution, 1775–1784* (Jefferson: McFarland and Company, 2003), 14; Stephenson, *Patriot Battles,* 27; James C. Neagles, *Summer Soldiers: A Survey and Index of Revolutionary War Courts-Martial* (Salt Lake City: Ancestry Incorporated, 1986), 208.

34. Stephenson, *Patriot Battles,* 25; Horton and Horton, *In Hope of Liberty,* 64.

35. Wanton went on to substitute for Abner Durfee and David Duffee in the state militia before enlisting for one year with Colonel John Topham's Rhode Island state regiment. RWPR William Wanton.

36. Sweet, 203, 199.

37. The term "mustee" has been used to categorize people of mixed race ancestry. In Rhode Island, officials began to use the term to identify individuals of color who were of Native American ancestry. RWPR Winsor Fry; RISA, *Regimental Book Rhode Island Regiment for 1781;* Rita Elaine Souther, ed., *Minority Military Service Rhode Island, 1775–1783* (Washington, DC: National Society Daughters of the American Revolution, 1988), 12; *U.S. Federal Census, Rhode Island Heads of Families, First Census, 1790 Rhode Island* (Washington, DC: GPO, 1908), 46; Ruth Wallis Herndon and Ella Wilcox Sekatau, "The Right to a Name: The Narragansett People and Rhode Island Officials in the Revolutionary Era," *Ethnohistory* 44, no. 3 (Summer 1997), 3.

38. Sweet, 201; Quarles, *The Negro in the American Revolution,* 52.

39. RWPR Winsor/Windsor Fry.

40. CSR Winsor/Windsor Fry.

41. The Slave Enlistment Act of 1778 was passed by the Rhode Island Assembly in February of that year to deal with low Rhode Island troop levels due to death, desertion, and disease. The act promulgated the recruitment and enlistment of slaves and other servants in lieu of their freedom. The act will be discussed in more detail in Chapter 5. Quarles describes the thirty-five soldiers listed on the return as free negroes. Regarding the Native Americans on the list, John Brown of the Narragansett Indian Tribe Historic Preservation Office (NITHPO) states that most soldiers of Indian descent fought *with* the Rhode Island regiments as representatives of a sovereign Narragansett nation, not as members of those regiments. In Brown's argument, those soldiers were motivated to defeat the British, not to support the American cause. The enlistment date of Jacob Ned (who appears on the list) of March 3, 1779, and his appearance with the First Rhode Island, Captain Dexter's Company of April 1779 indicate that the "Return of Freemen" list was possibly created in March 1779, since the enlistment dates of others on the list are prior to that date. RIHS, Military Papers IV; Quarles, *The Negro in the American Revolution,* 81 fn 49; Sidney Kaplan, *The Black Presence in the Era of the American Revolution 1770–1800* (New York: New York Graphic Society, 1973), 36. RIHS, Revolutionary War Military Papers, *Papers of Christopher Green, Rhode Island Military Papers,* "Return of Freemen inlisted during the War in First Rhode Island Battalion, commanded by Col. C. Greene." Joanne Pope Melish, "Recovering (from) Slavery: Four Struggles to Tell the Truth," in *Slavery and Public History: The Tough Stuff of American Memory,* ed. James Oliver Horton and Lois E. Horton (New York: The New Press: 2006, Kindle Edition), 129–130, location 2427; RISA, *Regimental Book Rhode Island Regiment for 1781; Rhode Island Heads of Families–First Census–1790* (Washington, DC: GPO, 1980); *Revolutionary War Pension Records,* National Archives; Bartlett, *Census of the Inhab-*

itants of the Colony of Rhode Island and Providence Plantations 1774, 184–191, 227–231; Souther, 11–14; Mildred Chamberlain, transcriber, *The Rhode Island 1777 Military Census* (Baltimore: Genealogical Publishing Company, 1985), 103, 105, 119; Maureen Taylor, *Runaways, Deserters, and Notorious Villains: From Rhode Island Newspapers, Volume I: The Providence Gazette, 1762–1800* (Rockport: Picton Press, 1994), 60; Jay Mack Holbrook, ed., *Rhode Island 1782 Census* (Oxford: Holbrook Research Institute, 1979), 38, 50.

42. Simon Barton is listed on the RIRWNI as a "slave enlisted into the Continental Battalion in 1778" (see Eric Grundset, ed., *Forgotten Patriots: African American and American Indian Patriots in the Revolutionary War: A Guide to Service, Sources and Studies* (Washington, DC: National Society Daughters of the American Revolution, 2008, 5), however, his name does not appear in other documents indicating slave status. The following records and studies detail the names of soldiers emancipated as a result of the Slave Enlistment Act of 1778: Lorenzo J. Greene, "Some Observations on the Black Regiment of Rhode Island in the American Revolution"; Sidney S. Rider, *An Historical Inquiry Concerning the Attempt to Raise a Regiment of Slaves by Rhode Island During the War of the Revolution* (Providence, 1880); RISA, *General Treasurer's Account, 1761–1781. Alphabet Book No. 6, 196–197* (C#00614); CSR Simon Barton; CSR Joseph Boyer; CSR Peter Dailey/Daily/Dayley; CSR Ceasar Finch; CSR Prince Limas/Limus/Lemus; CSR Toney Phillips; CSR Cuff Roberts; RWPR Winsor/Windsor Fry; RWPR James Greene/Green; RWPR Pharoah Hazzard/Hazard; RWPR John (Gideon) Harry; RWPR Richard Potter; RWPR Cuff Roberts; RWPR Rueben Roberts; RWPR Thomas Smith.

43. RIHS, "Return of Freemen"; RWPR Winsor (Windsor) Fry; RWPR James Greene/Green; RWPR Richard Potter; RWPR Thomas Smith; CSR Edward (Ned) Anthony/Anthoney, Jr.; CSR Simon Barton; CSR Jonathan (John) Charles; CSR Primus/Prince Childs/Chiles; CSR Toby Coys/Coies; CSR William Coopin/Cooping; CSR Peter Dailey/Daily/Dayley; CSR Benjamin Frank/Franck; CSR William Frank/Franck; CSR Asa Gardner/Gardiner; CSR Frances Gould/Gold; CSR Gideon Harry/Harrey; CSR Toney Phillips; CSR Elijah (Elisha) Waggs/Woggs; CSR Solomon Wanton; Ronald Vern Jackson, ed., *Index of Rhode Island Military Census, 1776* (West Jordan: Genealogical Services, 1988), 43.

44. Grundset, 211; Sweet, 199; Vern Jackson, 43; Walker, *So Few the Brave,* 8, 103, 105, 122–124; George F. G. Stanley, *Canada Invaded* (Toronto: A. M. Hakkert, 1973),104; Robert McConnell Hatch, *Thrust for Canada. The American Attempt on Quebec in 1775– 1776* (Boston: Houghton Mifflin, 1979), 64.

45. Amos is listed on the regimental payroll for 1776. Ronald Vern Jackson, editor, *Index Rhode Island Military Census, 1776,* 3; RWPR Richard Potter; Walker, *So Few the Brave,* 111–112.

46. CSR James Daley; CSR Frances Gould/Gold.

47. RISA, *Regimental Book Rhode Island Regiment for 1781*; CSR William Frank/Franck; RISA, Rhode Island Military Papers, "Return of all the noncommissioned officers and privates, inlisted for the War in the 5th Company of the Rhode Island Battalion commanded by Lieut. Col. Commandant Olney."

48. Christian M. McBurney, *Kidnapping the Enemy: The Special Operations to Capture Generals Charles Lee and Richard Prescott* (Yardley, PA: Westholme Publishing, 2013), 296 fn 96; Virgil D. White, ed. *Genealogical Abstracts of Revolutionary War Pension Files, Volume II: F–M* (Waynesboro: National Historical Publishing Company, 1991), 1257; *Historic and Architectural Resources of Tiverton, Rhode Island: A Preliminary Report* (Providence: Rhode Island Historical Preservation Commission [RIHPC]), 1983), 1, 10.

49. RISA, "Military Returns, Volume I," 106; Francis B. Heitman, *Historical Register of Officers of the Continental Army During the War of Revolution* (Washington, DC: Rare Book Shop Publishing Company, 1914), 514; McBurney, *Kidnapping the Enemy*, 110; Sweet, 205; CSR William Frank/Franck; Horton and Horton, *In Hope of Liberty*, 64.

50. CSR Benjamin Frank/Franck; Bartlett, *Census of the Inhabitants of the Colony of Rhode Island and Providence Plantations 1774*, 228.

51. Reiss, 239; Walker, *So Few the Brave*, 20; Souther, 5.

52. Heitman, 581; RISA, "Military Returns, Volume I," 106; Jencks, 340; Stephenson, 27; James Kirby Martin, "A 'Most Undisciplined, Profligate Crew': Protest and Defiance in the Continental Ranks, 1776–1783," *Arms and Independence: The Military Character of the American Revolution*, ed. Ronald Hoffman and Peter J. Albert (Charlottesville: University Press of Virginia, 1984), 125; Astor, 8.

53. Charles Patrick Neimeyer, *America Goes to War: A Social History of the Continental Army* (New York: New York University Press, 1996), 85, 132; James Kirby Martin, "A 'Most Undisciplined, Profligate Crew,'" 124–125; Lanning, *Defenders of Liberty*, 103.

54. Lorenzo J. Greene, *The Negro in Colonial New England*, 304–305.

55. RIBHS, *Creative Survival*, 31–32; Lanning, *Defenders of Liberty*, 45; RWPR William Frank.

56. Bartlett, *Census of the Inhabitants of the Colony of Rhode Island and Providence Plantations 1774*, 38–53; Jay Coughtry, *The Notorious Triangle: Rhode Island and the African Slave Trade 1700–1807* (Philadelphia: Temple University Press, 1981), 6; Lorenzo J. Greene, *The Negro in Colonial New England*, 304–305; Cottrol, 29.

57. RIHS, "2 June 1777, Isaac Paine's bond as surety to the town on Daniel Tefft's servant, Francis, being freed," Mss 214, sg1, series 1, vol. 3, no. 1240, Providence Town Papers, bond.

58. Benjamin Quarles, "The Revolutionary War as a Black Declaration of Independence," in *Slavery and Freedom in the Age of the American Revolution*, Ira Berlin and Ronald Hoffman, eds. (Charlotteville: University Press of Virginia, 1982), 292.

59. Quarles, "The Revolutionary War as a Black Declaration of Independence," 292–293.

60. Peter M. Voelz, *Slave and Soldier: The Military Impact of Blacks in the Colonial Americas* (New York: Garland Publishing, 1993), 392.

61. Joseph Plumb Martin, *Ordinary Courage: The Revolutionary War Adventures of Joseph Plumb Martin*, 2nd edition, ed. James Kirby Martin (St. James: Brandywine Press, 1999), 5.

62. Joseph Plumb Martin, *Ordinary Courage*, 13.

63. Jeremiah Greenman, *Diary of a Common Soldier in the American Revolution, 1775–1783, An Annotated Edition of the Military Journal of Jeremiah Greenman*, ed. Robert Bray and Paul Bushnell (DeKalb: Northern Illinois University Press, 1978), xv.

64. Greenman, 294.

65. Voelz, 7.

66. RWPR Winsor Fry.

67. RWPR William Wanton.

68. Caroline Cox, "'Boy Soldiers of the American Revolution: The Effects of War on Society," In *Children and Youth in a New Nation*, ed. James Marten (New York: New York University Press, 2009), 13–29; John Resch, *Suffering Soldiers: Revolutionary War Veterans, Moral Sentiment, and Political Culture in the Early Republic* (Amherst: University of Massachusetts Press, 1999), 219.

69. Chapin, *Rhode Island in the Colonial Wars*, 68; Lorenzo J. Greene, *The Negro in Colonial America*, 309–310.

70. Mechal Sobel, *Teach Me Dreams: The Search for Self in the Revolutionary Era* (Princeton: Princeton University Press, 2000), 162; James J. Schaefer, "The Whole Duty of Man: Charles Lee and the Politics of Reputation, Masculinity, and Identity during The Revolutionary Era, 1755–1783" (PhD diss., University of Toledo, 2006), 99–100.

71. Maggie Montesinos Sale, *The Slumbering Volcano: American Slave Ship Revolts and the Production of Rebellious Masculinity* (Durham: Duke University Press, 1997), 12, 14–15.

72. Schaefer, 114.

73. Sobel, 160–161.

74. Voelz, 402.

75. Sobel, 135.

76. Stokes, 21–22; Clark-Pujara, 6.

77. James Oliver Horton, "Freedom's Yoke: Gender Conventions among Antebellum Free Blacks," in *African-American Activism Before the Civil War: The Freedom Struggle in the Antebellum North*, ed. Patrick Rael (New York: Routledge, 2008), 174; Sobel, 140–141.

78. G. W. Offley, "A Narrative," in *Five Black Lives*, ed. Arna Bontemps (Middletown, CT: Wesleyan University Press, 1971), 136.

79. Sobel, 140.

80. William Grimes, *Life of William Grimes, The Runaway Slave*, ed. William L. Andrews and Regina E. Mason (New York: Oxford University Press, 2008), 106.

81. John W. Blassingame, editor, *Slave Testimony: Two Centuries of Letters, Speeches, Interviews, and Autobiographies* (Baton Rouge: Louisiana State University Press, 1977), 170; James Oliver Horton and Lois E. Horton, "Violence, Protest, and Identity: Black Manhood in Antebellum America," in *Free People of Color*, ed. James Oliver Horton (Washington, DC: Smithsonian Institution Press, 1993), 82.

82. Wallace, 61–62.

83. Taylor, Maureen Alice, *Runaways, Deserters, and Notorious Villains: From Rhode Island Newspapers, Volume I: The Providence Gazette, 1762–1800*, 28–29.

84. Taylor, *Runaways, Deserters, and Notorious Villains: From Rhode Island Newspapers, Volume I: The Providence Gazette, 1762–1800*, 29.

85. Maureen Alice Taylor and John Wood Sweet, *Runaways, Deserters, And Notorious Villains From Rhode Island Newspapers Volume 2: Additional notices from The Providence Gazette, 1762–1800 as well as advertisements from all other Rhode Island Newspapers from 1732–1800* (Rockport: Picton Press, 2001), 77.

86. Taylor, *Runaways, Deserters, and Notorious Villains: From Rhode Island Newspapers, Volume I: The Providence Gazette, 1762–1800*, 29, 33; Taylor and Sweet, 60.

87. Taylor, *Runaways, Deserters, and Notorious Villains: From Rhode Island Newspapers, Volume I: The Providence Gazette, 1762–1800*, 33.

88. Taylor and Sweet, 83.

89. Wallace, 53–54; Kaplan, 183; Wallace, 54.

90. Wallace, 65.

91. Wallace, 56.

92. Quarles, "The Revolutionary War as a Black Declaration of Independence," 292.

93. RIHS, *Providence Town Papers*, 4:72.

94. Venture Smith, "A Narrative of the Life and Adventures of Venture, A Native of Africa, Related by Himself," in *Making Freedom: The Extraordinary Life of Venture Smith*, ed. Chandler B. Saint and George A. Krimsky (Middletown, CT: Wesleyan University Press, 2009), 29.

95. Venture Smith, 27.

96. Venture Smith, 25.

97. Venture Smith, 32.

98. Venture's son, Cuff, purchased by his father out of slavery for $200, enlisted in the Continental army in 1781. Venture Smith, 98–99.

99. CSR Winsor (Windsor) Fry; CSR Caesar Sabins; CSR Prime Babcock; CSR Plato Vandorum; RISA, *Regimental Book Rhode Island Regiments for 1781.*

100. RISA, *Regimental Book Rhode Island Regiments for 1781.*

101. William Cooper Nell, *Services of Colored Americans in the Wars of 1776 and 1812* (Boston: Prentiss and Sawyer, 1851), 18.

102. John Thornton, *Africa and Africans in the Making of the Atlantic World, 1400–1680,* 280, 293; Voelz, 399.

103. RWPR Andrew Frank; White, *Genealogical Abstracts of Revolutionary War Pension Files, Volume II: F–M,* 1257; *Heads of Families–First Census–1790 Rhode Island* (Washington, DC: Government Printing Office, 1908), 32.

CHAPTER FOUR: BROTHERS AT WAR

1. Greenman, 73–78.

2. Israel Angell, *Diary of Colonel Israel Angell, Commanding the Second Rhode Island Continental during the American Revolution 1778–1781.* Transcribed from the Original Manuscript Together with a Biographical Sketch of the Author and Illustrative Notes by Edward Field, A.B. Historian of the Rhode Island Society of the Sons of the American Revolution (Providence: Preston & Rounds Company, 1899, Reprinted Arno Press, 1971), xii. Uniforms and equipment issued upon enlistment became ragged after continual and consistent use. Angell's "lousy" remark did not mean bad or terrible. It referred to the problem of lice within his ranks. The lack of proper cleaning of uniforms often resulted in lice-ridden clothing. The term "naked" meant the lack of proper clothing and footwear for his subordinates. Ray Raphael, *A People's History of the American Revolution: How Common People Shaped the Fight for Independence* (New York: Perennial, 2002, originally published: New York: The New Press, 2001), 111–112.

3. Sweet, 217; James Kirby Martin and Mark Edward Lender, A *Respectable Army: The Military Origins of the Republic, 1763–1789* (Wheeling: Harlan Davidson, 1982), 90–91, 95.

4. Louise Lewis Lovell, *Israel Angell, 1740–1832: Colonel of the 2nd Rhode Island Regiment* (Providence: Knickerbocker Press, 1921), 19; Walker, *So Few the Brave,* 34–36, 128–143.

5. *Regimental Book Rhode Island Regiments for 1781;* Walker, *So Few the Brave,* 5.

6. National Archives, Revolutionary War Rolls, 1775–1783, "A Muster Roll of Capt. Thos. Hughes in the Second Battalion for the State of Rhode Island Commanded by Col. Israel Angell in the Service of the United States for the Month of Dec 1777"; National Archives, Revolutionary War Rolls, 1775–1783, "Muster Roll of Capt. William Potter's Company in the Second Battalion from the State of Rhode Island Commanded by Col. Israel Angell in the Service of the United States for the Month of January 1778"; CSR Benjamin Frank/Franck; CSR William Frank/Franck; RIHS, "Return of Freemen"; RISA, *Regimental Book Rhode Island Regiment for 1781.*

7. Hughes married Welthian Greene, the daughter of Colonel Christopher Greene, during the war on February 27, 1782. Thomas Hamilton Murray, *Irish Rhode Islanders in the American Revolution* (Providence: American-Irish Historical Society, 1903), 22–23; Charles A. Battle, *Negroes on the Island of Rhode Island* (Newport: Newport's Black Museum, 1932), 3;

Bartlett, *Census of the Inhabitants of the Colony of Rhode Island and Providence Plantations, 1774,* 1–37; Elaine Forman Crane, *A Dependent People: Newport, Rhode Island in the Revolutionary Era* (New York: Fordham University Press, 1985), 5, 57, 76, 82; Carp, 99; RWPR Thomas Hughes; Bamberg, *Elder John Gorton and the Six Principle Baptist Church of East Greenwich, Rhode Island,* 289; Walker, *So Few the Brave,* 103, 115–117, 136–138, 158; Heitman, 307.

8. Narragansett Leader John Brown of the Narragansett Indian Tribe Historic Preservation Office (NITHPO) has acknowledged that some men of Native American descent who fought in the First Rhode Island were formerly enslaved and some may have been of African as well as Native American descent. Joanne Pope Melish, "Recovering (from) Slavery: Four Struggles to Tell the Truth," 129–130; Clark-Pujara, 34; CSR Jonathan (John) Charles; CSR William Coopin/Coopen/Cooping; CSR Gideon Harry/Harrey; CSR Toby/Tobey Coys/Coies; CSR Joseph Nocake/Nocage; RISA, *"Regimental Book Rhode Island Regiment for 1781";* "Rhode Island Soldiers – Men of Color," DAR Library, "Forgotten Patriots" File Collection; Grundset, 210, 211, 217, 223; Souther, 12; Boyle, 119, 131–132; Taylor, 60; Jay Mack Holbrook, *The 1782 Rhode Island Census,* 38; Charles Richard Smith, *Marines in the Revolution: A History of the Continental Marines in the American Revolution, 1775–1783* (Washington, D.C.: History and Museum Division, Headquarters, U.S. Marine Corps, 1975), 74, 411; Chamberlain, 13.

9. RIHS, "Return of Freemen"; CSR Edward (Ned) Anthony/Anthoney; CSR Fortune Sailes/Sayles; CSR Cuff Peckham; CSR Richard Pomp; Souther, 11; Boyle, 154; Grundset, 224, 225, 230; Chamberlain, 105; Boyle, 147, 149–150, 154.

10. There are two William Potter households listed in the 1774 Rhode Island Census, both located in South Kingstown. One household included eleven Blacks, an indication that head of household William Potter was a slaveholder. However, Captain William Potter did not own slaves. Bartlett, *Census of the Inhabitants of the Colony of Rhode Island and Providence Plantations 1774,* 90; CSR William Potter; RWPR William Potter; Walker, *So Few the Brave,* 101, 117, 138.

11. The 1774 Rhode Island Census lists one Black residing in the Providence household of Daniel Tefft. In June 1777, Isaac Paine posts surety bond on the occasion of Daniel Tefft's servant, Francis, being freed. Boyle, 120; Grundset, 211, 212, 218, 231; Boyle, 118, 120, 133, 156; CSR Francis Tift/Tifft/Tefft; RIHS, MSS 214 sg1, Providence Town Papers, Bond, 2 June 1777; Bartlett, *Census of the Inhabitants of the Colony of Rhode Island and Providence Plantations 1774,* 51; CSR John Daniels; CSR Ceasor (Caesar) Cook/Cooke; CSR Henry Hazzard/Hazard; CSR Noah Sisco/Sischo/Sisko/Siskoe.

12. Lanning, *Defenders of Liberty,* 109–110; Paul Barnett, "The Black Continentals," *Negro History Bulletin,* 33 (1970), 6.

13. Lanning, *Defenders of Liberty,* 107–109.

14. Lanning, *Defenders of Liberty,* 105–106.

15. Ibid., Lanning, *Defenders of Liberty,* 104.

16. Lanning, *Defenders of Liberty,* 104–105.

17. After the start of war, Army officials added four ounces of rum or whiskey, known as a "gill," to the daily ration list. Shoat is a term used to define a young pig. Nancy Fisher Chudacoff, "The Revolution and the Town of Providence, 1775–1783," *Rhode Island History* 35, no. 3, 1976, 76; Lanning, *Defenders of Liberty,* 104–105; Brace, 161.

18. Lanning, *Defenders of Liberty,* 106.

19. Lanning, *Defenders of Liberty,* 102.

20. Angell, 106.
21. Walker, *So Few the Brave*, 70.
22. Most historians of the Revolutionary War cite the constant problem within the Continental army regarding provisioning of Continental regulars. See Ray Raphael, *A People's History of the American Revolution: How Common People Shaped the Fight for Independence* (New York: Harper Perennial, 2002, originally published: New York: The New Press, 2001), 108–116; Charles Royster, *A Revolutionary People at War: The Continental Army and American Character, 1775–1783* (Chapel Hill: University of North Carolina Press, 179), 73.
23. Quoted in Astor, 13.
24. Martin and Lender, 90–91.
25. Quoted in Douglas R. Egerton, *Death Or Liberty*, 77, 114; Astor, 13.
26. Lanning, *Defenders of Liberty*, 97, fn 1; Joseph Plumb Martin, *Ordinary Courage*, 141, 76–77.
27. Lanning, *Defenders of Liberty*, 109; Voelz, 416.
28. Greenman, 73.
29. Quoted in Lanning, *Defenders of Liberty*, 115.
30. Lanning, *Defenders of Liberty*, 115.
31. Chudacoff, 76; Bonnie S. Ledbetter, "Sports and Games of the American Revolution," *Journal of Sport History* 6, no. 3 (Winter 1979), 35.
32. Lovell, 241; Chudacoff, 76.
33. Lovell, 241.
34. James R. Byrd, *Sacred Scripture, Sacred War: The Bible and the American Revolution* (New York: Oxford University Press, 2013), 7, 166; Lovell, 231; Jack Darrell Crowder, *Chaplains of the Revolutionary War: Black Robed American Warriors* (Jefferson: McFarland & Company, 2017), 5; John W. Brinsfield, "Military Chaplains: A Historian's View from the American Revolution to Iraq," *Christian Science Monitor*, https://www.csmonitor.com/2007/1030/p25s02-usmi.html; General Orders, February 15, 1783; "Founders Online, National Archives, https://founders.archives.gov/documents/Washington/99-01-02-10643.
35. Ebenezer David, *A Rhode Island Chaplain in the Revolution: Letters of Ebenezer David to Nicholas Brown 1775–1778*, ed. Jeannette D. Black and William Greene Roelker (Providence: Rhode Island Society of the Cincinnati, 1949), 37–38; Stephenson, 83–84.
36. Lovell, 240.
37. Angell, xii.
38. James Kirby Martin, "A 'Most Undisciplined, Profligate Crew': Protest and Defiance in the Continental Ranks, 1776–1783," 126.
39. Chudacoff, 76; Angell, 68.
40. Lovell, 226.
41. Lanning, *Defenders of Liberty*, 114; Angell, 28; Greenman, 73, 78 fn 64.
42. Lovell, 230, 236.
43. Lovell, 244.
44. Lovell, 241.
45. Lanning, *Defenders of Liberty*, 114.
46. John Smith, "Thro Mud and Mire Into the Woods, The 1777 Continental Diary of Sergeant John Smith."
47. John Smith, "Thro Mud and Mire Into the Woods, The 1777 Continental Diary of Sergeant John Smith."
48. Lovell, 231.
49. James Kirby Martin, "A 'Most Undisciplined, Profligate Crew': Protest and Defiance in

the Continental Ranks, 1776–1783," 128.

50. Angell, xii.

51. James Kirby Martin, "A 'Most Undisciplined, Profligate Crew': Protest and Defiance in the Continental Ranks, 1776–1783," 130–131.

52. The incomplete muster and pay rolls are silent about the assignment of the Frank brothers during the month of October 1777. However, after their action at the Battle of Red Bank both Rhode Island regiments were ordered to winter quarters at Valley Forge and made immediate march to that location. Both brothers are listed on the Valley Forge muster rolls with the combined Rhode Island forces. This evidence indicates that both brothers served in their respective regiments during the battle. *Chevaux de fries* are fortifications of sharp stones standing on edge. During the Revolutionary War, they were used as obstacles for the British naval fleet. The typical marine *chevaux de fries* used in the Delaware River was, according to Jeanne Willoz-Egnor, curator of the National Maritime Museum, "a thirty-foot square open-top box constructed of huge logs and lined with two-inch thick pine planks and included two or three 17 to 20-inch diameter poles tipped with large iron spikes were placed diagonally in the box." CSR William Frank/Franck; CSR Benjamin Frank/Franck; Henry B. Carrington, *Battles of the American Revolution 1775–1781. Historical and Military Criticism, with Topographical Illustration* (New York: A. S. Barnes and Company, 1877), 393; Lesser, 54–55; "Frames of Destruction," Mariner's Museum and Park (accessed April 25, 2023), https://www.marinersmuseum.org/2021/10/frames-of-destruction/.

53. Greenman, 79; Walker, *So Few the Brave*, 39; Thomas J. McGuire, *The Philadelphia Campaign Volume II: Germantown and the Roads to Valley Forge* (Mechanicsburg, PA: Stackpole Books, 2007, Kindle edition), 138.

54. John Smith, "Thro Mud and Mire Into the Woods, The 1777 Continental Diary of Sergeant John Smith."

55. Carrington, 394–395; Smith, "Thro the Muck and Mire Into the Wood, The 1777 Continental Diary of Sergeant John Smith."

56. Carrington, 394–395; David, 52–53.

57. It is unknown whether the Frank brothers were part of that detachment. McGuire, 159; Greenman, 80.

58. John Smith, "Thro Mud and Mire Into the Woods, The 1777 Continental Diary of Sergeant John Smith."

59. John Smith, "Thro Mud and Mire into the Woods, The 1777 Continental Diary of Sergeant John Smith." Affiliated forces refer to the "boat crew" which was more than likely affiliated with locals and not the Rhode Island regiments.

60. McGuire, 159.

61. Greenman, 82.

62. Greenman, 82. Abbatis were a type of fortification built using trees cut to point in the direction of the enemy, with the tips of the trees sharpened into spikes.

63. Carrington, 394–395; Walker, *So Few the Brave*, 40, 44.

64. Carrington, 395; Walker, *So Few the Brave*, 43–44.

65. Philander D. Chase and Edward G. Lengel, eds., *The Papers of George Washington, Revolutionary War Series, vol. 11, 19 August 1777–25 October 1777* (Charlottesville: University Press of Virginia, 2001), 590–592.

66. RIHS, *Colonel Greene's Book of Returns (1777 July 24–July 29 1780)* "Clothing Inventories of Soldiers Killed in the Action at Fort Mercer October 22, 1777 Belonging to Captain

Thomas Arnold's Company in Colonel Christopher Greene's Regiment," MSS673 SG2 Box 1, Folder 3.

67. Greenman, 65.

68. Voelz, 402.

CHAPTER FIVE: INTEGRATING FREE AND ENSLAVED

1. Greenman, 88; Lovell, 118–119.

2. "From George Washington to Major General Israel Putnam, 6 February 1778," Founders Online, National Archives, https://founders.archives.gov/documents/Washington/03-13-02-0382. [Original source: *The Papers of George Washington, Revolutionary War Series, vol. 13, 26 December 1777–28 February 1778*, ed. Edward G. Lengel. Charlottesville: University Press of Virginia, 2003, 464.]

3. Albigence Waldo, *Valley Forge, 1777–1778. Diary of Surgeon Albigence Waldo, of the Connecticut Line* (Philadelphia: Pennsylvania Magazine of History and Biography, 1897), 13.

4. "From George Washington to William Buchanan, 7 February 1778," Founders Online, National Archives, https://founders.archives.gov/documents/Washington/03-13-02-0385. [Original source: *The Papers of George Washington, Revolutionary War Series, vol. 13, 26 December 1777–28 February 1778*, ed. Edward G. Lengel. Charlottesville: University Press of Virginia, 2003, 465–466.]

5. "Letters of William Barton," http://www.americanrevolution.org/vlyfrgeltrs.htm.

6. Boyle, *"Death Seem'd to Stare": The New Hampshire and Rhode Island Regiments at Valley Forge* (Baltimore: Clearfield, 2005), xi.

7. Greenman, 88.

8. Greenman, 88.

9. George Weedon, *Valley Forge Orderly Book of General George Weedon of the Continental Army under Command of General George Washington in the Campaign of 1777–8* (New York: Dodd, Mead, 1902), 172.

10. Catherine M. A. Cottreau-Robins, "Domestic Architecture of the Black Loyalists in Nova Scotia, 1783–1800" (M.A. thesis, Dalhousie University, 2002), 66, 72.

11. Boyle, *"Death Seem'd to Stare,"* xiii; CSR Benjamin Frank/Franck; CSR William Frank/Franck.

12. Weedon, 169.

13. Weedon, 169.

14. Quoted in Douglas Southall Freeman, *George Washington, Volume IV: Leader of the Revolution* (New York: Scribner, 1951), 576.

15. Michael C. Harris and Gary Ecelbarger, "A Reconsideration of Continental Army Numerical Strength at Valley Forge," *Journal of the American Revolution* (May 18, 2021) (accessed January 18, 2022, at allthingsliberty.com); CSR William Frank/Franck; "Valley Forge Muster Rolls," Valley Forge National Historical Park (accessed 7 February 2008), http://valleyforgemusterroll.org; Lorenzo J. Greene, "Some Observations on the Black Regiment of Rhode Island in the American Revolution," *Journal of Negro History* 37, no. 2 (April 1952), 145; Royster, 109; Raphael, 128.

16. Library of Congress, *George Washington Papers*, "George Washington to Continental Congress, December 23, 1777."

17. Lorenzo J. Greene, "Some Observations on the Black Regiment of Rhode Island in the American Revolution," 145.

18. Lovell, 125–126.

19. RISA, "General Varnum to Nicholas Cooke, 7 March 1778," *Letters*, vol. 12, page 31.

20. "Israel Angell to Unidentified, not dated," in Joseph Lee Boyle, *Writings from the Valley Forge Encampment of the Continental Army December 19, 1777–June 19, 1778*, 46–47 (Bowie, MD: Heritage Books, 2003), 45–46; CSR Henry (Henery) Pisquish; CSR Quam (Quom) Cook; CSR Jack Allen/Allin; CSR William Archer; CSR Peter Bristol; CSR James Edwards; CSR Prince Jackson; CSR Abraham Nocake; CSR Richard Pomp; CSR Francis Tifft/Tift/Tefft.

21. At the time of their desertion, both served in Colonel Richmond's Rhode Island State Regiment. Their desertion was carried in the *Providence Gazette*, dated 26 April 1777— "Deserted the 26th of February . . . two Indians, viz. John Daniels, about 20 years of age, 5'7", long hair, belongs to Charlestown. Toby Coys, about 17 years of Age, 5'6", belongs to Charlestown." Both were retaken or returned to duty. Later, Coys is listed as a private, dead on 14 January 1782, on the casualty register. The cause of his death is unknown. It is curious to note that Coys is also listed as being discharged on 1 July 1780 in his Compiled Service Record. Whether this is an indication that he reenlisted after his 1780 discharge or not is unclear. He must have reenlisted, and this stint of service resulted in his death. CSR Toby Coys/Coies; CSR John Daniels; Taylor, 60; Boyle, *"Death Seem'd to Stare,"* 119; RISA, Military Papers, "Register of all casualties that have happened . . . since 1/1/1781."

22. Lorenzo J. Greene, "Some Observations on the Black Regiment of Rhode Island in the American Revolution," 145; Bartlett, *Records of the State of Rhode Island and Providence Plantations in New England, Volume VIII, 1776–1779* (Providence: Cooke Jackson & Company, Printers to the State, 1863), 641.

23. Bartlett, *Records of the State of Rhode Island and Providence Plantations in New England, Volume VIII*, 641.

24. RISA, Digital Archives, Black Rhode Islanders Collection 1652–1885, "February 1778 Slaves Enlisting in the Army," http://sos.ri.gov/archon/?p=digitallibrary/digitalcontent&id=448.

25. RISA, "February 1778 Slaves Enlisting in the Army."

26. Lorenzo J. Greene, "Some Observations on the Black Regiment of Rhode Island in the American Revolution," 142, 152; RISA, "February 1778 Slaves Enlisting in the Army"; Lanning, *Defenders of Liberty*, Appendix H.

27. A colonial census shows a Black population in North Kingstown as 184 and in South Kingstown as 380. The Black population in Providence totaled 225. Evarts B. Greene and Virginia D. Harrington, *American Population Before the Federal Census of 1790* (New York: Columbia University, 1932), 66; Lorenzo J. Greene, *The Negro in Colonial New England*, 344; Jones, 157; Lorenzo J. Greene, "Some Observations on the Black Regiment of Rhode Island in the American Revolution," 157–159.

28. Sweet, 207.

29. It is difficult to ascertain the actual number of slaves recruited during the period of authorization. Lorenzo Greene places the number at approximately 110, based upon the state treasurer's records detailing payments to slaveowners. Michael Lanning reports eighty-eight enslaved men joining the regiment from February 14, 1778, to June 10, 1778. Lorenzo J. Greene, "Some Observations on the Black Regiment of Rhode Island in the American Revolution," 157–158; Lanning, *Defenders of Liberty*, 75–76; Stephenson, 186; Horton and Horton, *In Hope Of Liberty*, 68; "A List of Negro Slaves Inlisted into the Continental Battalions and to Whom They Belonged, 1778," *Rhode Island Roots* 6, no. 3 (1980), 56.

30. RISA, "Camp Verplank's Point 23 Sept 1782 At a board of officers convened . . . Rhode Island Regiment to inspect the Company returns of Said regiment to determine . . . are entitled to Honorary Badges agreeable to General Orders"; RISA, *Regimental Book Rhode Island Regiment for 1781*; "Register of Non-Commissioned Officers and Privates in the 5th Company Rhode Island Battalion, inlisted for the War, and furloughed on the General Order of the 22nd of June 1783," RISA; RWPR Cato Greene; Neagles, 157; RISA, "Return of all non-commissioned officers and privates inlisted for the War in the 5th Company of the Rhode Island Battalion, Commanded by Lt. Col. Jeremiah Olney"; RISA, "Return of Non-commissioned Officers and Privates inlisted for War in the 6th Company of the Rhode Island Battalion, Commanded by Lt. Col. Jeremiah Olney"; Stephenson, 186; Horton and Horton, *In Hope Of Liberty*, 68; "A List of Negro Slaves Inlisted into the Continental Battalions and to Whom They Belonged, 1778," *Rhode Island Roots* 6, no. 3 (1980), 56.

31. Brace, 159.

32. Brace, 71.

33. Lanning, *Defenders of Liberty*, Appendix H, 205; Lorenzo J. Greene, "Some Observations on the Black Regiment of Rhode Island in the American Revolution," 143, 157–159, 162; Reiss, 241–242; Kai Wright, *Soldiers of Freedom: An Illustrated History of African Americans in the Armed Forces* (New York: Black Dog and Leventhal Publishers, 2002), 27; Walker, *So Few the Brave*, 51.

34. CSR Ebenezer Caesar; CSR Ceasor Cole; CSR Ceasar Cook; CSR Richard Pomp; CSR Ceaser Sabins; CSR Pomp Watson.

35. Freeman Toney Phillips enlisted on May 20, 1778, but the location of his enlistment is unknown. Lorenzo J. Greene, "Some Observations on the Black Regiment of Rhode Island in the American Revolution," 165 fn 86; RIHS, "Return of Freemen; CSR Simon Barton; CSR Peter Dailey/Daily/Dayley; CSR Ceasar Finch; CSR Prince Limas/Limus/Lemus; CSR Cuff Roberts; CSR Joseph Boyer/Bouyer.

36. Judith Van Buskirk argues that Rhode Island freed its slaves and made a "distinguishable black regiment of them." Joseph Boyle concludes that the massive reassignment of white and Black soldiers indicated a reorganization based on race. Robert K. Wright, Jr., *The Continental Army* (Washington, DC: Center of Military History, United States Army, 1983), 149; Van Buskirk, 108; Boyle, *"Death Seem'd to Stare,"* vi.

37. RISA, Digital Archives, African American Collection, "February 1778 Slaves Enlisting in the Army," http://sos.ri.gov/archon/?p=digitallibrary/digitalcontent&id=448.

38. Bartlett, *Records of the State of Rhode Island and Providence Plantations in New England, Volume VIII*, 641.

39. In explaining another realignment of the Rhode Island troops in 1781, military historian Robert K. Wright, Jr., describes the realignment during the Valley Forge winter as an "experiment in segregation." Wright, Jr., *The Continental Army*, 162.

40. Boyle, *"Death Seem'd to Stare,"* 104–171; Van Buskirk, 112; Lanning, *Defenders of Liberty*, 97, fn1, 100; Caroline Cox, *A Proper Sense of Honor: Service and Sacrifice in George Washington's Army* (Chapel Hill: University of North Carolina Press, 2004), 17; RWPR William Champlin; Wright, Jr. *The Continental Army*, 162; Daniel Popek, *They "...fought bravely, but were unfortunate": The True Story of Rhode Island's "Black Regiment" and the Failure of Segregation in Rhode Island's Continental Line, 1777–1783* (Bloomington: AuthorHouse, 2015, Kindle edition), location 2874.

41. National Archives, Revolutionary War Rolls, 1775–1783, "A Muster Roll of Capt. Thos. Hughes in the Second Battalion for the State of Rhode Island Commanded by Col. Israel

Angell in the Service of the United States for the Month of Dec 1777"; National Archives, Revolutionary War Rolls, 1775–1783, "Muster Roll of Capt. William Potter's Company in the Second Battalion from the State of Rhode Island Commanded by Col. Israel Angell in the Service of the United States for the Month of January 1778"; CSR Benjamin Frank/Franck; CSR William Frank/Franck; RIHS, "Return of Freemen"; RISA, *Regimental Book Rhode Island Regiment for 1781.*

42. Prince Jackson's service with the Continentals did not last much past his detail at Radnor. He is listed on the muster roll of Arnold's detachment in May 1778. However, he died on June 11, 1778, at the Yellow Springs Army Hospital at present-day Chester Springs, PA, approximately ten miles from the encampment. National Archives, "Muster Roll of Detachment from the 1st Rhode Island Battalion Commanded by Col. Christ. Greene in the Service of the United States for the Month of June, 1778; Francis James Dallett, with revisions by Phil Graham in 2014, *The War of the Revolution in Radnor (1777–1778)* (Radnor: Radnor Historical Society, 2014), 5, 24.

43. Heitman, 76; Walker, *So Few the Brave,* 124.

44. Van Buskirk, 111–112; John U. Rees, *"They Were Good Soldiers": African-Americans Serving in the Continental Army, 1775–1783* (Warwick, UK: Helion, 2019), 73; Walker, *So Few the Brave,* 46.

45. Stephenson, 282–285; Walker, *So Few the Brave,* 47; Rees, 73–74; James J. Schaefer, "The Whole Duty of Man: Charles Lee and the Politics of Reputation, Masculinity, and Identity during the Revolutionary Era, 1755–1783" (PhD Diss., University of Toledo, 2006), 181, 189; Dominick Mazzagetti, *Charles Lee: Self Before Country* (New Brunswick: Rutgers University Press, 2013), 156.

46. Christopher Booker, *"I Will Wear No Chain!": A Social History of African American Males* (Westport: Praeger, 2000), 43–44.

47. Battalions were generally composed of four companies with 35 men each. The 150-member First Rhode Island fits this configuration. CSR Benjamin Frank/Franck; CSR William Frank/Franck; Kaplan, 55; RIHS, "Return of Freemen"; Lorenzo J. Greene, "Some Observations on the Black Regiment of Rhode Island in the American Revolution," 164; Boyle, *"Death Seem'd to Stare,"* 104–171; Voelz, 401; Sobel, 140–141; John U. Rees, "Put up for winter quarters at Valley Forge," African American Soldiers at the 1777–1778 Overwintering Camp, Presentation given at "African Americans During the American Revolution: African American military and civilian participation in the Philadelphia Campaign and the Valley Forge Encampment in the winter of 1777–1778" (April 10, 2021), Spring Research Symposium organized by National Park Service—Valley Forge National Park and Association for the Study of African American Life and History, 26–27.

48. David O. White, *Connecticut's Black Soldiers 1775–1783* (Chester, CT: Pequot Press, 1973), 32; Lanning, *Defenders of Liberty,* 83; Horton and Horton, *In Hope of Liberty,* 69; Knoblock, *Strong and Brave Fellows: New Hampshire's Black Soldiers and Sailors of the American Revolution, 1775–1784* (Jefferson, NC: McFarland, 2003), 5.

49. White, *Connecticut's Black Soldiers,* 31–32; Lanning, *Defenders of Liberty,* 81–82; Nell, 11.

50. Lanning, *Defenders of Liberty,* 76–78; Van Buskirk, 113–115.

51. Greenman, 103; Lanning, *Defenders of Liberty,* 76–78; Van Buskirk, 113–115.

52. Walker, *So Few the Brave,* 52–53; McBurney, *The Rhode Island Campaign: The First French and American Operation in the Revolutionary War* (Yardley, PA: Westholme, 2011), 107; Appendix E, 240–243.

53. Quoted in George Washington Greene, *The Life of Nathanael Greene, Major-general in the Army of the Revolution · Volume 2* (New York: Hurd and Houghton, 1871), 99–100.

54. McBurney, *The Rhode Island Campaign*, 112–114.

55. For a more extensive study of the storm and siege of Newport, see *The Rhode Island Campaign* by Christian M. McBurney. CSR William Frank/Franck; CSR Benjamin Frank/Franck; Walker, *So Few The Brave*, 53–55; Robert A. Geake with Loren Spears, *From Slaves To Soldiers: The 1st Rhode Island Regiment in the American Revolution* (Yardley, PA: Westholme, 2016), 53–57; McBurney, *The Rhode Island Campaign*, 124–127.

56. Greenman, 127.

57. Angell, 8–9; Lanning, *Defenders of Liberty*, 76; Barnett, 7; Geake, 53–57; McBurney, *The Rhode Island Campaign*, 171, 187–191.

58. Angell, 9.

59. Quoted in Walker, *So Few the Brave*, 63; Lanning, *Defenders of Liberty*, 76–78; McBurney, *The Rhode Island Campaign*, 187–191.

60. Lanning, *Defenders of Liberty*, 76–78; Barnett, 7; McBurney, *The Rhode Island Campaign*, 190–191.

61. Benjamin Quarles, *The Negro in the American Revolution*, 81.

62. Ward, John. "A Memoir of Lieut.-Col. Samuel Ward, First Rhode Island Regiment, Army of the American Revolution; with a Genealogy of the Ward Family" (New York: Privately printed, 1875); Reprinted from *New York Genealogical and Biographical Record*, 6 (July 1875), 121.

63. Lanning, *Defenders of Liberty*, 76–78.

64. Walker, *So Few the Brave*, 58–65; Lanning, *Defenders of Liberty*, 76–77; Benjamin Quarles, *The Negro in the American Revolution*, 81; Paul Dearden, *The Rhode Island Campaign of 1778: Inauspicious Dawn of Alliance* (Providence: Rhode Island Publication Society, 1980), viii–ix; CSR Benjamin Frank/Franck; CSR William Frank/Franck; Van Buskirk, 115.

65. Quoted from McBurney, *The Rhode Island Campaign*, 199.

66. Walter K. Schroeder, *The Hessian Occupation of Newport and Rhode Island, 1776–1779* (Westminister: Heritage Books, 2005), 172.

67. Quoted in Nell, 128–129.

68. Nell, 128–129.

69. Angell, 10–11.

70. RISA, "Military Returns, IV," 9; McBurney, *The Rhode Island Campaign*, 199, 372 fn 17; CSR Benjamin Frank/Franck; CSR Jonathan (John) Charles; CSR James Daley; CSR Peter Dailey/Daily/Dayley.

71. John Ward, "A Memoir of Lieut.-Col. Samuel Ward, First Rhode Island Regiment, Army of the American Revolution; with a Genealogy of the Ward Family," 121.

72. Sweet, 218–219.

73. Peter M. Voelz, *Slave and Soldier: The Military Impact of Blacks in the Colonial Americas* (New York: Garland, 1993), 401; Sobel, 140–141.

74. James Kirby Martin, "A 'Most Undisciplined, Profligate Crew': Protest and Defiance in the Continental Ranks, 1776–1783," 127–128.

75. Cowell, 175.

76. Lanning, *Defenders of Liberty*, 113; Walker, *So Few the Brave*, 67–68.

77. CSR William Frank/Franck; CSR Benjamin Frank/Franck; Lorenzo J. Greene, "Some Observations on the Black Regiment of Rhode Island in the American Revolution," 166.

CHAPTER SIX: THE POOR SOLDIER'S MARRIAGE . . . .

1. Ben Frank is listed in the marriage record as a negro soldier. A second Frank, Hannah Frank, probable sister of Ben, was also married by the Elder Gorton in January 1779. *Rhode Island Marriages, 1724–1916*, Database, FamilySearch; Bamberg, *Elder John Gorton and the Six Principle Baptist Church of East Greenwich, Rhode Island*, 270.

2. Sarah's surname is spelled Willbour in the marriage record. However, the name has also been captured in the records as Wilbour, Wilbur, and Wilbor. *Rhode Island Marriages, 1724– 1916*; Bamberg, *Elder John Gorton and the Six Principle Baptist Church of East Greenwich, Rhode Island*, 270.

3. Lisa Wilson, 7; Harry M. Ward, *The War for Independence and the Transformation of American Society* (London: UCL Press, 1999), 172; Resch, 228.

4. Prince Brown, David Greene, Prince Limas, Pero Morey, possibly Abraham Pearce, and Solomon Wanton were also married by Gorton. Only Wanton and Frank were actually married during the war and both men are listed as "negro" soldiers. The marriage record of Prince Brown in 1781 describes the former soldier as a "negro of Coventry." It does not provide a racial designation for his bride. The details of Prince Limas' marriage in 1783 include the racial designation for both bride and groom. Prince is listed as a "Negro Man" and his bride, Mercy Austin, "an Indian Woman." In the same year, Pero Morey and Marget Spencer are "Blacks Both of East greenwich." The 1790 marriage of David Green and Countes Reynolds details their status as "Blacks people." There is no mention of parental information in any of these records. Bamberg, *Elder John Gorton and the Six Principle Baptist Church of East Greenwich, Rhode Island*, 1, 29, 269, 270, 286, 303–304, 360, 364.

5. "An Act to Prevent Clandestine Marriages," *The Public Laws of the State of Rhode Island and Providence Plantation, As Revised by a Committee and Finally Enacted by the Honourable General Assembly, at their Session in January, 1798. To Which are Prefixed, the Charter, Declaration of Independence, Articles of Confederation, Constitution of the United States and President Washington's Address of September 1796* (Providence: Carter and Wilkinson, 1798), 483.

6. Providence Town Council records lists Sarah Willbour/Frank's hometown as Middleborough, Massachusetts. RISA, "Providence Town Council Records," 5:155; *Rhode Island Marriages, 1724–1916*; Bamberg, *Elder John Gorton and the Six Principle Baptist Church of East Greenwich, Rhode Island*, 270; 1774 Rhode Island Colonial Census; *Vital Records of Sandwich Massachusetts*, "Death Notices–1809," 1442, www.americanancestors.org (accessed October 9, 2010).

7. Rhode Island Historical Society, "A List of Negro Slaves Inlisted into the Continental Battalions and to Whom They Belonged, 1778," *Rhode Island Roots* 6, no. 3 (1980), 56; "Some Observations of the Black Regiment of Rhode Island in the American Revolution," 157.

8. Joan R. Gundersen, *To Be Useful to the World: Women in Revolutionary America, 1740– 1790* (Chapel Hill: University of North Carolina Press, 2006), 71, 80, 152; Adams and Pleck, 11.

9. Sarah was forced to seek financial assistance from Providence Town officials during the war. Adams and Pleck, 19–20.

10. Gundersen, 43.

11. Gundersen, 80.

12. Gundersen, 80; Adams and Pleck, 20.

13. Providence Town Council Records, 5:155; Adams and Fleck, 13; *Rhode Island Marriages, 1724–1916*.

14. See Chapter 2. Rufus Frank mustered out of Providence, Rhode Island, during the French and Indian War. "Johnston, Rhode Island," www.rihs.org/mssinv/Mss202.htm; Cottrol, 19.

15. Arnold, *Vital Records of Rhode Island, 1636–1850 1st Series, Births, Marriages and Death, Volume 4, Tiverton, Part VII.*, 54; Bartlett, *Census of the Inhabitants of the Colony of Rhode Island and Providence Plantations 1774*, 191; Daniel R. Mandell, "Shifting Boundaries of Race and Ethnicity: Indian-Black Intermarriage in Southern New England, 1760–1880," *Journal of American History*, 85, no. 2 (Sept. 1998), 467, 469; *Rhode Island Marriages, 1724–1916*; Bamberg, *Elder John Gorton and the Six Principle Baptist Church of East Greenwich, Rhode Island*, 269; RWPR William Wanton; 1790 United States Census, Rhode Island, Newport County, Tiverton.

16. Ruth Wallis Herndon and Ella Wilcox Sekatau, "The Right to a Name: The Narragansett People and Rhode Island Officials in the Revolutionary Era," *Ethnohistory* 44, no. 3 (Summer 1997), 437; Mandell, "Shifting Boundaries of Race and Ethnicity," 467, 469; Pope Melish, "Recovering (from) Slavery," 126.

17. Gundersen, 45.

18. Carol Berkin, *Revolutionary Mothers: Women in the Struggle For America's Independence* (New York: Alfred A. Knopf, 2005), 52; Holly A. Mayer, *Belonging to the Army: Camp Followers and Community during the American Revolution* (Columbia: University of South Carolina Press, 1996), 69; Gundersen, 198.

19. Mayer, 122, 140; Gundersen, 194–196; Berkin, 57–58.

20. Quoted in Ward, 118.

21. Lovell, 260.

22. A 1708 Proclamation by Parliament set the value of the silver coin at 0.4.6 (54d) sterling. This value remained constant throughout the Revolutionary War and was known as "Lawful Money." Michael Barbieri, "The Dollar in Revolutionary America," *Journal of the American Revolution*, September 2016 (accessed December 21, 2020), https://allthingsliberty.com/2016/09/dollar-revolutionary-america/; Lovell, 260.

23. Ward, 118; Mayer, 122, 140; Gundersen, 197–198; Sweet, 220.

24. Mayer, 122; Ward, 118.

25. Ward, 119.

26. Angell, 99.

27. CSR Briton Saltonstall; Boyle, 154; Linda L. Mathew, *Gleanings from Rhode Island Town Records: Providence Town Council Records, 1770–1788* [5:279] (Providence: Rhode Island Genealogical Society, 2006), 74; Providence Town Council Records, 5: 395–396.

28. David, 75–76.

29. Ward, 166–168.

30. Lovell, 119–120.

31. Lorenzo J. Greene, "Some Observations on the Black Regiment of Rhode Island in the American Revolution," 166.

32. Bamberg, *Elder John Gorton and the Six Principle Baptist Church of East Greenwich, Rhode Island*, 29; Rider, 81; CSR Simon Barton; Bruce Chadwick, *The First American Army: The Untold Story of George Washington and the Men Behind America's First Fight for Freedom* (Naperville: Sourcebooks, 2007), 177.

33. "A List of Negro Slaves Inlisted into the Continental Battalions and to Whom They Belonged, 1778," *Rhode Island Roots* 6, no. 3, 57; CSR Cato Greene; RWPR Cato Greene.

34. CSR Solomon Wanton; Bamberg, *Elder John Gorton and the Six Principle Baptist Church of East Greenwich, Rhode Island*, 269; Stephenson, 172–173, 174–175; RISA, Rhode Island Military Papers, "Register of all casualties that have happened . . . since January 1, 1781."

35. Adams and Pleck, 161; Providence City Archives, "Records of Marriages and Births, Volume 5, Marriages by Reverend Stephen Gano." Hannah Wanton, a Black, is listed as being married to John Jones on October 31, 1822 in Providence. Whether this is the same Hannah Frank Wanton cannot be proven.

36. Providence Town Council Records, 5:155; Ruth Wallis Herndon, *Unwelcome Americans: Living on the Margin in Early New England* (Philadelphia: University of Pennsylvania Press, 2001), 2, 17.

37. Herndon, *Unwelcome Americans*, 11–12, 15; Gundersen, 149–150; Mathew, 43.

38. Jean C. Stutz, transcriber, *South Kingstown, Rhode Island Town Council Records, 1771–1795* (Kingston: Pettaquamscutt Historical Society, 1988), 93.

39. Stutz, 119.

40. Stutz, 123.

41. Stutz, 120.

42. Lisa Wilson, 7; Royster, 296; Lorenzo J. Greene, "Some Observations on the Black Regiment of Rhode Island in the American Revolution," 166.

43. Quoted in Royster, 296.

44. Herndon, *Unwelcome Americans*, 17.

45. Herndon, *Unwelcome Americans*, 6.

46. Herndon, *Unwelcome Americans*, 28.

47. Providence Town Council Records, 5:176.

48. Herndon, *Unwelcome Americans*, 5.

49. Herndon, *Unwelcome Americans*, 9.

50. National Archives, United States Federal Census, 1820, Massachusetts, Nantucket, Nantucket, Series M33, Roll 52, Page 60. Additionally, the Vital Records of Massachusetts confirmed the death of Daniel Wilbur, age 60–70 of Sandwich, Massachusetts. The village of Sandwich was located on Cape Cod in the vicinity of Nantucket Island. A connection between the Wilburs of Nantucket and the Wilburs of Sandwich has not been proven. *Vital Records of Sandwich Massachusetts*, "Death Notices–1809," 1442, www.americanancestors.org (accessed October 9, 2010).

CHAPTER SEVEN: THE WINTER OF DISCONTENT . . .

1. RISA, *Providence Town Council Records*, 5:158–59.

2. "The Deserter," a poem dating from the mid-eighteenth century, may have summed up Ben's feelings at this point in his career. The poem illustrates the brutality under which enlisted men served. The second verse reads "When first I deserted I thought myself free, When my cruel companions informed against me: I quickly followed after, and brought back with speed, With chains I was loaded, heavy irons on me." Moore, 397.

3. Joseph Lee Boyle, *"He Loves a good deal of rum": Military Desertions during the American Revolution, Volume One, 1775–June 30, 1777* (Baltimore: Clearfield Company by Genealogical Publishing Company, 2009), v; Neagles, 8; Ward, *The War for Independence and the Transformation of American Society*, 135.

4. John U. Rees argues that advertisements for Black soldiers were only two percent of the total deserters as compiled by Joseph Lee Boyle in *"He Loves a good deal of rum...": Military Desertions during the American Revolution*, his work regarding that subject. CSR Benjamin Frank; Rees, 188.

5. Cowell, 20.

6. Royster, 25; James Kirby Martin, "A 'Most Undisciplined, Profligate Crew': Protest and Defiance in the Continental Ranks, 1776–1783," 122–123.

7. John Smith, "Thro Mud and Mire Into the Woods, The 1777 Continental Diary of Sergeant John Smith."

8. James Kirby Martin, "A 'Most Undisciplined, Profligate Crew': Protest and Defiance in the Continental Ranks, 1776–1783," 121–122; John Smith, "Thro Mud and Mire into the Woods: The 1777 Continental Diary of Sergeant John Smith"; Niemeyer, 141; Greenman, 138, 104.

9. Quoted in Niemeyer, 134–135.

10. Niemeyer reviewed courts-martial entries from 168 sets of orderly books from Continental forces. James Kirby Martin, "A 'Most Undisciplined, Profligate Crew': Protest and Defiance in the Continental Ranks, 1776–1783," 138; Niemeyer, 134–135.

11. Ward, 135; CSR Benjamin Frank; Royster, 60; James Kirby Martin, "A 'Most Undisciplined, Profligate Crew': Protest and Defiance in the Continental Ranks, 1776–1783," 129–130.

12. James Kirby Martin, "A 'Most Undisciplined, Profligate Crew': Protest and Defiance in the Continental Ranks, 1776–1783," 123.

13. James Kirby Martin, "A 'Most Undisciplined, Profligate Crew': Protest and Defiance in the Continental Ranks, 1776–1783," 124; Royster, 61.

14. Quoted in Ward, 118.

15. Angell, xiii.

16. Angell, 91.

17. Worthington Chauncey Ford, editor, "Articles of War; September 20, 1776," *Journals of the Continental Congress 1774–1779* (Washington, DC: Government Printing Office, 1905), https://avalon.law.yale.edu/ 18th_century/contcong_09–20–76.asp (accessed June 20, 2021); Mike Matheny, "'The Predicament We Are In': How Paperwork Saved the Continental Army," *Journal of the American Revolution,* May 3, 2021, https://allthingsliberty.com/ 2021/05/the-predicament-we-are-in-how-paperwork-saved-the-continental-army/ (accessed June 20, 2021); Mayer, 59.

18. Greenman, 75–78.

19. Greenman, 76.

20. Greenman, 75–76.

21. John Smith, "Thro Mud and Mire into the Woods: The 1777 Continental Diary of Sergeant John Smith."

22. Historians have asserted that the desertion rate for Black troops was substantially lower than the average desertion rate among the Continental troops. Benjamin Quarles argued that African Americans deserted less because there was less for them to desert to. Donald Robinson agrees that Blacks had less motivation to return to civilian life. Glen Knoblock uses the lower desertion rates of Black soldiers as an indicator of their importance to America's fight for independence—that they were a stable presence in an army comprised of militiamen. Knoblock makes this argument by comparing the 5 percent desertion rate of New Hampshire's Black soldiers to the 33 percent desertion rate for Continental soldiers. However, John Wood Sweet acknowledges that a "considerable number" of Black soldiers of Rhode Island deserted, especially when their companies left the confines of their state. Sweet argues that these Black soldiers deserted for the same reasons as white soldiers: low morale, financial concerns, and malfeasance on the part of their superior officers. Quarles,

The Negro in the American Revolution, 79; Knoblock, *"Strong and Brave Fellows": New Hampshire's Black Soldiers and Sailors of the American Revolution, 1775–1784*, 21; Sweet, 220.

23. Sobel, 160–161.

24. RIBHS, *Creative Survival*, 30.

25. Neimeyer, 85; RIHS, "Return of Freemen"; RISA, *Regimental Book Rhode Island Regiment for 1781*; CSR Elijah Waggs; CSR Solomon Wanton; RWPR Winsor Fry; RWPR Richard Potter.

26. Gerzina, 132–133.

27. Angell, xiii; Chudacoff, 76; Brace, 161.

28. Greenman, 168.

29. Neagles, 139.

30. Quarles, *The Negro in the American Revolution*, 71; Lanning, *Defenders of Liberty*, 78; RIHS, "Return of Freemen"; CSR Thomas Amos; CSR Edward Anthony; CSR Simon Barton; CSR Joseph Boyer; CSR Jonathan Charles; CSR Primus Childs; CSR William Coopin; CSR Toby Coys; CSR Peter Dailey/Dayley/Daily; CSR James Daley; CSR Wilford Dick; CSR Caesar Finch; CSR Benjamin Frank; CSR William Frank; CSR Winsor Fry; CSR Asa Gardner; CSR Frank Gould; CSR James Greene; CSR Gideon Harry; CSR Charles Henly; CSR Pharoh Hazzard; CSR Prince Limas; CSR Toney Phillips; CSR Richard Potter; CSR Thomas Reynolds; CSR Cuff Roberts; CSR Rueben Roberts; CSR George Rogers; CSR Thomas Smith; CSR Josiah Sole; CSR Elijah Waggs; CSR Solomon Wanton.

31. Quoted in Royster, 241–242.

32. Quoted in Kaplan, 57.

33. Martin, "A 'Most Undisciplined, Profligate Crew': Protest and Defiance in the Continental Ranks, 1776–1783," 130.

34. As stated previously by Benjamin Quarles in his historic study of African American service and more recently reiterated by Robert A. Geake, these new soldiers deserted less than their counterparts. In his study, Geake also refers to previous works by Sidney S. Rider and Daniel M. Popek, who position the formerly enslaved soldiers as not adequately fulfilling their assignments, especially during the Battle of Rhode Island. I argue that the formerly enslaved did not desert in the same numbers as their counterparts. I also argue that the previously free soldiers of color did leave their service after serving longer periods than their white counterparts and after their terms and conditions of service were drastically changed. Quarles, *The Negro in the American Revolution*, 79; Robert A. Geake with Loren Spears, *From Slaves to Soldiers: The 1st Rhode Island Regiment in the American Revolution* (Yardley, PA: Westholme, 2016), 66–67; Sidney S. Rider, *An Historical Inquiry into the 1st Rhode Island Regiment; They Fought Bravely, but Were Unfortunate: The True Story of Rhode Island's Continental Line, 1777–1778* (Bloomington, IN: AuthorHouse, 2015); CSR James Clarke; CSR Jack Fones; CSR Sharpo Gardner; CSR William Greene; Thomas Lafavour; CSR Isaac Rodman; Van Buskirk, 125–126.

35. CSR Ed Anthony; CSR William Coopin; CSR Toby Coys; CSR Milford Dick; CSR Benjamin Frank; CSR Winsor Fry; CSR Asa Gardner; CSR Francis Gould; CSR James Greene; CSR Gideon Harry; CSR Richard Potter; CSR Cuff Roberts; CSR Rueben Roberts; CSR Thomas Smith; CSR Josiah Sole; CSR Elijah Waggs; CSR Solomon Wanton.

36. Heitman, 440.

37. Taylor, 60.

38. Coys is listed as a private, dead January 14, 1782, on the casualty register. It is unknown

as to the cause of his death. It is curious to note that Coys is also listed as being discharged on July 1, 1780, in his Compiled Service Record. Whether this is an indication that he reenlisted after his 1780 discharge or not is unclear. Boyle, 119; RISA, Rhode Island Military Papers, "Register of all casualties that have happened . . . since 1/1/1781"; CSR Asa Gardner; Neagles, 157.

39. Royster, 299; Providence Town Council Records, 5:158–159.

40. Greenman, 145.

41. Royster, 297.

42. Greenman, 168.

43. "From George Washington to Major Henry Lee, Jr., 9 July 1779," Founders Online, National Archives, https://founders.archives.gov/documents/Washington/03-21-02-0330. [Original source: *The Papers of George Washington, Revolutionary War Series, vol. 21, 1 June–31 July 1779*, ed. William M. Ferraro (Charlottesville: University Press of Virginia, 2012), 401–403.]

44. Stephenson, 99–100.

45. Walker, *So Few the Brave*, 71–72.

46. Fascines were long bundles of sticks bound together and used in the building or strengthening of military earthworks and batteries. Washington was very explicit in the types of timber used for these fortifications, twelve to eighteen feet in length and ten inches thick. Don N. Hagist, "Building and Attacking Redoubts," *Journal of the American Revolution*, June 24, 2015 (accessed May 5, 2018), https://allthingsliberty.com/2015/06/building-and-attacking-redoubts/; Angell, 74, 89, 100–101; Van Buskirk, 125; Edward G. Lengel, *The Battles of Connecticut Farms and Springfield* (Yardley, PA: Westholme, 2020), 61–62.

47. William T. Fontaine, *Reflections on Segregation, Desegregation, Power, and Morals* (Springfield, IL: Charles C. Thomas, 1967), 60.

48. Van Buskirk, 125–126; Robert G. Parkinson, *The Common Cause: Creating Race and Nation in the American Revolution* (Chapel Hill: University of North Carolina Press, 2016), 336; Lanning, *Defenders of Liberty*, 81.

49. Quoted from Christian M. McBurney, "Mutiny! American Mutinees in the Rhode Island Theater of War, September 1778–July 1779," *Rhode Island History* 69, no. 2 (Summer/Fall), 62; 60–64.

50. John A. Nagy, *Rebellion in the Ranks: Mutinies of the American Revolution* (Yardley, PA: Westholme, 2008), 12–13; McBurney, "Mutiny! American Mutinees in the Rhode Island Theater of War, September 1778–July 1779," 60–64.

51. "Christopher Greene to George Washington, March 27, 1780," *George Washington Papers at the Library of Congress, 1741–1799: Series 4. General Correspondence, 1697–1799.*

52. Neagles, 26; CSR Fry; Stephenson, 98. Fry's court-martial occurred between the months of March and May 1780.

53. Fry's courts-martial occurred between the months of March and May 1780. Regarding the initial court-martial, Washington did not agree with Greene's recommendation, but only due to a technicality. Washington responded on April 12, 1780, that Fry could not be charged and found guilty because a "Court Martial for the trial of a Continental officer or soldier can only be ordered by the Commander-in-Chief" and since Fry's court martial had not conformed to this practice Washington disapproved the sentence. "George Washington to Christopher Greene, April 12 1780," *George Washington Papers at the Library of Congress, 1741–1799: Series 4, General Correspondence. 1697–1799;* Van Buskirk, 121; Neagles, 26,

139; CSR Fry; LOC, "Christopher Greene to George Washington, March 27 1780," George Washington Papers; LOC, "George Washington to Christopher Greene, April 12 1780," George Washington Papers; RISA, Rhode Island Military Papers, "Register of Non-Commissioned Officers and Privates in the 5th Company of Rhode Island Battalion, inlisted for War and furloughed on the General Order of the 2nd of June, 1783."

54. Angell, xiii.

55. Judith Van Buskirk argues that Greene interceded on the behalf of his men less often than Israel Angell, who defended his men more often. Van Buskirk, 121, 140.

56. Prior to his departure, Allen was listed as sick absent in December. Soldiers listed as "sick absent" were 3rd Company, Olney's Regiment, June 15, 1783.

57. CSR Robert Allen; CSR Cuff Peckham; CSR George Thompkins; CSR Louden Thompson.

58. There was a cluster of five desertions by white soldiers from Camp Warren in April 1779. CSR John Taylor; CSR John Pillar; CSR John Law; CSR Alexander Howden; CSR Nathan Howard. A total of twenty-eight members of the First Rhode Island left in 1780. CSR Thomas Amos; CSR Edward (Ned) Anthony left in November 1780; CSR John Charles; CSR James Daley; CSR Milford/Wilford Duk/Dick; CSR Benjamin Frank; CSR Winsor Fry; CSR Frank Gould/Gold; CSR James Greene; CSR Gideon Harry; CSR Richard Potter; CSR Cezar/Caesar Sabens/Sabins; CSR Thomas Smith; CSR Josiah Sole/Soule; CSR Solomon Wanton. Van Buskirk, 128; Lanning, *Defenders of Liberty*, 177.

59. CSR James Daley.

60. Joseph Lee Boyle, *"He loves a good deal of rum . . .": Military Desertions during the American Revolution, 1775–1783, Volume Two, June 30, 1777–1783* (Baltimore: Clearfield, 2009), 234.

61. A second Wanton family, headed by William, also resided in Tiverton before the war. William, like Solomon, also headed a mixed household of Native Americans and Blacks. William Wanton's household included six Native Americans and one Black. RIHS, *Papers of Christopher Greene*, "Return of Casualties since 24th Dec 1779"; Bartlett, *Census of the Inhabitants of the Colony of Rhode Island and Providence Plantations 1774*, 191; Bamberg, *Elder John Gorton and the Six Principle Baptist Church of East Greenwich, Rhode Island*, 269; CSR Solomon Wanton; RIHS, "Muster Roll 1st Rhode Island Battalion June-July 1, 1778, Captain Arnold's Company"; RISA, Rhode Island Military Papers, "Register of all casualties that have happened . . . since 1/1/1781."

62. CSR Richard Potter; RWPR Richard Potter.

63. CSR Frank Gould.

64. RISA, Rhode Island Military Papers, "Register of all casualties that have happened . . . since 1/1/1781."

65. CSR Jonathan Charles.

66. CSR Gideon Harry; RWPR John (Gideon) Harry.

67. RWPR John (Gideon) Harry.

68. James Greene, 2nd is also listed on this register. I am unsure of the enlistment date of this James Greene, as well as additional military documentation. CSR James Greene; RISA, Rhode Island Military Papers, "Register of Levies who served in the Rhode Island Regiment, the Campaign of 1782 and are discharged."

69. Boyle, 115; CSR Benjamin Frank; CSR Jonathan Charles; CSR James Daley; CSR Winsor Fry; CSR Richard Potter; RISA, Rhode Island Military Papers, "Register of all casualties that have happened . . . since 1/1/1781."

70. CSR William Coopin; Boyle, *Death Seem'd to Stare*, 118; RISA, "Return of Casualties Since 24 Dec 1779"; *Massachusetts Soldiers and Sailors of the Revolutionary War: A Compilation from the Archives, Prepared and Published by the Secretary of the Commonwealth In Accordance with Chapter 100, Resolves of 1891*, Volume 3, C-Cor (Boston: Wright and Potter Printing Company State Printers, 1896), 984.

71. Knoblock, *"Strong and Brave Fellows": New Hampshire's Black Soldiers and Sailors of the American Revolution, 1775–1784*, 15.

72. Quoted in Lovell, 148–149.

73. Knoblock, *"Strong and Brave Fellows": New Hampshire's Black Soldiers and Sailors of the American Revolution, 1775–1784*, 15.

74. Royster, 71–72.

75. Excerpt taken from the Narrative of James Fergus. Fergus and his company were near Savannah, Georgia, and marching to Charleston. John C. Dann, editor, *The Revolution Remembered: Eyewitness Accounts of the War for Independence* (Chicago: University of Chicago Press, 1980), 183.

76. Niemeyer, 144–145; Neagles, 122; Rhode Island Historical Society, *Papers of Colonel Christopher Greene*, "Casualties Colonel Christopher Greene's Battalion January 1, 1777–January 1, 1778."

77. Quarles, *The Negro in the American Revolution*, 119.

78. Quoted in Quarles, *The Negro in the American Revolution*, 113.

79. Quarles, *The Negro in the American Revolution*, 113.

80. Graham Russell Hodges, *The Black Loyalist Directory: African Americans in Exile After the American Revolution* (New York: Garland, 1996), 170.

CHAPTER EIGHT: BROTHERS DIVIDED

1. CSR William Frank; Sobel, 140–141.

2. Wallace, 56.

3. CSR William Frank.

4. Cowell, 199.

5. Walker, *So Few the Brave*, 74.

6. Lovell, 139–140.

7. RIHS, "Return of Freemen"; CSR Charles Henly/Henley/Hebley/Handy/Handley; Grundset, 218; CSR Asa Gardner; Boyle, *"Death Seem'd to Stare,"* 127.

8. CSR Asa Gardner; CSR Charles Henly; Ronald Vern Jackson, editor, *Index Rhode Island Military Census, 1776* (West Jordan: Genealogical Services, 1988), 36.

9. Lanning, *Defenders of Liberty, 79;* CSR William Frank/Franck; Van Buskirk, 139; CSR Winsor (Windsor) Fry; RISA, "Return of all non-commissioned officers and privates inlisted for the War in the 6th Company of the Rhode Island Battalion"; CSR Edward (Ned) Anthony/Anthoney, Jr.; CSR Simon Barton; CSR Joseph Boyer/Bouyer; CSR Primus (Prince) Childs; CSR Toby Coys/Coies; CSR Peter Dailey/Daily/Dayley; CSR Ceasar Finch; CSR William Frank/Franck; CSR Pharoh Hazzard/Hazard; CSR Prince Limas/Limus/Lemus; CSR Jacob Ned; CSR Toney Phillips; CSR Thomas Reynolds; CSR Cuff Roberts; CSR George Rogers; CSR Elijah (Elisha) Waggs/Woggs; CSR Solomon Wanton.

10. CSR Edward (Ned) Anthony/Anthoney, Jr.

11. RISA, *Regimental Book Rhode Island Regiment for 1781;* RISA, "Return of all the Non-Commissioned Officers and Privates inlisted for the War in the 4th Company of the Rhode

Island Battalion Commanded by Lt. Colonel Olney"; RISA, "Register of Non-commissioned Officers and Privates in the 5th Company of Rhode Island Battalion, inlisted for War and furloughed on the General Order of the 2nd of June, 1783."

12. CSR Rueben/Ruben Roberts; CSR Elijah (Elisha) Waggs/Woggs; RISA, *Regimental Book Regiment for 1781;* RISA, "Return of all Non-Commissioned Officers and Privates in the 4th Company Commanded by Lt. Colonel Jeremiah Olney"; "Register of Non-Commissioned Officers and Privates . . . inlisted for War and furloughed on the General Order of the 2nd of June, 1778."

13. Coys's date of death is listed as January 14, 1782. Asa Gardner died October 26, 1780. Solomon Wanton died on December 28, 1781. His death is discussed in Chapter 6, "The Marriage of a Poor Soldier." CSR Jonathan (John) Charles; CSR James Daley; CSR Benjamin Frank/Franck; CSR Winsor (Windsor) Fry; CSR Richard Potter; CSR Rueben/Ruben Roberts; CSR Elijah (Elisha) Waggs/Woggs; CSR Toby Coys/Coies; CSR Asa Gardner/Gardiner; CSR Solomon Wanton; RISA, Rhode Island Military Papers, "Register of all casualties that have happened . . . since 1/1/1781."

14. A. J. Williams-Myers, "Out of the Shadows: African Descendants-Revolutionary Combatants in the Hudson River Valley; a Preliminary Historical Sketch," *Afro-Americans in New York Life and History* 31, no. 1 (2007), http://www.questia.com/read/1G1-158529011/out-of-the-shadows-african-descendants-revolutionary, 27–29; Allison Albee, *The Nasty Affair at Pines Bridge,* edited by Monica Doherty (Yorktown Heights, NY: Yorktown Historical Society, 2005), 16–17.

15. Greenman, 208.

16. Williams-Myers, 29; Walker, *So Few the Brave,* 78; Lanning, *Defenders of Liberty,* 78–79.

17. CSR Primus (Prince) Childs/Chiles; RISA, Rhode Island Military Papers, "Register of all casualties that have happened…since 1/1/1781"; Geake, 69–70.

18. Lanning, *Defenders of Liberty,* 79.

19. Rider, 47.

20. Greenman, 208.

21. RISA, Rhode Island Military Papers, "Register of all casualties that have happened… since 1/1/1781."

22. RIHS, "Return of Freemen."

23. Sweet, 233, 209; Walker, *So Few the Brave,* 155; CSR William Frank/Franck.

24. RISA, "Rhode Island Military Papers," Clothing Book.

25. Walker, *So Few the Brave,* 82.

26. Samuel Smith, *Memoirs of the Life of Samuel Smith, Being an Extract of a Journal Written by Himself From 1776 to 1786* (Middleborough, MA, 1853).

27. Walker, *So Few the Brave,* 82; Ruth Wallis Herndon, *Unwelcome Americans: Living on the Margins in Early New England* (Philadelphia: University of Pennsylvania Press, 2001), 171.

28. Van Buskirk, 141; Lanning, *Defenders of Liberty,* 79; Walker, *So Few the Brave,* 85, 91–92; Lanning, *The African American Soldier,* 15; Catherine R. Williams, *Biography of Revolutionary Heroes; Containing the Life of Brigadier Gen. William Barton, and Also, of Captain Stephen Olney* (Providence: Catherine R. Williams, 1839), 278; Ellen McCallister Clark, Sandra L. Powers, and E. K. Hong, *Rhode Island in the American Revolution* (Washington, DC: Society of Cincinnati, 2000), 28–29.

29. Walker, *So Few the Brave,* 53, 90–92; Sweet, 220.

30. Wanton's death is discussed in a previous chapter. RISA, Rhode Island Military Papers, "Register of all Casualty's that have happened In the Rhode Island Regmt. Since 1 Jan 1781"; CSR Toby Coys/Coies.

31. Samuel Smith, *Memoirs of Samuel Smith, A Soldier of the Revolution, 1776–1786, Written by Himself with Preface and Notes by Charles L. Bushnell* (New York: Privately Printed, 1860), 22.

32. Lanning, *Defenders of Liberty,* 79–80; Larry Lowenthal, *Marinus Willett: Defender of the Northern Frontier* (Fleischmanns, NY: Purple Mountain Press, 2000), 72–73; Reiss, 243; Samuel Smith, *Memoir;* RIHS, "Register of all casualties"; Geake, 85.

33. Lanning, *Defenders of Liberty,* 78; CSR William Frank/Franck; RISA, Rhode Island Military Papers, "Register of Non-commissioned Officers and Privates in the 5th Company of Rhode Island Battalion, inlisted for War and furloughed on the General Order of the 2nd of June, 1783."

34. Quoted in Bernard C. Nalty, *Strength for the Fight: A History of Black Americans in the Military* (New York: The Free Press, 1986), 15.

35. Quoted in Lorenzo J. Greene, "Some Observations on the Black Regiment of Rhode Island in the American Revolution," 171.

36. The soldiers of the Rhode Island Consolidated Regiment were discharged without money or clothes. Lorenzo J. Greene, "Some Observations on the Black Regiment of Rhode Island in the American Revolution," 171; Lanning, *Defenders of Liberty,* 92; "Certificates of the Rhode Island Line (1784), C#00164"; RISA, *Regimental Book Rhode Island Regiment for 1781,* 35.

37. As stated in the Introduction and Preface, according to the Franklin oral tradition, military, census, and marriage records, Ben Frank of Johnston, Rhode Island, is Ben Franklin of Granville, Nova Scotia. In loyalist records and documents, I believe Ben is listed as Ben Frankham in *Book of Negroes* and Ben Frankum on the "1784 Muster Roll of Birchtown, Nova Scotia." Regarding the possibility of a Ben Frankham in revolutionary South Carolina, an analysis of records detailing free "negroes" in that period does not include a listing for a Ben Frankham. See Paul Heinigg's work, *Free African Americans of North Carolina, Virginia, and South Carolina: From the Colonial Period to About 1820* (Baltimore: Clearfield Company, 2002). As an additional avenue of research, the South Carolina Free Negro Capitation Tax Books contain the names and other information about free Blacks residing in South Carolina, since the inception of the tax in 1756. However, the ledgers from 1756 until 1810 no longer exist. Letter to Mrs. Hattie Gilton from Finn Bower, Curator Shelburne County Museum, June 24, 2000; Graham Russell Hodges, *The Black Loyalist Directory: African Americans in Exile After the American Revolution* (New York: Garland, 1996), 170; LAC, *Shelburne Town Records Collection,* "Muster Book of Free Black Settlement of Birchtown, 1784 Captain Bridges' Company who have drawn provisions at Port Mouton"; Nic Butler, "South Carolina's Capitation Tax, 1756–1864," January 28, 2022, *Charleston's Time Machine,* Charleston County Public Library, www.ccpl.org/charleston-time-machine/south-carolinas-capitation-tax-free-people-of-color–1756–1864; *State Free Negro Capitation Tax Books,* Charleston, South Carolina, ca. 1811.

38. Other studies examine this idea as well. Carol Berkin argues that for African American women the chances and opportunities for "meaningful independence" rested with a British victory. Alfred and Ruth Blumrosen argue that the enslaved looked to the British for freedom and equality, especially given the Somerset Decision of 1774—in a belief that Great Britain had freed its slaves. Brown and Senior add that escaped slaves and free Blacks who

turned to the British cause were worried about the security of their freedom in an American republic. Their lives as enslaved and free Blacks in colonial America had not convinced them of their chance to obtain the goals of freedom and equality espoused by the American rebels. Cowell, 180; Neil MacKinnon, *This Unfriendly Soil: The Loyalist Experience in Nova Scotia, 1783–1791* (Kingston: McGill-Queen's University Press, 1986), 75; Wallace Brown, *The Good Americans: The Loyalists in the American Revolution* (New York: William Morrow, 1969), 29, 45–49; Maya Jasonoff, *Liberty's Exiles: American Loyalists in the Revolutionary World* (New York: Vintage Books, 2012), 8–9. Carol Berkin, *Revolutionary Mothers: Women in the Struggle For America's Independence* (New York: Alfred A. Knopf, 2005); Alfred W. and Ruth G. Blumrosen, *Slave Nation: How Slavery United the Colonies and Sparked the American Revolution* (Naperville: Sourcebooks, 2005); Wallace Brown and Hereward Senior, *Victorious in Defeat: The Loyalists in Canada* (Slingsby, UK: Methuen, 1984). Other important works about Blacks in Canada and Black loyalism include the following: Harvey Amari Whitefield, *Blacks on the Border: The Black Refugees in British North America, 1815–1860* (Burlington: University of Vermont Press, 2006); Cassandra Pybus, *Epic Journeys of Freedom: Runaway Slaves of the American Revolution and Their Global Quest for Freedom* (Boston: Beacon Press, 2006); Mary Louise Clifford, *From Slavery to Freetown: Black Loyalists After the American Revolution* (Jefferson, NC: McFarland, 1999); Graham Russell Hodges, *The Black Loyalist Directory: African Americans in Exile After the American Revolution* (New York: Garland, 1996); James W. St. G. Walker, *The Black Loyalists: The Search for a Promised Land in Nova Scotia and Sierra Leone* (Toronto: University of Toronto Press, 1992, originally published London: Longman, 1976); Ruth Holmes Whitehead, *Black Loyalists: Southern Settlers of Nova Scotia's First Free Black Communities* (Halifax: Nimbus Publishing, 2013).

39. Walker, *The Black Loyalists: The Search for a Promised Land in Nova Scotia and Sierra Leone, 1783–1870*, 5; Michael McDonnell, "Other Loyalists: A Reconsideration of the Black Loyalist Experience in the American Revolutionary Era," *Southern Historian* 16 (1995), 13.

40. "Philipsburg Proclamation," June 30, 1779, Manuscript letter, Henry Clinton Papers, Clements Library, University of Michigan; Littlefield, 47.

41. There are three registers listing Continental deserters among the Clinton Papers at the Clements Library at the University of Michigan. Of particular interest to this study is the register that lists 100 deserters, for a three- or four-week period in January/February 1780. For further reference, the spelling of names is taken directly from the documents in the Clinton Papers and there may be a variation and/or different spelling of surnames on muster rolls and compiled service records. Writer James Mitchell, Nature Deserter's Deposition, October 8, 1780, Vol. 125, Folder 28, Henry Clinton Papers; Lesser, *The Sinews of Independence,* ix.

42. Writer John Stapleton to Oliver DeLancey, Nature Deserter's Deposition, October 23, 1780, Vol. 126, Folder 43, Henry Clinton Papers.

43. CSR Anthony Manual; Writers Anthony Manual, Jacob Dilloe, and Joseph Swatheridge, Nature Deserters' Deposition, October 27, 1780, Vol. 127, Folder 7, Henry Clinton Papers.

44. Writer John Porter, Nature Deserter's Deposition, October 30, 1780, Vol. 127, Folder 35, Henry Clinton Papers.

45. CSR Adam Happle; CSR John Chesley; Writers Adam Happele and John Chesley, Nature Deserters' Deposition, November 7, 1780, Vol. 128, Folder 52, Henry Clinton Papers.

46. Writer Joe, Nature Deserter's Deposition, November 6, 1780, Vol. 128, Folder 43, Henry Clinton Papers.

47. Writer William Ormsby, Nature Deserter's Deposition, April 21, 1781, Vol. 153, Folder 4, Henry Clinton Papers.

48. Writer Alexander Ross, May 18, 1780, Vol. 99, Folder 33, Henry Clinton Papers.

49. The On-Line Institute for Advanced Loyalist Studies, "Other Facts/Records Rebel Deserters to the Loyalist Cause," www.royalprovincial.com/military/facts/ofrdeserters.htm (accessed December 15, 2008), maintained by Nan Cole, Todd Braisted.

50. Littlefield, 47; Astor, 11; Walker, *The Black Loyalists: The Search for a Promised Land in Nova Scotia and Sierra Leone, 1783–1870*, 5–6; Todd W. Braisted, "The Black Pioneers and Others," in *Moving On: Black Loyalists in the Afro-Atlantic World*, ed. John W. Pulis (New York: Garland, 1999), 27–29.

51. Edward Ely Curtis, *The Origins of the British Army in the American Revolution* (New Haven: Yale University Press, 1926), 135; Braisted, 27–29.

52. The Black Pioneer Corps evacuated from New York in the fall of 1783. See upcoming paragraphs in reference to the Black Pioneers. Ben Frankham was among a group that left in October 1783. Additionally, he was among a group of Black loyalists who were allocated land grants of 50 acres or more. See Marion Gilroy's *Loyalists and Land Settlement in Nova Scotia*, Publications No. 4, Published by the Public Archives of Nova Scotia, 5; Simon Schama, *Rough Crossings: The Slaves, the British, and the American Revolution* (New York: HarperCollins, 2006), 114–116; Quarles, *The Negro in the American Revolution*, 147–148; Astor, 11; Charles Johnson and Patricia Smith and the WGBH Series Research Team, *Africans in America: America's Journey Through Slavery* (New York: Harcourt Brace, 1998), 181–182; James W. St. G. Walker, *The Black Loyalists: The Search for a Promised Land in Nova Scotia, 1783–1820*, 5–6.

53. Stephen Davidson, *Birchtown and the Black Loyalist Experience From 1775 to the Present* (Halifax: Formac, 2019), 52; "Black Pioneer Formation Orders," University of Michigan, William L. Clements Library, Henry Clinton Papers, Volume 263, Miscellaneous Correspondence, 1776–1782; Gary B. Nash, *The Unknown American Revolution: The Unruly Birth of Democracy and the Struggle to Create America* (New York: Penguin, 2005), 166.

54. Writer Great Britain Army in America, Nature, Return of Deserters sent to Lieutenant Willington...between 1st January and 7th August 1781, August 7, 1781, Vol. 169, Folder 15, Henry Clinton Papers; LAC, "Muster Roll of the Black Pioneers for 61 days," 1781, Vol. 25.

55. Lorenzo J. Greene, "Some Observations on the Black Regiment of Rhode Island in the American Revolution," *Journal of Negro History* 37, no. 2 (April 1952), 157; CSR Sharper Gardner.

56. "Black Pioneer Formation Orders."

57. Braisted, 11–12; McDonnell, 6, 14–15.

58. Hodges, 170.

59. Braisted, 15–16; Littlefield, 40.

60. Walker, *So Few the Brave*, 84–85.

61. James W. St. G. Walker, *The Black Loyalists: The Search for a Promised Land in Nova Scotia, 1783–1820*, 9; Mary Louise Clifford, *From Slavery to Freetown: Black Loyalists After the American Revolution* (Jefferson, NC: McFarland, 1999), 33; Pybus, 59.

62. "An Account of the Life of David George," http://collections.ic.gc.blackloyalists/documents/diaries/george_a_life.htm.

63. Clifford, 24.

64. "Memoirs of Boston King," http://collections.ic.gc.ca/blackloyalists/documents/diaries/king-memoirs.html.
65. Pybus, 59.
66. Pybus, 32, 57.
67. John W. Pulis, editor, *Moving On: Black Loyalists in the Afro-Atlantic World* (New York: Garland, 1999), xv; Hodges, xiv; Pybus, 32; Ellen Gibson Wilson, *The Loyal Blacks* (New York: Capricorn, 1976), 62–63.
68. Pybus, 28–29; D. G. Bell, "African American Refugees to Annapolis Royal and Saint John, 1783: A Ship Passenger List," *Nova Scotia Historical Review* 16, no, 2 (July 1996): 71–81, 71.
69. Neil MacKinnon, *This Unfriendly Soil: The Loyalist Experience in Nova Scotia, 1783–1791* (Kingston: McGill-Queen's University Press, 1986), 4–5.
70. Boston King, *Memoirs of Boston King.* http://www.collections.ic.gc.ca/blackloyalists/documents/diaries/king-memoirs.htm (accessed September 22, 2004).
71. Simon Schama argues that Carleton and other British leaders were influenced by the 1774 Somerset Decision as decided by Judge William Murray Mansfield. The decision ruled that an owner could not restrain a fugitive slave, and given that fact an enslaved person in England could liberate him or herself. Schama, 150–151; Blumrosen, 12–13; Johnson and Smith, 194; Hodges, xvii.
72. Johnson and Smith, 194–195; Hodges, xviii-xix.
73. Ellen Gibson Wilson argues that several different individuals captured the information contained in the *Book of Negroes*. Given that fact, she argues that the information may be "unreliable" in some cases, regarding geography and spelling. Additionally there is dispute among historians regarding the ethnicity of Samuel Fraunces. In some works, he is classified as a free Black; in other works he is designated as white. Ellen Gibson Wilson, 69; Clifford, 34–35, 37; Hodges, xi, xvii, xviii, Johnson and Smith, 195; Schama, 147, 151; Carp, 65.
74. Hodges, xix.
75. Hodges, 170.

CHAPTER NINE: WILLIAM FRANK, AFRICAN AMERICAN
1. Sarah J. Purcell, *Sealed With Blood: War, Sacrifice and Memory in Revolutionary America* (Philadelphia: University of Pennsylvania Press, 2002), 55–56; Horton and Horton, *In Hope of Liberty,* xi.
2. Wright, Jr., *The Continental Army,* 175.
3. "General Orders, 7 August 1782," *Founders Online,* National Archives, https://founders.archives.gov/documents/Washington/99-01-02-09056.
4. Sources stipulate that the term "with reputation" indicates a soldier who served with honor and had a good character. RISA, "Camp Verplank's Point 23 Sept. 1782. At a board of officers convened agreeable to the orders of Colonel Olney of the Rhode Island Regiment to inspect the Company returns of Said regiment to determine and report the names of the Non Commissioned Officers and Soldiers who are intitled to Honorary Badges agreeable to General Orders. Major Olney, Captain Hughes, Captain Humphrey, Members. The Board met agreeable to orders and reports as follows"; RISA, "Register of Non Commis. Officers and privates Intitled to Honorary Badges of Distinction for long and Faithful Service who were not Included in the Report of the Board given in the 1st Sept. 1782 as Entered..."; RISA, "Return of all the Non Commissioned Officers and Privates inlisted for the War in the 5th Company of the Rhode Island Battalion commanded by Lieut. Col.

Olney," dated June 1783; Rees, "'He Come Out with Us This Time as a Volunteer . . .': Soldiers Serving Without Pay in the Second New Jersey Regiment, 1777–1780," revwar75.com/library/rees/volunteer.htm; Worthington Chauncey Ford, ed., *Journals of the Continental Congress 1774–1789, Volume VIII, 1777 May 22 to October 2* (Washington, DC: Government Printing Office, 1907), 556.

5. There is a listing for Frances Goold, a Black in the 1800 U.S. Federal Census, living in New York City, the head of household of two. Barbara Kay Armstrong, compiler, *Index to the 1800 Census of New York* (Baltimore: Genealogical Publishing Company, 1984), 148; "U.S. Inflation Calculator from 1635 to 2021," https://www.officialdata.org/; Herndon, 171; RISA, Rhode Island Military Papers, dated 1784, "Account of Public Certificates received by John Singer Dexter for and paid to the Officers and Soldiers of the Rhode Island Line, being the balance due to them for Arrears of Pay, Subsistence, the Gratuity to the Men engaged for the War and the Commendation to the Officers, on a final Settlement of Accounts with the United States"; RISA, "Register of All Casualties."

6. Welcome Arnold Greene, et al., *The Providence Plantations for Two Hundred and Fifty Years of the City of Providence, With a Graphic Description of the City at the Present Time, and of Its Industries, Commerce, Manufactures, Business Interests, Educational, Religious, And Charitable Institutions, Civic, Scientific, And Military Organizations; Also, Sketches of the Cities of Newport and Pawtucket, and Other Towns of the State* (Providence: J. A. & R. A. Reid, Publishers and Printers, 1886), 400.

7. Welcome Arnold Greene, et al., *The Providence Plantations*, 400.

8. Irving H. Bartlett, "The Free Negro in Providence Rhode Island," *Negro History Bulletin* 14, no. 3 (December 1950), 51–54, 66–67; RIBHS, *Creative Survival*, 33.

9. Foner, 515; Joanne Pope Melish, *Disowning Slavery: Gradual Emancipation and "Race" in New England, 1780–1860* (Ithaca: Cornell University Press, 1998), 120–128.

10. Quoted in Palmer, 190.

11. RIBHS, *Creative Survival*, 33.

12. RIBHS, *Creative Survival*, 33–34.

13. Grummick is also spelled "Grummuck" in the records. Cherry Fletcher Bamberg, editor, *Rhode Island Roots: Gleanings from Rhode Island Town Records: Warwick Town Council Records, 1781–1801* (Greenville, RI: Rhode Island Genealogical Society, 2013), 38, 86; Bamberg, editor, *Rhode Island Roots: Gleanings from Rhode Island Town Records: East Greenwich Town Council Records, 1775–1800* (Greenville, RI: Rhode Island Genealogical Society, 2009), 101, 121; Gabriel J. Loiacono, "Warned Out: How Cuff Roberts Was Banished by Poor Law Officials," in *How Welfare Worked in the Early United States: Five Microhistories* (New York: Oxford University Press, 2021), 78–80, 82–84, 89; "Deaths Registered in the City of Boston, 1801 to 1848," Town and City Clerks of Massachusetts. Massachusetts Vital and Town Records (Provo, UT: Holbrook Research Institute).

14. Lorenzo J. Greene, *The Negro in Colonial New England*, 75–76, 98.

15. 1790 Federal Census; Virgil D. White, ed., *Genealogical Abstracts of Revolutionary War Pension Files, Volume II: F-M.* (Waynesboro: National Historical Publishing Company, 1991), 1257; RIBHS, *Creative Survival*, 40; Joanne Pope Melish, *Disowning Slavery: Gradual Emancipation and "Race" in New England, 1780–1860*, 128.

16. Bamberg, *Elder John Gorton and the Six Principle Baptist Church of East Greenwich, Rhode Island*, 303.

17. 1790 Federal Census; RISA, *Regimental Book Rhode Island Regiment for 1781*; Robert Ewell Greene, *Black Courage 1775–1783: Documentation of Black Participation in the Amer-*

ican Revolution (Washington, DC: National Society of the Daughters of the American Revolution, 1984), 79–82.

18. Horton and Horton, *In Hope of Liberty*, 80; Lanning, *The African American Soldier*, 17.

19. James C. Neagles and Lila L. Neagles, *Locating Your Revolutionary War Ancestor: A Guide to the Military Records* (Logan: Everton, 1983), 36–37; Louis Wilson, "Genealogical and Military Data of Blacks, Indians, Mustees From Rhode Island in the American Revolutionary War," Rhode Island Historical Society, undated; RWPR William Frank; 1800 Federal Census; 1810 Federal Census. Congress passed pension legislation during and after the war. Most Revolutionary War pension records contain files resulting from the 1818 and 1820 legislation. Both acts liberalized the pension laws only requiring nine months or more of service with the Continental army as a requirement to receive monthly pension payments. Qualified enlisted pensioners received eight dollars a month as a result of the 1818 legislation. Pensioners also received back payments of owed pension.

20. Neagles and Neagles, 37; RWPR Simon Barton; RWPR Peter Dailey; RWPR Ceaser Finch; RWPR Winsor Fry; RWPR Ruben Roberts.

21. Brace, 177.

22. RWPR Cato Greene; "A List of Negro Slaves Inlisted into the Continental Battalions and to Whom They Belonged, 1778," *Rhode Island Roots* 6, no. 3, 57; Ewell Greene, 38,73, 75.

23. Neagles and Neagles, 34–35; Dann, xvii.

24. RIBHS, *Creative Survival*, 44.

25. Brace, 168.

26. RWPR Richard Potter.

27. RWPR Richard Potter.

28. Mercy Limas is also listed as Mary Limas in the records. Prince Limas is not listed in 1790 Federal Census. *U.S. Revolutionary War Bounty Land Warrants Used in the U.S. Military District of Ohio and Relating Papers (Acts of 1788, 1803, and 1806), 1788–1806;* Microfilm Publication M829, National Archives, Washington, DC, "Land Warrants Issued Prior to 1800"; RWPR Prince Limas; East Greenwich Rhode Island Town Clerk Land and Property Records, East Greenwich Land Evidence Records, Volume 10, Page 27 (10:27), 1783–1801; Bamberg, *Elder John Gorton and the Six Principle Baptist Church of East Greenwich, Rhode Island*, 303, fn 218.

29. RWPR Cuff Roberts.

30. RWPR Winsor (Windsor) Fry; CSR Winsor (Windsor) Fry; *Rhode Island Heads of Families-First Census–1790 Rhode Island Census* (Washington, DC: Government Printing Office, 1908), 46; Lowell M. Volkel, *An Index to the 1800 Federal Census of Rhode Island*, 1970), 27; Ronald Vern Jackson, editor, *Rhode Island 1810 Federal Census Index* (Salt Lake City: A.G.E.S., 1976), 12; Ronald Vern Jackson, Gary Ronald Teeples, and David Schaeffermeyer, eds., *Rhode Island 1820 Federal Census Index* (Bountiful: Accelerated Indexing Systems, 1976), 13.

31. RWPR Winsor Fry; Bruce Campbell MacGunnigle, "Winsor Fry of East Greenwich, Rhode Island and His Descendants (Part One)," *Rhode Island Roots* 41, no. 1 (March 2015), 31–32.

32. Pinkster is a holiday that was celebrated over several days by African and Dutch New Yorkers throughout the 1700s. "Pinkster" is the Dutch name for Pentecost, an important festival in the Christian calendar celebrated seven weeks after Easter, in May or early June. Because of its timing, Pinkster was also associated with the renewal of life in spring, so it combined religious and secular components. Lanning, *The African American Soldier*, 17; Ben-

jamin Quarles, "Black History's Antebellum Origins," in *African American Activism Before the Civil War: The Freedom Struggle in the Antebellum North* (New York: Routledge, 2008), 88; Purcell, 104.

33. Horton and Horton, *In Hope of Liberty*, 69.

34. Brace, 172.

35. Brace, 173–174.

36. Brace, 175.

37. Venture Smith, 29; David Richardson, "Becoming African in America," paper presented at the American Historical Association annual conference, Boston, January 6–9, 2011.

38. Purcell, 76–77; Ward, *The War for Independence and the Transformation of American Society*, 186.

39. Nell, 128–129.

40. Quoted in Nell, 130.

41. Quoted in Purcell, 76–77.

42. Purcell, 76–77.

43. RIBHS, *Creative Survival*, 30.

44. Quoted in Lanning, *The African American Soldier: From Crispus Attucks to Colin Powell*, 15–16.

45. William Cooper Nell, *The Colored Patriots of the American Revolution, With Sketches of Several Distinguished Colored Persons: To Which Is Added A Brief Survey of the Conditions and Prospects of Colored Americans* (Boston: Robert F. Wallcut, 1855), 5.

46. Pope Melish, "Recovering (from) Slavery," 121–131.

47. Other Frank families populated Johnston in the 1790 Federal Census. Along with William is Andrew Frank, who headed a household of nine individuals. Andrew's service during the Revolutionary War has been discussed earlier in the book. Additionally, another household of two headed by Betty Frank is also listed in the census. The second individual listed in that residence is Tobey Frank. I am unable to identify Betty and Tobey's relationship with William and Ben. It is not documented whether she is possibly the widow of Rufus Frank who headed a household of five, with three juveniles and one adult female.

48. RISA, Rhode Island Military Papers, "Account of Public Certificates received by John Singer Dexter for and paid to the Officers and Soldiers of the Rhode Island Line, being the balance due to them for Arrears of Pay, Subsistence, the Gratuity to the Men engaged for the War and the Commendation to the Officers, on a final Settlement of Accounts with the United States"; "Land Warrants Issued Prior to 1800," RWPR William Frank.

CHAPTER TEN: BEN FRANKLIN, BLACK LOYALIST

1. University of Sydney, Black Loyalist Repository, http://www.blackloyalist.info/source-image-display/display/85 (accessed February 16, 2015); Hodges, 170; Harvey Amani Whitfield, *North to Bondage: Slavery in the Maritimes* (Vancouver: UBC Press, 2016), 118.

2. Bridglal Pachai, *Beneath the Clouds of the Promised Land: The Survival of Nova Scotia's Blacks Volume 1: 1600–1800* (Halifax: Black Educators Association, 1987), 50.

3. Stephen Kimber, *Loyalists and Layabouts: The Rapid Rise and Faster Fall of Shelburne, Nova Scotia: 1783–1792* (Toronto: Doubleday Canada, 2008), 104–105.

4. Brown and Senior, 50; John Pulis, editor, *Moving On: Black Loyalists in the Afro-Atlantic World* (New York: Garland, 1999), xiii; Charles Wetherell and Robert W. Roetger, "Notes and Comments: Another Look At The Loyalists of Shelburne, Nova Scotia, 1783–1795,"

Canadian Historical Review, 70, no. 1 (1989): 76; John N. Grant, "Black Immigrants into Nova Scotia, 1776–1815," *Journal of Negro History* 58, no. 3 (July 1973), 255.

5. Pachai, 41–43; Pybus, 59

6. The following ships transported groups of Black loyalists to Port Mouton during this period: sloop *Elk,* brig *Jenney,* ship *Nisbet,* and the brig *Elijah.* The composition of the brig *Jenney* is unique among this grouping since its six passengers are listed as the property of John Nash. The remaining transports contained a diversity of loyalists who were assigned to the Wagon Master General's Department, listed as former slaves, or carried as free persons. Ellen Gibson Wilson, 69; *Black Loyalists: Our History, Our People,* the *Book of Negroes, Book Two* http://collections.ic.gc.ca/blackloyalists/documents/ (accessed November, 2008); Brown and Senior, 36–37.

7. Brown and Senior, 32; Hodges, 170, xix–xx.

8. Ruma Chopra, *Unnatural Rebellion: Loyalists in New York City During the Revolution* (Charlottesville: University Press of Virginia, 2011), 213–214; McDonnell, 17; Sylvia Frey, "Between Slavery and Freedom: Virginia Blacks in the American Revolution," *Journal of Southern History* 49, no. 3 (Aug. 1983), 390; James W. St. G. Walker, *The Black Loyalists: The Search for a Promised Land in Nova Scotia and Sierra Leone, 1783–1870* (Toronto: University of Toronto, 1992, originally published London: Longman, 1976), 7.

9. Nova Scotia Archives and Records Management Library(NSARM), *An Ongoing Database for Nova Scotia Black Cultural History: Subset Database: The Book of Negroes: Inspection Rolls of Blacks Leaving New York with the British Army, 1783;* Kimber, 139; Ellen Gibson Wilson, 69; Hodges, xvii–xviii, 191.

10. Hodges, 191.

11. Ellen Gibson Wilson, 76.

12. Ellen Gibson Wilson, 69, 87; Clifford, 37; Hodges, 169–171; Canada's Digital Collections Program, *Black Loyalists: Our History, Our People: Documents Book of Negroes, Book Two,* http://blackloyalist.com/canadiandigitalcollection/index.htm (accessed April 25, 2005).

13. Curtis, 135; Braisted, 27–28.

14. Hodges, 169–171; Canada's Digital Collections Program, *Black Loyalists: Our History, Our People: Documents Book of Negroes, Book Two,* http://blackloyalist.com/canadiandigital-collection/index.htm (accessed April 25, 2005).

15. Littlefield, 47.

16. Hodges, 170–171; Johnson and Smith, 194.

17. One hectare is equal to 2.5 acres. Pachai, 44; Brown and Senior, 36–37; J. M. Bumsted, "1763–1783: Resettlement and Rebellion," in *The Atlantic Region to Confederation: A History,* ed. Philip A. Buckner and John G. Reid (Toronto: University of Toronto Press, 1994), 167; Harvey Amani Whitfield, *Blacks on the Border: The Black Refugees in British North America, 1815–1860* (Burlington: University of Vermont Press, 2006), 15; Ellen Gibson Wilson, 71, 81.

18. Bumsted, 183; Sylvia Hamilton, "Naming Names, Naming Ourselves: A Survey of Early Black Women in Nova Scotia," in *We're Rooted Here and They Can't Pull Us Up: Essays in African Canadian Women's History,* ed. Peggy Bristow (Toronto: University of Toronto Press, 1994), 14–15; Bridglal Pachai, *Traditional Lifetime Stories: A Collection of Black Memories, Volume 1* (Dartmouth: Black Cultural Centre for Nova Scotia, 1987), 13; Pachai, *Beneath the Clouds of the Promised Land: The Survival of Nova Scotia's Blacks Volume 1: 1600–1800,* 39–40, 44.

19. Pachai, *Beneath the Clouds of the Promised Land: The Survival of Nova Scotia's Blacks Volume I: 1600–1800*, 45; Neil MacKinnon, *This Unfriendly Soil: The Loyalist Experience in Nova Scotia, 1783–1791* (Kingston: McGill-Queen's University Press), 4–5; Ellen Gibson Wilson, 106.

20. A substantial portion of loyalists were settled in these areas because pre-loyalists had already possessed the best farming lands and remaining available lands were located in areas near Digby, Port Roseway, and Port Mouton. Neil MacKinnon, "A Dearth of Miracles: Governor John Parr and the Settling of the Loyalists in Nova Scotia," *Nova Scotia Historical Review* 15, no. 1 (1995), 33, 35; MacKinnon, *This Unfriendly Soil*, 17–18.

21. Ellen Gibson Wilson, 72; Pachai, *Beneath the Clouds of the Promised Land: The Survival of Nova Scotia's Blacks Volume I: 1600–1800*, 46.

22. As quoted in Ellen Gibson Wilson, 71–72.

23. Hodges, 170; MacKinnon, *This Unfriendly Soil*, 76.

24. Pachai, *Beneath the Clouds of the Promised Land: The Survival of Nova Scotia's Blacks Volume I: 1600–1800*, 46; MacKinnon, *This Unfriendly Soil*, 21–23; Marion Robertson, *King's Bounty: A History of Early Shelburne, Nova Scotia.* (Halifax: Nova Scotia Museum, 1978), 77, 88.

25. Kimber, 116, 295; Quoted in Ellen Gibson Wilson, *The Loyal Blacks*, 86; Hodges, xxi.

26. Leslie Hannon, *Redcoats and Loyalists, 1760–1815* (Toronto: Natural Science of Canada Limited, 1978), 50; MacKinnon, *This Unfriendly Soil*, 62–63; Wetherell and Roetger, 64; Ellen Gibson Wilson, 103.

27. Clifford, 44; Hodges, 80–89.

28. "Extract from William Booth's Diary," *Black Loyalists, Our History, Our People, Canada's Digital Collection*, https://blackloyalist.com/cdc/documents/diaries/booth_diary.htm.

29. Hodges, xxiii; Barry Cahill, "Stephen Blucke: The Perils of Being a 'White Negro' in Loyalist Nova Scotia," *Nova Scotia Historical Review* 11, no. 1 (1991), 130; Schama, 116, 155, 236.

30. "Benjamin Marston's Shelburne Journal," *Black Loyalists, Our History, Our People, Canada's Digital Collection*, https://blackloyalist.com/cdc/documents/diaries/marston_journal.htm#survey.

31. Robertson, 87–88.

32. MacKinnon, *This Unfriendly Soil*, 50; Robertson, 87–88.

33. Ellen Gibson Wilson, 81; Robertson, 87.

34. The four other companies were led by Captains James Read, Scott Murray, George Fractions, and Jacob Wyth. LAC, *Shelburne Town Records Collection*, "Militia Muster Roll, 1784 A List of Those Mustered At Shelburne, N.S. in the Summer of 1784 By William Porter, Deputy Commissary Of Musters"; Robertson, 88.

35. The results of realignment gathered by comparison of Brig Elijah's passenger manifest list and the Birchtown Muster Roll of 1784; LAC, *Shelburne Town Records Collection* "Muster Book of Free Black Settlement of Birchtown, 1784 Captain Robert Bridges' Company who have drawn provisions at Port Mouton with Colonel Mollison to the 30 April 1784 from 1st May to the 24 July 1784"; Canada's Digital Collections Program *Black Loyalists: Our History, Our People: Documents The Book of Negroes, Book Two* http://blackloyalist.com/canadiandigitalcollection/index.htm (accessed April 25, 2005); Ellen Gibson Wilson, 81; Pachai, *Beneath the Clouds of the Promised Land: The Survival of Nova Scotia's Blacks Volume I: 1600–1800*, 48.

36. Robertson, 88.

37. Boston King, *Memoirs of Boston King,* http://blackloyalist.com/canadiandigitalcollection/ (accessed September 22, 2004).

38. Clara Dennis, *Down in Nova Scotia, My Own, My Native Land* (Toronto, 1934), 356, 359.

39. Laird Niven and Stephen A. Davis, "Birchtown: The History and Material Culture of an Expatriate African-American Community," in *Moving On: Black Loyalists in the Afro-Atlantic World,* ed. John W. Pulis (New York: Garland, 1999), 65.

40. Cottreau-Robins, 66, 72.

41. Joanna Brooks, "John Marrant's Journal: Providence and Prophecy in the 18th Century Atlantic," *The North Star: A Journal of African American Religious History* 3, no. 1 (Fall 1999), 5; Kimber, 125–126, 174, 218; Cahill, "Stephen Blucke: The Perils of Being a 'White Negro' in Loyalist Nova Scotia," 130.

42. Ellen Gibson Wilson, 87; Library and Public Archives of Canada, "Muster Book of Free Black Settlement of Birchtown, 1784, Captain Bridges' Company who have drawn provision at Port Mattoon with Colonel Mollison to the 30 April 1784 from 1st May to the 24 July 1784"; W. Bryan Rommel-Ruiz, "Colonizing the Black Atlantic: The African Colonization Movements in Postwar Rhode Island and Nova Scotia," *Slavery and Abolition* 27, no. 3 (December 2006), 360.

43. Ellen Gibson Wilson, 87.

44. Hodges, xxi–xxii, xxv; Douglas R. Egerton, *Death or Liberty: African Americans and Revolutionary America* (New York: Oxford University Press, 2009), 207; Robertson, 77, 88.

45. Evelyn B. Harvey, *The Negro Loyalists: Arrival and Departure* (Ottawa: Carleton University, Institute of Canadian Studies, no date), 11–11a; Ellen Gibson Wilson, 74–75.

46. NSARM, Gideon White Papers, "Letter from Jas Courtney to Archibald Cunningham on Arriving at Shelburne (Port Roseway)," dated July 1, 1783.

47. "Muster Book of Free Black Settlement of Birchtown, 1784," Library and Archives Canada/MG9-B9-14, Volume 1, 148–149; Marion Gilroy, compiler, *Loyalists and Land Settlement in Nova Scotia* (Campbellville: Global Heritage Press, 2006), 82–115.

48. Hodges, xxv; Niven and Davis, 60; Ellen Gibson Wilson, 87, 103; Robertson, 91.

49. Hodges, xxii.

50. Diary and Letters of Captain Booth of the Royal Engineers Stationed in Shelburne, 1789.

51. Frances Henry, *Forgotten Canadians: The Blacks of Nova Scotia* (Don Mills: Longman Canada, 1973), 20; MacKinnon, *This Unfriendly Soil,* 147; Ellen Gibson Wilson, 87.

52. Robertson, 93; Ellen Gibson Wilson, 88–89.

53. Egerton, 208; James St. G. Walker, "On the Record: the Testimony of Canada's Black Pioneers, 1783–1865," in *Emerging Perspectives on the Black Diaspora,* ed. Aubrey W. Bonnett and G. Llewellyn Watson (Lanham: University Press of America, 1990), 86.

54. Hodges, xxiii; Robertson, 89–90; Kimber, 184; Ellen Gibson Wilson, 92–93; Jim Power, "To Nova Scotia in Search of Liberty," *American Visions* 3 (1988): 23.

55. Marston's Journal.

56. Robin W. Winks, *The Blacks in Canada: A History* (Montreal: McGill-Queen's University Press, 1971), 39; Power, 23; Kimber, 186.

57. Alan Taylor, "'The Hungry Year': 1789 on the Northern Border of Revolutionary America," in *Dreadful Visitations: Confronting Natural Catastrophe in the Age of Enlightenment* (New York: Routledge, 1999), 154, 146–147.

58. As quoted in Alan Taylor, 151–152 (William Clark to Reverend Samuel Peters, 23 June 1789), MG1 (Reverend Samuel Peters Papers), Reel 10958, PANS.

59. Quoted in Brooks, 13.

60. Brooks, 12.

61. "Memoirs of Boston King," *Black Loyalists: Our History, Our People*, http://collections.ic.gc.ca/blackloyalists/documents/diaries/king-memoirs.htm (accessed September 22, 2004).

62. "John Marrant's Journal," *Black Loyalists: Our History, Our People*, http://blackloyalist.com/canadiandigitalcollection/documents/diaries/journal/44–53.htm (accessed May 21, 2009), 48.

63. Brooks, 11–12.

64. "Booth's Diary March 14th 1789," *Black Loyalists: Our History, Our People*, http://blackloyalist.com/canadiandigitalcollection/index (accessed September 22, 2004).

65. Kimber, 244.

66. Kimber, 179, 293.

67. "Memoirs of Boston King."

68. By the mid-1780s, population estimates of these Black settlements are as follows: Brindley Town at 211 individuals; Chedabucto at 350 individuals; Little Tracadie at 172 individuals; and Preston at 300 individuals. MacKinnon, *This Unfriendly Soil,* 50; Brown and Senior, 20; Pachai, *Beneath the Clouds of the Promised Land: The Survival of Nova Scotia's Blacks Volume I: 1600–1800,* 46–48; Walker, *The Black Loyalists,* 39.

69. Pachai, *Beneath the Clouds of the Promised Land: The Survival of Nova Scotia's Blacks Volume I: 1600–1800,* 50.

70. Ellen Gibson Wilson, 94; Clifford, 49; MacKinnon, 75; Robertson, 96; Hodges, xxiii; Kimber, 202.

71. LAC, "Extracts from the Special Sessions of Shelburne, Nova Scotia," *Shelburne Nova Scotia Court Records,* MG9, B 9–14, volume 6.

72. Clifford, 51; Kimber, 203–204.

73. PANS, "Shelburne Transcripts, MG 4, volume 141, Extracts from Special Sessions of Shelburne Court General Sessions," 9.

74. Kimber, 203–204.

75. Davidson, 33; James W. St. G. Walker, "On the Record: The Testimony of Canada's Black Pioneers, 1783–1865," 95; Hodges, xxv; Robertson, 99.

76. Quoted in Hodges, xxiv; Robertson, 99.

77. J. M. Bumsted, *Henry Alline, 1748–1784* (Toronto: University of Toronto Press, 1971), 46–55; Brooks, 6.

78. Walker, "On the Record: The Testimony of Canada' Black Pioneers, 1783–1865," 93, 95; Brooks, 6.

79. Robertson, 98; Hodges, xxv; Brooks, 5; Kimber, 219.

80. Hodges, xxv–xxvi; Cedrick May, "John Marrant and the Narrative Construction of an Early Black Methodist Evangelical," *African American Review* (Winter 2004), 556.

81. Hodges, xxvii; Pachai, *Beneath the Clouds of the Promised Land: The Survival of Nova Scotia's Blacks Volume I: 1600–1800,* 51–52.

82. Wilkinson had a tenuous relationship with Blucke, the leader of Birchtown. This relationship also played out in court in a 1786 court case "Moses Wilkinson vs Col. Bluck, Moses is ordered to deliver up to Col. Bluck, one Richard Wilkinson, a Negro boy the bound servant of Col. Bluck." Nova Scotia Museum, *Birchtown/South Shore Court Records*

in *Nova Scotia Museum Research, Black Loyalists, Black Communities, 1998–2000, Master Finding Aid.* (Halifax: Nova Scotia Museum, 2000), 3; Hodges, xxvi; Kimber, 141; Pachai, *Beneath the Clouds of the Promised Land: The Survival of Nova Scotia's Blacks Volume I: 1600–1800*, 51; Brooks, 6.

83. Jackson and his family are not listed in the Black Loyalist Directory—an indication that they arrived before the mass evacuation of loyalists at the end of the war. AHS, "The Edward Jackson Family of Granville."

84. The Benjamin James farm was located near present-day Bridgetown. This may have been the origins of the Inglewood Black community per local historian and genealogist Ian Lawrence. LAC, "Muster Roll of Disbanded Officers, Discharges and Disbanded Soldiers and Loyalists taken in the County of Annapolis betwist the 18th and 24th of June 1784," Ward Chipman Papers, MG 23, D1, series 1, volume 24, page 48.

85. AHS, Annapolis County Deeds, Volume 5, 1784–1786, 374; Ian Lawrence, unpublished pamphlet titled "Deeds Involving Blacks."

86. Ian Lawrence, "Deeds Involving Blacks."

87. AHS, "The Litch Family of Grandville Township," https://annapolisheritage society.com/genealogy/family-histories/litch-family-granville-township/.

88. "Booth's Diary March 14th 1789," http://blackloyalist.com/canadiandigitalcollection/index (accessed September 22, 2004).

89. Robert Dunfield, interview by Shirley Green, August, 2009. Transcript in possession of this writer. Lawrencetown: Nova Scotia Community College Centre of Geographic Sciences, "Mapannapolis," Karsdale/Thorne's Cove, http://mapannapolis.ca/black-loyalists; Brenda Thompson, *Finding Fortune: Documenting and Imagining the Life of Rose Fortune* (Halifax: SSP Publications, 2019), 111–112.

90. It appears that these two young men arrived at Port Roseway (Shelburne) separate from their possible father, Edward Jackson. Both held certificates of freedom from Benjamin James, an indication of his prior ownership of the young men. James eventually sold his farm to officials of the church in 1799. A. W. Savary, *Supplement to the History of the County of Annapolis Correcting and Supplying Omissions in the Original Volume* (Toronto: William Briggs, 1913), 38–39, 111; W. A. Calnek, completed and edited by A. W. Savary, *History of Annapolis County Including Old Port Royal and Acadia with Memoirs of the Representatives in the Provincial Parliament, and Biographical and Genealogical Sketches of Its Early English Settlers and Their Families* (Toronto: William Briggs, 1897), 212, 534; Hodges, 69; LAC, "Muster Roll of Disbanded Officers, Discharges and Disbanded Soldiers and Loyalists taken in the County of Annapolis betwist the 18th and 24th of June 1784," Ward Chipman Papers, MG 23, D1, Series 1, volume 24, page 48.

91. Ben appears in the records as Ben Franklin from this point. The county's borders were changed in 1836 and 1837 to create the counties of Digby and Yarmouth. Calnek, xii–xiii; Gilroy, 27.

92. Lawrence, "The Franklin Family of Granville Township, N.S."; Morse, 53, 55; Charles Bruce Fergusson and the Public Archives of Nova Scotia, *Place-Names and Places in Nova Scotia* (Halifax: Mika Publishing Company, 1967), 256–257.

93. Nova Scotia Births and Baptisms, 1710–1896; Morse, 53, 55; Lawrence, "The Franklin Family of Granville Township, N.S."

94. Benjamin Marston, *Benjamin Marston's Journal*, Entry for 17 December 1784, Winslow Papers, University of New Brunswick Libraries.

95. Brinley Town was named after white loyalist George Brinley, who Blacks residing at Brinley Town believed was sympathetic to their cause. The settlement is often referred to as Brindley Town, a distinction that started to appear on maps after 1785. Amanda Doucette, "There's a lot of unanswered questions: Halifax man traces roots back to Digby County," *Tri-County Vanguard,* 10 October 2018; Walker, *The Black Loyalists,* 24; Taunya Padley, *The Church of England's role in Settling the Loyalists in the Town of Digby, 1783–1810,* Master's Thesis, Acadia University, 1991, 4, 13; Thompson, *Finding Fortune,* 50, 111.

96. Walker, *The Black Loyalists,* 25–27; Thompson, *Finding Fortune,* 50; *Black Loyalists: Our History, Our People, The Book of Negroes, Book Two,* http://collections.ic.gc.ca/blackloyalists/documents/ (accessed November 2008).

97. Ellen Gibson Wilson, 108; MacKinnon, 20; Brooks, 6; Walker, *The Black Loyalists,* 68–69; Thompson, *Finding Fortune,* 67.

98. Walker, *The Black Loyalists,* 80–82.

99. Ellen Gibson Wilson, 34–35; Charles Bruce Fergusson, editor, *Clarkson's Mission to America, 1791–1792* (Halifax: Public Archives of Nova Scotia, 1971), 17–18; Clifford, 62.

100. Gilroy, 27; Clifford, 62–63.

101. Clifford, 94; Thompson, *Finding Fortune,* 27.

102. Walker, *The Black Loyalists,* 127; "Black Pioneers," www.footnote.com/page/1407_black_pioneers/ (accessed June 22, 2009).

103. NSARM, Gideon White Papers, "Draft of Letter from Gideon White to Nathaniel Whitworth."

104. Pachai, *Beneath The Clouds of the Promised Land: The Survival of Nova Scotia's Blacks Volume I: 1600–1800,* 54–55; Walker, *The Black Loyalists,* 124–126; Anthony Kirk-Greene, "David George: The Nova Scotian Experience," *Sierra Leone Studies* (December 1960), 112–113; Clifford, 94–95.

105. Clifford, 95; Morse, 55, 57.

106. Walker, *The Black Loyalists,* 384–385.

107. Morse, 53, 55; Lawrence, "The Franklin Family of Granville Township, N.S."

108. Rommel-Ruiz, 358.

109. By this time, Blucke had become unpopular among the remaining Black loyalist population. He was also accused of the misappropriation of funds. A short time after he filed the petition, Blucke left Birchtown. His disappearance from Birchtown is a matter of conjecture. A popular myth is that his torn and bloody clothing was found a short distance from the settlement, possibly indicating his death was caused by wild animals. However, Blucke's family also left the settlement with him, so the myth is not logical. "Blucke's Petition 1792," http://blackloyalist.com/canadiandigitalcollection/documents/official/blucke_petition–1791 (accessed June 30, 2009); Schama, 311; Laird Niven, *Was This the Home of Stephen Blucke? The Excavation of AkDi–23, Birchtown, Shelburne County* (Halifax: Nova Scotia Museum, 2000), 16.

110. Walker, *The Black Loyalists,* 385.

111. NSARM, Nova Scotia Commissioner of Crown Lands fonds, "Mortgage Indenture between Benjamin Franklin and George Wood," 22 March 1796, MF 17697, Book 1B, 604.

112. NSARM, Nova Scotia Commissioner of Crown Lands fonds, "Discharge of Mortgage to George Wood," 29 March 1799, MF 17698, Book 2, 83.

113. Pachai, *Traditional Lifetime Stories: A Collection of Black Memories, Volume 1,* 15, 17; Walker, *The Black Loyalists,* 385, 388.

114. Walker, *The Black Loyalists*, 388–389.

115. LAC, "Nova Scotia–Granville–Town Register of births, marriages, deaths and ear-marks, 1720–1881," MG9, B9, Volume 1.

116. Ben was not the only member of the Black loyalist community to have a large family. Two of Ben's daughters, Isabella and Hannah, married into large families. The family of John Pomp had eight children and the family of Samuel Brothers had ten children. AHS, "The Family of John Pomp"; AHS, "The Family of Samuel Brothers"; NSARM, Nova Scotia Commissioner of Crown Lands fonds, "Sale of farm lot between Benjamin and Margaret Franklin to Robert Marshall," 11 June 1812, MF 17299, Book 5, Pg. 36.

117. Rommel-Ruiz, 358.

118. NSARM, Land Papers Index, "Jordan, Abedingo and others land grant," 5 August 1809; NSARM, Nova Scotia Land Grants, 1732–1864, M.G. 9, B 5.

119. NSARM, Nova Scotia Commissioner of Crown Lands fonds, "Relinquishment of grant lands to Trinity Church in the Parish of Digby," 3 January 1817.

120. Ibid.

121. John Croscup was the eldest son of Ludwick Croscup, loyalist and part of the migration to Nova Scotia after the war. John received and purchased land from his father at Thorne's Cove in present-day Karsdale. At the time of his death, he was a prosperous farmer and a documented slaveholder. Cora Greenaway, "The Croscup Family of Karsdale, Annapolis County and Their Painted Room," *Nova Scotia Historical Review* 9, no. 2 (1989), 106, 110, 113; Lawrence, "The Franklin Family of Granville Township N.S."

122. Rachel B. Herrman, *No Useless Mouth: Waging War and Fighting Hunger in the American Revolution* (Ithaca: Cornell University Press, 2019), 136.

123. Quoted in Herrman, *No Useless Mouth*, 145.

124. *No Useless Mouth*, 145.

125. *No Useless Mouth*, 147.

126. *No Useless Mouth*, 147

127. *No Useless Mouth*, 146–147.

128. Lawrence, "The Brothers Family," Hodges, 6; LAC, "Return of Loyalists and dis-charged soldiers taken in Annapolis County Between 18th and 29th June, 1784..."; LAC, "Record of Negroes and their families mustered in Annapolis County, betwist the 28th day of May and the 30th day of June 1784, copied from the Muster Rolls," Ward Chipman Papers, MG23 D1, Series 1, volume 24, page 72; Morse, 41.

129. Married by banns indicated an announcement of an impending marriage at the couple's parish church. Wayne W. Walker, *Annapolis and Digby Counties Marriages, Volume 3:1821–1840* (Ottawa: IGI: 1988 extraction), record 512, 59–60; Hodges, 201; LAC, Carleton Papers, *Book of Negroes, 1783;* Karen E. McKay, compiler, *1838 Census Index of Digby Co., Nova Scotia* (Halifax: Publication No. 19 Genealogical Association of Nova Scotia, 1995), 12.

130. AHS, "Register of marriages at Clements, Granville, and Dalhousie 1806, 1813, 1817–1834," MG 9, B8, Volume 3, page 5.

131. The family name was changed after 1871 from Pomp to Stevenson. Family members indicated that ancestors viewed the name of Pomp as derogatory in some way. Hodges, 166; AHS, "The Pomp/Stevenson Family of Annapolis and Granville Townships, N.S."

132. Listed as Anthony Buttler in *Book of Negroes*, Guy Carleton, 1st Baron Dorchester: Papers, The National Archives, Kew (PRO 30/55/100, Nova Scotia Archives; Sherri Borden Colley, "Halifax Man traces roots to the black loyalists of Digby," https://www.cbc.ca/news/

canada/nova-scotia/black-loyalists-barton-african-nova-scotians-history–1.3986843, Halifax, CBC News, 2017; Lawrence, "The Franklin Family of Granville Township, N.S.";Gilroy, 26.

133. In early nineteenth-century Nova Scotia, the poor or those in need of government assistance were unable to work and were either sick, disabled, elderly, or abandoned children. In order to receive assistance under Nova Scotian law, Ben had to prove residency or "settlement" in the designated poor district within his township. To do so, he had to reside there for five consecutive years, after the age of twenty-one and without receiving prior aid from the Overseers of the Poor of that district. Cynthia Simpson, "The treatment of Halifax's poor house dead during the nineteenth and twentieth centuries" (Master's Thesis, Saint Mary's University, Halifax, Nova Scotia), 11–12, 14, 17; T. D. MacDonald, "The Nova Scotia Poor Law," *Public Affairs: A Maritime Quarterly for the Discussion of Public Affairs* 1, no. 1, August (1937), 70; NSARM, *Census Returns*, 1838; Lawrence, "The Franklin Family of Granville Township, N.S."; Judith Fingard, "The Relief of the Unemployed Poor in Saint John, Halifax, and Saint John's, 1815–1860," *Acadiensis* 5, no. 1 (Autumn 1975), 33; Brenda Thompson, "Paupers Outside: Poor Houses in Nova Scotia," https://poorhousesofnovascotia.com/ 2018/06/12/ paupers-outside/; Thompson, *A Wholesome Horror: Poor Houses in Nova Scotia* (Halifax: SSP Publications, 2017, Kindle edition), Locations 260, 1442, 1446; Karen E. McKay, compiler, *1838 Census Index of Annapolis Co., Nova Scotia* (Halifax: Publications Number 20 Genealogical Association of Nova Scotia, 1999), 41.

134. Rommel-Ruiz, 361.

EPILOGUE: MY GRANDFATHER CAME FROM CANADA

1. 1891 Census of Canada, Annapolis County, Lequille, LAC; "Obituary for Thomas Henry Franklyn," *Annapolis Spectator* (1929).

2. "Obituary for Thomas Henry Franklyn," *Annapolis Spectator* (1929).

3. Woodtor, 9; Tony Burroughs, *Black Roots: A Beginner's Guide to Tracing the African American Family Tree* (New York: A Fireside Book, 2001), 36–37.

4. James St. G. Walker, *The Black Loyalists*, 384.

5. Gene Smith, "Black Nova Scotians," *American Legacy*, Summer, 2003, 28.

6. The Black Loyalist Heritage Centre and Society at https://blackloyalist.com.

7. Whitfield, *Blacks on the Border: The Black Refugees in British North America 1815–1860*, 4–5.

8. Benjamin R. Franklin, personal interview with writer. Lynn, Massachusetts, 12 July 2000; "United States World War I Draft Registration Cards, 1917–1918 for John Franklin," 12 July 2021, http://familysearch.org; *R. L. Polk & Co.'s Trow General Directory of New York City Embracing The Boroughs of Manhattan and The Bronx, 1916* (New York: R.L. Polk & Co., 1916), 1437.

9. "Delap's Cove" (accessed June 8, 2021), https://www.mapannapolis.ca/black-loyalists-annapolis-county; 1860 United States Federal Census, Robbinston, Washington County, Maine, accessed 6 June 2021, http://familysearch.org; U.S., City Directories, 1822–1995, Lynn, Massachusetts (accessed June 6, 2021), http://ancestry.com; Lawrence, "The Brothers Family of Annapolis, Nova Scotia."

10. 1880 United States Federal Census, Lynn, Essex County, Massachusetts, accessed June 6, 2021, http://familysearch.org; Franklin A. Dorman, *Twenty Families of Color in Massachusetts, 1742–1998* (Boston: New England Historical Society, 1998), 47; *The Book of Negroes, Book One*, http://collections.ic.gc.ca/blackloyalists/ documents (accessed June 5, 2021); Thompson, *Finding Fortune*, 61.

11. John Franklin, Sr. enlisted as a nondeclarant alien meaning prior to his service, he did not officially declare his intention to become a naturalized citizen. Personnel Records of the First World War, "Service Record for Peter Franklin," LAC; "Honorable Discharge from the United States Army for John Franklin," Certified dated July 1919, Private Papers of Benjamin R. Franklin, Lynn, Massachusetts; "New York, U.S., Abstracts of World War I Military Service, 1917–1919 for John Franklin," (accessed July 12, 2021), http://ancestry.com; "United States World War I Draft Registration Cards, 1917–1918 for John Franklin," July 12, 2021, http://familysearch.org; Nancy Gentile Ford, *Americans All! Foreign-born Soldiers in World War I* (College Station: Texas A&M University Press, 2001), 56, 63, 66; Arthur E. Barbeau and Florette Henri, *The Unknown Soldiers: African American Troops in World War I* (Boston: Da Capo Press, 1996), xiv; Kai Wright, *Soldiers of Freedom: An Illustrated History of African Americans in the Armed Forces* (New York: Black Dog and Leventhal Publishers, 2002), 137; Lanning, *The African-American Soldier: From Crispus Attucks to Colin Powell* (New York: Citadel Press, 2004), 133, 137–139; Gail Buckley, *American Patriots: The Story of Blacks in the Military from the Revolution to Desert Storm* (New York: Random House, 2001), 218–219; National Archives at St. Louis, MO; *Applications for Headstones, 1/1/1925–6/30/1970*; NAID: *NAID 596118*; Record Group Number: *92*; Record Group Title: *Records of the Office of the Quartermaster General.*

12. Benjamin R. Franklin, personal interview with writer, Lynn, MA, July 12, 2000.

13. Historian Matti Peltonen has described the concept of the "typical exception" or "normal exception" nature of the new microhistory as it relates to perspective and how emphasis is given to small units (persons, places, and things) and how those units serve as a means to unite the micro and macro levels of history. Matti Peltonen, "Clues, Margins, and Monads: The Micro-Macro Link in Historical Research," *History and Theory* 40, no. 3 (Oct. 2001), 356–357.

Bibliography

PRIMARY SOURCES

AFRICAN AMERICANS IN THE EARLY REPUBLIC

American Ancestors. *Vital Records of Sandwich Massachusetts*, "Death Notices–1809."

Grimes, William. *Life of William Grimes, The Runaway Slave.* Edited by William L. Andrews and Regina E. Mason. Oxford: Oxford University Press, 2008.

Holbrook, Jay Mack, editor. *Rhode Island 1782 Census.* Oxford: Holbrook Research Institute, 1979.

Jackson, Ronald Vern, editor. *Rhode Island 1810 Federal Census Index.* Salt Lake City: AGES, 1976.

Jackson, Ronald Vern, David Schaeffermeyer, and Gary Ronald Teeples, editors. *Rhode Island 1820 Federal Census Index.* Bountiful: Accelerated Indexing Systems, 1976.

Jackson, Ronald Vern, and Gary Ronald Teeples, editors. *Rhode Island 1830 Census Index.* Bountiful: Accelerated Indexing Systems, 1977.

Offley, G. W. "A Narrative." In *Five Black Lives.* Edited by Arna Bontemps. Middletown: Wesleyan University Press, 1971.

Rhode Island Heads of Families–First Census–1790 Rhode Island. Washington, D.C.: Government Printing Office, 1908.

United States Federal Census, 1800.

United States Federal Census, 1810.

United States Federal Census, 1820.

Volkel, Lowell M., *An Index to the 1800 Federal Census of Rhode Island.* Volkel Publishing, 1970.

COLONIAL AND REVOLUTIONARY RHODE ISLAND

Arnold, James N. *Vital Record of Rhode Island 1636–1850. First Series. Births, Marriages, Deaths: A Family Register for the People, Vol. 2, Providence County.* Providence: Narragansett Historical Publishing Company, 1892.

———. *Vital Record of Rhode Island 1636–1850. First Series Births, Marriages and Deaths. A Family Register For The People. Vol. 7. Friends and Ministers.* Providence: Narragansett Historical Publishing Company, 1895.

———. *Vital Record of Rhode Island 1636–1850. First Series: Births, Marriages and Deaths. A Family Register for the People. Vol. 10. Town and Church.* Providence: Narragansett Historical Publishing Company, 1898.

———. *Vital Record of Rhode Island, 1636–1850. 1st Series. Births, Marriages and Death, Vol. 4, Tiverton, Part VII.* Providence: Narragansett Historical Publishing Company, 1895.

Bartlett, John Russell. With index by E. E. Brownell. *Census of the inhabitants of the Colony of Rhode Island and Providence Plantations, 1774.* Baltimore: Genealogical Publishing Company, 1969.

Cushing, John D., editor. *The Earliest Acts and Laws of the Colony of Rhode Island and Providence Plantations, 1647–1719.* Wilmington, DE: Michael Glazier, 1977.

Early Records of the Town of Providence Volume V Being Part of the Third Book of The Town of Providence Otherwise Called the Book with Brass Clasps. Providence: Snow and Farnham City Printers, 1894.

Early Records of the Town of Providence Volume IX Being Part of the Book of Records of Town Meetings Number 3 1677–1750 and other Papers. Providence: Snow and Farnham City Printers, 1895.

Evans Early American Imprint Collection. Ann Arbor: Text Creation Partnership, 2011.

Family History Center. *Record of Births, Marriages, and Deaths, Vol. 5 Years 1678–1859. Register of St. John's Church.* Narragansett, Rhode Island.

Family History Center. *Rhode Island Marriages, 1724–1916.* Database. Salt Lake City, Utah.

Providence Old City Hall Archives. *Book of Marriages.*

———. *Wills and Probate Records, 1582–1932.*

"Samuel Cranston, December 5, 1708, Newport, Rhode Island to the Board of Trade." In Records of the Colony of Rhode Island and Providence Plantations in New England, Volume IV, 1707–1740. Providence: Knowles, Anthony & Co., 1859.

Stutz, Jean C., transcriber. *South Kingstown, Rhode Island Town Council Records, 1771–1795.* Kingston: The Pettaquamscutt Historical Society, 1988.

Trans-Atlantic Slave Trade Database, "Voyages Database." http://slavevoyages.org/tast/index.faces (accessed 10 October 2010).

FAMILY HISTORY AND RECORDS

Franklin, Benjamin R. Interview by author, 12 July 2000, Lynn, Massachusetts.

"Obituary for Thomas Henry Franklin." *Annapolis Spectator,* 1929.

FRENCH AND INDIAN WAR

Chapin, Howard M. *Nine Muster Rolls of Rhode Island Troops Enlisted During The Old French War To Which is added The Journal of Captain William Rice in The Expedition of 1746.* Providence: Printed for the Society by the Standard Printing Company from original MSS in the Library of the R.I. Historical Society, 1915.

———. *Rhode Island in the colonial wars. A list of Rhode Island soldiers and sailors in the old French and Indian war, 1755–1762.* Providence: Printed for the Society, 1918.

Lucier, Armand Francis, editor. *French and Indian War Notices Abstracted from Colonial Newspapers Volume 3: January 1, 1758 – September 17, 1759.* Bowie: Heritage Books, 1999.

MacGunnigle, Bruce Campbell. *Red Coats and Yellow Fever: Rhode Island Troops at the Siege of Havana, 1762.* Providence: Printed for the Society of Colonial Wars in the State of Rhode Island and Providence Plantations by Webster Press, Inc., 1991.

Rhode Island Historical Society. Colonial Militia Records. *An Account of Cash pd. Officers and Soldiers Belonging to Captain Burkitt and Eddy Companies pd. at Providence, 12/26/1759.*

———. Colonial Militia Records. *An Account of Cash pd. Officers and Soldiers Belonging to Col. Chris. Harris Company 1760. Vol. 6, p. 72.*

———. Colonial Militia Records. *An Account of Cash pd. Captain Ebenezer Jenckes Company pd at providence, 12/27/1757, Vol. 6, p. 69.*

———. Colonial Militia Records. *Captain Daniel Wall's company paid at Providence 1/12/1758, Vol. 6, p. 71.*

———. *Nine Muster Rolls of Rhode Island Troops Enlisted During The Old French War To Which is added The Journal of Captain William Rice in The Expedition of 1746.* Providence: Printed for the Society by the Standard Printing Company from original MSS in the Library of the R.I. Historical Society, 1915.

Sandel, Edward, editor. *Black Soldiers in the Colonial Militia Documents from 1639 to 1780.* Roseland: Tabor-Lucas Publications, 1994.

LOYALISTS

Annapolis Historical Society and Genealogy Centre. *Annapolis County Deeds*, Volume 5, 1784–1786.

Bell, D. G. "African American Refugees To Annapolis Royal and Saint John, 1783: A Ship Passenger List." *Nova Scotia Historical Review*, Volume 16, Issue 2 (1996): 71–81.

Braisted, Todd W. "The On-Line Institute for Advanced Loyalist Studies." www.royalprovincial.com.

Canadian Digital Collections. Black Loyalists, Our History, Our People, Documents: Diaries: Booth's Diary. "William Booth's Diary." http://collections.ic.gc.ca/blackloyalists/documents/diaries/booth_diary.htm. Accessed 22 September 2004.

———. Black Loyalists, Our History, Our People, Documents: Diaries: David George's Life. "An Account of Life of Mr. David George from S.L.A. given by himself." http://collections.ic,gc,ca/blackloyalists/documents/diaries/george_a_life.htm. Accessed 22 September 2004.

———. Black Loyalists, Our History, Our People, Documents: Diaries: Dyott's Diary. "William Dyott's Diary." http://blackloyalist.com/canadiandigitalcollection/documents/diaries/dyottsdiary. htm. Accessed 30 June 2009.

———. Black Loyalists, Our History, Our People, Documents: Diaries: Jessop's Diary. "William Jessop's Diary." http://blackloyalist.com/canadiandigitalcollection/documents/diaries/jessop_ excerpt.htm. Accessed 30 June 2009.

———. Black Loyalists, Our History, Our People, Documents: Diaries: King–Memoirs. "Memoirs of Boston King." http://collections.ic.gc.ca/blackloyalists/documents/diaries/king-memoirs.htm. Accessed 22 September 2004.

———. Black Loyalists, Our History, Our People, Documents: Diaries: Marston's Journal. "Benjamin Marston's Shelburne Journal." http://collections.ic.gc.ca./blackloyalists/documents/diaries/marston_journal.htm. Accessed 22 September 2004.

Gilroy, Marion, compiler. *Loyalists and Land Settlement in Nova Scotia.* Campbellville: Global Heritage Press, Inc., 2006.

Hodges, Graham Russell. *The Black Loyalist Directory: African Americans in Exile After the American Revolution.* New York: Garland Publishing, Inc., 1996.

Lawrence, Ian. *Deeds Involving Blacks*. Annapolis Royal: Annapolis Historical Society and Genealogy Centre, n.d.

————. *The Edward Jackson Family of Granville*. Annapolis Royal: Annapolis Historical Society and Genealogy Centre, n.d.

————. *The Franklin Family of Granville Township, Nova Scotia*. Annapolis
Royal: Annapolis Historical Society and Genealogy Centre, n.d.

Library and Archives of Canada. "List of Black People in the County of
Annapolis who wishes to make Application to Government for Lands."
RG 20, Series C, Volume 85, Micro 9340, no date.

————. *Ward Chipman Papers*, MG 23, D1, Series 1, volume 24. "Muster
Roll of Disbanded Officers, Discharges and Disbanded Soldiers and
Loyalists taken in the County of Annapolis betwist the 18th and 24th of
June 1784."

————. *Ward Chipman Papers* MG 23, D1, Series 1, volume 25. "Muster
roll of Captain Allen Stewart's Company of Black Pioneers for 61 days."

————. *Ward Chipman Papers*, MG 23, D1, Series 1, Volume 25. "Muster
roll of the Black Pioneers for 61 days."

Nova Scotia Archives. Nova Scotia Commissioner of Lands fonds.

————. *Crown Land Grants Book G*. mfm 13029.

————. *Crown Land Grants: Index A to G, 1730–1937*. mfm 12926.

————. *Crown Land Grants: Index H to Z, 1730–1937*. mfm 12927.

————. *Crown Land Grants, Old book 16*, mfm 13042.

————. *Nova Scotia and Cape Breton, 1790 Dec 1 to 1792 July 12*, "List of
the Blacks in Birchtown Who Gave In Their Names For Sierra Leone
in November, 1791." C.O.217/63, mfm 13863.

————. *Original Correspondence, Secretary of State, No. 63*.

Newman, Debra Lynn. "An Inspection Roll of Negroes Taken On Board
Sundry Vessels at Staten Island Bound for Nova Scotia, 1783." *Journal of
the Afro-American Historical and Genealogical Society* 1 (1960): 72–79.

Smith, Leonard H. Jr. and Norma H. Smith. *Nova Scotia Immigrants to
1867*. Baltimore: Genealogical Publishing Company, 1992.

Walker, Wayne. *Annapolis and Digby County Marriages, Volume 1 1750–
1800*. Annapolis Royal: Annapolis Historical Society, n.d.

Whitehead, Ruth Holmes. *Black Loyalists: A Short Biography of All Blacks
Emigrating to Shelburne County, N.S. after the American Revolution 1783*.
Halifax: Nova Scotia Museum, 2000.

Wright, Esther Clark. *The Loyalists of New Brunswick*. Moncton: Moncton
Publishing Company, 1972.

MISCELLANEOUS

Ancestry.com. U.S., City Directories, 1822–1995 [database on-line]. Lehi, Utah. Ancestry.com Operations, Inc., 2011.

REVOLUTIONARY WAR

American Revolution.org. Valley Forge Letters. "Letters of William Barton." www.americanrevolution.org/vlyfrgeltrs.html (accessed 20 October 2004).

Angell, Israel. *Diary of Colonel Israel Angell, Commanding the Second Rhode Island Continental during the American Revolution 1778–1781. Transcribed from the Original Manuscript Together with a Biographical Sketch of the Author and Illustrative Notes by Edward Field, A.B. Historian of the Rhode Island Society of the Sons of the American Revolution.* Providence: Preston & Rounds Company, 1899. Reprint, Arno Press, 1971.

Bamberg, Cherry Fletcher. *Elder John Gorton and the Six Principle Baptist Church of East Greenwich, Rhode Island.* Greenville: Rhode Island Genealogical Society, 2001.

_____. *Rhode Island Roots: Gleanings from Rhode Island Town Records: East Greenwich Town Council Records, 1775–1800.* Greenville, RI: Rhode Island Genealogical Society, 2009.

_____. *Rhode Island Roots: Gleanings from Rhode Island Town Records: Warwick Town Council Records, 1781–1801.* Greenville, RI: Rhode Island Genealogical Society, 2013.

Bartlett, John Russell, editor. *Records of the State of Rhode Island and Providence Plantations by Order of the General Assembly, Volume 11, 1664–1677.* Providence: A. Crawford Greene and Brothers State Printers, 1857.

_____. *Records of the Colony of Rhode Island and Providence Plantations in New England, Volume VII, 1770–1776.* Providence: A. Crawford Greene, State Printer, 1862.

_____. *Records of the State of Rhode Island and Providence Plantations by Order of the General Assembly, Volume VIII, 1776–1779.* Providence: Cooke, Jackson & Company, Printers to the State, 1863.

Blassingame, John W. editor. *Slave Testimony: Two Centuries of Letters, Speeches, Interviews, and Autobiographies.* Baton Rouge: Louisiana State University Press, 1977.

Boyle, Joseph Lee. *"Death Seem'd to Stare": The New Hampshire and Rhode Island Regiments at Valley Forge.* Baltimore: Clearfield Company, 2005.

————. *"He Loves a good deal of rum": Military Desertions during the American Revolution, Volume Two, June 30, 1777–1783.* Baltimore: Clearfield Company by Genealogical Publishing Company, 2009.

————. *Writings from the Valley Forge Encampment of the Continental Army December 19, 1777–June 19, 1778.* Bowie, MD: Heritage Books, 2003.

Brace, Jeffrey. *The Blind African Slave Or Memoirs of Boyrereau Brinch, Nicknamed Jeffrey Brace, as told to Benjamin F. Prentiss, Esq.* Edited by Kari J. Winter. Madison: University of Wisconsin Press, 2004.

Brinch, Boyrereau. *The Blind African Slave, or Memoirs of Boyrereau Brinch, Nicknamed Jeffrey Brace. Containing an Account of the Kingdom of Bow-Woo, in the Interior of Africa; with the Climate and Natural Productions, Laws, and Customs Peculiar to That Place. With an Account of His Captivity, Sufferings, Sales, Travels, Emancipation, Conversion to the Christian Religion, Knowledge of the Scriptures, &c. Interspersed with Strictures on Slavery, Speculative Observations on the Qualities of Human Nature, with Quotation from Scripture.* [book on-line] (Chapel Press: University of North Carolina, 2001) http://docsouth.unc.edu/neh/brinch/brinch.html (accessed 10 August 2004).

Chamberlain, Mildred M., transcriber. The Rhode Island 1777 Military Census. Baltimore: Genealogical Publishing Company, 1985.

Chase, Philander D., editor. *The Papers of George Washington, Revolutionary War Series, vol. 2, 16 September 1775–31 December 1775.* Charlottesville: University Press of Virginia, 1987.

Chase, Philander D. and Edward G. Lengel, editors. *The Papers of George Washington, Revolutionary War Series, vol. 11, 19 August 1777–25 October 1777.* Charlottesville: University Press of Virginia, 2001.

Dann, John C., editor. *The Revolution Remembered: Eyewitness Accounts of the War for Independence.* Chicago: University of Chicago Press, 1980.

David, Ebenezer. *A Rhode Island Chaplain in the Revolution: Letters of Ebenezer David to Nicholas Brown 1775–1778.* Edited by Jeannette D. Black and William Greene Roelker. Providence: Rhode Island Society of the Cincinnati, 1949.

Donnan, Elizabeth, editor. *Documents Illustrative of the History of The Slave Trade to America, Volume I, 1441–1700.* New York: Octagon Books, 1965.

Force, Peter, editor. *American Archives, Fourth Series Containing a Documentary History of the English Colonies in North America From the King's Message of March 7, 1774 to the Declaration of Independence by the United States, Volume III.* Washington: M. St. Clair Clarke and Peter Force Publishers, 1840.

Ford, Worthington Chauncey, editor. "Articles of War; September 20, 1776." *Journals of the Continental Congress 1774–1779*. Washington, DC: Government Printing Office, 1905. Available at https://avalon.law. yale.edu/18th_century/contcong_09-20-76.asp. Accessed 20 June 2021.

———. Journals of the Continental Congress 1774–1789, Volume VIII, 1777 May 22 to October 2. Washington, DC: Government Printing Office, 1907.

Friends of Valley Forge Park. Valley Forge Legacy: The Muster Roll Project. "Valley Forge Muster Roll." http://valleyforgemusterroll.org (accessed 22 September 2004).

Greenman, Jeremiah. *Diary of a Common Soldier in the American Revolution, 1775–1783, An Annotated Edition of the Military Journal of Jeremiah Greenman*. Edited by Robert Bray and Paul Bushnell. DeKalb: Northern Illinois University Press, 1978.

Gunning, Kathryn McPherson, editor. *Selected Final Pension Payment Vouchers 1818– 1864 Rhode Island*. Westminster: Willow Bend Books, 1999.

Henry Clinton Papers. William L. Clements Library. University of Michigan, Ann Arbor.

Hutchinson, William T. and William M. E. Rachal, editors. *The Papers of James Madison, vol. 2, 20 March 1780–23 February 1781*. Chicago: University of Chicago Press, 1962.

Jackson, Ronald Vern, editor. *Index Rhode Island Military Census, 1776*. West Jordan: Genealogical Services, 1988.

Lengel, Edward G., editor. *This Glorious Struggle: George Washington's Revolutionary Letters*. New York: HarperCollins, 2007.

Lesser, Charles H., editor. *The Sinews of Independence: Monthly Strength Reports of the Continental Army*. Chicago: University of Chicago Press, 1976.

Library of Congress. American Memory, The George Washington Papers, 1697–1799: Series 4, General Correspondence. "Greene, Christopher to George Washington, 27 March 1780." http:// www.lcweb2loc.gov/cgi-bin/query/P?mgw.27/temp/~ammem_zoe (accessed 20 September 2006).

Martin, Joseph Plumb. *Ordinary Courage: The Revolutionary War Adventures of Joseph Plumb Martin*. 2nd ed. Edited by James Kirby Martin. St. James: Brandywine Press, 1999.

Massachusetts Soldiers and Sailors of the Revolutionary War: A Compilation From The Archives. 17 vols. Boston: 1896–1908.

Mathew, Linda L. *Gleanings from Rhode Island Town Records: Providence Town Council Records, 1770–1788*. Providence: Rhode Island Genealogical Society, 2006.

Millar, John F., editor. "A British Account of the Siege of Rhode Island, 1778, the Journal of Peter Anthony Reina, British Midshipman on the Frigate Juno." *Rhode Island History* 38, no. 3 (1779): 79–85.

Moore, Frank, compiler. *The Diary of the American Revolution 1775–1781*. New York: Washington Square Press, 1967.

National Archives. "Compiled Service Records of Soldiers Who Served in the American Army during the Revolutionary War." M881/Roll 843. RG 93.

———. "Revolutionary War Pension Records." Series M805, Selected Rolls.

———. "Revolutionary War Rolls, 1775–1783." M246. RG 93.

Neagles, James C. *Summer Soldiers: A Survey and Index of Revolutionary War Courts-Martial*. Salt Lake City: Ancestry Incorporated, 1986.

Rhode Island Historical Society. *Jeremiah Olney Papers 1781–1783*. "Return of Invalid Pensioners belonging to the State of Rhode Island . . . commencing on the 5th of March 1789 . . . figured by Jer. Olney and John S. Dexter . . . dated February 1st, 1790."

———. *Jeremiah Olney Papers 1781–1783*. "Return of Officers and Soldiers Transferred from the Rhode Island Line to Serve in the following Independent Corps."

———. *Jeremiah Olney Papers 1781–1783*. "Time When the following Invalids were Discharged."

———. Johnston Town Records Collection. *Town Council Meeting Records. 1761–1777*.

———. "Military Papers, Volume 4."

———. "Muster Roll 1st Rhode Island Battalion June–July 1, 1778, Captain Arnold's Company."

———. Papers of Colonel Christopher Greene, 1737–1781.

———. Providence Town Council Records, June 1777.

———. *Rhode Island Land Evidence, Volume I, 1648–1696 Abstracts*. Providence: Rhode Island Historical Society, 1921.

Rhode Island State Archives. *Rhode Island Military Papers*. "Camp Verplank's Point 23rd Sept 1782. At a board of officers convened . . . to determine the names of . . . officers who are entitled to Honorary Badges."

———. "Certificates of the Rhode Island Line (1784), C#00164."

———. Digital Archives, African American Collection.

———. Providence Town Council Records, 1770–1788 [5:155].

———. *Rhode Island Military Papers.* "Register of all casualties that have happened . . . since 1/1/1781."

———. "Register of Furloughs Granted in the Rhode Island Regt. Since Jan. 1, 1782."

———. "Register of Levies who served in the Rhode Island Regiment, the Campaign of 1782 and are discharged."

———. "Military Returns, Volumes 1–4."

———. "Regimental Book Rhode Island Regiment for 1781, Regimental Book, 1–38."

———. "Return of all the noncommissioned officers and privates, inlisted for the War in the 5th Company of the Rhode Island Battalion commanded by Lieut. Col. Commandant Olney."

———. "Register of Non-commissioned Officers and Privates in the 5th Company of Rhode Island Battalion, inlisted for War and furloughed on the General Order of the 2nd of June, 1783."

———. "Return of all non-commissioned officers and privates inlisted for the War in the 6th Company of the Rhode Island Battalion, Commanded by Lt. Col. Jeremiah Olney."

Smith, John. "Thro Mud and Mire into the Woods, The 1777 Continental Diary of Sergeant John Smith, First Rhode Island Regiment (Colonel Christopher Greene, commanding Varnum's Brigade)." http://www.revwar75.com/library/bob/smith.htm (accessed 10 October 2004).

Smith, Joseph Jencks. *Civil and Military Lists of Rhode Island, 1647–1800: A list of all officers elected by the General assembly from the organization of the legislative government of the colony to 1800.* Providence: Preston and Rounds Company, 1900.

Smith, Samuel. *Memoirs of the Life of Samuel Smith, Being an Extract of a Journal Written By Himself From 1776 to 1786.* Middleborough, MA: 1853.

Smith, Venture. "A Narrative of the Life and Adventures of Venture, A Native of Africa, Related by Himself." In *Making Freedom: The Extraordinary Life of Venture Smith,* eds. Chandler B. Saint and George A. Krimsky. Middletown: Wesleyan University Press, 2009.

Souther, Rita Elaine. *Minority Military Service Rhode Island 1775–1783.* Washington, DC: National Society Daughters of the American Revolution, 1988.

Taylor, Maureen Alice. *Runaways, Deserters, And Notorious Villains: From Rhode Island Newspapers, Volume 1: The Providence Gazette, 1762–1800.* Camden: Picton Press, 1994.

Taylor, Maureen Alice and John Wood Sweet. *Runaways, Deserters, And Notorious Villains: From Rhode Island Newspapers, Volume 2: Additional notices from The Providence Gazette, 1762–1800 as well as advertisements from all other Rhode Island Newspapers from 1732–1800.* Rockport: Picton Press, 2001.

Waldo, Albigence. *Valley Forge, 1777–1778. Diary of Surgeon Albigence Waldo, of the Connecticut Line.* Philadelphia: The Pennsylvania Magazine of History and Biography, 1897.

Ward, John. A Memoir of Lieut.-Col. Samuel Ward, First Rhode Island Regiment, Army of the American Revolution; with a Genealogy of the Ward Family. New York: Privately printed, 1875. Reprint New York Genealogical and Biographical Record, 6 (July 1875): 113–128.

Weedon, George. *Valley Forge Orderly Book of General George Weedon of the Continental Army under Command of General George Washington in the Campaign of 1777–8.* New York: Dodd, Mead and Company, 1902.

White, Virgil D., editor. *Genealogical Abstracts of Revolutionary War Pension Files, Volume II: F–M.* Waynesboro: National Historical Publishing Company, 1991.

Wilson, Louis. "Genealogical and Military Data of Blacks, Indians, Mustees From Rhode Island in the American Revolutionary War." Providence: Rhode Island Historical Society, not dated.

SECONDARY SOURCES

Adams, Catherine and Elizabeth H. Pleck. *Love of Freedom: Black Women in Colonial and Revolutionary New England.* New York: Oxford University Press, 2010.

Albee, Allison. *The Nasty Affair at Pines Bridge.* Edited by Monica Doherty. Yorktown Heights, NY: Yorktown Historical Society, 2005.

Allen, Ernest Jr. "Afro-American Identity: Reflections on the Pre-Civil War Era." In *African-American Activism Before the Civil War: The Freedom Struggle in the Antebellum North.* Edited by Patrick Rael. New York: Routledge, 2008.

Alt, William E. and Betty L. Alt. *Black Soldiers, White Wars: Black Warriors from Antiquity to the Present.* Westport: Praeger Publishing, 2002.

Archer, Richard. *Jim Crow North: The Struggle For Equal Rights In Antebellum New England.* New York: Oxford University Press, 2017.

Astor, Gerald. *The Right to Fight: A History of African-Americans in the Military.* New York: Presidio Press, 1988.

Bailey, Sarah Loring. *Historical Sketches of Andover.* Boston: Houghton, Mifflin, 1880.

Baker, John F. Jr. *The Washingtons of Wessyngton Plantation: Stories Of My Family's Journey to Freedom*. New York: Atria Books, 2009.

Bamberg, Cherry Fletcher. "The 1774 Census of Rhode Island: Tiverton." *Rhode Island Roots* 33, No. 4 (2007): 169–193.

Barbieri, Michael. "The Dollar in Revolutionary America." *Journal of the American Revolution*. September, 2016. Accessed 21 December 2020. https://allthingsliberty.com/2016/09/dollar-revolutionary-america/.

Barnett, Paul. "The Black Continentals." *Negro History Bulletin* 33 (1970): 6–9.

Baron, Donna Keith, J. Edward Hood, and Holly V. Izard. "They Were Here All Along: The Native American Presence in Lower-Central New England in the 18th and 19th Centuries." *William and Mary Quarterly*, 3rd Series, 53, no. 3, Indians and Others in Early America (July 1996): 561–586.

Bartlett, Irving H. "The Free Negro in Providence, Rhode Island." *Negro History Bulletin* 14, no. 3 (December 1950): 51–54, 66–67.

Battle, Charles A. *Negroes on the Island of Rhode Island*. Newport: Newport's Black Museum, 1932.

Berkin, Carol. *Revolutionary Mothers: Women in the Struggle for America's Independence*. New York: Alfred A. Knopf, 2005.

Berlin, Ira. "Coming to Terms with Slavery in 21st Century America." In *Slavery and Public History: The Tough Stuff of American Memory*. Edited by James Oliver Horton and Lois E. Horton. New York: The New Press, 2006.

———. "From Creole to African: Atlantic Creoles and the Origins of African-American Society in Mainland North America." *William and Mary Quarterly* 53, no. 2 (April 1996): 251–288.

———. *The Making of African America: The Four Great Migrations*. New York: Viking Press, 2010.

———. *Many Thousands Gone: The First Two Centuries of Slavery in North America*. Cambridge: Belknap Press of Harvard University Press, 1998.

Blakeley, Phyllis R. "A Negro Loyalist Who Sought Refuge In Nova Scotia." *Dalhousie Review* 48, no. 3 (1968): 347–356.

Blumrosen, Alfred W. and Ruth G. Blumrosen. *Slave Nation: How Slavery United the Colonies and Sparked the American Revolution*. Naperville: Sourcebooks, 2005.

Bolster, W. Jeffrey. "An Inner Diaspora: Black Sailors Making Selves." In *Through a Glass Darkly: Reflections On Personal Identity In Early America*. Edited by Ronald Hoffman, Mechal Sobel, and Fredrika J. Teute. Chapel Hill: Published for the Omohundro Institute of Early American History and Culture by the University of North Carolina Press, 1997.

———. *Black Jacks: African American Seamen in the Age of Sail.* Cambridge: Harvard University Press, 1998.

Booker, Christopher. *"I Will Wear No Chain!": A Social History of African American Males.* Westport: Praeger, 2000.

Braisted, Todd W. "The Black Pioneers and Others: The Military Role of Black Loyalists in the American War for Independence." In *Moving On: Black Loyalists in the Afro-Atlantic World.* Edited by John W. Pulis. New York: Garland, 1999.

Brigham, Clarence S., compiler. *Seventeenth-Century Place Names of Providence Plantations, 1636–1700.* Providence: Rhode Island Historical Society, 1903.

Brooks, Joanna. "John Marrant's Journal: Providence and Prophecy in the 18th Century." *The North Star: A Journal of African American Religious History* 3, no. 1 (Fall 1999): 1–21.

Brown, Wallace. "The Black Loyalists in Sierra Leone." In *Movin' On: Black Loyalists In the Afro-Atlantic World.* Edited by John W. Pulis. New York: Garland, 1999.

———. *The Good Americans: The Loyalists in the American Revolution.* New York: William Morrow, 1969.

Brown, Wallace and Hereward Senior. *Victorious in Defeat: The Loyalists in Canada.* Toronto: Methuen, 1984.

Bumsted, J. M. "1763–1783: Resettlement and Rebellion." In *The Atlantic Region to Confederation: A History.* Edited by Philip A. Buckner and John G. Reid. Toronto: University of Toronto Press, 1994.

———. *Henry Alline, 1748–1784.* Toronto: University of Toronto Press, 1971.

Burroughs, Tony. *Black Roots.* New York: A Fireside Book, 2001.

Byrd, James R. *Sacred Scripture, Sacred War: The Bible and the American Revolution.* New York: Oxford University Press, 2013.

Cady, John Hutchins. *Rhode Island Boundaries, 1636–1936.* Providence: Rhode Island Tercentenary Commission, 1936.

Cahill, Barry. "Stephen Blucke: The Perils of Being a 'White Negro' in Loyalist Nova Scotia." *Nova Scotia Historical Review* 11, no. 1 (1991): 129–134.

———. "The Black Loyalist Myth in Atlantic Canada." *Acadiensis* 29, no. 1 (1999): 76–87.

Cardoso, Jack J. "The Black Man As A Soldier." In *The Negro Impact on Western Civilization.* Edited by Joseph S. Roucek and Thomas Kiernan. New York: Philosophical Library, 1970.

Carp, Benjamin. *Rebels Rising: Cities and the American Revolution.* New York: Oxford University Press, 2007.

Carpenter, Daniel Hoogland. *History and Genealogy of the Carpenter Family in America: From Settlement At Providence, Rhode Island, 1637–1901.* Jamaica, NY: The Marion Press, 1901.

Carrington, Henry B. *Battles of the American Revolution 1775–1781. Historical and Military Criticism, with Topographical Illustration.* New York: A.S. Barnes and Company, 1877.

Chadwick, Bruce. *The First American Army: The Untold Story of George Washington and the Men Behind America's First Fight for Freedom.* Naperville: Sourcebooks, 2007.

Chudacoff, Nancy Fisher. "The Revolution And the Town: Providence, 1775–1783." *Rhode Island History* 35, no. 3 (1976): 71–89.

Clark, Ellen McCallister, Sandra L. Powers, and E. K. Hong. *Rhode Island in the American Revolution.* Washington, DC: Society of the Cincinnati, 2000.

Clark-Pujara, Christy. *Dark Water: The Business of Slavery in Rhode Island.* New York: New York University Press, 2016.

Clegg, Claude A. "The Promised Land, Inc.: Company-Repatriate Relations during the Founding of Freetown, Sierra Leone." In *Movin' On: Black Loyalists In the Afro-Atlantic World.* Edited by John W. Pulis. New York: Garland, 1999.

Clifford, Mary Louise. *From Slavery to Freetown: Black Loyalists After the American Revolution.* Jefferson, NC: McFarland, 1999.

Coleman, Theodore. "Camp Hill, Hardscrabble, and Addison's Hollow in Early Providence." April 22, 2023. *Small State Big History.* http://smallstatebighistory.com/camp-hill-hardscrabble-and-addisons-hollow-in-early-providence/

Conley, Patrick T. "The Battle of Rhode Island, 29 August 1778: A Victory for the Patriots." *Rhode Island History* 62, no. 3 (Fall 2004): 51–65.

Cottreau-Robins, Catherine, M.A. "Domestic Architecture of the Black Loyalists in Nova Scotia, 1783–1800." Master's Thesis, Dalhousie University, 2002.

Cottrol, Robert J. *The Afro-Yankees: Providence's Black Community in the Antebellum Era.* Westport: Greenwood Press, 1982.

Coughtry, Jay. *The Notorious Triangle: Rhode Island and the African Slave Trade 1700–1807.* Philadelphia: Temple University Press, 1981.

Cowell, Benjamin. *Spirit of '76 in Rhode Island or Sketches of the Efforts of the Government and People in the War of the Revolution.* Boston: A. J. Wright, Printer, 1850.

Cox, Caroline. *A Proper Sense of Honor: Service and Sacrifice in George Washington's Army.* Chapel Hill: University of North Carolina Press, 2004.

———. "'Boy Soldiers of the American Revolution: The Effects of War on Society." In *Children and Youth in a New Nation.* Edited by James Marten. New York: New York University Press, 2009.

Crane, Elaine Forman. *A Dependent People: Newport, Rhode Island in the Revolutionary Era.* New York: Fordham University Press, 1985.

———. *Ebb Tide in New England: Women, Seaports, and Social Change, 1630–1800.* Boston: Northeastern University Press, 1998.

Crowder, Jack Darrell. *Chaplains of the Revolutionary War: Black Robed American Warriors.* Jefferson, NC: McFarland, 2017.

Cutter, William Richard. *Genealogical and Family History of Western New York: A Record of the Achievements of Her People in the Making of a Commonwealth and the Building of a Nation Volume I.* New York: Lewis Historical, 1912.

Dallett, Francis James with revisions by Phil Graham in 2014. *The War of the Revolution in Radnor (1777–1778).* Radnor: Radnor Historical Society, 2014.

David, James Corbett. *Dunmore's New World: The Extraordinary Life of a Royal Governor in Revolutionary America—with Jacobites, Counterfeiters, Land Schemes, Shipwrecks, Scalping, Indian Politics, Runaway Slaves, and Two Illegal Royal Weddings.* Charlottesville: University Press of Virginia, 2013.

Davidson, Stephen. *Birchtown and the Black Loyalist Experience From 1775 to the Present.* Halifax: Formac, 2019.

Dennis, Clara. *Down in Nova Scotia, My Own, My Native Land.* Toronto: Ryerson Press, 1934.

Desrochers, Robert E. Jr. "'Not Fade Away': The Narrative of Venture Smith, an African American in the Early Republic." In *A Question of Manhood, Volume 1: Manhood Rights: The Construction of Black Male History and Manhood, 1750–1870.* Edited by Darlene Hine and Earnestine Jenkins. Bloomington: Indiana University Press, 1999.

Dunfield, Robert, staff volunteer at Annapolis Historical Society and Genealogy Centre. Interview by author, August 2009, Annapolis Royal, Nova Scotia.

Eaton, Amasa M. "The Development of the Judicial System in Rhode Island." *Yale Law Journal* 14, no. 3 (January 1905): 148–170.

Egerton, Douglas R. *Death or Liberty: African Americans and Revolutionary America.* New York: Oxford University Press, 2009.

Eltis, David and David Richardson. *Atlas of the Transatlantic Slave Trade.* New Haven: Yale University Press, 2010.

FamilyTreeDNA. "Understanding Matches." https://familytreedna.com/my-ftdna/understanding-matches.aspx?pf=y. Accessed 6 October 2010.

Fergusson, Charles Bruce, editor. *Clarkson's Mission To America, 1791–1792.* Halifax: Public Archives of Nova Scotia, 1971.

Fick, Carolyn E. *The Making of Haiti: The Saint Domingue Revolution from Below.* Knoxville: University of Tennessee Press, 1990.

Fingard, Judith. "The Relief of the Unemployed Poor in Saint John, Halifax, and Saint John's, 1815–1860." *Acadiensis,* 5, no. 1 (Autumn/Automne 1975): 32–53.

Foner, Philip S. *History of Black Americans: From Africa to the Emergence of the Cotton Kingdom.* New York: Greenwood Press, 1975.

Fontaine, William T. *Reflections on Segregation, Desegregation, Power, and Morals.* Springfield, IL: Charles C. Thomas, 1967.

Franklin, John Hope and Evelyn Brooks Higginbotham. *From Slavery to Freedom: A History of African Americans,* Ninth Edition. New York: Mc-Graw-Hill, 2011.

Freeman, Douglas Southall. *George Washington Volume IV: Leader of the Revolution.* New York: Scribner, 1951.

Gates, Henry Louis. *Finding Oprah's Roots, Finding Your Own.* New York: Crown, 2007.

———. *Finding Your Roots.* Season 1, episode 9, "John Legend/Wanda Sykes/Margarett Cooper." Public Broadcasting System, 13 May 2012.

———. *Life Upon These Shores: Looking at African American History, 1513–2008.* New York: Alfred A. Knopf, 2011.

Geake, Robert A. with Loren Spears. *From Slaves to Soldiers: The 1st Rhode Island Regiment in the American Revolution.* Yardley, PA: Westholme, 2016.

Geggus, David. "The French Slave Trade: An Overview." *William and Mary Quarterly* 58, no. 1 (January 2001): 119–138.

Gerzina, Gretchen Holbrook. *Mr. and Mrs. Prince: How An Extraordinary Eighteenth Century Family Moved out of Slavery into Legend.* New York: HarperCollins, 2008.

Gilje, Paul A. *Liberty on the Waterfront: American Maritime Culture in the Age of Revolution.* Philadelphia: University of Pennsylvania Press, 2004.

Gomez, Michael A. *Exchanging Our Country Marks: The Transformation of African Identities in the Colonial and Antebellum South.* Chapel Hill: University of North Carolina Press, 1994.

Grant, John N. "Black Immigrants into Nova Scotia, 1776–1815." *Journal of Negro History* 58, no. 3 (July 1973): 253–270.

Greenaway, Cora. "The Croscup Family of Karsdale, Annapolis County and Their Painted Room." *Nova Scotia Historical Review* 9, no. 2 (1989): 106–125.

Greene, Evarts B. and Virginia D. Harrington. *American Population Before the Federal Census of 1790.* New York: Columbia University, 1932.

Greene, George Washington. *The Life of Nathanael Greene Major-General in the Army of the Revolution, Volume 2.* New York: Hurd and Houghton, 1871.

Greene, Lorenzo J. "Some Observations on the Black Regiment of Rhode Island in the American Revolution." *Journal of Negro History* 37, no. 2 (April 1952): 142–172.

———. "Slave-Holding New England and Its Awakening." *Journal of Negro History* 13, no. 4 (1928): 492–533.

———. *The Negro in Colonial New England.* New York: Atheneum, 1968.

Greene, Robert Ewell. *Black Courage 1775–1783: Documentation of Black Participation in the American Revolution.* Washington, DC: National Society of the Daughters of the American Revolution, 1984.

Greene, Samuel Arnold. *History of the State of Rhode Island and Providence Plantations: From the Settlement of the State, 1636 to the Adoption of the Federal Constitution, 1790.* Providence: Preston & Rounds, 1899.

Greene, Welcome Arnold, et al. *The Providence Plantations for Two Hundred and Fifty Years of the City of Providence, With a Graphic Description of the City at the Present Time, and of Its Industries, Commerce, Manufactures, Business Interests, Educational, Religious, and Charitable Institutions, Civic, Scientific, and Military Organizations; Also, Sketches of the Cities of Newport and Pawtucket, and Other Towns of the State.* Providence: J. A. & R. A. Reid, Publishers and Printers, 1886.

Gundersen, Joan R. *To Be Useful to the World: Women in Revolutionary America, 1740–1790.* Chapel Hill: University of North Carolina Press, 2006.

Hagist, Don N. "Building and Attacking Redoubts." *Journal of the American Revolution*, 24 June 2015. Available at https://allthingsliberty.com/2015/06/building-and-attacking-redoubts/. Accessed 5 May 2018.

Hall, Gwendolyn Midlo. *Slavery and African Ethnicities in the Americas: Restoring the Links.* Chapel Hill: University of North Carolina Press, 2005.

Hamilton, Sylvia. "Naming Names, Naming Ourselves: A Survey of Early Black Women in Nova Scotia." In *We're Rooted Here and They Can't Pull*

Us Up: Essays in African Canadian Women's History. Edited by Peggy Bristow. Toronto: University of Toronto Press, 1994.

Hannon, Leslie. *Redcoats and Loyalists, 1760–1815*. Toronto: Natural Science of Canada Limited, 1978.

Harbold, Judith C. "The 1774 Census of Rhode Island: Johnston." *Rhode Island Roots* 32, no. 4 (2006): 109–134.

Hardesty, Jared Ross. *Black Lives, Native Lands, White Worlds: A History of Slavery in New England*. Amherst: Bright Leaf, an imprint of University of Massachusetts Press, 2019.

Harris, Leslie M. *In the Shadow of Slavery: African Americans in New York City, 1626–1863*. Chicago: University of Chicago Press, 2003.

Harvey, Evelyn B. *The Negro Loyalists: Arrival and Departure*. Ottawa: Carle- ton University Institute of Canadian Studies, no date given.

Haskins, George L. "The Beginnings of Partible Inheritance in the American Colonies." *Yale Law Journal* 51 (1942). Available at: https://digital-commons.law.yale.edu/ ylj/vol51/iss8/5.

Hatch, Robert McConnell. *Thrust for Canada: The American Attempt on Quebec in 1775–1776*. Boston: Houghton Mifflin, 1979.

Heitman, Francis B. *Historical Register of Officers of the Continental Army During the War of Revolution*. Washington, DC: Rare Book Shop, 1914.

Henry, Frances. *Forgotten Canadians: The Blacks of Nova Scotia*. Don Mills: Longman Canada, 1973.

Herndon, Ruth Wallis. *Unwelcome Americans: Living on the Margin in Early New England*. Philadelphia: University of Pennsylvania Press, 2001.

Herndon, Ruth Wallis and Ella Wilcox Sekatau. "The Right to a Name: The Narragansett People and Rhode Island Officials in the Revolutionary Era." *Ethnohistory* 44, no. 3 (Summer 1997): 433–462.

Herrman, Rachel B. *No Useless Mouth: Waging War and Fighting Hunger in the American Revolution*. Ithaca: Cornell University Press, 2019.

Hill, Lawrence. "Freedom Bound." *Beaver* 87, no. 1 (2007): 16–23.

Hine, Darlene Clark and Earnestine Jenkins. "Black Men's History: Toward a Gendered Perspective." In *A Question of Manhood, Volume 1: Manhood Rights: The Construction of Black Male History and Manhood, 1750–1870*. Edited by Darlene Clark Hine and Earnestine Jenkins. Bloomington: Indiana University Press, 1999.

Hodges, Graham Russell. *Root & Branch: African Americans in New York and East Jersey, 1613–1863*. Chapel Hill: University of North Carolina Press, 1999.

Hoffer, Peter Charles. *Law and People in Colonial America*. Baltimore: Johns Hopkins University Press, 1992.

Horton, James Oliver. "Freedom's Yoke: Gender Conventions Among Antebellum Free Blacks." In *African-American Activism Before the Civil War: The Freedom Struggle in the Antebellum North*. Edited by Patrick Rael. New York: Routledge, 2008.

Horton, James Oliver and Lois E. Horton. *In Hope of Liberty: Culture, Community and Protest Among Northern Free Blacks, 1700–1860*. New York: Oxford University Press, 1997.

———. "Violence, Protest, and Identity: Black Manhood in Antebellum America." In *Free People of Color*. Edited by James Oliver Horton. Washington, DC: Smithsonian Institution Press, 1993.

Howell, Barbara Thompson. *How to Trace Your African-American Roots*. Secaucus: Citadel Press, 1999.

Jackson, Buzzy. *Shaking the Family Tree: Blue Bloods, Black Sheep, and Other Obsessions of an Accidental Genealogist*. New York: Touchstone, 2010.

Jasonoff, Maya. *Liberty's Exiles: American Loyalists in the Revolutionary World*. New York: Vintage Books, 2012.

Johnson, Charles and Patricia Smith and the WGBH Series Research Team. *Africans in America: America's Journey Through Slavery*. New York: Harcourt Brace, 1998.

Johnson, Walton R. and D. Michael Warren, eds. *Inside the Mixed Marriage: Accounts of Changing Attitudes, Patterns, and Perceptions of Cross-Cultural and Interracial Marriages*. Lanham: University Press of America, 1994.

Jones, Rhett S. "Plantation Slavery in the Narragansett Country of Rhode Island, 1690– 1790: A Preliminary Study." *Plantation Society in the Americas* 2, no. 2 (1986): 157–170.

Kammen, Carol. *On Doing Local History*. Nashville: American Association for State and Local History, 1986.

Kaplan, Sidney. *The Black Presence in the Era of the American Revolution 1770–1800*. New York: New York Graphic Society, 1973.

Kennedy, Hazel Wade. *Fragments of Time in Pawtuxet*. Cranston: Modern Press, 1986.

Kimball, Gertrude Selwyn. *Providence in Colonial Times*. Boston: Houghton Mifflin, 1912.

Kimber, Stephen. *Loyalists and Layabouts: The Rapid Rise and Faster Fall of Shelburne, Nova Scotia: 1783–1792*. Toronto: Doubleday Canada, 2008.

Kirk-Greene, Anthony. "David George: The Nova Scotian Experience." *Sierra Leone Studies* (December 1960): 93–120.

Kiven, Arline Ruth. *Then Why the Negroes: The Nature and Course of the Anti-Slavery Movement in Rhode Island: 1637–1860.* Providence: Urban League of Rhode Island, 1973.

Knoblock, Glenn A. *African American Historic Burial Grounds and Gravesites of New England.* Jefferson, NC: McFarland, 2016.

———. *"Strong and Brave Fellows": New Hampshire's Black Soldiers and Sailors of the American Revolution, 1775–1784.* Jefferson, NC: McFarland, 2003.

Kolchin, Peter. *American Slavery, 1619–1877.* New York: Hill and Wang, 2003.

Kyvig, David E. and Myron A. Marty. *Nearby History.* Walnut Creek: AltaMira Press, 2000.

Lanning, Michael Lee. *The African-American Soldier: From Crispus Attucks to Colin Powell.* New York: Citadel Press, 2004.

———. *Defenders of Liberty: African-Americans in the Revolutionary War.* New York: Citadel Press Kensington Publishing, 2000.

Ledbetter, Bonnie S. "Sports and Games of the American Revolution." *Journal of Sports History* 6, no. 3 (Winter 1979): 29–40.

Lemisch, Jesse. "'Jack Tar on the Streets': Merchant Seamen in the Politics of Revolutionary America." *William and Mary Quarterly* 25, no. 3 (July 1968): 371–407.

Lemons, J. Stanley. "Rhode Island and the Slave Trade." *Rhode Island History* 60, no. 4 (2002): 95–104.

Lengel, Edward G. *The Battles of Connecticut Farms and Springfield.* Yardley, PA: Westholme, 2020.

Lengel, Edward G., editor. *This Glorious Struggle: George Washington's Revolutionary War Letters.* New York: HarperCollins, 2007.

Levesque, George A. "Interpreting Early Black Ideology: A Reappraisal of Historical Consensus." In *African-American Activism Before the Civil War: The Freedom Struggle in the Antebellum North.* Edited by Patrick Rael. New York: Routledge, 2008.

Linebaugh, Peter and Marcus Rediker. *The Many Headed Hydra: Sailors, Slaves, Commoners, and the Hidden History of the Revolutionary Atlantic.* Boston: Beacon Press, 2000.

Littlefield, Daniel. *Revolutionary Citizens: African-Americans, 1776–1804.* New York: Oxford University Press, 1997.

Loiacono, Gabriel J. *How Welfare Worked in the Early United States: Five Microhistories.* New York: Oxford University Press, 2021.

Lovell, Louise Lewis. *Israel Angell, 1740–1832: Colonel of the 2nd Rhode Island Regiment.* Providence: Knickerbocker Press, 1921.

Lowenthal, Larry. *Marinus Willett: Defender of the Northern Frontier.* Fleischmanns, NY: Purple Mountain Press, 2000.

MacDonald, T. D. "The Nova Scotia Poor Law." *Public Affairs: A Maritime Quarterly for the Discussion of Public Affairs* 1, no. 1 (August 1937): 30–32.

MacGunnigle, Bruce C. "Winsor Fry of East Greenwich, Rhode Island and His Descendants (Part One)." *Rhode Island Roots* 41, no. 1 (March 2015): 30–36.

MacKinnon, Neil. "A Dearth of Miracles: Governor John Parr and the Settling of the Loyalists in Nova Scotia." *Nova Scotia Historical Review* 15, no. 1 (1995): 33–44.

———. "The Nova Scotia Loyalists: A Traumatic Community." In *Loyalists and Community in North America.* Edited by Robert Calhoon, Timothy M. Barnes, and George A. Rawlyk. Westport: Greenwood Press, 1994.

———. *This Unfriendly Soil: The Loyalist Experience in Nova Scotia 1783–1791.* Kingston: McGill-Queen's University Press, 1986.

Mandell, David R. "Shifting Boundaries of Race and Ethnicity: Indian-Black Intermarriage in Southern New England, 1760–1880." *Journal of American History* 85, no. 2 (Sept. 1998): 466–501.

Manegold, C.S. *Ten Hills Farm: The Forgotten History of Slavery in the North.* Princeton: Princeton University Press, 2010. Kindle.

Mari, Francesca. "The Microhistorian." *Dissent Magazine.* https://www.dissentmagazine.org/article/the-microhistorian-2. Accessed 19 August 2016.

Martin, James Kirby. "A 'Most Undisciplined, Profligate Crew': Protest and Defiance in the Continental Ranks, 1776–1783." In *Arms and Independence: The Military Character of the American Revolution.* Edited by Ronald Hoffman and Peter J. Albert. Charlottesville: University Press of Virginia, 1984.

———. *A Respectable Army: The Military Origins of the Republic, 1763–1789.* Wheeling: Harlan Davidson, 1982.

Maslowski, Peter. "National Policy Toward The Use of Black Troops in the Revolutionary War." In *Slavery, Revolutionary America and the New Nation.* Edited by Paul Finkelman. New York: Garland, 1990.

Matheny, Mike. "'The Predicament We Are In': How Paperwork saved the Continental Army." *Journal of the American Revolution,* 3 May 2021. Available at https://allthingsliberty.com/2021/05/the-predicament-we-are-in-how-paperwork- saved-the-continental-army/. Accessed 20 June 2021.

Mathew, Linda L. "Smallpox in Providence, 1776–1779." *Rhode Island Roots* 38, no. 1 (2012): 1–22.

May, Cedrick. "John Marrant and the Narrative Construction of an Early Black Methodist Evangelical." *African American Review* (Winter 2004): 554–570.

Mayer, Holly A. *Belonging to the Army: Camp Followers and Community during the American Revolution.* Columbia: University of South Carolina Press, 1996.

Mazzagetti, Dominick. *Charles Lee: Self Before Country.* New Brunswick: Rutgers University Press, 2013.

McBurney, Christian M. *Dark Voyage: An American Privateer's War on Britain's African Slave Trade.* Yardley: Westholme, 2022.

———. *Kidnapping the Enemy: The Special Operations to Capture Generals Charles Lee and Richard Prescott.* Yardley, PA: Westholme, 2013.

———. *The Rhode Island Campaign: The First French and American Operation in the Revolutionary War.* Yardley, PA: Westholme, 2011.

McDonnell, Michael. "Other Loyalists: A Reconsideration of the Black Loyalist Experience in the American Revolutionary Era." *Southern Historian* 16 (1995): 5–25.

McGowan, Louis H., and the Johnston Historical Society. *Images in America: Johnston.* Dover, NH: Arcadia Publishing, 1997.

McManus, Edgar. *Black Bondage in the North.* Syracuse: Syracuse University Press, 1973.

Melish, Joanne Pope. *Disowning Slavery: Gradual Emancipation and "Race" in New England, 1780–1860.* Ithaca: Cornell University Press, 1998.

———. "The Manumission of Nab." *Rhode Island History* 68, no. 1 (2010): 37–42.

———. "Recovering (from) Slavery: Four Struggles to Tell the Truth." In *Slavery and Public History: The Tough Stuff of American Memory.* Edited by James Oliver Horton and Lois E. Horton. New York: The New Press, 2006.

Minardi, Margot. *Making Slavery History: Abolitionism and the Politics of Memory in Massachusetts.* New York: Oxford University Press, 2010.

Moore, George H. *Historical Notes on the Employment of Negroes in the American Army of the Revolution.* New York: Charles T. Evans, 1862.

Morgan, Philip D. and Andrew Jackson O'Shaughnessy. "Arming Slaves in the American Revolution." In *Arming Slaves: From Classical Times to the Modern Age.* Edited by Christopher Leslie Brown and Philip D. Morgan. New Haven: Yale University Press, 2006.

Morris, Richard B. "The Emergence of the American Laborer." In *The History of the American Worker*. Edited by Richard B. Morris. Princeton: Princeton University Press, 1983.

Morse, William Inglis. *Gravestones of Acadie*. London: A. Smith and Company, 1929.

Mozingo, Joe. *The Fiddler on Pantico Run: An African Warrior, His White Descendants, a Search for Family*. New York: Free Press, 2012.

Mumford, Kevin. "After Hugh: Statutory Race Segregation in Colonial America, 1630–1725." *American Journal of Legal History* 43, no. 3 (1999): 280–305.

Murray, Thomas Hamilton. *Irish Rhode Islanders in the American Revolution*. Providence: American-Irish Historical Society, 1903.

Nalty, Bernard C. *Strength for the Fight: A History of Black Americans in the Military*. New York: The Free Press, 1986.

Nash, Gary B. *The Forgotten Fifth: African Americans in the Age of Revolution*. Cambridge: Harvard University Press, 2006.

Neagles, James C. *Summer Soldiers: A Survey and Index of Revolutionary War Courts-Martial*. Salt Lake City: Ancestry Incorporated, 1986.

Neagles, James C. and Lila L. Neagles. *Locating Your Revolutionary War Ancestor: A Guide to the Military Records*. Logan: Everton Publishers, 1983.

Neimeyer, Charles Patrick. *America Goes to War: A Social History of the Continental Army*. New York: New York University Press, 1996.

Nell, William C. *The Colored Patriots of the American Revolution, with sketches of several distinguished colored persons: to which is added a brief survey of the Condition and Prospects of Colored Americans*. Boston: Robert F. Wallcut, 1855.

———. *Services of Colored Americans in the Wars of 1776 and 1812*. Boston: Prentiss and Sawyer, 1851.

Nelson, William E. *The Common Law in Colonial America, Volume 1, The Chesapeake and New England, 1607–1660*. New York: Oxford University Press, 2008.

Newell, Margaret Ellen. *Brethren by Nature: New England Indians, Colonists, and the Origins of American Slavery*. Ithaca: Cornell University Press, 2015.

Niven, Laird and Stephen A. Davis. "Birchtown: The History and Material Culture of an Expatriate African-American Community." In *Moving On: Black Loyalists in the Afro-Atlantic World*. Edited by John W. Pulis. New York: Garland, 1999.

Nye, Eric. "Pounds Sterling to Dollars: Historical Conversion of Currency." Accessed at www.uwyo.edu/numimage/currency.htm, 17 October 2022.

Pachai, Bridglal. *Beneath the Clouds of the Promised Land, Volume I: 1600–1800*. Halifax: McCurdy Printing, 1987.

———, editor. *Traditional Lifetime Stories: A Collection of Black Memories, Volume 1*. Dartmouth: Black Cultural Centre for Nova Scotia, 1987.

Padley, Taunya. *The Church of England's role in Settling the Loyalists in the Town of Digby, 1783–1810*. Master's Thesis, Acadia University, 1991.

Palmer, Colin A. *Passageways: An Interpretive History of Black America, Volume I: 1619–1863*. Fort Worth: Harcourt Brace College Publishers, 1998.

Parkinson, Robert G. *The Common Cause: Creating Race and Nation in the American Revolution*. Chapel Hill: University of North Carolina Press, 2016.

Peltonen, Matt. "Clues, Margins, and Monads: The Micro-Macro Link in Historical Research." *History and Theory* 40, no. 3 (October 2001): 347–359.

Perl-Rosenthal, Nathan. *Citizen Sailors: Becoming American in the Age of Revolution*. Cambridge: Belknap Press of Harvard University Press, 2015.

Peterson, Carla L. *Black Gotham: A Family History of African-Americans in Nineteenth-Century New York City*. New Haven: Yale University Press, 2011.

Piersen, William D. *Black Yankees: The Development of an Afro-American Subculture in 18th Century New England*. Amherst: University of Massachusetts Press, 1988.

Popek, Daniel. *They "…fought bravely, but were unfortunate:" The True Story of Rhode Island's "Black Regiment" and the Failure of Segregation in Rhode Island's Continental Line, 1777–1783*. Bloomington: AuthorHouse, 2015.

Power, Jim. "To Nova Scotia in Search of Liberty." *American Visions* 2, no. 2 (1988): 22–25.

Public Broadcasting System. African American Lives. "African American Lives, Science, The Tests, Lineage Testing." http://www.pbs.org/wnet/aalives/2006/ p_science_tests2.html (accessed 7 February 2008).

Pulis, John. editor. *Moving On: Black Loyalists in the Afro-Atlantic World*. New York: Garland, 1999.

Purcell, Sarah J. *Sealed with Blood: War, Sacrifice, and Memory in Revolutionary America*. Philadelphia: University of Pennsylvania Press, 2002.

Pybus, Cassandra. *Epic Journeys of Freedom: Runaway Slaves of the American Revolution and Their Global Quest for Liberty*. Boston: Beacon Press, 2006.

Quarles, Benjamin. "Black History's Antebellum Origins." In *African-American Activism Before the Civil War: The Freedom Struggle in the Antebellum North*. Edited by Patrick Rael. New York: Routledge, 2008.

————. "The Colonial Militia and Negro Manpower." *Mississippi Valley Historical Review* 45, no. 4 (March 1959): 643–652.

————. *The Negro in the American Revolution*. Chapel Hill: University of North Carolina Press, 1961.

————. "The Revolutionary War as a Black Declaration of Independence." In *Slavery and Freedom in the Age of the American Revolution*. Edited by Ira Berlin and Ronald Hoffman. Charlottesville: University Press of Virginia, 1982.

Raphael, Ray. *A People's History of the American Revolution: How Common People Shaped the Fight for Independence*. New York: Harper Perennial, 2002. Originally published: New York: The New Press, 2001.

Rappleye, Charles. *Sons of Providence: The Brown Brothers, The Slave Trade, and the American Revolution*. New York: Simon and Schuster Paperbacks, 2006.

Reed, Harry. *Platform for Change: The Foundations of the Northern Free Black Community, 1775–1865*. East Lansing: Michigan State University Press, 1994.

Rees, John U. "He Come Out with us this time As a Volunteer . . .": Soldiers Serving Without Pay in the Second New Jersey Regiment, 1777–1780. https://revwar75.com/library/rees/volunteer.htm. Accessed July 7 2023.

————. *"They Were Good Soldiers": African Americans Serving in the Continental Army, 1775–1783*. Warwick, UK: Helion and Company, 2019.

Reeve, Tapping. *The Law of Baron and Femme Of Parent and Child, Guardian and Ward, Master and Servant, And of the Powers of Courts of Chancery, with an Essay on the Terms Heir, Heirs, and Heirs of the Body*. Burlington: Chauncey Goodrich, 1846.

Reiss, Oscar. *Blacks in Colonial America*. Jefferson: McFarland, 1997.

Resch, John. *Suffering Soldiers: Revolutionary War Veterans, Moral Sentiment, and Political Culture in the Early Republic*. Amherst: University of Massachusetts, 1999.

Rhode Island Black Heritage Society. *Creative Survival: The Providence Black Community in the 19th Century*. Providence: Rhode Island Black Heritage Society, 1985.

Rhode Island Historical Society. "Johnston, Rhode Island." www.rihs.org/mssinv/Mss202.htm. Accessed 20 September 2006).

Rhode Island Historical Preservation Commission. *Historic and Architectural Resources of Tiverton, Rhode Island: A Preliminary Report*. Providence: Rhode Island Historical Preservation Commission RIHPC.

Rider, Sidney. *An Historical Enquiry concerning the attempt to raise a regiment of slaves by Rhode Island during the war of the revolution. With several tables prepared by Lt.-Col. Jeremiah Olney, commandant.* Providence: S. S. Rider, 1880.

Robertson, Marion. King's Bounty: *A History of Early Shelburne, Nova Scotia.* Halifax: Nova Scotia Museum, 1983.

Rommel-Ruiz, W. Bryan. "Colonizing the Black Atlantic: The African Colonization Movements in Postwar Rhode Island and Nova Scotia." *Slavery and Abolition* 27, no. 3 (December 2006): 349–365.

Rose, James M. and Alice Eichholz. *Black Genesis: A Resource Book for African-American Genealogy.* Baltimore: Genealogical Publishing Company, 2003.

Royster, Charles. *A Revolutionary People At War: The Continental Army and American Character 1775–1783.* Chapel Hill: University of North Carolina Press, 1979.

Sammons, Mark J. and Valerie Cunningham. *Black Portsmouth: Three Centuries of African American Heritage.* Durham: University of New Hampshire Press, 2004.

Savary, A. W. *Supplement to the History of the County of Annapolis Correcting and Supplying Omissions in the Original Volume.* Toronto: William Briggs, 1913.

Schaefer, James J. "The Whole Duty of Man: Charles Lee and the Politics of Reputation, Masculinity, and Identity during The Revolutionary Era, 1755–1783." PhD dissertation, University of Toledo, 2006.

Schama, Simon. *Rough Crossings: The Slaves, the British, and the American Revolution.* New York: HarperCollins, 2006.

Schomberg Center for Research in Black Culture. *In Motion: The African American Migration Experience*, "The Transatlantic Slave Trade, The Development of the Trade." http://www.inmotionaame.org/migrations/topic.cfm?migration=1&topic=2.

Schroder, Walter K. *The Hessian Occupation of Newport and Rhode Island, 1776–1779.* Westminister: Heritage Books, 2005.

Shy, John W. "A New Look at Colonial Militia." *William and Mary Quarterly*, 3rd series, 20, no. 2 (April 1963): 176–185.

Smith, Charles Richard. *Marines in the Revolution A History of the Continental Marines in the American Revolution, 1775–1783.* Washington, DC: History and Museum Division, Headquarters, U.S. Marine Corps, 1975.

Smith, Gene. "Black Nova Scotia." *American Legacy*, Summer 2003.

Smolenyak, Megan. *Who Do You Think You Are? The Essential Guide to Tracing Your Family History.* New York: Viking, 2009.

Sobel, Mechal. *Teach Me Dreams: The Search for Self in the Revolutionary Era.* Princeton: Princeton University Press, 2000.

Stanley, George F.G. *Canada Invaded.* Toronto: A. M. Hakkert, 1973.

Staples, William Read. *Annals of the Town of Providence From Its First Settlement, to the Organization of the City Government in June 1832.* Providence: Knowles and Vose, 1843.

Stephenson, Michael. *Patriot Battles: How the War of Independence Was Fought.* New York: Harper Perennial, 2007.

Stewart, James Brewer. "The Emergence of Racial Modernity and the Rise of the White North, 1790–1840." In *African-American Activism Before the Civil War: The Freedom Struggle in the Antebellum North.* Edited by Patrick Rael. New York: Routledge, 2008.

Stewart, Rowena. *A Heritage Discovered: Blacks in Rhode Island.* Providence: Rhode Island Black Historical Society, 1975.

Stokes, Keith W. and Theresa Guzman Stokes. *A Matter of Truth: The Struggle for African Heritage & Indigenous People Equal Rights in Providence, Rhode Island (1620–2020).* Middleton: Rhode Island Black Historical Society and 1696 Heritage Group, 2021.

Sweet, John Wood. *Bodies Politic: Negotiating Race in the American North, 1730–1830.* Baltimore: Johns Hopkins University Press, 2003.

Taylor, Alan. "'The Hungry Year': 1789 on the Northern Border of Revolutionary America." In *Dreadful Visitations: Confronting Natural Catastrophe in the Age of Enlightenment.* Edited by Alessa Johns. New York: Routledge, 1999.

Thompson, Brenda. *A Wholesome Horror: Poor Houses in Nova Scotia.* Halifax: SSP Publications, 2017.

———. *Finding Fortune: Documenting and Imagining the Life of Rose Fortune (1774–1864).* Halifax: SSP Publications, 2019.

———. "'Paupers Outside', Poor Houses in Nova Scotia." Accessed at poorhousesofnovascotia.com (12 June 2018).

Thornton, John K. *Africa and Africans in the Making of the Atlantic World, 1400–1800.* New York: Cambridge University Press, 1998.

Van Buskirk, Judith. *Standing in Their Own Light: African American Patriots in the American Revolution.* Norman: University of Oklahoma Press, 2017.

Voelz, Peter. *Slave and Soldier: The Military Impact of Blacks in the Colonial Americas.* New York: Garland, 1993.

Walcott, Robert L. "Husbandry in Colonial New England." *New England Quarterly* 9, no. 2 (June 1936): 244–245.

Walker, Anthony. *So Few the Brave: Rhode Island Continentals, 1775–1783.* Newport: Seafield Press, 1981.

Walker, James W. St. G. *The Black Loyalists: The Search for a Promised Land in Nova Scotia and Sierra Leone, 1783–1870.* Toronto: University of Toronto Press, 1992, originally published London: Longman, 1976.

———. "Myth, History and Revisionism: The Black Loyalists Revisited." *Acadiensis* 29, no. 1 (1999): 88–105.

———. "On The Record: The Testimony of Canada's Black Pioneers, 1783–1865." In *Emerging Perspectives on the Black Diaspora,* ed. Aubrey W. Bonnet and G. Llewellyn Watson. Lanham: University Press of America, 1990.

Wallace, Maurice O. *Constructing the Black Masculine: Identity And Ideality in African American Men's Literature and Culture, 1775–1995.* Durham: Duke University Press, 2002.

Ward, Harry M. *The War for Independence and the Transformation of American Society.* London: UCL Press, 1999.

Warren, Wendy Anne. *New England Bound: Slavery and Colonization In Early America.* New York: Liveright, 2016.

———. "'The Cause of Her Grief': The Rape of a Slave in Early New England." *Journal of American History* 93, no. 4 (March 2007): 1031–1049.

Wax, Darold D. "Preferences for Slaves in Colonial America." *Journal of Negro History* 58, no. 4 (1973): 311–401.

Wetherell, Charles and Robert W. Roetger. "Notes and Comments: Another Look at the Loyalists of Shelburne, Nova Scotia, 1783–1795." *Canadian Historical Review,* 70, no. 1 (1989): 76–91.

White, David O. *Connecticut's Black Soldiers, 1775–1783.* Chester: Pequot Press, 1973.

Whitehead, Ruth Holmes. *Black Loyalists: Southern Settlers of Nova Scotia's First Free Black Communities.* Halifax: Nimbus, 2013.

Whitfield, Harvey Amani. *Blacks on the Border: The Black Refugees in British North America, 1815–1860.* Burlington: University of Vermont Press, 2006.

———. *North to Bondage: Slavery in the Maritimes.* Vancouver: UBC Press, 2016.

Whiting, Gloria McCahon. "Power, Patriarchy, and Provision: African Families Negotiate Gender and Slavery in New England." *Journal of American History* 103, no. 3 (December 1, 2016): 583–605.

Wiencek, Henry. *An Imperfect God: George Washington, His Slaves, and the Creation of America.* New York: Farrar, Straus and Giroux, 2003.

Williams, Catherine R. *Biography of Revolutionary Heroes; Containing the Life of Brigadier Gen. William Barton, and Also, of Captain Stephen Olney.* Providence: Catherine R. Williams, 1839.

Williams-Myers, A. J. "Out of the Shadows: African Descendants-Revolutionary Combatants in the Hudson River Valley; a Preliminary Historical Sketch." *Afro- Americans in New York Life and History* 31, no. 1 (2007). Available at http://www.questia.com/read/1G1-158529011/out-of-the-shadows-african- descendants-revolutionary.

Wilson, Ellen Gibson. *The Loyal Blacks.* New York: Capricorn Books, 1976.

Wilson, Joseph T. *The Black Phalanx: African Americans in the War of Independence, the War of 1812, and the Civil War.* Hartford: American Publishing Company, 1890. Reprint, New York: DaCapo Press, 1994.

Wilson, Lisa. *Ye Heart of a Man: The Domestic Life of Men in Colonial New England.* New Haven: Yale University Press, 1999.

Winks, Robin W. *The Blacks in Canada: A History.* Montreal: McGill-Queen's University Press, 1971.

Winson, Gail I. "Researching the Laws of the Colony of Rhode Island and Providence Plantations: From Lively Experiment to Statehood." *Roger Williams University Law Library Staff Publications 3* (2005). https://docs.rwu.edu/law_lib_sp/3.

Withey, Lynne. *Urban Growth in Colonial Rhode Island: Newport and Providence in the 18th Century.* Albany: State University of New York Press, 1984.

Wolin, Jeremy L. "Hard Scrabble and Snow Town." *Demolition and Amnesia: Roger Williams National Monument Online Project.* Providence: Brown University, 2017.

Wood, Betty. *The Origins of American Slavery: Freedom and Bondage in the English Colonies.* New York: Hill and Wang, 1997.

Wood, Peter H. *Strange New Land: Africans in Colonial America.* New York: Oxford University Press, 2003.

Woodtor, Dee Palmer. *Finding a Place Called Home: A Guide to African-American Genealogy and Historical Identity.* New York: Random House, 1999.

Wright, Kai. *Soldiers of Freedom: An Illustrated History of African Americans in the Armed Forces.* New York: Black Dog and Leventhal Publishers, 2002.

Wright, Robert K. Jr. *The Continental Army.* Washington, DC: Center of Military History, United States Army, 1983.

Zilversmit, Arthur. *The First Emancipation: The Abolition of Slavery in the North.* Chicago: University of Chicago Press, 1967.

Acknowledgments

THIS BOOK ABOUT MY AMAZING AND UNIQUE ANCESTORS was a long time in the making. This project originated in my desire to investigate the oral tradition of my maternal ancestors—the Franklins of Nova Scotia. My familial connections to the subjects held this author to an additional layer of scrutiny and review. I not only had to meet the standards of my profession, but also convince family members that my research and analysis was fair and accurate. As such, my gratitude and thanks go to many people who have helped to make this book a reality.

This book began as part of my PhD program at Bowling Green State University, where I received great instruction and guidance. I would like to thank my former advisor and friend, Ruth Wallis Herndon, for her mentorship, support, and expertise. Along that line, I also valued the advice and insight from professors Rebecca Mancuso, Lillian Ashcraft-Eason, and Gretchen Holbrook Gerzina.

Much thanks to good friends and colleagues Chris Eisel and James Schaefer who read many drafts of the book and offered wonderful counsel and support.

I greatly appreciate the assistance from the archivists and staff at the following: Rhode Island Historical Society; Rhode Island State Archives; University of Michigan's Clements Library; The Genealogy Center at Allen County Public Library of Fort Wayne, Indiana; Research & Genealogy Centre of the Annapolis Heritage Society of Annapolis Royal, Canada; Nova Scotia Archives; and the Library and Archives of Canada.

Many thanks to friends and members of the genealogy community for listening to the story of the Frank brothers and offering encouragement and instruction, especially members of the Journey African American Genealogy group of Toledo, Ohio, and the instructors and staff of the Midwest African American Genealogy Institute (MAAGI).

Thanks also to Todd W. Braisted and Christian M. McBurney for their valuable insight and feedback. I also wish to thank Noreen O'Connor-Abel and Bruce H. Franklin of Westholme Publishing for their guidance and assistance.

This book would not have been possible without the knowledge and support of two Franklin descendants, my uncle Ben Franklin and my aunt Hattie Franklin Gilton. Ben Franklin, the keeper of the Frank brothers' story, passed along their story and legacy to a new generation. Hattie Franklin Gilton's initial research into our family history provided the catalyst for further research and investigation. I am extremely grateful to both.

Last and certainly not least, I thank Franklin descendants and family members scattered throughout Ohio, California, Massachusetts, Rhode Island, and Canada. I especially thank my son, Michael, Jr. and my grandchildren, Michael, III, Mylake, Xakar, Kimberly, Naya, and Isaiah for their constant love and support.

Index

Harris, Andrew, 232
Harris, Cesar, 171
Harris, Christopher, 17, 19, 20
Harris, Dr., 98–99, 178–179
Harris, Hannah Middleton, 232
Harris, William, 6, 12
Harrison, Francis, 222
Harry, Gideon, 59, 88, 139
Haskell, Charles, 180
Hastings, Selena, 212
Havana, Cuba, siege at, 21
Hazard, Peter, 84, 131
Hazzard, Henry, 59, 60, 88
Hazzard, Pharoah, 39, 40, 148, 168–169
Heath, William, 64, 131, 134–135, 150
Henly, Charles, 147–148
heroic artisan ideal, 48–49, 51–52
Hessian troops, 74, 76, 94–95, 98
Hill, Nancy, 111
Hitchcock, Daniel, 30, 57, 60
homesickness, 124–125
Honorary Badges of distinction, 168
horses, ownership of, 12
housing. *See* shelter and housing
Howe, Richard, 93
Howe, William, 70, 159
Hughes, Thomas, 59, 88, 140
Humphrey, David, 91
Huntingdon Church, 218
Huntingdonian Connexion, 211–212
Hutchens, Elizabeth, 194
Hutchings, Colonel, 111

indentured servitude, 2, 3–4, 203, 219, 220. *See also* slavery
Innes, Alexander, 159
interracial marriage, 26, 105

Jackson, Ann, 222
Jackson, Edward, 212–214, 219, 222
Jackson, Isabella, 212–213
Jackson, James, 214, 221
Jackson, Lydia, 203
Jackson, Margaret. *See* Franklin, Margaret Jackson
Jackson, Patience. *See* Warrington, Patience Jackson

Jackson, Prince, 88
Jackson, Thomas, 222
James, Benjamin, 213, 214
James, Elizabeth, 214
Joe (deserter), 158
Johnson, Ann. *See* Franklin, Ann Johnson
Johnson, George, 200, 202
Johnson, Lucy, 188
Johnston, Rhode Island
    Andrew Frank in, 31, 55
    free Blacks in, 23–24, 171–172
    militia company of, 57–58
    and removal of Sarah Frank from Providence, 117
    Rufus Frank's family in, 15, 22–23, 27
    Sarah Frank in, 107
    William Frank in, 169, 171, 182
Johnston, Robert, 222
Jones, Samuel, 186
Jordan, Abedingo, 222
Jordan, Isaac, 222
justice system, 12–14, 208–209

Kelley, Jenny, 224
Kelley, Moses (Morris), 224–225
Kelly, Abella. *See* Franklin, Abella Kelly
Kench, Thomas, 90
King, Boston
    on Article VII, 163–164
    on Birchtown, 197, 205
    as Black Methodist, 212
    on decline of Shelburne, 206–207
    in evacuation of Charleston, 161–162
    occupations of, 202–203
King, Violet, 212
Kinnicutt, Anthony, 25, 44, 45, 52, 128

L'Abondance (ship), 194–195, 202, 225
land ownership
    allotments promised to enlistees, 44, 172–173
    by Ben Frank, 220, 221
    in Birchtown, 195–196, 201–202
    in Brinley Town, 217
    by Frank Nigro, 2, 9, 11
    in Nova Scotia, 190–191
    by William Carpenter, 5–7
    by William Frank, 172, 182